Fourth Edition

Analyzing Financial Statements

By Thomas P. Carlin
Albert R. McMeen, III

1120 Connecticut Avenue, N.W.
Washington, D.C. 20036

This publication is designed to provide accurate and authoritative information in regard to the subject matter covered. It is sold with the understanding that the publisher is not engaged in rendering legal, accounting, or other professional service. If legal advice or other expert assistance is required, the services of a competent professional person should be sought.

From a Declaration of Principles jointly adopted by a Committee of the American Bar Association and a Committee of Publishers and Associations.

Library of Congress Cataloging-in-Publication Data
Carlin, Thomas P.
Analyzing financial statements/by Thomas P. Carlin, Albert R. McMeen.—4th ed.

p. cm.
Rev. ed.: Analyzing financial statements/John E. McKinley . . . [et al.], 3rd ed. 1988.

Includes index.
ISBN 0-89982-315-7
1. Financial statements. I. McMeen, Albert R., 1942- II. Analyzing financial statements. III. Title.
HF5681.B2C354 1993
657'.3—dc20 93-10976
CIP

Fourth Edition, 1993

Printed in the United States of America

Table of
Contents

PREFACE 

Analyzing Financial Statements is a practical introduction to financial analysis from the viewpoint of the commercial loan analyst. One of the key skills of an effective loan analyst is the ability to understand a borrower's or prospective borrower's past performance and creditworthiness.

Chapter 1 serves as an introduction, defining financial analysis and explaining its purpose. This chapter emphasizes the structure that financial analysis adds to the loan process. Chapter 2 discusses the importance of thoroughly understanding a company's industry and operating environment and describes the various cyclical patterns of the economy and their impact on various industries.

The remaining chapters focus on specific analytical areas and techniques and use examples based on actual companies to show how data might be interpreted. Chapters 3 through 5 focus on the three basic analytical areas that enable a loan analyst to analyze and interpret a company's past performance. These are

- analysis of balance sheets,
- analysis of income statements, and
- analysis of statements of cash flow.

Chapters 6 through 9 focus on analytical techniques that help a loan analyst predict a company's future performance. These techniques include

- calculation and interpretation of ratios.
- preparation and analysis of cash budgets,
- preparation of long-term forecasts, and
- review of additional financial-management analytical techniques.

Chapter 2 presents two detailed case studies; it and the remaining chapters ask questions about how to apply the principles explained in the chapters to the case studies. The appendix gives the answers to the questions about one of the case studies. Together, these elements show how a comprehensive financial analysis would proceed step-by-step, using all the techniques explained in the book to reach a sound judgement concerning a borrowing company's credit needs and its ability to repay loans.

Throughout, the text emphasizes the importance of both technical analysis (manipulating the numbers) and interpretive, or critical, analysis (getting behind the numbers to raise questions and draw conclusions about the financial viability of a company). The text also stresses that financial analysis does not in itself provide answers, but rather helps the loan analyst to focus on the most vulnerable aspects of a company's operation and to identify important questions requiring answers from the company's management. The ultimate decision, however, still must take into account the loan officer's subjective judgement of such factors as management's capabilities and the market situation.

Analyzing Financial Statements provides beginning analysts with an understanding of the fundamentals of financial analysis. However, to become a proficient lender, the loan analyst will have to hone the basic skills presented here through diligent application, further study, and—perhaps most important of all—practical experience.

The American Bankers Association is grateful to the bankers who generously gave of their time and expertise to review this new edition of *Analyzing Financial Statements*. Appreciation for their important contributions is extended to

Jerry Clark
Senior Vice President
NationsBank
Atlanta, Georgia

Robert de Buys
Senior Vice President
South Trust Bank
Birmingham, Alabama

Donald B. Ferega
Assistant Vice President
Norwest Bank Bear Valley
Denver, Colorado

Mark A. Truitt
Banking Officer
Colorado National Bank
Denver, Colorado

Robert E. Taylor
Vice President
INB Banking Company
Jeffersonville, Indiana

Lester A. Hoeflich
Assistant Vice President
M & T Bank
Buffalo, New York

In addition, appreciation is extended to the many bankers, AIB chapter leaders, instructors, and students who suggested ways to make this edition an even more useful resource for commercial lenders.

ABOUT THE AUTHORS

Thomas P. Carlin is president of the Financial Training Group Ltd., which designs and implements training systems for the financial services industry. Mr. Carlin has worked both domestically and internationally as a line lending officer and as a consultant to banks in the design and implementation of technical training programs. He earned a B.A. degree from Villanova University and a masters degree in international management from the American Graduate School of International Management.

Albert R. McMeen, III, is president of Training Associates, Inc. He is a financial training consultant for banks, life insurance companies, and other financial services industries and a professor at New York University, Stern Graduate School of Business, and Long Island University School of Business, Accounting, Public Affairs, and Computer Science. Formerly an executive at several financial institutions, Mr. McMeen is also the author of *Equipment Leasing Guide for Lessees* and *Debt Repayment Capacity*.

FINANCIAL STATEMENT ANALYSIS: AN OVERVIEW

LEARNING OBJECTIVES

After studying this chapter, you will be able to

- define financial statement analysis,
- explain how financial statement analysis helps structure the commercial lending decision,
- refer to relevant accounting principles,
- discuss the technical and interpretive aspects of analysis,
- list sources of financial data and reliability,
- explain the basic steps of financial statement analysis, and
- identify the limitations of financial statement analysis.

INTRODUCTION

Banks frequently invest much of their assets in loans made to commercial customers. For this reason, banks depend on their commercial loan officers to make sound judgments about the financial stability of the businesses applying for loans. Financial statement analysis gives the loan officer much of the information required to make sound lending decisions.

When making loan decisions, the loan officer must be concerned with the needs of the business as well as the community. Through careful financial statement analysis and sound lending decisions, the commercial loan officer can contribute to the profitability of the bank and to the growth of local businesses while meeting the needs of the community.

Chapter 1 provides a broad overview of financial statement analysis as it applies to credit analysts, defines financial statement analysis, discusses the concept of risk, and presents the sequence of steps involved in analyzing financial statements.

Birth of Modern Financial Statement Analysis

Prior to the Great Depression, less debt was outstanding among businesses than there is today. Then, most business firms depended for their capital funds on the equity markets or on short-term lending from commercial banks. The large part played by the unregulated stock market, its cyclical swings, and the lack of diligent analysis by lenders who extended credit based solely on the market value of collateral or the state of the economy, periodically created severe financial distress. Since little consistent or reliable financial information was available, a drop in confidence by investors could sweep unimpeded throughout the economy.

The collapse of the stock market in 1929 was a tremendous blow to many hundreds of new businesses seeking additional capital to expand. A chain reaction extended into the commercial banking industry because banks had extended short-term credit against planned stock issues that never occurred because the stock market collapsed. Thus, the commercial banks were faced with undercapitalized borrowers and, in many cases, defaulting loans that caused the banks to nervously call in their loan portfolios. The resulting bank and business failures cooled the booming economy and caused large capital losses, resulting in the Great Depression of the 1930s.

As a consequence of the Great Depression, the federal government established the Securities and Exchange Commission (SEC), which published regulations about how business firms should report their financial condition and the results of their operations. Among the SEC's many regulations was one requiring the accounting profession to create rules for business accounting, called generally accepted accounting principles (GAAP). Initially coordinated by the American Accounting Association and the American Institute of Certified Public Accountants, GAAP is currently administered by the Financial Accounting Standards Board (FASB) in Stamford, Connecticut.

After GAAP, there was a reasonable basis upon which to engage in financial statement analysis. While not eliminating the personal interaction vital to any bank and borrower relationship, GAAP made it possible to examine a business firm's past performance on a consistent basis from year to year. With the introduction of GAAP, there was also a reasonable prospect that different firms would use the same concepts in accounting for their activities. Even though many firms today do not issue financial statements backed up by an independent audit, most banks require that firms prepare their statements in accordance with GAAP.

Increasing Use of Debt

Another reason for studying financial statement analysis is the increasing use of debt to finance business. The analysis of a firm's debt and its capacity to safely acquire more debt is the subject of this book. The importance of debt markets continues to grow because debt allows owners of businesses to obtain capital without diluting their equity. That is, for a firm with rapidly increasing sales and profits, shareholders wish to defer bringing in new shareholders and thereby dividing the profits. By borrowing at an interest rate unrelated to these growing profits, the firm can avoid new sales of common stock. This deferral of sharing of a growing base can bring greater rewards in the future when additional stock is sold.

The Glass-Steagall Act of 1933 segregated the commercial banks from the equity markets, leaving the tightly regulated investment banking firms to serve as the sole source of equity financing. Because of the competition among investment bankers, commercial banks, insurance companies, and others, innovative debt instruments became common in the aggressive debt markets. One example of debt instrument innovation is commercial paper. Commercial paper permits the most credit-worthy companies to borrow on a short-term basis directly from individuals and institutions, bypassing the commercial banks. With the advent of this borrowing instrument, commercial banks lost an important portion of their prime credit-worthy borrowers to the direct market. Another example of debt instrument innovation is revolving credit, which allows principal to be advanced and repaid as needed. A third example is subordinated-convertible debt that offers equity incentives in exchange for reduced interest rates. Convertible debt is usually subordinated to other senior lenders, but purchasing it is still safer than purchasing common stock of higher-risk firms. Later, as dividends increase and the market price rises nearly to the conversion equivalent price, it can be converted to equity at a preset price.

Another major factor behind an increase in demand for debt was the advent of corporate income taxes. Corporate treasurers quickly recognized that being able to deduct interest expenses made borrowing a less expensive source of capital, after taxes, than equity with its nondeductible dividends.

Commercial banks, becoming more aggressive in their pursuit of income sources, relaxed their credit standards, especially in the markets for loans to developing countries and for real estate development. Moreover, intensified corporate acquisition and the related leveraged buyout activity in the 1980s increased the demand for corporate debt. In many corporate acquisitions and leveraged buyouts, most of a company's equity is replaced by debt. In the case of the RJR buyout, the issuance of new debt was $27 billion. In a paradox of defense against unfriendly acquisitions, some corporations acquired substantial debt to make themselves less likely takeover candidates. These substitutions of debt for common stock reportedly have removed an average of $100 billion from the stock markets annually over the entire decade of the 1980s. Therefore, for nearly 20 years the debt markets have been the major supplier of net new capital to businesses.

DEFINITION OF FINANCIAL STATEMENT ANALYSIS

A critical component of the commercial lending process, *financial statement analysis* helps the loan officer decide whether a loan should be made and under what terms and conditions. The commercial lending process normally begins with an interview between the commercial client and the loan officer and continues through the stages of credit investigation, financial statement analysis, loan structuring and pricing, loan negotiation, loan documentation and closing, and loan follow-up. Thus, financial statement analysis is an important factor not only in the lending decision, but also in the monitoring process after the loan is closed.

Financial statement analysis focuses on the company's past and current financial performance as reflected in its financial statements, rather than on such factors as the company's management style and credit history. Nevertheless, such nonfinancial considerations do help establish the direction and depth the financial statement analysis should take.

Financial statement analysis involves the systematic examination and interpretation of information to assess a company's past performance for the purpose of predicting future viability. Financial statement analysis helps pinpoint unique characteristics—operating or financial—that affect a business's likelihood of success or failure. It presents a picture of the company that includes the following:

- *Financial Structure*—the assets the company maintains and the liabilities it has incurred to acquire and keep those assets, including the company's capacity or flexibility to deal with both planned and unplanned change;
- *Operating Cycle*—the stages the business goes through to bring its products or services to the market; and
- *Trends and Comparative Performance*—the direction that the business operation is going, as evidenced by comparison of financial results from more than one year and with other companies in the same industry and size.

Technical vs. Interpretive Aspects of Analysis

Commercial credit analysts examine the financial information available to them by applying techniques based on sound logic and accounting principles. They perform many technical operations that include calculating ratios, reformatting information for clarity, evaluating the company's goals, comparing statistics with those of other businesses, and projecting future operating results.

This technical manipulation of the data is only a small part, however, of what is needed to complete a comprehensive and effective financial statement analysis of a company. Once the credit analyst has crunched the numbers (calculated ratios, analyzed trends, and compared firms), the results must be interpreted to determine the reasons behind the numbers. The goal is to learn not only *what* is happening, but *why* it is happening. It is also important to consider how past events and current trends might affect the company's future repayment ability.

The crux of financial statement analysis, then, is to understand and correctly interpret the results of the technically manipulated data. To accomplish this, the analyst must first obtain considerable background information about

- the company's ownership,
- its management,
- its lines of business,
- its competition and the markets in which the company operates,
- its operational aspects,
- the characteristics of the industry,
- the company's position within the industry,
- pertinent government regulations,

- the company's susceptibility to adverse changes in the general economy, and
- the extent to which demographic trends and consumer preferences may affect the company's operations.

Understanding these organizational and environmental factors provides meaning to the abstract numbers derived in the technical examination. This information, along with the financial information, helps the loan officer reach a conclusion as to the risks of a proposed loan.

Analysis of Risk

The bank's role as commercial lender provides a limited return on funds of depositors. It earns its contracted-for rate of interest on the loan regardless of the borrower's profitability. This limited return—coupled with the thin margin between the bank's interest return and its cost of funds and its typical high leverage—requires the bank to take only a restrained risk in the extension of credit.

Nevertheless, risk is an inescapable part of commercial lending. The principal risk—called *credit risk* by bankers—is that the borrower will not meet the terms of the loan and that secondary repayment sources, such as collateral, will be insufficient to cover the losses. Credit management attempts to manage the credit risk in the lending portfolio by establishing lending, analysis, and work-out guidelines or policies appropriate for the institution. Financial statement analysis is one of the parts of credit decision making: assessing the risk that companies will not be able to repay their loans as agreed. The loan officer can frequently lessen the hazard of loss by accurately appraising a customer's creditworthiness—ability to repay—and then ensuring that the loan is properly secured, structured, and monitored.

To evaluate risk, attempt to identify the uncertainties the commercial borrower faces to see if its financial strengths and weaknesses are balanced. If the borrower's strengths exceed its weaknesses by a margin sufficient to cover the perceived uncertainties, the loan represents an acceptable credit risk. This concept is often expressed as a formula:

Strengths - Weaknesses > Uncertainties = Acceptable credit risk.

Some of the risks that will be examined throughout the book include

- *liquidity*—the ability of a firm (1) to respond quickly to unexpected financial problems and opportunities, (2) to increase assets if sales grow, and (3) to repay short-term debt from normal conversion of assets to cash;
- *net cash flow*—the generation of cash for long-term purposes such as fixed asset replacements, net additions to current assets, and repayment of long-term debt;

- *operating profit*—the evidence of operations successful enough to reassure investors about the firm's survival and growth in the future; and

- *leverage*—the extent of debt, as a source of the funds used to operate the business, and loan repayment requirements, relative, respectively, to the equity cushion and variability of cash flow.

Functions of Financial Statement Analysis

The scope and focus of financial statement analysis will vary somewhat depending on the specific purpose of the examination. For example, whether the company is seeking long-term or short-term financing or whether the analysis is being done as part of the ongoing monitoring of an existing loan will affect the nature of the financial statement analysis.

Determining the Depth and Focus of the Analysis

Both the size of the requested loan (relative to the size of the firm) and its terms affect the financial statement analysis. A large loan will require relatively more effort on the part of the bank to assure itself that an analysis of sufficient depth has been completed. This is not to say that a small loan cannot have great uncertainty surrounding its repayment. Nevertheless, the smaller interest payment on the small loan may not profitably permit extended analysis, and thus the financial statement analysis may have to be more cut-and-dried.

Companies requesting loans generally need to finance either current assets (such as accounts receivable and inventory) or fixed assets (equipment, buildings, or land). A basic tenet of lending dictates that a temporary or seasonal increase in current assets should be financed by short-term loans, while increases in fixed assets should be financed by long-term loans. Here is why: the principal on short-term loan is payable in full with the conversion of inventory and accounts receivable assets to cash during the operating cycle. Normally, this occurs within one year; therefore, short-term loans are listed on the balance sheet in the current liabilities section. An example of this is the farmer borrowing seed money and repaying the loan at harvest. In contrast, long-term loans are usually payable over the life of the asset they helped finance. They have maturities of one year or longer and are reported as long-term liabilities. An example of this is the farmer financing a tractor over three or four years. Thus, in most cases, the term of the loan and the type of the analysis will be determined by the purpose of the loan.

Monitoring Process

Financial statement analysis is an important part of both the initial decision to approve a loan and the ongoing monitoring process during the entire period that a loan is outstanding. It is particularly useful in identifying problem loan situations early on. With early detection of a problem situation, the bank can often help the company take prompt action to turn the situation around. In addition, banks often monitor their larger borrowers—to whom they may have given credit lines—even when the borrowers have no loans currently outstanding.

The Loan Approval Process

The loan approval process in most institutions involves one or more decision makers, sometimes in the form of a committee, who approve the loan. Generally, the loan officer is referred to as the person, or one of the persons, with loan approval authority who signs for the loan. The credit analyst has the responsibility of preparing information for these decision makers in the desired format and according to the policies of the individual institution. Sometimes, the analyst works closely with the senior credit officer or loan officer to prepare the analysis in written form. At other times, the analyst works directly with the prospective borrower and then makes a presentation to the decision makers, sometimes assembled into a loan committee. This is often the case when the analyst and loan officer are one and the same person, but with insufficient authority to commit the bank to the specific loan.

In either case the written credit analysis is a digest of both the facts concerning the financial and nonfinancial information, as the analyst (and, sometimes, as the loan officer) sees them, and the evaluation of those facts for the purpose of predicting the likelihood of future repayment of the loan, as the analyst interprets it. The full-fledged credit presentation, possibly dwelling on economic conditions or market competition, goes beyond the scope of this book, which concentrates on examination of the financial statements themselves. While these are viewed in light of the nonfinancial information, the primary focus is on how the information they impart can be useful to the full credit analysis, a larger issue. Thus, financial statement analysis is a subset of credit analysis.

SEQUENTIAL STEPS OF FINANCIAL STATEMENT ANALYSIS

The fashioning of a financial statement analysis starts with a preliminary investigation of a company and moves to an in-depth examination of its operating performance and financial structure as evidenced by its historical and projected financial statements. Most banks have a systematic approach for obtaining the various documents, organizing and presenting the information contained therein, and then evaluating and interpreting the data using the standard analytical techniques. The basic steps in financial statement analysis are presented in detail in the following chapters in the order in which they are normally considered. The text is arranged in such a way that each chapter presents an in-depth look at a different tool of financial statement analysis. A brief overview of the entire financial statement analysis process follows.

Obtaining and Spreading the Statements

Banks always ask prospective commercial borrowers to submit detailed financial data, usually prepared in conformity to GAAP, in support of their loan requests. Most banks have established guidelines as to the type and number of financial statements that should be obtained to do a comprehensive examination. Generally, a bank requires three or more year-end income statements, balance sheets, and statements of cash flows as well as comparable interim statements available since the year end. The lender may also specify one to five years of forecast financial statements (sometimes called pro forma statements) and, especially for seasonal lending, a monthly cash budget. Other financial data that lenders may ask commercial borrowers to submit in support of their loan requests include

- a business or marketing plan,
- tax returns,
- operating and capital budgets,
- inventory summary or listing,
- accounts receivable agings,
- backlog and contract status reports,
- accounts payable agings, and
- sales and expense breakdowns.

If any of this documentation is not readily available, it will usually be prepared at the loan officer's request. In some cases, the credit analyst may have to construct some of the items—such as the statement of cash flows or cash budget—on the basis of available data.

Management's Involvement in Statement Preparation

There are different goals among various users of financial statements, and these goals can shape the appearance of the financial statements. The interests of entrepreneurial owners versus those of nonowning managers is a prime example of how these goals can conflict.

Entrepreneurial owners want the financial statement prepared so as to confirm their own understanding of the firm's performance for the year and to meet certain requirements for paying taxes to the Internal Revenue Service. Outside of conforming to the tax rules, the information in the financial statements is useful essentially for the owners' purposes. Even if the financial statements do not show much income or liquidity and show only the historical purchase price of fixed assets, the entrepreneurs' shrewd understanding of their business and that of their competitors allows them to discern how well they are doing and their chances for continued success.

In contrast to these motivations are those of the professional managers. As corporations grow larger, different areas of the company are often decentralized into departments or divisions whose performance is measured separately. These divisions are headed by managers who do not have their personal wealth at stake in the corporation. Managers attempt to achieve specific targets laid out by the board of directors or by the shareholders of a small corporation. Often, these guidelines are integrated into the results presented in the financial statement and are set up by owners or shareholders in an attempt to align the efforts of managers with their own interests. Frequently, bonus programs are offered to managers to obtain this alignment, the bonuses being based on such established benchmarks of financial performance as net income. While the managers may have a different set of goals in mind, such as job security, the bonus program focuses their attention on the results reported in the financial statements.

Moreover, the professional (nonowning) manager of public corporations must be responsive to government regulations. One of the most important of these regulations is supplying financial and nonfinancial information to shareholders. Therefore, the objectives of the nonowning managers include providing a "report card" on their activities for the purposes of both earning compensation and complying with information requirements of shareholders, investors, lenders, and regulators.

The opportunity to prepare one's own report card creates temptations that are difficult to resist. As George Foster states in *Financial Statement Analysis*,[1] "No matter how detailed the set of rules issued by accounting policy bodies, creative managers or their advisers will find means of structuring transactions that do not give rise to reported expenses or reported liabilities even though, in spirit, expenses or liabilities exist. This is but one of several reasons why the disclosures in annual reports need not represent either a complete or an unbiased representation of the underlying transactions and events affecting the firm."

Throughout a financial statement analysis, the analyst must remember that **the statements are those of management** and that accountants reviewed them only to see that they conform to broad standards and meet certain statistical tests of validity. In the preparation of the financial statements, owners and managers have a great deal of leeway by which they can make themselves look good. One way management can make its efforts look better is to choose the best time of the year for preparing the statements. For instance, by having the fiscal year end in the summer, when inventories and receivables are much lower than in December (their peak), retail businesses can produce financial statements that indicate a more favorable financial condition.

Examining the Auditor's Opinion

Auditors review financial statements to test whether they are in accordance with the principles and policies promulgated by the Securities and Exchange Commission and by the Financial Accounting Standards Board. In contrast, management is tempted to prepare the financial statements to present the company's performance in the most favorable light. Another pressure helping to make the results of an audit relatively muddy is the auditors' desire to continue to be the accounting firm for the business they are auditing. Because of these factors, the result of an audit is more appropriately described by the word *fair* than it is by the word financial analysts would like to see: *accurate*.

After examining the financial statements of management, auditors must express an opinion on the quality of the statements. Four types of opinions are given: *unqualified opinion*, *qualified opinion*, *disclaimer opinion*, and *adverse opinion*.

An *unqualified opinion* means that the management receives the highest accolade for "presenting fairly the financial position and results of operations and changes in financial position for the period involved." Footnoted disclosures accompanying an audited statement may result in significant information being available to a firm's creditors. In effect, the footnotes allow the auditor to comment on the statements relative to the GAAP standards. A financial statement that the auditors have declared to conform to GAAP standards has the best credentials that an analyst can obtain. Securing such a financial statement should be required for every unsecured loan request over $100,000.

Even here, the conflicts between the goals of management, the best efforts of auditors, and the needs of readers of financial information produce predicaments. The list of unqualified opinions of financial statements during the 1980s contains cases where, it later turned out, substantial deviations from the truth were included in the statements. Here are examples of some financial statements that were inappropriately given unqualified-opinion ratings:

- In 1982, Stauffer Chemical reduced its earnings by 25 percent as a result of a postaudit review of its financial statements. It had prematurely recognized as real sales orders that had not been shipped.

- AM International Incorporated in 1980 changed its earnings from a $10 million profit to a $190 million loss shortly after its financial statement was issued with an unqualified opinion from a major accounting firm. It had neglected to take an accounting adjustment for discontinuing a line of office computer equipment that was not selling.
- In 1982, Touche Ross was censured by the SEC for allowing Litton Industries to postpone losses from cost overruns on Navy contracts from 1972 through 1977—five years after the fact.
- Ernst & Whinney gave an unqualified opinion to the United American Bank of Knoxville in January 1983. Within three weeks of the release of the financial statements the bank declared insolvency, setting off a chain reaction that hurt many other financial institutions that had deposits with United American.
- In early December 1992, Ernst and Young, a successor firm to Ernst & Whinney, agreed to pay three federal regulatory agencies $400 million to settle claims of improper auditing of many banks and thrifts that subsequently became insolvent.

These examples make it clear that reliance only on audited statements will not prevent a bank from lending to a company that may have significant problems. The audit itself does not prevent management from misrepresentation. In conclusion, the accountant's job is a complicated, maybe even impossible, one. Although many regulatory authorities attempt to keep financial reporting to investors at a high standard, financial statements need to be approached from a wary perspective.

A *qualified opinion* means that the statements present fairly the financial position and results of operations, but that there are certain qualifications about the scope of the auditor's engagement at the audited firm or that there are uncertainties about the future which cannot be resolved or the effect of which cannot be estimated. These reservations, usually phrased "except for" and "subject to," are exemplified below:

> As discussed in Note B, because of the uncertainty of mining plans it may be necessary at some indeterminate future date to write off a significant amount of net book investment in the Company's Questa mine and mill.
>
> In our opinion, subject to the realization of the Company's investment in Questa property referred to above, ... the accompanying financial statements present fairly ....[2]

A *disclaimer opinion* means that because of limitations in the scope of the auditing firm's engagement or because of uncertainties about the future that cannot be resolved or the effect of which cannot be estimated, the accountants cannot express an opinion. A disclaimer opinion includes the *review* and *compilation opinions*, which means that the auditors consolidated the statements and prepared the acknowledgments without independently verifying the data, an important part of any audit.

An *adverse opinion* means that the statements *do not* present fairly the financial position or results of operations in conformity with generally accepted accounting principles. This type of opinion is rarely encountered.

For analysis purposes, the qualified opinion is comparable to an unqualified opinion and, depending on the reason for the qualification, is usually suitable. A financial statement with the disclaimer opinion would be considered unaudited, but could be prepared substantially in accordance with GAAP and should be treated as discussed in the next section. The adverse opinion is of questionable value.

Unaudited Statements

Audited financial statements differ from unaudited statements in one highly important way—the degree of confirmation of asset, liability, sales, and expense account balances. For example, in the normal course of an audit engagement, inventory levels are physically sampled, and statistically selected accounts receivable are confirmed.

Confirmation is not done, or is not done with the same thoroughness or independence, in the preparation of unaudited statements.

Many firms do not have their financial statements prepared by an outside accountant or accounting firm because they claim not to be able to justify the cost of a full audit, approximately $15,000 or more. Instead, statements are generated in house from books and records that have not been independently verified. The following questions may be suggested to the credit analyst:

- ❒ How experienced or competent is the preparer?
- ❒ Are the financial records of the firm accurate and complete?
- ❒ Have all the liabilities been identified and reported?
- ❒ Even if the person who prepares the information is qualified and the data are both available and reliable, how independent is the preparer?
    - Is the preparer in the day-to-day employ of the enterprise?
    - Can the preparer be objective about the value of inventory or the collectibility of receivables?
    - Can the preparer be unduly influenced by the owner of the business?

The professional standards of certified public accountants require independence from the client or disclosure of business or family relationships that might inhibit the exercise of independent judgment. The presence of audited financials (and their implications) gives a certain comfort level to the creditors of the enterprise. The reliance by creditors on analysis of less than audited statements needs to be clearly understood, and the bank must be protected with collateral or personal guarantees of the owners or other appropriate consideration.

A readily available alternative source of financial information is the firm's income tax return submitted to the Internal Revenue Service. Some play down the accuracy of these returns, claiming that the income errs on the conservative side. Nevertheless, these statements are prepared for the IRS, which will prosecute fraudulent submissions. Assuming the proper reporting, there is significant information in the tax return, which should be certified as a *conformed*, or exact, copy.

Spreading the Financial Statements

Basically, *statement spreading* is the process by which information from financial statements is recorded on a standard form, or spreadsheet. Many banks use a standard spreadsheet for income statements, balance sheets, and statements of cash flows. Use of a spreadsheet enables the analyst to review a number of years all at once, to spot trends in the company's account balances, and to make comparisons.

In many banks, spreading and common-sizing of financial statements and ratio calculations are done by accessing computerized databases available through private firms and even such government organizations as the Securities and Exchange Commission. This practice can result in some loss of the type of analytical input to be discussed in the following three chapters. Thoughtful preparation of data on computers to clarify the analytical input and to make the results more useful has always differed from copying other analyst's work from a publication by Moody's Investors Service or Standard & Poor's.

With the goal being to interpret a company's past financial performance and to project its likely future performance in order to gauge its ability to repay the requested loan (or the existing loan in a problem credit analysis), *the credit analyst may err by concentrating on the three financial statements without incorporating the information from the footnotes.* Because of the issues just discussed, the analyst needs to reconcile the financial statements for his or her own use, incorporating footnote information or reliable external information, such as appraisals by certified appraisers. Spreading the statements can be the opportunity for making these adjustments.

Since the key to successful financial statement analysis lies in the credit analyst's ability to determine not simply what has happened in the past or even why it happened, but what it bodes for the future, all available financial information needs to be interpreted and integrated. However, it cannot be overemphasized that financial statement analysis does not purport to be an exact science that can be used to predict with certainty a company's future. Unknown factors abound, and subjective judgment is necessarily involved in drawing conclusions from the analyzed data and making the final credit decision.

Balance Sheet Analysis

The *balance sheet* is the first part of the financial statements to be analyzed in this book. It is a point-in-time financial picture of the company—usually as of the last day of the company's fiscal year. The basic structure of the balance sheet can be stated as a simple equation:

Assets = Liabilities + Net worth.

Balance sheet analysis entails an evaluation of the company's assets followed by an evaluation of its liabilities (debt) and, the difference between the two, its net worth (or equity).

Income Statement Analysis

Next to be analyzed is the *income statement*—also called a profit and loss statement or earnings statement. One of the most important sources of information about a company, it begins with total revenues (or sales) and then categorizes the various expenses leading to the net profit (or loss) for the period. The accountant's goal is to analyze the net profit or net income, that is, to estimate the wealth generated by the firm during the period. The analysis consists of examining the quality and consistency of revenue and truthfulness of the expenses.

Statement of Cash Flow Analysis

The third financial statement to be analyzed is the *statement of cash flow* (stemming from the sources and uses of funds statement and, its predecessor, the sources and applications of funds statement). As its name implies, this model of the company's business operations shows how a company obtains and uses its cash resources, ignoring the accrual accounting, wealth-generating model.

Since debt is repaid with cash, the statement of cash flow helps the lender determine both the company's funding needs and its sources of repayment. The statement of cash flow shows inflows and outflows of cash categorized as operating funds flows, investing activities, and financing activities. Like an income statement, it is dynamic (normally covering a fiscal year).

Every client should be required to submit as part of its financial documentation a statement of cash flows prepared, if possible, in accordance with the Statement of Financial Accounting Standards (SFAS) No.95. Some clients, especially those submitting statements that have not been reviewed by outside auditors, can not or will not prepare a statement of cash flow. In this case the analyst may approximate the information in the spreading process.

Ratio Analysis

Ratios are not only the best known and most widely used of all the financial statement analysis tools, they are also the most overrated and most widely misused. Ratios allow the lender to study the relationship and trends over time between various components of financial statements, such as assets and liabilities or expenses and revenues. While ratios are easily calculated, their correct interpretation is more problematic. The specific ratios used by a particular bank may vary, but the major categories of ratios reflect the major aspects of a company's operations that a lender needs to consider:

- *Liquidity*—the ability to meet current obligations and convert assets to cash.
- *Leverage*—the relationship between liabilities and the company's net worth.
- *Solvency*, or *Coverage*—the company's capacity to meet its continuing payment obligations.
- *Profitability*—the company's ability to sell its products or provide a service at a price that exceeds its expenses.
- *Activity*—the efficiency with which a company uses its assets (which will vary over time, particularly for a company that is cyclical in nature).

Trend Analysis

Determining trends and making industry comparisons are two basic analytical techniques that will be discussed in detail throughout the text. Trend analysis compares information over comparable periods or at comparable times for the same company. It is used to detect favorable or unfavorable changes in operating policies as reflected in revenues, expenses, and asset or liability accounts.

Comparative Analysis

Comparative analysis parallels the ratios and other financial information of at least two companies, preferably of the same size and industry. This allows the analyst to draw conclusions about the relative performance of the firms. By using the *Annual Statement Studies* by Robert Morris Associates, many firms may be matched to the subject firm and statistical conclusions drawn.

Preparing Forecasts

Forecasts are basic to the loan analysis and put into numerical form something that the granting of any loan implicitly assumes—that the borrower will be able to repay the principal. Two tools used in this analysis are short-term and long-term forecasts. Some analysts call them cash budgets and pro formas, the latter term being used especially to describe a one-year forecast of the three financial statements.

The types of projections shown herein forecast the future based upon the technique of percentage of sales relationships; everything is forecast based upon its historic relationship to sales. Therefore, the entire forecast is predicated on (1) an accurate-as-possible prediction of the sales levels and (2) the company's operating structure not changing in ways that disturb the historical relationships between sales and expenses or asset levels, as identified by the analyst.

Cash Budget

The *cash budget* is an important financial statement analysis tool. Presented in the form of a one-year financial forecast, a cash budget forecasts a company's cash receipts and payments, generally on a month-to-month basis. The cash budget enables the lender to gauge a business's peak credit needs and its ability to generate sufficient cash to repay short-term loans over the term of its operating cycle. The cash budget also helps a lender determine whether a company's borrowing needs are long term or short term. Cash budgets are especially useful in determining the financial needs of borrowers with seasonal operating cycles (such as a toy store that rings up half of its total sales in the last two months of each year).

Long-term Forecasts

The examination of three- to five-year forecasts of income statements and balance sheets forces the analyst to apply what has been learned from analysis of the historical financial statements to the future, given an estimated level of sales. Examination of a company-provided forecast involves evaluating the company's underlying assumptions as well as the expected economic, competitive, and regulatory environment in which the company will operate.

Normally, the projections depend on the size and term of the requested loan. However, since management-submitted pro formas tend to be biased, credit analysts often create their own prognosis for a company based on what they consider more-likely assumptions (such as lower profit margins).

Other Advanced Analytical Techniques

Besides the essential analytical tools described above, several more-advanced analytical techniques are available. These techniques include

- *working investment analysis*, which measures the impact of sales growth on financing requirements and a company's ability to expand sales;
- *sustainable growth analysis*, which measures a company's ability to expand its sales without changing its proportional use of debt;
- *sensitivity analysis*, which uses multiple scenarios to examine a company's areas of greatest vulnerability; and
- *industry factor*, which considers the variability of the borrowing firm's cash flows by comparing them to the cash flows of other companies in its industry.

These techniques are invaluable in refining and focusing the financial statement analysis process and in evaluating a company's ability to grow. With practice, credit analysts will gain skill in using them and in interpreting the results as well as in determining what types of advanced analysis are useful in a particular situation.

Ideally, sound conclusions should be reached efficiently—that is, with minimum effort. The amount of work entailed will vary greatly with the commercial credit analyst's level of experience. For instance, a senior loan officer with 25 years of experience may be able to quickly scan and understand financial information, do technical and interpretive analyses mentally, and promptly reach a conclusion. The beginning credit analyst, by contrast, can afford few shortcuts.

LIMITATIONS OF ANALYSIS

Although financial statement analysis is a critical tool in commercial lending activities, it has some important limitations. First, its success depends upon the reliability and completeness of the information being analyzed. Yet, even with unqualified audit opinions, financial statement analysis is not an exact science that can be used to arrive at absolute conclusions. Because it deals with future uncertainty, analysis is much better at formulating questions and projecting possibilities than it is at providing definitive answers.

Technical analysis alone cannot provide a complete understanding of the borrower. Banks do not make loan decisions based on financial statement analysis alone; the nonfinancial strengths and weaknesses of the borrower must also be considered. In addition, pricing, negotiation of specific terms, the bank's willingness to assume risk, and the availability of funds are also important aspects of the decision to extend or deny credit.

Accounting Methods

Generally accepted accounting principles (GAAP) prescribe methods of reporting accounting or financial information in order to facilitate comparisons among companies. Nevertheless, in preparing financial statements, many different accounting techniques are accepted. For example, financial statements can be prepared on a cash or an accrual basis, using LIFO (last in, first out) or FIFO (first in, first out) inventory valuation methods, and using accelerated depreciation or straight-line depreciation of fixed assets.

Although the accounting methods used are usually described in the footnotes to accountant-prepared financial statements, differences in accounting methods can make it difficult to make valid comparisons even between companies in the same industry. Comparing financial statements of a company over time may also yield invalid conclusions if the company has changed any of its accounting methods during the period being analyzed. Moreover, many accounting rules allow leeway in recognizing income and charging expenses; thus, the analyst must be on the alert for management's self-serving selection of these alternatives to make its performance look better than it is.

Financial Condition

In assessing a business's financial condition, the accountant is concerned with the reporting of assets (what is owned), liabilities (what is owed), and owner's equity (the investment by the stockholder). There are two very important points to note here. The first is that *assets are normally recorded at historical cost,* the market value at the time of purchase. In periods of inflation or deflation, recording assets at historical cost can produce differences between carrying value in terms of accounting and current value in real economic terms because increases in value (or reductions in value occurring more slowly than originally estimated for depreciation purposes) are not reflected. Possible exceptions to the recording of assets at original cost will be discussed later in chapter 3.

The other key point is the concept of *liquidity,* which refers to the ability to quickly convert an asset to cash (at or near market value) or to how soon a liability will have to be paid in cash. Assets and liabilities are listed on the balance sheet and on the spreadsheet in descending order of liquidity. If on the one hand a borrower collects its accounts receivable within the 30 days that is standard within its particular industry, the receivable would be judged quite liquid. On the other hand, if the company's new warehouse was designed to meet its specialized needs and constructed next to its factory, the warehouse is quite illiquid by comparison with the accounts receivable. The company could sell the warehouse, but to find a buyer quickly for such a distinct structure the company probably would have to offer a discount or some other financial incentive.

Any asset expected to convert to cash in the firm's normal operating cycle is called a *current asset*. Unfortunately, GAAP's rules for determining current status are not consistently based on the operating cycle; they include most assets and liabilities that will convert to cash or are required to be paid within one year. This difference makes the current status of assets and liabilities on audited financial statements subject to interpretation. Clearly, this is more a problem in some industries than others. For example, farmers, toy manufacturers, and ski clothing retailers have a well-defined annual business cycle. Except for such obvious seasonality, most business firms whose statements an analyst will spread have operating cycles of less than one year, and this complicates the fact that a firm's *current position* is analyzed in terms of the difference between current assets and current liabilities. The difference is *net* working capital, but it is customarily shortened and just called *working capital*.

The owner's equity account can be viewed from two perspectives:

- *accounting*, the owner's initial and subsequent investments and whatever net income has been retained in the business from its inception; or
- *financial*,the net difference between the value of assets and the obligations of liabilities. This latter definition causes analysts to be aware of the value of the assets in the marketplace, which is important for collateral protection as well as for the potential revenue that may be produced from any firm's assets.

Results of Operations

The results of operations are measured by revenues and expenses; revenues are sales, while expenses are described in accounting terms as the costs to produce revenues. In this book, the terms *costs* and *expenses* are used interchangeably. The difference between the effort (cost) and the result (revenue) is net profit or net loss.

Costs should be thought of in two broad categories: those costs directly related to production of sales, and those costs only indirectly related. Examples of directly related costs include sales commissions and costs incurred in the manufacturing or production process, such as raw materials, manufacturing, labor, and so on. These are more commonly referred to as *cost of sales* or *cost of goods sold*. Indirect costs include those not directly tied to the production of revenue, such as accounting or legal fees, administrative and secretarial salaries, rent, utilities, interest on borrowed funds, and the like. These are more commonly referred to as *selling*, or *general administrative costs*. As discussed in chapter 4, the relative proportions of these types of costs to sales and the ratio of net income to sales is of considerable analytical significance.

Accountants attempt to present information on an interpretive basis by matching revenues with their related expenses. This idea includes depreciation, the accounting process of allocating the cost of a fixed asset over the asset's estimated useful life. Depreciation is usually considered to be a direct expense, since production activity directly causes wear—if not economic obsolescence—on a fixed asset.

Manufacturers include depreciation in cost of goods sold. However, depreciation is not an outflow of cash like the money spent to acquire an asset. Through depreciation, the cost of acquiring the fixed asset is distributed over time in an attempt to match it with the revenues generated by the asset over more than a single operating cycle. This is a prime example of the differences between cash accounting and accrual accounting, which are discussed in chapters 4 and 5.

Continuity

The concept of continuity presupposes that the enterprise will remain in business in its present form for a long enough time to use its assets for their intended purpose and to pay liabilities in the ordinary course of business. This concept is also known as the *going concern*. If an enterprise can not be termed a going concern, then the immediate practical problems for the financial statement analyst are to determine whether the firm's assets are properly valued for financial presentation and—if they are not—whether the owner's equity is overstated.

The assumption underlying continuity is that assets will be used for their original purpose of generating future revenues and long-term net cash flow. If the business fails, the assets might have to be liquidated for the sole purpose of repaying debt immediately; such a set of distressed circumstances would produce a dollar result substantially less than any value that appears on the financial statements. If there is reason to question the ability of the enterprise to maintain a going concern status, the accountant must bring this question to the attention of the reader of the financial statements; however, such a statement by accountants is rare unless the audited firm is already in default on its obligations.

Presented Fairly

The phrase *presented fairly* in an audit opinion is not precise. GAAP state that principal assumptions should be disclosed, that their form and substance should be comparable to those of the prior year, and that all matters of a nature deemed material by the accountants should be addressed or disclosed where appropriate. Because of the accountant's focus on income generation as production of wealth, GAAP insist that revenues and related costs be properly matched in each reporting period.

Generally accepted accounting principles is a term that came into use in the 1930s as a result of professional and regulatory reforms to formalize and standardize accounting practices, including financial statement presentations. GAAP encompass those practices generally in use and commonly found in business and those with regulatory and authoritative professional support for their continued use. GAAP are defined as such by the accounting profession and are followed (or exceptions noted) by all reputable accountants. GAAP have evolved to adapt to increasingly complex business environments.

Throughout the history of accounting, there has been a consistent trend toward conservative presentation of financial information. If an asset's value on the open market declines, for example, the accountant will normally write it down to its realizable value. If, however, an asset increases in value, the accountant will not show the increase. This treatment of writing assets down to net realizable value is typically applied to marketable securities and inventories, although it is sometimes extended to other assets. A significant loss of a fixed asset's value due to economic obsolescence would constitute an appropriate reason for a markdown.

As the foregoing discussion has shown, standard practices and principles govern accounting and accounting's final product—the financial statements. To be designated a *certified public accountant* (CPA), a practitioner of accounting must meet the standards of the profession and be certified or licensed. Each of the fifty states certifies, but the professional standards nationally are virtually identical. Even though standards are rigorous and high, not all certified public accountants are equally qualified by industry, size of client, or years of professional experience. Furthermore, accounting practice requires judgment, and not all situations are necessarily obvious.

While accounting appears to be very precise because of its quantitative terms (sometimes to the penny), it is often much less than precise. Fortunately, most users of financial information understand these issues and recognize that presentation of reliable financial information requires competence, conservatism, and consistency. The purpose of this book is to review basic ideas and to alert you to that which may either enhance or compromise the quality of financial information. The goal is to assist you in making your efforts more productive more quickly.

Adequacy of Information

Some relevant information may not show up on a company's financial statements. For example, a listing of sales backlogs or contractual orders of capital goods may be important considerations that only an experienced loan officer or one knowledgeable about the company or industry might know to look for.

Often the data in financial statements are aggregated. For example, a company with various product lines usually shows a single total sales figure on the income statement. The credit analyst may need to request breakdowns of sales and expenses by product line or by geographical area.

Moreover, many important factors cannot be quantified and listed on a financial statement. Thus, loan interviews and credit checks supplement the financial statement analysis of a company to assess such nonfinancial characteristics of the borrower as evidence of the company's willingness to repay past debts and an overall consideration of the character traits of management.

SUMMARY

Financial statement analysis involves both the technical manipulation and the interpretation of financial information to assess a company's past performance, present condition, and future viability as a means of determining the amount of risk involved in a lending situation. This assessment is expressed in the formula

Strengths – Weaknesses > Uncertainties = Acceptable credit risk.

The scope of the examination may be influenced by the size, purpose, and term of the loan or, in the case of a problem loan, the specific circumstances surrounding that loan. Financial statement analysis involves the following sequential steps:

1. Obtain the requisite financial statements.
2. Evaluate the various income statement and balance sheet accounts and then spread them.
3. Evaluate these historical statements by centering on the company's operations as seen in its income statements and on its financial structure as seen in its balance sheets.
4. Review a company's statement of cash flow to assess the company's sources and uses of cash.

5. Use ratios to conduct trend analysis (comparing a company's results over time) and comparative analysis (comparing a company's results with that of other companies in the same industry).
6. Especially for short-term loans, create or review the company's monthly cash budget (its projected receipts and expenditures) in order to determine the company's seasonal or other short-term funding needs.
7. Predict the firm's future performance and, thus, its ability to repay the loan in question. This involves the creation or review of a company's projected financial statements (or pro formas), the value of which depend in large part on their being based on a realistic sales projection. Often the credit analyst will rework the pro formas using different assumptions.
8. Finally, the lender may select from several more-advanced analytical techniques that may show, for example, a company's ability to undergo rapid growth.

After completing all of these analytical steps, the analyst must interpret the information in light of the company's nonfinancial strengths and weaknesses and the total environment in which the company operates.

EXERCISES

Important Terms to Define

The following terms are italicized in the text to help you locate definitions for them.

- financial statement analysis
- financial structure
- trends and comparative performance
- credit risk
- liquidity
- leverage
- unqualified opinion
- qualified opinion
- disclaimer opinion
- adverse opinion
- balance sheet
- income statement
- statement of cash flow
- solvency, or coverage
- profitability
- generally accepted accounting principles (GAAP)
- historical cost
- current asset
- working capital
- going concern
- presented fairly
- certified public accountant

Review Questions

1. To better understand the concept of financial analysis, imagine that you are a doctor using an electrocardiograph on a patient. The machine prints out a chart showing how the patient's heart is performing, and you interpret the chart to diagnose the patient's health. What other methods might you use to interpret the likelihood that the patient will remain healthy? Compare this analysis to the factors you might consider in determining the likelihood that a business will remain healthy. Finally, list several factors that might have an unexpected adverse effect on the health of the patient and the business.

2. Consider how the concept of uncertainty affects a loan officer's assessment of risk. What aspects of society can be accurately predicted? For example, can the economy, weather, or election results be accurately predicted? List some historic trends that can be studied to narrow the uncertainty gap, such as leading indicators, pressure zones, or opinion polls. Next, draw some conclusions about how well historic trends predict the future and compare them to the accuracy of predictions you might reach when analyzing the financial statements of a company.

3. Prepare a list of factors that contribute to the stability of an organization seeking a loan. For example, a company with little or no debt can better withstand a recession and the drop in sales because it has less interest and loan principal payments than a company with significant debt.

NOTES

1. *Financial Statement Analysis*, 2nd Edition [1986] pp. 158-159.
2. *Financial Statement Analysis*, Leopold A. Bernstein

The Industry Environment

LEARNING OBJECTIVES

After studying this chapter, you will be able to explain

- the characteristic operating cycles—also called cash flows cycles—of different types of industries and how they are distinguished from the annual accounting for income;
- why a company's type of business, legal structure, size, and management strategies, as well as its external environment, are important considerations in financial statement analysis;
- how a company's cash flow cycle can affect debt requirements and repayment; and
- the typical distribution of assets and liabilities for manufacturers, wholesalers, retailers, and a number of different service companies.

INTRODUCTION

Before examining specific financial data, the credit analyst should have a good understanding of the company and its operating environment. This understanding provides a context for the financial statement analysis and enables the analyst to put the figures in a meaningful perspective.

The primary factor that a lender should take into consideration from the outset is the type of business in which the loan applicant is engaged—that is, whether it is a manufacturing, merchandising, service, or agricultural enterprise. Each category of business operation has characteristic operating cycles, types of credit needs, and sources of financing or repayment. This chapter discusses the following steps that an analyst can take to help describe the basic qualities of the individual business:

- *Identifying the operating cycle*—defining the time it takes a business to add value to raw materials or labor, sell the product or service, and collect the cash from the sale.
- *Analyzing the cash flow cycle*—understanding how it affects the need for outside financing and the timing of loan repayment. A company's fixed asset cycle and profit cycle are related concepts.
- *Describing management's objectives*—describing the firm's goals, including its market tactics, profit objectives, growth targets, and business ethics and reviewing its management style.
- *Assessing industry risk*—comparing the riskiness of different industries and business strategies.
  - *Studying the marketplace*—determining whether competition is a significant factor in setting the stage for financial statement analysis.
  - *Understanding the macroeconomic environment*—ascertaining whether the industry is vulnerable to economic downturns, and knowing its regulatory environment.
- *Learning the size*—finding out whether the company is run by one manager or operates with divisions of responsibilities or operating facilities.
- *Learning the legal status*—determining whether the company is organized as a proprietorship, a partnership, or a corporation.

DISTINCTIONS AMONG BUSINESS OPERATIONS

Most businesses can be categorized as manufacturing, merchandising, service, or agricultural enterprises. Businesses of the same type tend to have certain similarities such as operating cycles of the same duration, requirements for cash or credit, and asset and liability structures. The fact that many businesses today are diversified—that is, they operate in more than one type of business—complicates the examination significantly. For example, if a company that manufactures suits also retails them, the analyst should review the various components of the company separately. This requires prodding the firm for unconsolidated or separate statements by division and, most important for the lending financial institution, committing extra time and analysis to gain an understanding of the credit risk associated with the borrower.

Understanding the type of business in which a company is engaged is also important because the length of a company's operating cycle affects the risk of a loan and will thus enter into the loan officer's decision as to the amount, term, and structure of a loan. The length of the operating cycle is usually expressed in the average number of days involved in converting raw materials or service capabilities to usable products or services, selling these products or services, and collecting the accounts receivable generated by the sales. Furthermore, the lender must be aware of any factors that may disrupt the operating cycle and, therefore, the company's cash flow. In addition, an experienced loan officer will come to know what to expect, and hence what is out of line, when looking at financial statements for a given type of company.

Exhibit 2.1 demonstrates that currently only 15 percent of the work force is directly involved in production of goods. The bulk of employment in the United States at this time is centered on service and professional occupations, which requires the analyst to understand how to assess professional and service occupations in financial statement analysis.

Manufacturers

Manufacturers make products for sale by changing raw materials or purchased parts into salable goods. For example, a paper mill is a manufacturer that converts wood pulp, a raw material, into paper. A furniture company, on the other hand, might purchase wood, glue, nails, and screws to produce desks or tables.

The operating cycle of manufacturers starts with cash or trade credit that is used to finance the purchase of raw materials. Using these raw materials, inventory is manufactured and then sold and recorded as an increase in

Exhibit 2.1 Employment by Occupation

Occupation	Millions	Percent
Managerial and professional specialty	**30,398**	**25.16**
Executive, administrative and managerial	14,848	12.29
Professional specialty	15,550	12.87
Technical, sales and administrative support	**36,127**	**29.90**
Technicians and related support	3,645	3.02
Sales occupations	14,065	11.64
Administrative support, including clerical	18,416	15.24
Service occupations	**15,556**	**12.87**
Private household	872	0.72
Protective service	1,960	1.62
Service, except private household and protective	12,724	10.53
Precision production, craft, and repair	**13,818**	**11.44**
Mechanics and repairers	4,550	3.77
Construction trades	5,142	4.26
Other precision production, craft, and repair	4,126	3.41
Operators, fabricators, and laborers	**18,022**	**14.91**
Machine operators, assemblers, and inspectors	8,248	6.83
Transportation and material moving occupations	4,886	4.04
Handlers, equipment cleaners, helpers, and laborers	4,888	4.05
Total, all Federal Government Agencies	**3,497**	**2.89**
Total	**120,839**	**100.00**

Source: Bureau of Labor Statistics for 1989.

accounts receivable. When the accounts receivable are collected, cash is generated, which is then used to repay trade creditors—or the bank debt which allowed earlier repayment and purchase—or to order more raw materials, perhaps on credit, thus beginning the cycle again.

In general, manufacturers are inventory and fixed asset intensive, requiring a large amount of debt to carry out their operations (which typically entails buying and equipping a plant). Manufacturers request loans for many reasons, such as to

- purchase equipment related to their production process,
- fund inventory purchases,
- carry accounts receivable, or
- make plant improvements.

Historically, banks have been partial to manufacturing operations with regard to lending terms. Accounts receivable derived from physical products shipped, inventories of raw materials, finished goods, and even work in process were looked upon as collateral that could be liquidated relatively easily. Lending financial institutions have thought of plant and equipment as the "bricks and mortar" that maintain or even increase their value as collateral over time. The reason for this predisposition towards manufacturers was the ability to sell the firm's physical assets, against which the bank would take a lien. Liens are called the secondary source of repayment, the back door out of a bad loan transaction.

Today, manufacturing is diminishing in importance to the economy and becoming vulnerable to international competition at the same time. The speed with which plant and equipment can become obsolete challenges the traditional, often unsophisticated, reliance on collateral value. Thus, future financial statement analysis will depend on examination of the cash flows that can be generated from these assets, not their historical cost.

In commercial bond rating agencies, *market* share is regarded as the best indicator of a company's stability, or at least survivability, especially during macroeconomic crises like recessions. Manufacturing businesses tend to have a larger share of their market than do their counterparts in the service, transportation, and reselling industries. This stability entitles manufacturers that have substantial market share to preferential treatment on loan terms.

Wholesalers

Wholesalers do not produce but resell marketable goods—either manufactured or nonmanufactured—to retailers, to other wholesalers, or to major users of the product. The major risk for wholesalers is getting caught with merchandise that is no longer in demand by the market or is available elsewhere at lower prices. While manufacturing styled clothing is subject to some risk, the difference between production cost and selling price makes it less risky than wholesaling, where the profit margins are narrower. Wholesaling is more common in durable, nonstyled goods, including everything from producers' supplies to alcoholic beverages.

The operating cycle of a wholesaler begins with the use of cash or trade credit to purchase inventory. When the inventory is sold, accounts receivable are created, which are converted to cash upon payment, thus completing the cycle. A notable characteristic of the operating cycle of wholesalers is the large amount of inventory that is purchased and sold. This high rate of inventory turnover means that a wholesaler's profit as a percentage of sales is usually low.

Accounts receivable typically constitute another important asset and accounts payable constitute an important liability for wholesalers. Since wholesalers do not typically require substantial amounts of equipment or other fixed assets, the majority of loan requests relate to working capital requirements—that is, amounts required to carry inventory and accounts receivable.

Retailers

Retailers purchase finished products from wholesalers or directly from manufacturers for resale to consumers. Retail businesses are diverse, ranging from department stores to small specialty boutiques. The operating cycle of retailers begins with cash or accounts payable used to purchase inventory (a finished product), which in turn is generally sold directly to the public for cash or on credit. Thus, accounts receivable are usually minimal. The cash is used to purchase more inventory.

As with wholesalers, a key factor in evaluating a retailer is inventory turnover. Depending on the type of retailer, either inventory or fixed assets may be the primary asset. Retail businesses typically request loans to increase their inventory or expand their retail outlets. Inventory loans predominate at peak seasons, especially Christmas. The amount of capital required to finance a retail operation varies greatly according to sales volume and the particular industry involved. Net profit margins for retailers are smaller than they are for manufacturers, but greater than for wholesalers. Rapidly growing sales volume usually requires a significant amount of inventory.

More recently, the expansion of chains of stores across the country, especially in suburban shopping centers, has resulted in numerous retail outlets of the same company. The substantial capital for these new facilities has generally come from the real estate investment markets. Rarely do retailers own these facilities; generally, they are owned by real estate syndicates or partnerships and leased, on a long-term basis, to the retailer. Frequently these lease commitments are equivalent to long-term debt, but for accounting purposes they are carried only in the footnotes of the financial statement. The bond rating agencies, such as Standard & Poor's, expend considerable effort to construct balance-sheet-equivalent debt numbers from these leasing obligations to enable comparison between firms. The existence of this off-balance-sheet debt is of concern to the lending financial institution.

In addition, the expansion of chain stores has caused a rapid increase in inventory and made it more difficult to control the inventory. Inventory pilferage has caused the demise of more than one electronics retailer. The capital required for this expansion frequently has come from eager manufacturers and wholesalers who are not aware of their commitment to what is, in effect, a long-term inventory base. Eventually, banks are requested to provide interim funding, and they need to be aware of the issue of inventory required for seasonal versus base-level expansion.

Transportation Companies

Transportation firms are an extremely diverse lot, including everything from railroads to taxis. Their business is transporting the goods of other businesses and consumers. Their primary similarity is a substantial requirement for fixed equipment, from railroad rolling stock to aircraft to titled vehicles.

Transportation companies often use their equipment for set periods, ranging from 1 year for a car owned by an automobile rental company to 25 years for a jet owned by a commercial airline. Although the equipment in both of these examples have useful lives beyond the periods mentioned, the purchasers intend to recapture a portion of their investment upon resale of the equipment to the used-equipment market. Thus, part of the fixed asset flow of funds comes from selling assets into what can be a volatile used-equipment marketplace. Vacillation in the used-equipment market can destabilize transportation firms, depending upon their need for new equipment. In general, however, the value of this equipment holds up well and reduces the risk for any lending financial institution.

Since transportation equipment has a useful life of at least one year, financing is generally provided long-term. Furthermore, as recent recessions have fallen short of catastrophic declines in trade, the cash flow of transportation firms tends to be relatively stable, if low margin. Moreover, as some areas of the industry have stopped growing rapidly, capital-equipment acquisitions may be primarily for replacement, resulting in relatively predictable returns.

Finally, the high leverage and fixed costs of these operations require lenders to be vigilant in assessing the net operating profit margin, the primary health gauge for transportation firms.

Financial Services

Financial services firms are a diverse group and include such firms as stock brokers, insurance companies, and consumer credit-card companies. Naturally, banks themselves are in this category. These firms generally provide an intermediary service, which means they obtain money from depositors and lend it to borrowers. This *intermediation*, as it is called, is illustrated in Exhibit 2.2

Intermediation

Exhibit 2.2

Provide Loans or Equity Investments with These Characteristics	*By Intermediating Using These Sources of Funds*
Long-term repayment	Short-term sources of funds
Large dollar amounts	More numerous small depositors or investors
Diversified investments	One source obligation for depositors

Compared to forecasting profits of manufacturers and transportation companies, forecasting whether the profit margin of financial services firms will continue into the future is difficult. The difficulty arises because these firms are highly leveraged, have substantial debt relative to their equities, and advance considerable funds relative to their small net return. If only a few of their obligors or investments do not repay the principal, many times that number of good investments are required to make up for the loss. Furthermore, many financial services firms are not diversified into different types of business or geographic regions, and a downturn in one area can cause a series of losses that can wipe out a firm with a small equity base. Finally, employees of some of these firms are not well trained in identifying safe investments, and the regulators from government agencies and the accountants who audit the books of these firms are not always able to forestall problems.

Because of the above factors, and because so much of the value of a financial services firm's assets depends on collecting principal from specific investments, the financial statements of these firms tend to be less useful in predicting the future than those of other types of business. In addition, the character of the officers of financial services firms must be absolutely above reproach to reduce the danger of defalcation (embezzlement).

As a result of all these factors, during the late 1980s, the losses in principal in just the commercial and savings bank portion of the financial services industry were catastrophic. Because agencies of the federal government guarantee depositors' funds, the financial burden of those losses fell on the taxpayer. Current estimates are that losses net of recoveries will amount to over $300 billion, nearly 10 percent of the total $3 trillion in loans outstanding from commercial and savings banks.

In summary, knowledge of the specifics of the financial service institution's investment portfolio is essential for proper financial statement analysis.

Construction

Construction firms contract with clients to build real estate, generally to order. Except for a few large public firms, these companies tend to be small, entrepreneurial businesses. There are three major risks to this type of business. First, most one-time contracts are for custom configurations (not suitable for commodity sale). Second, during the considerable time required to complete a project, costs can escalate beyond initial estimates, rendering the entire project profitless. Third, many construction firms run into financial difficulties because they build facilities on the speculation that the real estate market will continue to be strong. Naturally, the changeable real estate market adds risk to assessing the value of the work-in-progress account. An additional complexity is the difficulty of estimating the cost of custom projects. Many contractors fail because they underestimate the cost, but must complete the project because of the contract.

Most construction projects frequently lap over the fiscal year end of the contractor. Accountants debate whether the percentage of completion income recognition method is dependable, but most lending financial institutions prefer it because it provides some indication of how the costs and expenses are aligned. Tax laws also encourage percentage-of-completion accounting for tax purposes.

Because of the difficulty in measuring the profits of projects before they are completed, consummation of a large project should signal the analyst to review the statements, even if they are interim ones. Fiscal year statements are important only if the contractor generally operates by building many small projects and is nonseasonal; analyzing quarterly statements, if not monthly statements, is highly advised.

Construction firms have substantial assets invested in equipment and work in progress. The latter is of practically no value to a lending firm in the event of a collapse of the construction firm. Banks financing accounts receivable for contractors must monitor the ongoing projects to achieve proper *due diligence*. (Due diligence means that a reasonable investigation was undertaken to ensure that the reported facts are validated.) Lending institutions that are financing equipment need to investigate the market to determine the equipment's usefulness to other contractors and its marketability (*fungibility*).

Health Services

Health services is a substantial and growing industry. Frequently, a health service business is set up as a not-for-profit firm. The activity of providing health care is straightforward from an accounting point of view. The largest expense is labor cost, much of it fixed. A large asset is the accounts receivable, coming primarily from so-called third-party reimbursement. If calculated with the appropriate contractual requirements and adjustments, these are secure assets, owed by government sponsored and private insurance companies. Increasingly, charges for services provided are regulated by the these third-party agencies.

Hospitals and nursing homes have the largest investment in fixed assets in this industry, but many other firms are inventorying and renting equipment to be used in patients' homes. Thus, the heavy investment in fixed assets is a primary focus of any financial statement analysis. The revenue-producing capabilities of these assets are of primary importance; if a hospital has too many beds or expensive diagnostic equipment that is underutilized, cash flow may be insufficient to cover required debt payments. Furthermore, as in all fixed-asset-intensive businesses, equipment leasing hides assets and the associated equivalent debt from the financial statements.

Governmental and Quasi-Governmental Organizations

Governments and their authorities organize to achieve certain specific objectives. Because their objectives frequently are user oriented (for example, providing postal service), these governmental organizations have their own peculiar analysis issues. Like business organizations, they issue financial statements. Unfortunately, these statements are less useful than those of business organizations for predicting the future because the legislative authorities that create the expenditure programs not only can create revenues by increasing taxes, but can also dramatically increase the expenditures. These increases are difficult to predict because they may be based upon constituency demands rather than on market or historic realities. A clear sense of the political environment is central to forecasting repayment of financing.

The most frequent government borrowings are, first, long-term bonds frequently used to finance fixed assets such as bridges and, second, short-term tax anticipation notes used to smooth cash flow before arrival of a tax payment date.

While *quasi-governmental organizations* are somewhat insulated from this process, the existence of long-term public bonds with restrictive covenants is central to their stability. The bonds issued by these authorities may be tied to revenues to be derived from providing a service directly to the public, such as a bridge, or indirectly through the local government, such as a sewer plant. Projections produced by the authorities may be only as accurate as the start-up business plans mentioned at the beginning of the chapter, but they have one advantage: they have a monopoly on the service to be provided. This monopoly and taxing capability reduce the market (revenue) risk for this type of business so that the bank can make a loan to an otherwise impossible project.

Personal Service Businesses

Personal service businesses—which include restaurants, law firms, and travel agencies, just to mention a few types—do not sell tangible products, but instead provide a service. The operating cycle of a service business differs from that of other companies in that no or little inventory of salable stock is involved. Instead, the performance of a service generates accounts receivable, which remain the main current asset. In analyzing the operating cycle of a service business, focus on accounts receivable since a concentration of accounts receivable or a large number of uncollected receivables can disrupt the operating cycle, thereby posing a risk to the lender.

Most personal service companies have few physical assets and thus relatively low fixed assets and long-term debt requirements. Risk in this industry is caused by the intensely personal nature of the service. Frequently, a single employee can make or break the firm. The prior year's financial statements need to be validated by surveying pivotal employees and customers about their intentions in the coming year or, even better, by obtaining work or sales contracts to ensure that the revenue stream is dependable.

Agricultural Businesses

Agricultural businesses produce crops or raise livestock. While the operating cycle of most farms is the traditional year, current emphasis on vegetables and animal products produced year round in technologically advanced settings are changing the nature of the industry. The operating cycle commences when cash is used to purchase seeds, fertilizer, and animal food for the production of inventory. The product is sold at market, creating accounts receivable which when paid generate cash. The addition of government price-support regulations and commodity futures markets provides some stability to this business, which is frequently quite cyclical because of weather and competitive variables.

Like manufacturing firms, agricultural businesses generally borrow long-term for equipment needs and short-term for seasonal financing needs that arise from the timing differences between payment of cultivation costs and receipt of revenues from sale of the harvested crops. For the lending financial institutions, the risk in farming in recent years has been in financing land acquisition. The 1980s saw gyrations in the value of land, predicated on pricing of agricultural products on the world markets in dollar terms. Farmers were tempted to expand or mortgage their land at these higher market values, only to fall into default when the dollar's improved value priced U.S. products out of the market. The importance of cash flow analysis is again pivotal in avoiding failure.

OTHER ENVIRONMENTAL ISSUES

The Company's Marketplace

A lender must also understand the larger environment in which a company operates. This includes the marketplace, the regulatory environment, the effect of the nation's economy on the business, and the business' vulnerability to the almost innumerable uncertainties that every company faces to some extent—be it the vagaries of the weather or technological and social change.

Market Characteristics

To put a company's financial results in perspective requires the credit analyst to understand the structure of the market in which the company competes. Here are some questions to guide the analyst's investigations:

- Does the company have many competitors or only a few?
- How easy is it for new competitors to enter the market? Does product differentiation play a major role in a company's success in this industry?
- To what extent can the company control the price of its products?
- Is the company an industry leader, or must it be ready to follow the leader's strategy on price, regardless of its own costs?
- To what extent do demographic and consumer preference trends affect the company?
- Is the market for the company's product expanding, stable, or contracting?

If a company's sales fluctuate with the seasons, it faces an external factor called *seasonality*. A boat dealer, for example, usually sees heavy sales from spring through summer, with business almost nonexistent for the remainder of the year. General merchandise retailers, on the other hand, encounter heavy sales in November and December due to holiday shopping. Recognizing seasonality is particularly important when analyzing interim income statements.

Products and services also have their own life cycles. They begin as an idea, are transformed into an entity for sale, and are marketed until they stop selling profitably. The business then discontinues the product or service. The product life cycle may be very short for a fad product or very long for a staple product. Consider at what stage of a company's life cycle its products or services are. This may be difficult to determine because unforeseen consumer trends and new technology may shorten a product's life cycle. For example, the demand for citizens band (CB) radios skyrocketed in the 1970s, then dropped precipitously after a few years when consumer interest waned. Nevertheless, evaluating the probability of continued profitable sales for a company's product or service is critical to an effective examination.

Economic Environment

Interest rates, inflation, tax policies, and the ups and downs of the national economy affect all companies to some extent. Some industries, however, are particularly vulnerable to changes in the general economy. For example, the automobile, construction, and capital goods industries are considered to be cyclical because they are so sensitive to economic downturns and recoveries. This sensitivity results in fluctuations in revenues between operating cycles caused by a reaction to the expansion or contraction of general business activity.

Regulatory Environment

Another important consideration is the extent to which *government regulations* affect a company. Even industries that are not subject to a high degree of regulation may be subject to import quotas, export bans, price supports, or subsidies. Other companies are subject to clean air and clean water regulations, which have added tremendously to their cost of doing business. Besides federal regulations, state and local laws may be an important consideration for some companies.

Management Objectives

Management policies and objectives are other factors that distinguish companies and affect their need for financing and their ability to repay loans. The operating policies of some businesses emphasize profits or cash flow over growth. Some firms have relatively strict accounts receivable and inventory controls, while others tend to incur more debt and favor higher accounts receivable and inventory in their quest to capture a larger share of the market—which, in turn, may lead to greater stability.

Growth-oriented companies might cut their selling prices without the benefit of lower costs in order to increase sales. Other companies are less concerned with short-term profits than with long-term maximization of equity. Understanding its objectives can help an analyst put a company's financial statements in perspective and evaluate the company's success in achieving its goals. In fact, using the financial statements to judge the company's success in reaching management's stated goals is a necessity for a complete credit analysis.

Some companies are created because of legal and tax considerations. As mentioned when discussing joint ventures above, many organizations set up separate companies for the sole purpose of owning property or other fixed assets that are then leased back to the organizations to lower their taxes. Other businesses, concerned with how their financial statements appear to creditors and investors, might create a separate company to provide off-balance-sheet financing for a portion of the organization's activities.

Only after understanding the objectives of the company can the credit analyst begin to answer the questions vital to a financial statement analysis:

- ❐ How successful is the company?
- ❐ Can the company meet its objectives?
- ❐ What financial needs does the company have as a result of trying to meet its objectives?
- ❐ Should the bank attempt to satisfy all or part of the financial needs of the company, and if so, how?

Type of Legal Structure

An important distinction among businesses is their legal status—that is, whether a company is set up as a proprietorship, a partnership, or a corporation. For example, officers of a corporation are not legally liable for the corporation's financial obligations to the bank unless they formally agree to accept such liability. The owners of a proprietorship or partnership, however, do assume responsibility for the company's financial obligations.

Sole Proprietorships

Many small businesses in the United States are *sole proprietorships*. For example, most doctors, lawyers, carpenters, and tradespeople operate as sole proprietorships. This is the easiest type of business structure to form. The owners of such businesses assume complete responsibility for their operations, including any financial obligations to banks. The assets, debt, and income of the owner and the business are legally one and the same. Thus, take into account both personal and business assets in evaluating the creditworthiness of a sole proprietorship.

The risks of these small businesses are great for reasons listed below in the section on company size. Moreover, the business records of these firms tend to lack sophistication and usefulness since the owners may treat the business operations and their own personal activities as indistinguishable. The willingness of the sole proprietor to work long hours and devote his or her life to the health of the business can sometimes outweigh the exposure to risk, enabling the bank to advance funds for seasonal needs or to finance a high-value-retaining piece of equipment on an installment basis or as an equipment lease.

Partnerships

A partnership is a business that is jointly owned by two or more individuals. In a *general partnership*, the profits and losses are divided among the partners according to the terms of the partnership agreement (often based on each partner's equity contribution), and all of the business income is regarded as personal income of the owners. All partners assume complete legal responsibility for all the liabilities of the partnership, and lenders can look at the personal assets of each partner as well as those of the partnership when evaluating creditworthiness.

In a *limited partnership*, certain owners may be designated as general partners and others as limited partners. General partners are liable for all partnership debts, whereas limited partners are similar to stockholders in corporations; their liability is limited to their equity contribution. Limited partnerships are particularly common in real estate investment ventures.

To a lending financial institution, the main advantage of partnerships is that they must prepare and file financial statements with the state and federal governments for tax purposes. Therefore, their financial reports are generally of higher quality than those produced by sole proprietors. Indeed, since they are cooperative enterprises, the financial reports tend to have more abstract validity because the different partners, who may not be involved in the financial aspects of the business, want to know what has transpired.

For bankers, the risks associated with partnerships are centered on the intensely personal-service aspect of most partnership operations. While the limited fixed assets and inventories required in service businesses should reduce risk, the individual partners frequently "own" the clients on an individual basis. Therefore, if financial problems erupt, individual partners may leave the firm, taking the revenue-producing clients with them. Unless they have considerable personal wealth, partners caught in a financial crisis may take the easy way out and file for personal bankruptcy. Finally, if one partner dies, the partnership dies too, and his or her estate is entitled to that interest. This lowers the likelihood that partnerships will survive over long periods.

Mention should be made of a type of organization that is taxed like a partnership, directly through to the owners, but is otherwise in the legal form of a corporation. This is the *S corporation*, and it provides the owners, who are like limited partners for all other intents and purposes, with limited liability. Because S corporations are owned by one person or a small group whose members frequently play major roles in operating the business, the lender is essentially dealing with a partnership. Thus, as in the case of the limited partnership, lending policies often require obtaining the guarantee of the owners. Moreover, because the tax liability is completely hidden from the financial statement, analysis is less definitive.

Corporations

Corporations are business organizations that are legally treated as individuals. Thus, unlike sole proprietorships and partnerships, corporations pay taxes, buy and sell assets, and incur liabilities. Highly regulated, corporations are owned by their stockholders—one person, a few individuals, or hundreds of thousands of shareholders in the case of a large publicly held company. An advantage of the corporate setup for the equity investor is that it protects its owners from personal exposure to indebtedness. Shareholders stand to lose no more than their investment in a company, even in the case of bankruptcy. For this reason, lenders may require owners of closely held corporations to personally guarantee any debt extended to the corporation.

Even though most corporations are privately held—that is, their stock is not publicly traded—they must prepare and file financial statements with the state and federal governments for tax purposes. Therefore, like partnerships, their financial reports are generally of higher quality than those produced by sole proprietorships. A corporation's income is taxed at corporate rates, and dividends to shareholders are then taxed again at individual rates. This double-taxation phenomenon causes corporations to reinvest a larger percentage of their profits (that is, retain them as equity) than do other types of businesses.

For the lending financial institution, corporate organizations pose substantially reduced risk because, generally, they

- ❒ are larger than proprietors or partnerships (see below for more on this issue),
- ❒ have greater management depth than do proprietors or partnerships,
- ❒ provide more structured financial reports than do proprietors or partnerships,
- ❒ provide less intensely personal service than do proprietors or partnerships, and
- ❒ possess unlimited life, unlike proprietors or partnerships, which die with their owners.

Another recently popular form of corporation is the *joint venture* whereby several corporations contract with each other to undertake some activity. The area of joint concern may be research and manufacturing, or one firm may be good at marketing and the other at manufacturing. Whatever the case, the purpose of the venture may be as much focused on tax and accounting issues as on substantive business reasons. As a byproduct of the tax and accounting issues, corporations may use the joint venture to disguise their investment or to limit their liability—something not beneficial to any lender.

Size of Company

A company's relative size, frequently indicated by the extent of its management organization, its stature in the community, and its clout in the marketplace, may also affect its financing needs and its ability to repay debt. The sophistication (or lack thereof) of a company's financial statements may also reflect its size.

One Manager

The manager of a small business is generally the *entrepreneur* who began the business. The owner-manager typically does not have all the expertise needed to run a company. He or she may have technical or sales expertise, but lack accounting or financial ability, or vice versa. Managers of small businesses often do not hire full-time financial experts, but instead use clerical bookkeepers or an accounting service. Therefore they may rely on their accountant or their banker to provide financial expertise and direction, a problematic course for the banker, given the conflict of interest in protecting both the client and the depositor's money.

Small businesses often direct their products or services to limited markets. The operation either introduces a new product to undeveloped markets or is a minor participant in a larger, more established market. Additionally, small companies often have unsophisticated operations and, unless their owners are wealthy, limited capital resources. Public equity markets are typically unavailable to them, and borrowing long-term money is difficult even in the venture capital market.

Moreover, the lack of management depth increases the risk of the business to a great degree. If an accident or ill health befalls the owner, the business will be likely to fail. If macroeconomic variables affect its market, a small firm is frequently unable to weather the problem due to the limited skills of its only manager.

Thus the bank usually serves a critical role in the funding of necessary capital for a small company's growth. The bank expects, in return, not only compensation for its risk (that is, payment of interest), but also substantial protection in terms of collateral, loan agreements, and a continued flow of information from the company. Even then, a bank encounters a relatively high degree of risk simply because the failure rate of small businesses is so high.

Multiple Managers Functioning in Different Areas

A successful small business typically grows into a medium-sized business. To improve its management, the company will begin to hire functional specialists, such as a controller or marketing experts. Hopefully, the company creates *management depth* so that, in the absence of the chief executive officer, two or more officers are available to deal with macroeconomic crises, like recessions.

As it becomes more sophisticated, the multiple manager company may diversify its lines of business. For example, a company that began by making paper cups may expand production to make milk cartons, or a retailer of women's clothing may take on a line of men's clothing as well. Such diversification usually requires additional capital. The company may also obtain access to venture capital equity markets or attract private investors. Access to private and public debt sources also increases.

As long as the company continues to grow, it will normally continue to have significant financing needs, and banks will continue to be a major source of funds, especially in seasonal businesses. This funding role is often shared among several banks if the business outgrows the local bank's individual lending capacity and comes, by virtue of its expansion, to have financial requirements greater than the lending policy limits of its initial bank. As the company grows, it also typically begins to fine-tune its financial operations to provide better and more useful information, especially audited financial statements that it gives to its financial sources.

Company Decentralized into Divisions

A medium-sized company eventually may become a large company. By then, its management is usually more functionally specialized. Besides employing a treasurer, the company may employ several financially astute people to deal exclusively with its ongoing capital needs and its long-range financial planning. Further, the managers in charge of divisions within the company may have significant knowledge of overall operations. They greatly reduce the risk that the company will fail; their combined knowledge helps the company see its way through times of crises and macroeconomic stress. Altogether, that makes lending money to larger companies less of a risk. In contrast, smaller companies have only one or, at best, a few functional specialists on whom to rely in hard times.

When a large company becomes a major economic force, able to control or influence its industry's markets, it may substantially affect product pricing and developmental trends. Operationally, large companies tend to be sophisticated and use the latest and most complex technology, possibly including the use of robotics and computer-based cost accounting. Large companies generally have the capitalization, visibility, and operating record to enable them to draw from a wide variety of financial resources, including public debt or equity markets. At this point, the bank is likely to be a secondary provider of funds since public debt markets offer large, successful firms a pricing advantage over borrowing from commercial banks.

CASH FLOW CYCLES

The various characteristics of a business discussed in the first part of this chapter are important to financial statement analysis in part because they affect cash flow, which in turn affects a company's need for bank financing and its ability to repay debt. Most business enterprises rely to some extent on bank loans as one of the sources of financing, or cash. This cash may be used to purchase inventory, which in turn is used in the production of goods or the delivery of services, and then returns to cash (or accounts receivable, and then cash). This cash enables the company to purchase more inventory, thus beginning the *cash flow cycle* again.

Understanding cash flows, including how cash is generated and used, is a critical if difficult part of the financial statement analysis process. That is because the accountant's accrual income model is not focused on cash! Indeed, the accountant's goal is to use the income statement to reflect the production of *wealth*, the increase in the value of the shareholder's net worth. The net worth account, itself, is almost always represented on the balance sheet by assets other than cash. While income is a major source of cash flow, its identification is only partially sufficient for detecting the overall cash flow that banks prefer for loan repayment.

Cash flow in financial statement analysis includes all the economic resources available to a company, not just the balance in the cash account. Although most business transactions do involve cash or cash equivalents, analysts also consider as part of cash flow such seemingly noncash economic resources as trade credit and accrued accounts payable. Trade credit results from the common practice of purchasing goods on account, meaning the goods are paid for sometime after they are received. During the time between the purchase of and payment for a supplier's goods, trade credit serves as a source of cash.

Accruals are another noncash economic resource involving a promise to pay later for a service performed now. A restaurant owner, for example, may pay dishwashers and busers weekly for work performed the previous week. Such owed, but unpaid, labor costs constitute another source of cash. The concept of cash flows, therefore, includes not only cash and cash-equivalent accounts, but other tangible resources or assets (such as inventory or machinery) and intangible economic power (such as the ability to incur debt in the form of trade credit and accruals).

Current Account Uses of Cash

To illustrate a simple cash flow cycle, consider the Anderson Light Company, a business that purchases and resells lamps at a profit. On day one, the Anderson Light Company has $50 in cash in its bank account. On day two, the company purchases a lamp from its wholesale suppliers for $50. Then, on day three, the company sells the lamp for $75 cash. Thus the company realizes a $25 profit for the work involved in purchasing and reselling the lamp. Exhibit 2.3 illustrates this simple cash flow cycle.

Most businesses, of course, involve more complex operations than simply purchasing and reselling a single product. Assume that Anderson Light Company buys unassembled lamp parts, employs a person to assemble the lamp in its shop, and then sells the completed lamp. Exhibit 2.4 illustrates this slightly longer cycle.

Exhibit 2.4 shows that on day one the Anderson Light Company has $50 in its account. On day two, the company pays $35 for lamp parts. On day three, the employee assembles the lamp and places it on the showroom floor. The employee is paid $15. On day four, the lamp is sold for $75 cash. Anderson

Exhibit
2.3

Cash Flow Cycle of Retailer

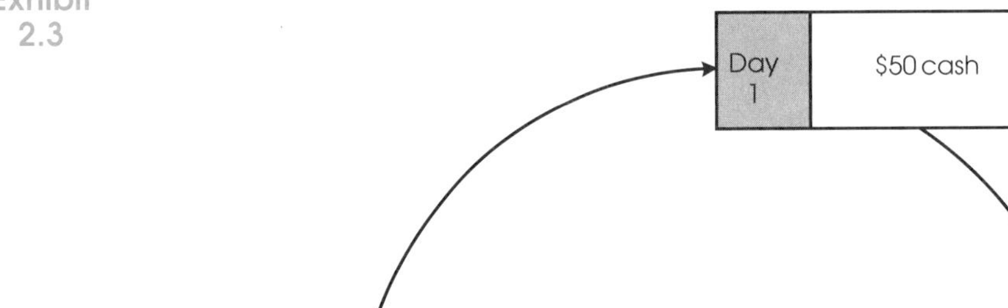

Exhibit
2.4

Cash Flow Cycle of Manufacturer

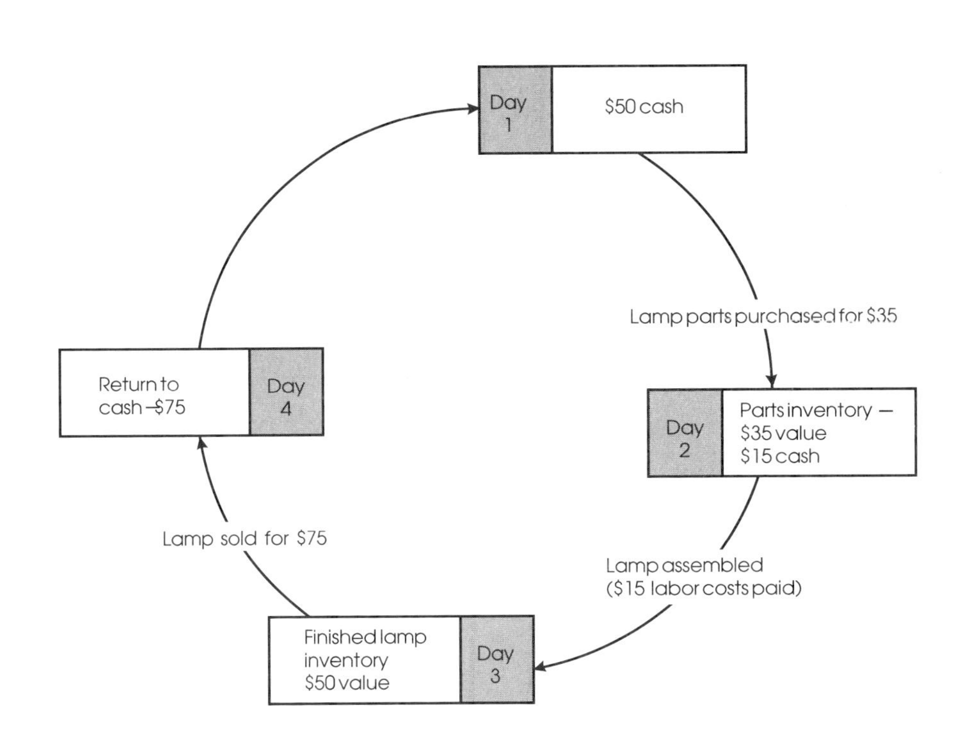

Exhibit 2.5

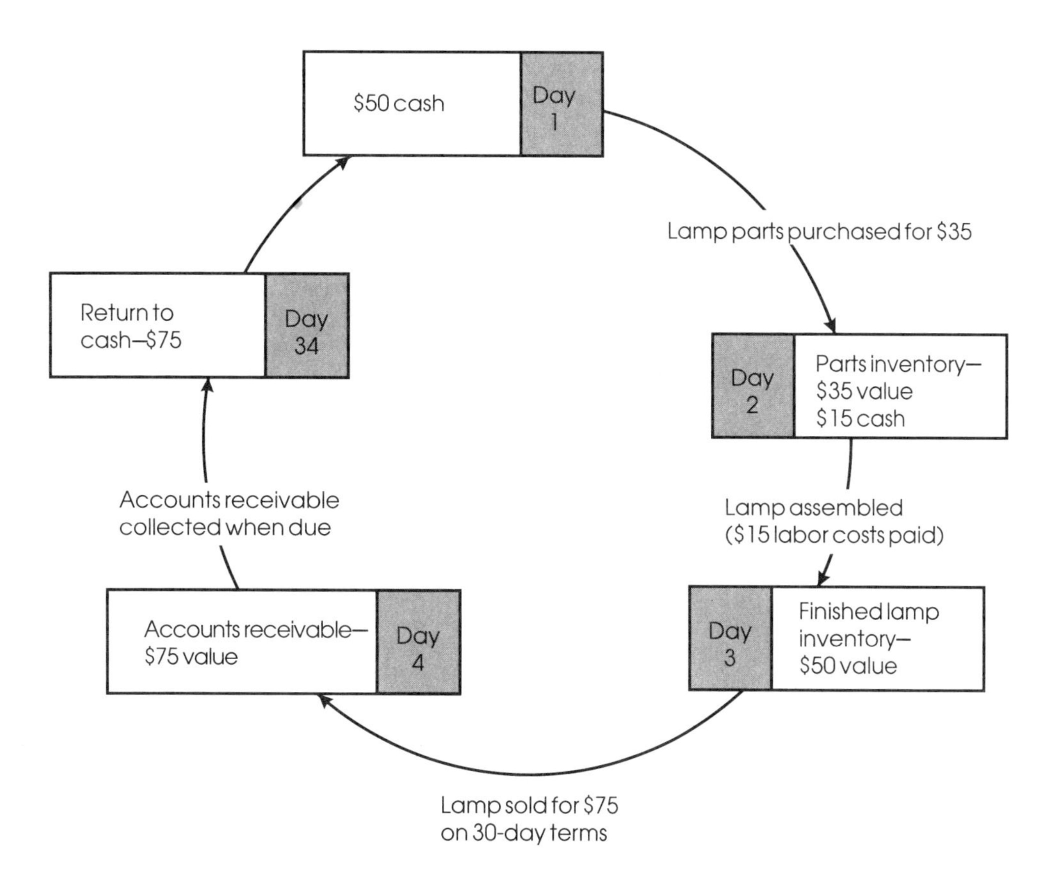

Light still makes a $25 profit on its original $50 investment, but the length of its cash flow cycle is increased when it assembles as well as retails lamps.

The length of the company's cash flow cycle further increases if the lamp is sold on credit, as Exhibit 2.5 illustrates.

In this third example, the lamp is sold on day four on 30-day terms. This creates accounts receivable and greatly lengthens the cash flow cycle, assuming the customer waits until day 34 to pay for the lamp. In the meantime, the company has no cash for purchasing parts for more lamps or for paying its employee.

The preceding examples illustrate that the cash flow cycle reflects the type of operation in which a company engages (in this case, a retail operation versus a manufacturing operation). It also illustrates how management decisions can affect the cash flow cycle (in this case, by its decision to sell the lamps on credit).

Current Account Sources of Cash

Up to this point, Anderson Light Company's use of cash in its operation (to buy inventory and pay for labor) has been considered, but not the question of where the cash came from (the *current account sources of cash*). It was assumed that the company had sufficient cash to purchase parts, pay for labor, and wait 30 days to collect the proceeds of a sale.

Equity

The amount of money invested in the Anderson Light's operation by the company's owner (the original $50) is considered invested equity. Invested equity is one of the major sources of cash available to businesses and may be the only source available to a new business. But what happens if a company does not have sufficient equity to sustain its entire cash flow cycle? Specifically, what would happen if the Anderson Light Company started out with only $40 worth of equity? Exhibit 2.6 illustrates this situation.

Exhibit 2.6

Cash Flow Cycle of Retailer

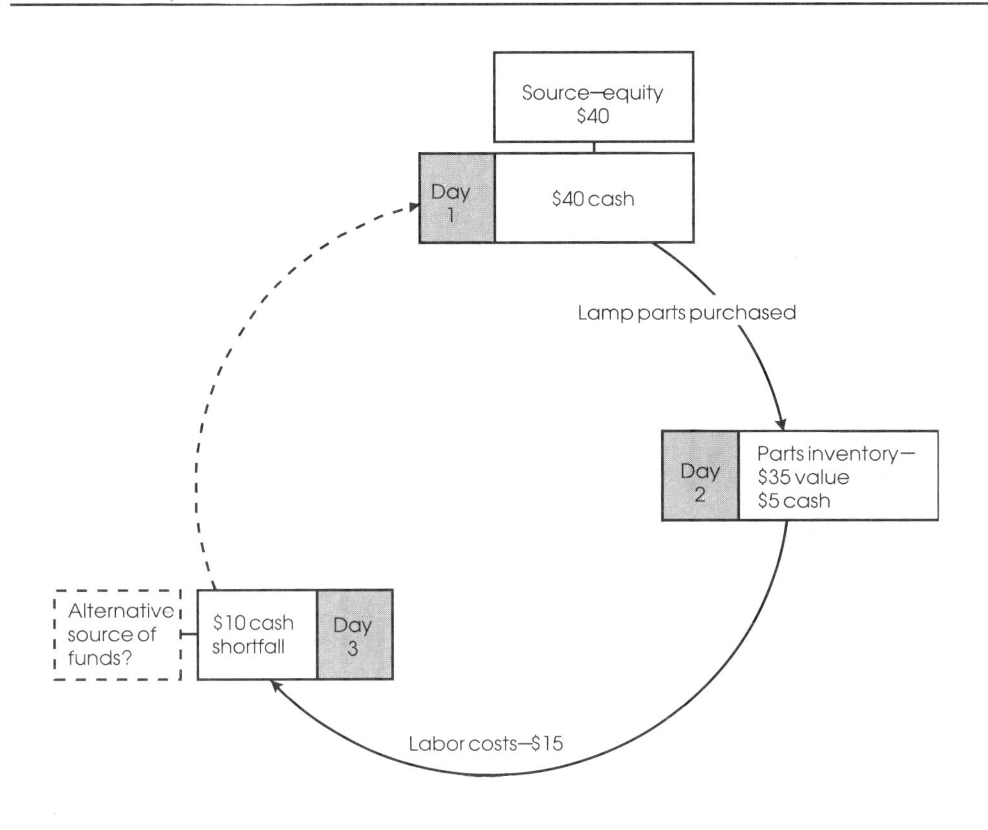

After spending $35 on lamp parts, the company has only $5 left, whereas labor to assemble the lamp costs $15. The Anderson Light Company here faces a classic business dilemma—a shortage of cash. The shortfall is only $10, but the company needs that money to hire the labor to assemble the lamp. Once assembled, the lamp can be sold for a profit and the worker paid. But if the company cannot complete its operating cycle, it fails. Failure to complete the operating cycle is a common cause of problem loans.

How can a company with insufficient equity raise money to enable it to complete its operating cycle? It could go to its bank and request a short-term loan. However, because loans cost money in the form of interest payments and thus reduce the company's profits, the company may consider other sources of cash first—such as trade credit, labor accruals, or a reduction of sale terms.

Trade Credit

The Anderson Light Company might try to negotiate credit terms with its supplier of lamp parts. If its supplier will allow 20-day payment terms, for instance, the resulting cash flow cycle is that illustrated in Exhibit 2.7.

Incomplete Cash Flow Cycle: Use of Trade Credit to Delay Shortfall

Exhibit 2.7

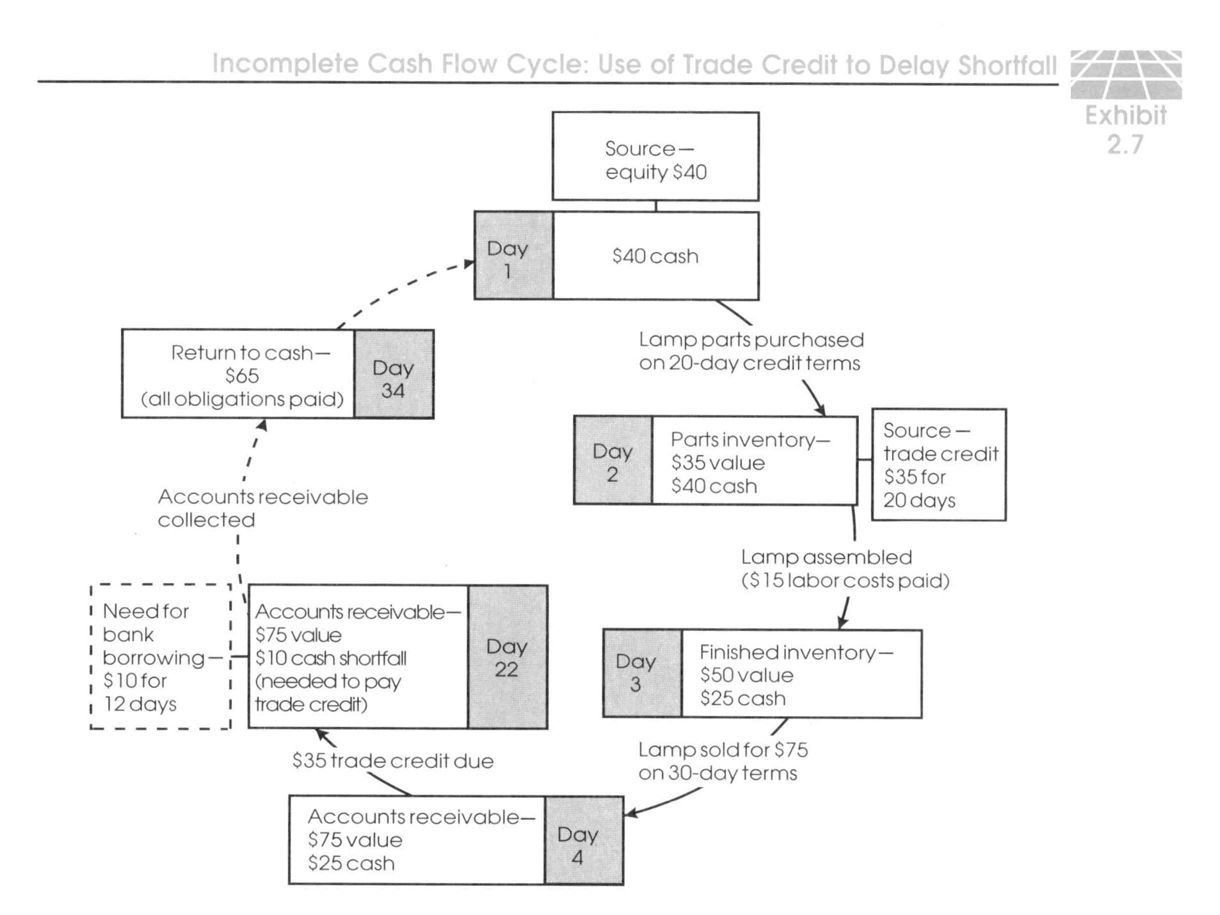

In this scenario, the Anderson Light Company has $40 in its account on day one. The next day, the company purchases $35 worth of lamp parts and promises to pay for them on day 22. Thus, the company still has $40 cash at its disposal. On the third day, Anderson Light Company uses $15 of its cash

reserves to hire a laborer to assemble the lamp parts. On the fourth day, the lamp is sold on 30-day terms. On day 22, the bill for lamp parts comes due and Anderson Light Company again faces a $10 shortfall. Unless the company can raise the additional $10, its supplier must wait for payment until day 34, when the customer's payment of $75 becomes due. If this fails to satisfy the supplier, the company may still need to request a short-term loan. However, the company now needs to borrow the $10 for only 12 days, rather than for 30 days (as required in the previous scenario).

Accruals

Another strategy Anderson Light Company might use to complete its cash flow cycle would be to adopt a policy of deferring the payment of its labor for a week. This is in effect a source of cash called labor accrual. The company's cash flow cycle would then look like that in Exhibit 2.8

Exhibit 2.8 Incomplete Cash Flow Cycle: Use of Labor Accrual to Delay Shortfall

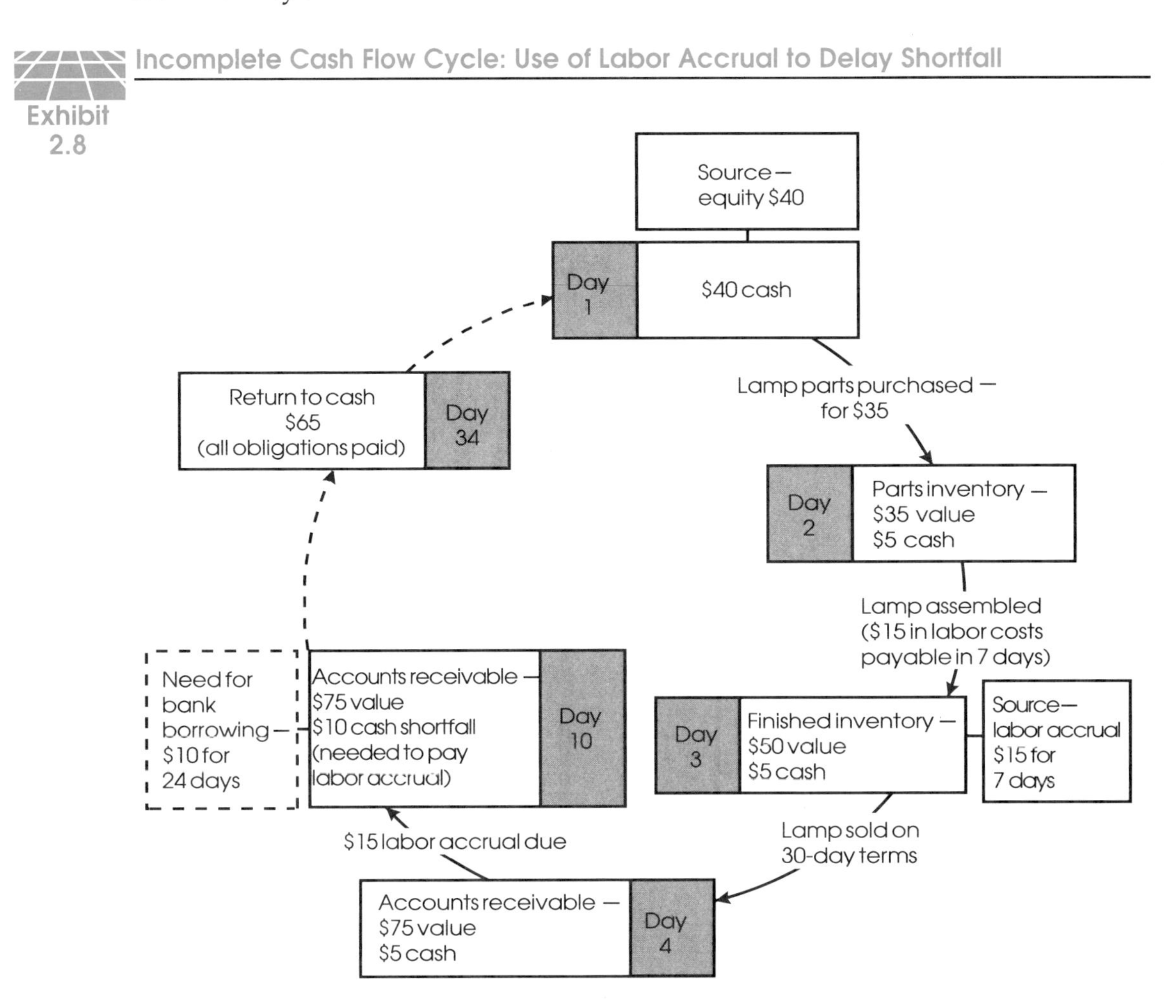

Again, the Anderson Light Company begins with $40 in equity and spends $35 for lamp parts. Since it pays cash for the supplies, it now has a $5 balance. On day three, the employee assembles the lamp but agrees to be paid one

week later. On the fourth day, a customer purchases the lamp on 30-day terms. On day 10, the $15 labor expense comes due, but the company has only a $5 cash balance. Again, the company finds itself $10 short and must borrow from the bank for 24 days until the customer's $75 payment comes due. While this is preferable to borrowing for 30 days, it is not as effective a solution in this case as negotiating trade credit terms.

Reduction of Credit Sale Terms

Another strategy that Anderson Light Company could adopt to alleviate its cash shortfall would be to reduce the credit terms offered to its customers. Suppose the company reduced the credit terms extended to its customers from 30 days to 18 days and was also able to negotiate a 20-day trade credit with its supplier. The company's cash flow cycle would now look like the one depicted in Exhibit 2.9.

Complete Cash Flow Cycle

Exhibit 2.9

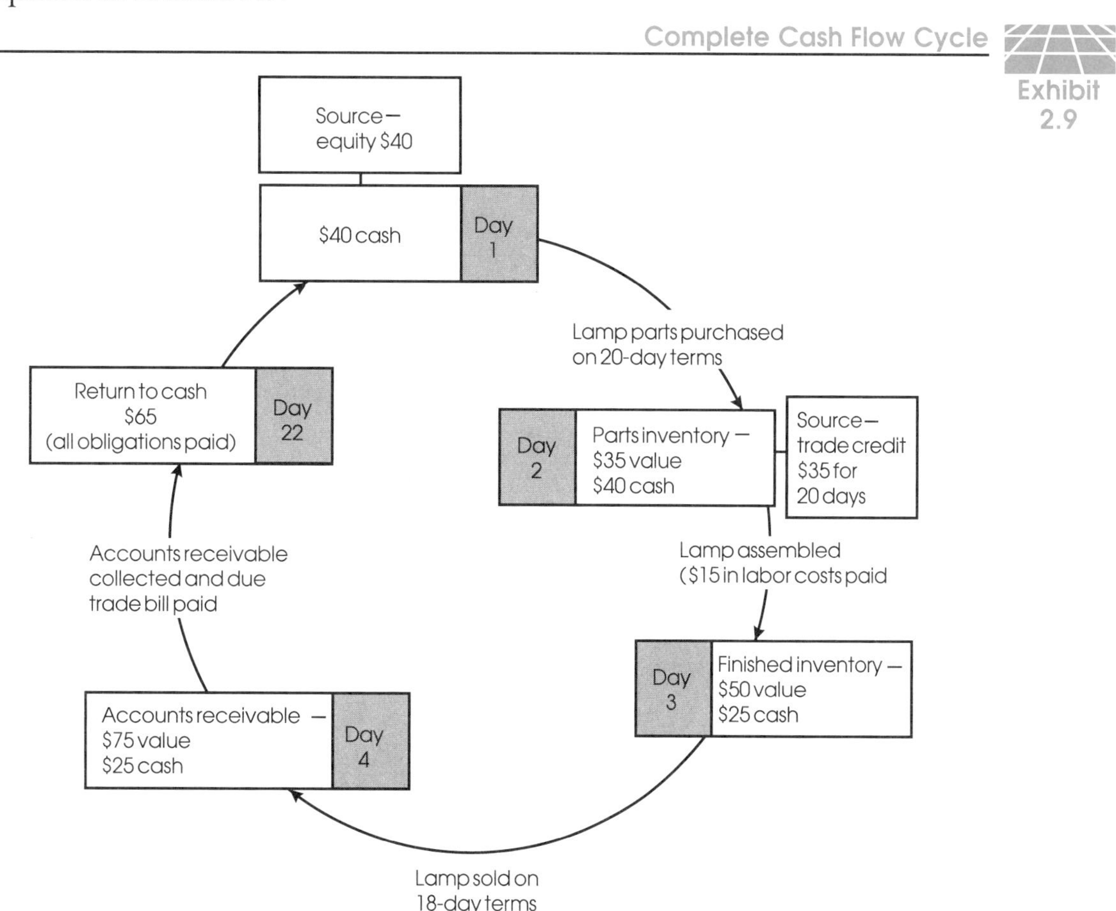

On day one, the company has $40 in its account. The next day, the company purchases $35 in lamp parts on credit, promising to pay for them in 20 days. The employee assembles the lamp on the third day and receives $15 in payment. On the fourth day, a customer purchases the lamp for $75 on 18-day terms. On day 22, both the company's $35 bill for parts and the customer's $75 payment for the lamp come due, enabling Anderson Light Company to meet its debt obligation (assuming the customer pays by the due date). Moreover, the company still makes a $25 profit on its original investment.

Long-term Uses of Cash

The discussion of cash flow thus far has been concerned with the current operating cycle, which involves the conversion of cash into operating assets and then back into cash within a short period. But that cash conversion process does not take place in a vacuum. Businesses need facilities to house their operations and tools to perform their tasks.

The Anderson Light Company, for example, might need offices for its sales and administrative staff, space for the assembly process, and a warehouse for its inventory. It might also need production equipment (such as a drill press) and other equipment (perhaps a delivery van). Assets needed to support, rather than be consumed by, a company's operation are referred to as fixed assets, which are also called capital assets. The acquisition, funding, use, and replacement of fixed assets is called the *investment cycle* because the company uses the assets again and again through a number of current operating cycles rather than expending them or converting them to cash within a single current operating cycle. Most fixed assets, however, are eventually expended through their repeated use in the production process and must be replaced. Because replacement is usually several years after the initial purchase, replacement cost is higher and needs to be considered in cash flow analysis.

The investment cycle, like the current operating cycle, begins with the expenditure of cash to acquire or create an asset. The company does not, however, directly convert the fixed asset back into cash by selling its drill press, for example, to create an account receivable that is later collected to produce cash. Nevertheless, fixed assets do play a critical part in the current operating cycle. The company's products cannot be created or its services delivered without the support of the company's fixed assets. Thus, the company recovers the original cash expenditure for the fixed asset, but only over time and only through the profitable sale of the products that the fixed asset helps create. During this time, the fixed assets generally depreciate in value.

Long-term Sources of Cash

A company must have adequate fixed assets to support its current operating cycle. Additionally, the company must structure its paying for those fixed assets to avoid disrupting the current operation of the business. Initial payment for the fixed assets can come from three sources: excess cash, equity contribution, or debt. Of these, debt and excess cash are the most common. Then, the company's current operating cycle generates the cash to repay the debt.

However, cash generated through the current operating cycle must first be used to replenish the company's current operating assets, such as inventory and receivables. To the extent that it is not used for some other purpose, the net cash flow from operations is normally available to purchase fixed assets or service debt. Therefore, the commercial loan officer should structure payment terms on loans for the purchase of fixed assets in such a way that companies can repay these debts with net cash flow generated through the use of the fixed assets over their useful lives.

Summary

The current operating cycle and the investment cycle comprise all the cash movements related to a company's basic operations. Those cycles must generate sufficient cash to replenish working capital, provide for growth, and repay debt incurred to acquire fixed assets. Any other cash requirements are outside the company's primary operation, and management should consider these needs only after the company has adequately provided for the funding requirements of the operating and investment cycles.

ACCRUAL ACCOUNTING VS. CASH ACCOUNTING

Another useful way of looking at a company's operations is in terms of its income statement. The components of the income statement involve a company's recognition of income and the expenses related thereto and the resulting profit or loss. It is important to understand that recognition of profit does not generally coincide with a company's cash flow. In fact, while all companies seek to maximize their cash flow (since this is the medium for paying bills, loans, salaries, dividends, and so on), not all companies try to maximize profits. In fact, many privately held companies try to minimize reported earnings to reduce taxes. However, because most financial statements are earnings-oriented rather than cash-oriented, it is important to understand both the income statement and the cash cycle—and to be able to make the transition between the two.

Most companies prepare their financial statements using accrual accounting rather than cash accounting. *Accrual accounting* recognizes revenues as earned when sales are transacted, regardless of when the company actually receives payment. Expenses are likewise recognized when they are incurred rather than when payment is made. *Cash accounting* recognizes revenues as earned when payment is received, regardless of the timing of the transaction. Likewise, the company expenses the cost associated with producing these revenues only when the cash is actually paid out. For example, if a company with a calendar-year fiscal period sold $2,000 worth of products on 20 December 1992, with payment due on 20 January 1993, the $2,000 would be recognized as 1992 revenue under the accrual method, but as 1993 revenue under the cash method.

Although cash accounting is of special interest to the lender, which will be repaid in cash, most companies use accrual accounting for financial reporting purposes because it matches related revenues and expenses, thus providing a more accurate measure of the company's ability to generate wealth. To illustrate this, assume that Photo Dealer, a wholesaler of photographic equipment, opened for business on 1 November 1992. Exhibit 2.10 shows the company's cash-basis income statement prepared for November and December. The company buys cameras for $125 each, paying for them at the time of purchase. It rents office and warehouse facilities for $500 per month and pays an average of $200 per month for utilities. The company pays both the rent and the utility bills on the 15th day of each month.

Exhibit 2.10

Cash-Basis Income Statement

Photo Dealer
Income Statement (Cash Basis)

Item	*Month Ended 11/30/92*	*Month Ended 12/31/92*
Sales (revenues)	—	$7,000
Purchases	$ 5,000	—
Gross Profit	(5,000)	7,000
Utilities and rent	700	700
Profit (loss)	$(5,700)	$6,300

On 1 November, Photo Dealer purchases 40 cameras for $125 each (or a total of $5,000). The next day, the company sells 30 cameras at $200 each. The cameras will be delivered to Photo Dealer's retail customers during November. The cameras are sold on 30-day terms, due 2 December. On 8 December, Photo Dealer sells 10 cameras at $100 each, a 50 percent pre-Christmas discount intended to clear remaining inventory. These cameras are delivered in December, with payment due upon receipt of the merchandise. On a cash basis, the business appears to have lost money in November, whereas profits in December were excellent.

Accrual accounting, which matches revenues with expenses, tells quite a different story. It shows that November was a profitable month for Photo Dealer, whereas December was unprofitable. Recall that during November Photo Dealer sold 30 cameras for $200 each, resulting in a $75 profit on each camera. However, in December the company sold 10 cameras for $100 each, for a $25 loss per camera. Although the business had excess cash in December (as shown in the cash-basis statement), the extra cash was not due to an effective sales strategy. Exhibit 2.11 shows the company's interim income statement calculated on an accrual basis.

Accrual-Basis Income Statement

Exhibit 2.11

Photo Dealer
Income Statement (Accrual Basis)

Item	*Month Ended 11/30/92*	*Month Ended 12/31/92*
Sales (revenues)	$6,000	$1,000
Purchases	$3,750	1,250
Gross Profit	$2,250	$ (250)
Utilities and rent	700	700
Profit (loss)	$1,550	$ (950)

In the two income statements for Photo Dealer, the total profit for the two-month period equals the amount of cash generated ($600 in each case). In an actual situation, the amount of profit or loss shown on an accrual-basis income statement would normally be quite different from the company's cash flow. That is why lenders analyze cash flow statements (discussed in chapter 5) and cash budgets (discussed in chapter 7) to determine the timing and amount of a company's cash requirements over time, information that may not be evident from examining a company's accrual-basis financial statements. Nevertheless, the income statement, as fashioned by the accrual method, is a better reflection of how efficiently a company has managed its assets. Therefore, both the income statement and the statement of cash flows are important to financial statement analysis.

SUMMARY OF MAJOR CONCEPTS

From the outset, it is important that the credit analyst have a good understanding of the company that is the subject of financial statement analysis. This requires first of all an understanding of the five basic types of businesses—manufacturers, wholesalers, retailers, service companies, and agricultural businesses—each of which has a characteristic operating cycle that creates differing funding needs. Other factors that an analyst needs to consider include the legal structure of the business, its size and rapidity of growth, its management policies and objectives, and its external environment—that is, the marketplace in which it operates. Together, these factors provide a meaningful context for the ensuing financial statement analysis.

An understanding of the company's business operations will also help a lender understand its operating cycle. As was illustrated by the various scenarios involving the Anderson Light Company, operating cycles may utilize various sources of cash—including equity, trade credit, accruals, and bank loans. The scenarios also showed how growth in sales tend to create the need for financing of additional current assets as well as fixed assets—an important concept underlying financial statement analysis.

A credit analyst must also understand a company's investment cycle and how it relates to the company's current operating cycle as well as its generation of income, including the distinction between profitability as shown by accrual-basis financial statements and actual cash flow.

EXERCISES

Important Terms to Define

manufacturers
wholesalers
retailers
transportation firms
financial services firms
construction firms
due diligence
fungibility
health service
personal service businesses
agricultural businesses
quasi-governmental organizations
market
government regulations
sole proprietorships
general partnership
limited partnership
S corporation
corporation
joint venture
entrepreneur
management depth
cash flow
wealth
cash flow cycle
current account sources of cash
long-term uses of cash
long-term sources of cash
accrual accounting
cash accounting

DEPENDABLE DOORS CASE STUDY

Company History

Dependable Doors is a manufacturer of patio doors for the residential, multifamily, and mobile home industries. Its headquarters are in Kingsport, Tennessee.

Paul Brookshire, the president of Dependable Doors, is a graduate of the University of North Carolina at Chapel Hill. Upon receiving his MBA in 1972, he returned with his wife and daughter to his home in Kingsport and began working for his uncle Bill Brookshire, who founded Dependable Doors. Paul worked in a variety of functions for his uncle and eventually took over the business when his uncle retired in 1983. Since that time, Paul has expanded the business from a privately owned basement operation to a publicly traded, over-the-counter company. He is an acknowledged workaholic with a strong personality.

Dependable Doors' main plant is in Kingsport, Tennessee, although it brought another large facility on line in St. Louis in February of 1991. This new facility is part of management's plan to shift capacity toward the multifamily home market (apartments and condominiums), which is the direction that housing market trends have been going, as shown below:

Changes in the U.S. Housing Mix by Percentage

Years	*Single-Family Homes*	*Multifamily Homes*	*Mobile Homes*
1970-1975	83	10	7
1976-1981	67	25	8
1982-1987	55	31	14
1987-1991	44	35	21

Note: These are not the actual figures for the years shown.

Dependable Doors is in a very competitive business. More than 250 companies engage in patio door manufacturing, most of them operating seasonally. Dependable Doors ranks among the top 10 firms in both of its patio door lines. It also leads in its other two product lines (closet doors and a new entry-door system).

A geographical breakdown of its sales shows that 81 percent of Dependable Doors' sales are east of the Mississippi River, with an additional 10 percent in Canada. The company's 17 full-time salespersons market to 600 building supply customers who maintain an inventory of its products. The salespersons also market directly to large multifamily and commercial contractors. The company's largest customer, Fleetwood Homes, which accounts for nearly 12 percent of Dependable Doors' total sales, decided in 1991 to stop carrying Dependable's door line. Dependable Doors expects to lose this account altogether in 1992. At the same time, it significantly increased its sales to a Canadian company from 3 percent of total sales in 1990 to 11 percent in 1991. None of the remaining accounts represents more than 3 percent of Dependable Doors' total sales.

The company's sales are seasonal, peaking in the early months of the calendar year in anticipation of late spring and summer construction. The company's treasurer, John Fitzsimmons, recently quit because of personality differences with Paul. He had provided the company with strong expense-control systems and accurate forecasting. The company has recently hired a replacement from its main competitor, Academy Doors.

1991 Fiscal Results

Housing starts were expected to increase dramatically in 1991. Based upon forecasts by government agencies and private economists, Dependable Doors projected a sales increase of 10 percent for 1991. Instead, continued sluggishness in the economy caused housing starts to decline somewhat over the prior year. Most of the decline occurred in the multifamily home market, as shown below:

Housing Starts in the United States

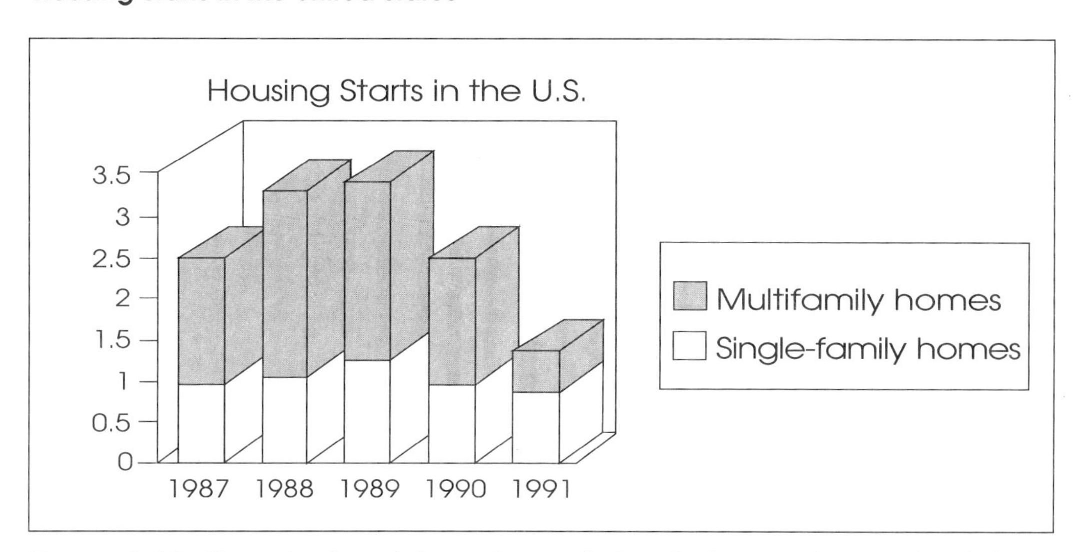

Dependable Doors' sales of doors for multifamily homes dropped, while its sales to single family homes increased by 12 percent.

On top of this weak market, Dependable Doors' materials, labor, and distribution expenses skyrocketed, shrinking its profit margins. The company had to bear the expenses associated with the start-up of the St. Louis plant (only 8 months in operation by year end) and a 3-month shutdown of the Kingsport facility due to a lack of sales. Nevertheless, the company managed to maintain its previous sales level. It was able to do so by increasing its market share as a result of a strong sales effort, increased product acceptance over larger geographic areas, and the introduction of new products. The company may also have engaged in price-cutting to maintain its market share.

Dependable Doors projects a strong recovery in 1992, including 50 percent more sales, based on

- a market recovery that will spur housing starts from approximately 30 percent,
- geographic expansion into Texas and Canada,
- expansion of wood-door production to meet the strong demand for wood doors in Texas and Canada,
- full use of all production facilities, and
- introduction of new products.

Chapter 7 — this affects cost budgets

Dependable Doors Consolidated Financial Statements

Dependable Doors
Income Statement
for the Fiscal Years Ending Sept. 30, 1988-1991
(in thousands of dollars)

	9/30/88	%	*9/30/89*	%	*9/30/90*	%	*9/30/91*	%
Net sales	15,469	100	19,578	100	20,540	100	20,055	100
Cost of goods sold	11,043	71	14,370	73	15,194	74	15,703	78
Gross profit/revenues	4,426	29	5,208	27	5,346	26	4,352	22
Selling expenses	1,016	7	1,259	6	1,529	7	1,443	7
General and administrative expenses	1,553	10	1,888	10	2,410	12	2,485	13
Total operating expenses	2,569	17	3,147	16	3,939	19	3,928	20
Operating profit	1,857	12	2,061	11	1,407	7	424	2
Interest expense	138	1	241	2	635	3	833	4
Profit before tax	1719	11	1,820	9	772	4	(409)	(2)
Income taxes	665	4	806	4	103	1	(234)	(1)
Net profit after tax	1,054	7	1,014	5	669	3	(175)	(1)
Ratios:								
Net profit-to-worth	N/A		20.17		11.68		Neg.	
Net profit-to-total assets	N/A		12.12		8.85		Neg.	
Funds flow-to-current maturities	28.31		18.95		9.51		Neg.	
Times interest earned	13.46		8.59		2.22		0.51	
Notes:								
Dividends	97		144		144		717	
Depreciation	770		760		750		859	

Dependable Doors
Balance Sheet
for the Fiscal Years Ending Sept. 30, 1988-1991
(in thousands of dollars)

	9/30/88	%	9/30/89	%	9/30/90	%	9/30/91	%
Assets								
Cash	202	2	109	1	409	2	548	3
Accounts receivable—net	3,056	34	3,422	34	3,662	21	4,161	23
Inventory	1,933	22	2,661	26	4,095	23	4,118	23
Income tax refund	—	—	—	—	297	2	426	2
Current assets	5,191	58	6,192	61	8,463	48	9,253	51
Fixed assets—net	3,336	38	3,503	35	8,285	47	8,294	47
Other assets	355	4	378	4	725	5	442	2
Noncurrent assets	3,691	42	3,881	39	9,010	52	8,736	49
Total assets	8,882	100	10,073	100	17,473	100	17,989	100
Liabilities and Net Worth								
Notes payable to banks	1,500	17	400	4	1,800	10	2,500	14
Accounts payable trade	709	8	558	6	1,530	9	1,434	8
Accruals	623	7	558	6 *	519	3	589	3
Current maturities LTD	61	1	86	—	134	1	147	1
Current-year income taxes	207	2	289	3	—	—	—	—
Current debt	3,100	35	1,891	19	3,983	23	4,670	26
Long-term debt secured	995	11	2,355	23	6,762	39	6,615	37
Total debt	4,095	46	4,246	42	10,745	62	11,285	63
Reserve—deferred income taxes	194	2	364	4	740	4	963	5
Capital stock—common	1,200	14	1,200	12	1,200	7	1,320	7
Paid-in surplus	1,524	17	1,524	16	1,524	9	2,049	12
Retained earnings	1,869	21	2,739	27	3,264	18	2,372	13
Net worth	4,593	52	5,463	54	5,988	34	5,741	32
Total liabilities and net worth	8,882	100	10,073	100	17,473	100	17,989	100
Working capital	2,091		4,301		4,480		4,583	
Ratios:								
Quick/current	1.05/1.67		1.87/3.27		1.10/2.12		1.10/1.98	
Debt-to-worth	0.89		0.78		1.79		1.97	
Sales-to-receivables (days)	—		60		63		71	
Cost of sales-to-inventory (days)	—		58		81		95	
Purchases-to-payables (days)	—		16		25		34	

Dependable Doors
Comparative Funds Flow Statement
for the Fiscal Years Ending Sept. 30, 1988-1991
(in thousands of dollars)

	9/30/89	*9/30/90*	*9/30/91*
Operating Funds:			
Net income	1,014	669	(175)
Add: Depreciation/amortization	760	750	859
Change in deferred tax liability	170	376	223
Change in accounts receivable	(366)	(240)	(499)
Change in inventory	(728)	(1,434)	(23)
Change in other current assets	—	(297)	(129)
Change in accounts payable	(151)	972	(96)
Change in accruals	(65)	(39)	70
Change in current-year income tax	82	(289)	—
Net cash flow from operations	716	468	230
Investment Flows:			
Change in other noncurrent assets	(23)	(347)	283
Increase in fixed assets	(927)	(5,532)	(868)
Total outflows from investments	(950)	(5,879)	(585)
Financing Flows:			
Dividends paid	(144)	(144)	(717)
Change in notes payable to banks	(1,100)	1,400	700
Change in commercial long-term debt	25	48	13
Change in long-term debt	1,360	4,407	(147)
Increase in capital accounts	—	—	645
Net financing flow	141	5,711	494
Change in cash/marketable securities	(93)	300	139

Notes to Financial Statements

1. Depreciation is taken on a straight-line basis over useful lives ranging from 3 to 15 years.
2. Deferred income taxes arise primarily from timing differences in the recognition of depreciation between the tax returns and management's financial statements. The Financial Accounting Standards Board (FASB) has issued Statement No. 96, Accounting for Income Taxes, which significantly changes the accounting for income taxes. The FASB requires that this Statement be implemented no later than the Company's 1992 fiscal year. The Statement requires a significantly different and more complex approach for the financial accounting and reporting of income taxes than is presently used. The Company does not believe that the application of the Statement will produce a significant adjustment to the Company's financial statements. The Company plans to implement this statement in 1992.
3. Revenue is recognized upon the shipment of the Company's products. At the same time, the Company provides for sales returns based upon experience.
4. Inventories are valued at the lower of cost (first-in, first-out) or market.
5. The Company has a trusted pension plan covering substantially all of its full-time employees. Pension expense is based on actuarial computations of current and future benefits. The Company's policy is to fund amounts that are required by applicable regulations and are tax deductible. The estimated amounts of future payments to be made under other retirement programs are being accrued currently over the period of active employment and are also included in pension expense.

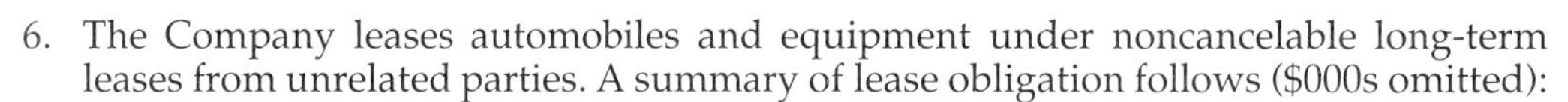

6. The Company leases automobiles and equipment under noncancelable long-term leases from unrelated parties. A summary of lease obligation follows ($000s omitted):

1992	$1,085
1993	$ 887
1994	$ 775
1995	$ 690

7. The income tax refund in 1990 was due to a research and development tax credit.

Report of Auditors

Stein and Stein, C.P.A.
8400 Center Street
Knoxville, Tennessee 34125
31 December 1991

The Board of Directors
Dependable Doors
2950 Jefferson Boulevard
Kingsport, Tennessee 34701

Gentlemen:

We have examined the consolidated balance sheets of Dependable Doors, Inc., (a Tennessee corporation) as of 30 September 1990 and 30 September 1991 and the related statements of operations and retained earning and cash flows for the years then ended. Our examinations were made in accordance with generally accepted auditing standards and, accordingly, included such tests of the accounting records and such other auditing procedures as we considered necessary in the circumstances.

In our opinion, the aforementioned financial statements present fairly the financial position of Dependable Doors, Inc., at 30 September 1990 and 30 September 1991 and the results of the company's operations and its cash flows for the periods then ended, in conformity with generally accepted accounting principles applied on a consistent basis.

Industry Information

An established method of looking at a company is to compare it with others in the same industry by referring to the Robert Morris Associates annual *Statement Studies,* which organizes Standard Industrial Classification (SIC) code and industry comparison data.

The astute analyst will read the Robert Morris Associates' disclaimer statement:

> RMA cautions that the *Studies* be regarded only as a general guideline and not as an absolute industry norm. This is due to limited samples within categories, the categorization of companies by their primary Standard Industrial Classification (SIC) number only, and different methods of operations by companies within the same industry. For these reasons, RMA recommends that the figures be used only as general guidelines in addition to other methods of financial analysis.

The sales mix of Dependable Doors is as follows:

Product	*1987*	*1988*	*1989*	*1990*	*1991*
Aluminum-framed patio doors	37%	37%	32%	32%	25%
Wood-framed patio doors	28%	33%	37%	40%	42%
Steel bifold closet doors	35%	30%	31%	28%	16%
Steel entry-door systems	-0-	-0-	-0-	-0-	17%

Dependable Doors, as do many companies these days, bridges more than one SIC code. It is closest to SIC code number 3442, which encompasses manufacturers of metal doors, sashes, frames, molding, and trim. However, as the sales mix of Dependable Doors indicates, almost 42 percent of its sales are wood-framed patio doors. Therefore, when comparing it to SIC code 3442, always remember that Dependable Doors' business mix is not exactly the same as the industry classification.

MANUFACTURERS - METAL DOORS, SASH, FRAMES, MOLDING & TRIM SIC #3442

Type of Statement			*Current Date Sorted By Sales*			
Unqualified		*2*	*1*	*9*	*11*	*14*
Qualified				*1*		
Reviewed	*1*	*14*	*13*	*11*	*4*	*1*
Compiled	*6*	*17*	*5*	*2*	*1*	
Other	*6*	*7*	*1*	*5*	*3*	*1*
	48 statements (6/30-9/30/89)		*88 statements (10/1/89-3/31/90)*			
	0-1MM	*1-3MM*	*3-5MM*	*5-10MM*	*10-25MM*	*25MM+*
NO. OF STATEMENTS	*13*	*40*	*20*	*28*	*19*	*16*
ASSETS	%	%	%	%	%	%
Cash & Equivalents	8.00	6.00	4.80	5.30	6.30	7.10
Trade Receivables -(net)	23.40	32.80	34.6	30.50	34.00	25.10
Inventory	36.50	40.50	28.50	30.70	30.30	24.40
All Other Current	4.20	2.70	0.40	1.50	2.50	2.70
Total Current	72.10	82.00	68.30	68.00	73.10	59.20
Fixed Assets (net)	23.40	12.70	24.70	25.40	18.70	29.80
Intangibles (net)	1.00	0.80	2.30	0.30	1.20	3.50
All Other Noncurrent	3.50	4.50	4.70	6.30	7.00	7.50
Total	100.00	100.00	100.00	100.00	100.00	100.00
LIABILITIES						
Notes Payable-Short Term	9.80	12.50	7.60	15.00	7.20	2.00
Cur. Mat.-L/T/D	4.00	3.20	4.50	4.10	3.50	2.40
Trade Payables	14.60	20.30	20.50	16.50	20.20	10.50
Income Taxes Payable	1.10	1.00	1.1	0.20	0.4	0.40
All Other Current	12.20	6.20	8.00	8.10	8.40	8.80
Total Current	41.70	43.20	41.60	43.90	39.70	24.00
Long-Term Debt	28.50	10.90	18.70	15.10	16.30	15.90
Deferred Taxes	0.00	0.50	0.20	0.40	0.30	1.8
All Other Noncurrent	5.20	2.60	3.80	1.80	0.20	5.90
Net Worth	24.60	42.70	35.60	38.70	43.50	52.40
Total Liabilities & Net Worth	100.00	100.00	100.00	100.00	100.00	100.00
INCOME DATA						
Net Sales	100.00	100.00	100.00	100.00	100.00	100.00
Gross Profit	33.60	30.00	29.10	26.20	26.50	25.60
Operating Expenses	29.70	26.30	26.90	22.40	22.30	20.00
Operating Profit	4.00	3.70	2.20	3.80	4.30	5.60
All Other Expenses (net)	1.9	1.20	1.10	1.10	0.30	1.60
Profit Before Taxes	2.10	2.50	1.10	2.70	4.00	4.00

RATIOS

Current		5.50		3.50		2.70		1.90		2.80		4.20
		2.50		1.80		1.70		1.70		2.10		2.30
		1.10		1.40		1.20		1.30		1.40		1.90
Quick		2.70		1.60		1.40		1.30		1.40		2.9
		1.10		0.80		0.90		0.90		1.10		1.10
		0.40		0.50		0.70		0.50		0.90		0.90
Sales/Receivables	**16**	23.40	**31**	11.80	**32**	11.50	**36**	10.30	**33**	10.90	**30**	12.20
	42	8.70	**43**	8.40	**45**	8.20	**49**	7.50	**46**	8.20	**41**	8.90
	70	5.20	**66**	6.50	**62**	5.90	**68**	6.30	**69**	6.40	**66**	6.60
Cost of Sales/Inventory	**66**	6.50	**43**	8.40	**33**	11.00	**41**	8.90	**51**	7.10	**36**	10.10
	81	4.50	**69**	5.30	**60**	7.30	**69**	5.30	**68**	5.40	**60**	6.10
	243	1.50	**111**	3.30	**73**	5.00	**85**	4.30	**94**	3.90	**66**	5.50
Cost of Sales/Payables	**6**	67.30	**13**	28.00	**17**	21.60	**20**	18.50	**28**	12.90	**16**	24.50
	37	9.90	**33**	11.00	**37**	10.00	**34**	10.60	**38**	9.50	**23**	16.00
	114	3.20	**67**	6.40	**60**	6.10	**46**	7.90	**57**	6.40	**40**	9.10
Sales/Working Capital		3.30		4.60		6.50		6.70		4.60		4.20
		5.70		7.50		9.50		9.30		5.90		6.10
		56.90		151		24.90		16.30		13.20		9.10
EBIT/Interest		2.40		4.90		4.10		5.80		5.50		11.00
	(12)	1.40	(36)	2.20	(17)	1.50	(26)	2.60	(15)	3.20	(14)	5.50
		-1.30		0.90		1.00		0.80		1.50		3.10
Net Profit + Depr. Dep., Amort./Cur. Mat. L/T/D				4.20		5.70		6.80		8.30		17.00
			(21)	2.50	(13)	2.2	(18)	2.1	(11)	3.2	(11)	7.20
				1.20		0.50		0.30		1.10		1.8
Fixed/Worth		0.20		0.10		0.20		0.30		0.20		0.40
		1.40		0.30		1.00		0.90		0.40		0.50
		NM		0.60		4.10		1.10		0.80		1.00
Debt/Worth		1.5		0.6		0.90		0.70		0.60		0.40
		3.50		1.50		1.70		1.70		1.7		0.80
		NM		4.10		4.90		4.00		2.8		2.10
% Profit Before Taxes/ Tangible Net Worth		19.80		40.30		28.10		23.60		26.60		34.20
	(10)	10.5	(39)	14.9	(16)	10.7	(27)	16		22.3	(15)	24.3
		-8.90		1.50		6.10		9.10		11.10		13.40
% Profit Before Taxes/ Total Assets		5.70		8.70		11.40		9.80		11.90		15.70
		2.40		4.80		3.20		5.10		7.40		10.30
		-2.70		0.10		0.70		0.10		2.30		1.90
Sales/Net Fixed Assets		108.60		49.80		40.10		17.40		26.40		11.80
		6.60		27.20		18.80		9.40		19.70		6.70
		5.00		15.90		7.80		5.70		7.20		4.30
Sales/Total Assets		2.70		3.30		3.30		2.5		3.20		2.50
		1.60		2.80		2.70		2.30		2.10		1.90
		0.70		2.20		1.80		1.90		1.80		1.60
% Depr. Dep. Amort./ Sales		1.70		0.80		1.00		1.10		0.90		1.20
	(10)	3.00	(37)	1.30	(19)	2.10		1.4	(18)	1.30	(16)	1.40
		5.10		1.90		3.10		1.9		2.3		3.30
% Officer's Comp/Sales				2.70		1.90						
			(27)	4.50	(13)	3.30						
				7.00		4.10						
Net Sales ($)		7652M		80487M		76813M		216233M		316092M		1968561M
Total Assets ($)		8004M		31496M		32184M		101366M		144612M		920469M

Questions About Dependable Doors

1. What type of operating cycle does Dependable Doors have?

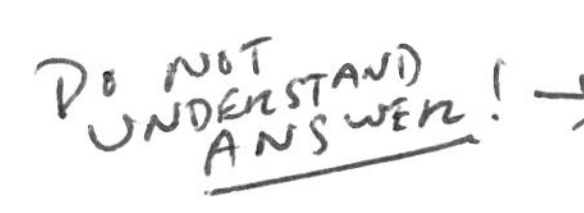

2. Is Dependable Door's distribution of assets and liabilities typical?
3. What type of financing needs might the company have?
4. As a lender, what other types of industry risks might concern you?
5. What kind of operating cash flow cycle might Dependable Doors have and how might it differ from its accounting for income?

The answers to these questions are in the appendix.

Company History

Engraph was organized in 1945 as a North Carolina corporation and was reincorporated in Delaware in 1987. The following is background information on the business, primarily from the firm's annual report.

Engraph is a manufacturer of packaging and product-identification materials for selected market segments within the multi-billion-dollar packaging materials market. It has seven divisions and two subsidiary companies, each of which produces a variety of products in the general field of packaging materials and identification products.

Engraph's target markets are consumer electronics, beverages, snack foods, textiles, personal care, and health care. It concentrates on four major areas:

1. labels and package inserts,
2. screen process printing,
3. paperboard cartons and specialties, and
4. flexible packaging.

The divisions that produce promotional labels and coupons make tear-off, instant-redemption coupons whose adhesive ceases to stick once the consumer peels the coupon off the package. This solves a sticky problem for retailers that store and sort coupons. Another product is a heat-shrinkable sleeve that can be used as a tamper-evidence device or as a means of delivering promotional messages and coupons. These divisions also produce a primary label with a protective pouch that contains technical data or other information about the product. This label is used primarily by the health care industry.

The divisions involved in screen process printing service the beverage industry, which needs high-quality graphics on its vending machines and fleet vehicles. They have to stock a variety of shapes and sizes of graphic panels to fit a wide range of vending machines and fleet vehicles.

The divisions that make paperboard cartons and specialties produce a variety of products, including

- paperboard covers for glassware in hotel rooms,
- beverage coasters for hotels and lounges,
- packaging for personal and health care products, and

- specialty packaging, including packages with windows for the textile and consumer electronics markets.

The divisions that produce flexible packaging work primarily with the candy, gum, and frozen fruit juice industries. The packaging for these industries requires eye-catching special effects and appetizing color photography.

Management's Analysis of Engraph's Financial Condition and the Results of its Operations

Acquisitions and Disposition

On 15 March 1991, the Board of Directors approved the sale of the Company's Package Products Flexible division ("Flexible"). On 18 April 1991, the Company sold Flexible to Gravure International Corporation. The selling price, net of transaction expenses, approximated book value. The Company received $9,200,000 in cash and a five-year note for approximately $5,711,000. Cash proceeds were used to reduce debt incurred to acquire Graphic Resources, Inc. ("Graphic Resources"). The financial statements reflect the operating results of Flexible separately from continuing operations, and prior year financial information has been appropriately restated.

On 22 February 1991, the Company purchased Graphic Resources, a leading producer of printed pressure-sensitive roll labels and folded and multilayer coupons. On 4 June 1990, the Company purchased Ariston Incorporated ("Ariston"), a leading producer of screen-printed identification materials that specializes in high-quality pictorial graphics. On 18 July 1990, the Company became a 50-percent partner in a joint venture called Ramallo, Escribano & Co., which serves Puerto Rico and the Caribbean basin market for roll labels and pharmaceutical-product inserts. The Company used the equity method of accounting to reflect its investment and the proportion of its earnings resulting from the partnership operation.

On 31 January 1989, the Company purchased the Patton Division of Afford Industries, Inc., a supplier of specialty labels and related application equipment. All of the acquisitions were accounted for under the purchase method of accounting. This section of acquisitions and disposition should be read in conjunction with the financial statements.

Results of Operations

Net sales in 1991 were $200,499,000, an increase of 19.5 percent from the $167,808,000 reported in 1990. Approximately $27,870,000, or 85.5 percent, of the increase resulted from the acquisition of Graphic Resources and Ariston. Market share gains and the slightly improved business climate in 1991 contributed to the remainder of the increase. Net sales in 1990 increased 0.5 percent over the $166,987,000 reported in 1989. The increase in net sales in 1990 resulted primarily from the net effect of the sales attributable to Ariston, offset by increased competition, a soft economy, and decisions by two major customers to produce their requirements internally.

The gross margin percentage increased to 26.0 percent in 1991 from 25.5 percent in 1990 and 24.1 percent in 1989. Operating efficiencies made in 1991 improved the gross margin from prior-year levels. Additionally, margins were improved by concentrating on higher-value-added products, controlling costs, and utilizing materials better. Reduced operating costs and improved productivity and product mix resulted in 1990's increased gross margin over 1989's.

The selling and administrative expense for 1991 was $34,275,000, or 17.1 percent of net sales, compared with $27,301,000, or 16.3 percent of net sales in 1990, and $25,793,000, or 15.4 percent of net sales in 1989. The increased selling and administrative expense in 1991 was primarily due to the change in the mix of business units. The increase in 1990's selling and administrative expense was largely attributable to the acquisition of Ariston, which had a high selling and administrative expense relative to net sales.

Interest-bearing debt at 31 December 1991 was $3,505,000 compared with $58,594,000 and $50,496,000 at December 1990 and 1989, respectively. The 1991 increase in debt was incurred to finance the acquisition of Graphic Resources, net of the cash proceeds from the sale of Flexible. The 1990 increase in debt was primarily due to the acquisition of Ariston. Interest expense in 1991 amounted to $4,344,000 compared with $3,107,000 in 1990 and $3,577,000 in 1989. Interest expense in 1990 decreased from 1989 due to a stock issuance of approximately $15,000,000 in July 1989 to institutional investors in the United Kingdom, the proceeds of which were used to partially repay term loans issued to finance the acquisition of Patton in January 1989.

The Company's effective tax rate was 41.9 percent for 1991, 37.5 percent for 1990, and 39.2 percent for 1989. The effective tax rate increased in 1991 due to the additional goodwill generated by the acquisition of Graphic Resources and Ariston, higher state income tax provisions, and the effect of certain nonrecurring items affecting the 1990 provision. The effective tax rate decreased in 1990 from 1989 due to slightly lower state income tax provisions.

Income from continuing operations was $7,913,000 in 1991, $7,854,000 in 1990, and $6,851,000 in 1989. The year-to-year increases of 0.8 percent in 1991 and 14.6 percent in 1990 resulted from essentially the same factors that affected net sales and gross margin.

Financial Condition

The Company continued in good financial condition. In the first quarter of 1991, the Company financed the purchase of Graphic Resources and refinanced certain Graphic Resources debt with borrowings under the Company's unsecured long-term credit agreements and its short-term lines of credit. In April 1991, the Company used the cash proceeds from the sale of Flexible to reduce the borrowings under the unsecured long-term credit agreements and the short-term line of credit.

In the third quarter of 1990, the Company issued $20,000,000 of senior unsecured promissory notes at interest rates ranging from 9.33 percent to 9.63 percent, due in varying annual installments beginning 1 September 1995 and ending 1 September 2001. The borrowings were used to repay term loans of $6,000,000, which had been used in the second quarter of 1990 to finance the purchase of Ariston and refinance certain Ariston debt. The remainder of the borrowings was used to repay moneys borrowed under the unsecured long-term credit agreements maintained by the Company. In April 1990, the Company issued 89,059 shares of common stock, valued at $708,000, to a group of former stockholders of Screen Graphics, Inc., as the final earnout payment in connection with the acquisition.

New debt was incurred in 1989 primarily to acquire Patton and to purchase major equipment for a business unit. In July 1989, the Company sold 1,821,136 shares of common stock to institutional investors in the United Kingdom, and the net proceeds of approximately $15,000,000 were used to partially repay term loans used to finance the Patton acquisition. In April 1989, the Company paid $2,735,000 in cash and issued 1,649,652 shares of common stock valued at $10,959,000 to the group of former stockholders of Screen Graphics, Inc., pursuant to an earnout agreement.

Working capital at the end of 1991 was $19,511,000 compared with $22,355,000 in 1990. The Company utilizes the working-capital-to-net-sales ratio as one of its primary measurements of the effectiveness of its short-term management of assets. At 31 December 1991, the working-capital-to-net-sales ratio was 9.1 percent compared with 11.2 percent in 1990. The improvement in the 1991 ratio was due primarily to the lower working capital levels maintained by Graphic Resources relative to other business units. The 1991 current ratio was 1.7 compared with 2.0 at the end of 1990.

Investing activities in 1991 included capital expenditures of $6,742,000, the acquisition of Graphic Resources for approximately $11,614,000 in cash, and the disposition of Flexible. The Company also made an additional capital contribution of approximately $120,000 to the Ramallo, Escribano & Co. joint venture. In 1990, investing activities included capital expenditures of $8,177,000 and the acquisition of Ariston for approximately $3,760,000 in cash, with approximately $1,662,000 payable in June 1992. In addition, approximately $2,324,000 was used to become a 50-percent partner in the Ramallo, Escribano

& Co. joint venture. In 1989, capital expenditures of $9,152,000 and the acquisition of Patton were the major investing activities. As discussed in note 15 to the Consolidated Financial Statements, the Company had signed contracts to purchase miscellaneous manufacturing equipment; these contracts require remaining future payments of $691,000 as of 31 December 1991. Subsequent to year end, the Company entered into commitments to acquire additional manufacturing equipment in the amount of approximately $4,575,000, of which approximately $1,095,000 has been paid.

Long-term debt increased from $36,894,000 in 1990 to $41,756,800 in 1991. The Company's ratio of long-term debt to capital was 33.0 percent in 1991 compared with 30.9 percent in 1990. The increase was primarily due to additional borrowings to finance the acquisition of Graphic Resources.

During 1991, 1990, and 1989, the Company used $3,612,000, $5,677,000, and $412,000, respectively, to repurchase shares, the majority of which were repurchased under existing agreements with certain groups of stockholders. The Company's agreements with these groups of stockholders grant them the right through years varying from 1995 to 2002 to require the Company (or its designee) to purchase up to 10 percent of the shares initially covered by such agreement in any year and, in certain cases, an additional 10 percent in any two nonconsecutive years, at a purchase price based on the average stock price for the 30 days preceding the purchase. Using the average stock price for the 30 days preceding 31 December 1991, the Company potentially could be required to purchase shares with a market value of $10,684,000 in 1992; $5,057,000 in 1993; $6,515,000 in 1994; $3,655,000 in 1995; $3,129,000 in 1996; and $4,003,000 thereafter. In prior years, the Company has been required to repurchase only a portion of the shares subject to current repurchase obligations pursuant to these agreements.

The Company maintains unsecured long-term credit agreements providing for loans up to $50,000,000. At 31 December 1991, $7,466,000 was borrowed under these agreements. The Company has two $5,000,000 short-term lines of credit with two principal lenders. In 1991, no borrowings were made under these short-term lines of credit. The Company's internal cash flow, combined with availability under its existing loan agreements, should adequately provide for near-term funding needs. However, the Company's long-term strategic objectives indicate that it could require all of its internally generated funds, current borrowings, and possibly additional financing to support future growth.

The Company has been informed that it is a potentially responsible party in regard to several environmental investigations. The Company has reviewed its potential liability relating to these environmental matters and believes, based upon known facts and the Company's prior experience, that, except with respect to the Rock Hill Chemical Company site in Rock Hill, South Carolina (the "Rock Hill site"), the costs of all outstanding claims are not material. The Company's information with respect to the Rock Hill site is incomplete; however, based on the information the Company does have and its experience in similar matters, the Company believes that the likelihood of incurring a material loss with respect to such site is remote.

The Financial Accounting Standards Board's release on Accounting for Income Taxes has been deferred to fiscal years beginning after 15 December 1992. The Company's current intentions are to adopt this standard in 1993 and to restate prior-years financial statements, expecting no significant affect on the Company's net income and balance sheet.

The Financial Accounting Standards Board has issued Statement of Financial Accounting Standards No. 106, "Employers' Accounting for Postretirement Benefits other than Pensions" (SFAS 106). The Company offers its employees no postretirement benefits; therefore, SFAS 106 had no impact on the Company's financial statements.

Inflation

Most of the Company's inventories are valued using the LIFO method. In 1991, the Company experienced inventory inflation of 1.3 percent compared with an inflation factor of 1.7 percent in 1990 and 2.1 percent in 1989.

Consolidated Financial Statements

Engraph, Inc., and Subsidiaries
Consolidated Statements of Income
(Dollars in thousands except share data)

	Years Ending December 31		
	1991	*1990*	*1989*
Net sales	$200,499	$167,808	$166,987
Cost of Sales	148,467	125,358	126,773
Gross margin	52,032	42,450	40,214
Selling and administrative expense	34,275	27,301	25,793
Operating income	17,757	15,149	14,421
Interest expense	(4,344)	(3,107)	(3,577)
Other income	217	522	428
Income from continuing operations before provision for income taxes	13,630	12,564	11,272
Provision for income taxes	5,717	4,710	4,421
Income from continuing operations	7,913	7,854	6,851
(Loss) Income from discontinued operation, net of income taxes of $115, $502, and ($667) in 1991, 1990, and 1989, respectively	(160)	(838)	1,033
Net income	7,753	7,016	7,884
Earnings per share			
Continuing operations	$0.46	$0.44	$0.40
Discontinued operation	(0.01)	(0.05)	0.06
Net income	0.45	0.39	0.46
Cash dividends per common share	$0.12	$0.11	$0.10
Weighted average number of common and common equivalent shares outstanding	17,270,000	17,864,000	17,045,000

The accompanying notes are an integral part of these statements.

Engraph, Inc., and Subsidiaries
Consolidated Balance Sheets
(Dollars in thousands except share data)

	Years Ending December 31 *1991*	*1990*
ASSETS		
Current assets:		
Cash and cash equivalents	$613	$70
Accounts receivable, less allowance for doubtful accounts of $730 in 1991 and $619 in 1990	23,446	20,798
Inventories	18,334	18,814
Deferred income taxes	3,232	2,273
Other current assets	1,376	2,226
Total Current Assets	47,001	44,181
Property, plant and equipment, net	60,887	65,271
Other assets:		
Goodwill and other intangible assets, net	36,734	26,212
Investments	7,839	3,905
Total assets	$152,461	$139,569
LIABILITIES AND STOCKHOLDERS EQUITY		
Current liabilities:		
Current maturities of long-term debt	$1,749	$1,700
Accounts payable	13,772	12,290
Accrued liabilities	12,169	7,836
Total current liabilities	27,690	21,826
Long-term debt, less current maturities	41,756	36,894
Deferred income taxes	5,391	4,975
Other deferred liabilities	2,576	4,044
Redeemable common stock, subject to repurchase agreements at cost; 3,604,569 shares in 1991 and 3,904,313 in 1990	12,463	14,566
Common stock, $1 par value; shares outstanding-13,342,619 in 1991 and 12,346,665 in 1990		
Shares held in treasury-349,485 in 1991 and 151,352 in 1990	13,343	12,347
Capital in excess of par value	36,642	30,776
Retained earnings	12,600	14,141
Total liabilities and stockholders' equity	$152,461	$139,569

The accompanying notes are an integral part of these statements.

Engraph, Inc., and Subsidiaries
Consolidated Statements of Cash Flows
(Dollars in thousands)

	Years Ending December 31		
	1991	*1990*	*1989*
CASH FLOWS FROM OPERATING ACTIVITIES:			
Income from continuing operations	$7,913	$7,854	$6,851
Adjustments to reconcile income from continuing operations to net cash provided by continuing operating activities	9,060	7,554	6,440
Depreciation and amortization	(543)	266	600
Loss (gain) on sales of property, plant and equipment	50	7	(64)
	16,480	15,681	13,827
Changes in assets and liabilities, net of effects from sale of Flexible, purchase of Graphic Resources, Inc., Ariston Incorporated and Patton, and sale of assets			
Accounts receivable	(1,990)	2,177	(2,372)
Inventories	(1,996)	(29)	(855)
Other assets	1,037	(526)	(1,322)
Accounts payable	3,091	(1,940)	(1,685)
Accrued liabilities	1,232	216	(1,608)
Other deferred liabilities	(1,900)	726	575
Net cash provided by continuing operating activities	15,945	16,305	6,560
Net cash provided (used) by discontinued operation	890	(3,386)	1,988
CASH FLOWS FROM INVESTING ACTIVITIES:			
Additions to property, plant and equipment	(6,742)	(8,177)	(9,152)
Net liabilities (assets) of businesses acquired	100	(4,147)	(22,087)
Additions to goodwill	(11,581)	(2,293)	(14,276)
Investment in joint venture	(120)	(2,324)	
Proceeds from disposals of property, plant and equipment	289	471	68
Proceeds from sale of assets	12,911		
Net cash used in investing activities	(5,143)	(16,470)	(45,447)
CASH FLOWS FROM FINANCING ACTIVITIES:			
Issuance of note receivable	(3,711)		
Issuance of long-term debt	28,128	27,774	32,620
Issuance of common stock	1,039	1,258	26,879
Payments of long-term debt, including current maturities	(29,672)	(21,992)	(20,667)
Shares repurchased	(3,612)	(5,677)	(412)
Dividends paid	(1,963)	(1,920)	(1,560)
Change in bank overdraft	(1,358)	1,820	(6)
Net cash (used) provided by financing activities	(11,149)	1,263	36,854
Net increase (decrease) in cash and cash equivalents	543	(2,288)	(45)
Cash and cash equivalents at beginning of year	70	2,358	2,403
Cash and cash equivalents at end of year	$613	$70	$2,358
SUPPLEMENTAL DISCLOSURES OF CASH FLOW/INFORMATION:			
Cash paid during the year for:			
Interest	$4,038	$3,088	$3,255
Income taxes	$4,058	$3,677	$4,777

The accompanying notes are an integral part of these statements.

Engraph, Inc., and Subsidiaries
Consolidated Statement of Stockholders' Equity
(Dollars in thousands)

	Redeemable Common Stock at Cost	*Common Stock at $1 Par Value*	*Capital in Excess of Par Value*	*Retained Earnings*
Balance at December 31, 1988	$6,272	$6,055	$16,991	$9,044
Shares issued in a private placement		1,388	13,774	
Additional shares issued for purchase of Screen Graphics, Inc	10,939		239	
Shares issued to employee benefit plans		20	(22)	
Options exercised		64	293	(1,560)
Dividends paid or reinvested		28		7,884
Net income				
Redeemable common stock put to Engraph or third party designee	(578)	210	(44)	
Shares issued under long-term incentive plan		14	142	
Four-for-three stock split, June 1989		2,041	940	(2,981)
Balance at December 31, 1989	16,633	9,820	32,313	12,387
Additional shares issued for purchase of Screen Graphics, Inc	708			
Options exercised		92	(41)	
Dividends paid or reinvested		39	252	(1,920)
Net income				7,016
Shares repurchased		(161)	(2,787)	
Shares issued under long-term incentive plan		18	190	
Redeemable common stock put to Engraph or third party designee	(2,775)	56	(10)	
Five-for-four stock split, June 1990		2,483	859	(3,342)
Balance at December 31, 1990	14,566	12,347	30,776	14,141
Options exercised		171	217	
Shares issued under long-term incentive plan		12	58	
Dividends paid or reinvested		32	244	(1,963)
Net income				7,753
Shares repurchased		(73)	(2,049)	
Shares issued under sales incentive plan		44	273	
Redeemable common stock put to Engraph or third party designee	(2,103)	180	452	
5% stock dividend, November 1991		630	6,691	(7,331)
Balance at December 31, 1991	$12,463	$13,343	$36,662	$12,600

The accompanying notes are an integral part of these statements.

Notes to Engraph's Consolidated Financial Statements

Engraph, Inc., and Subsidiaries

31 December 1991, 1990, and 1989

1. Significant Accounting and Financial Reporting Policies:

- Consolidation. The consolidated financial statements include those of Engraph, Inc., and its wholly owned subsidiaries. All significant intercompany accounts and transactions have been eliminated in consolidation.
- Revenue Recognition. Sales and related cost of goods sold are recognized upon shipment to customers or as specified by the terms of the related contracts.
- Statements of Cash Flows. For the purposes of the statements of cash flows, the Company considers all highly liquid instruments purchased with a maturity of three months or less to be cash equivalents.
- Inventories. Inventories are valued at the lower of cost or market. Cost is determined principally using the last-in, first-out (LIFO) method.
- Income Taxes. Deferred income taxes result primarily from timing differences of deductions for financial reporting and income tax purposes.
- Property, Plant and Equipment. Property is stated at cost and is depreciated using the straight-line method over the assets' estimated useful lives, ranging from 10 to 50 years for buildings and improvements, 3 to 10 years for land improvements, 3 to 15 years for machinery and equipment, and 2 to 3 years for vehicles. Assets under capital lease are depreciated over the lesser of the assets' useful lives or the terms of the leases. Maintenance, repairs, and minor renewals are charged to expense as incurred. Additions, replacements, and improvements are capitalized. Gains and losses from sales or other disposals of property and plant and equipment are included in other income.
- Goodwill and Other Intangible Assets. Excess of cost over net assets of businesses acquired is amortized on a straight-line basis over 40 years from the acquisition dates. Other intangible assets are amortized on a straight-line basis over the assets' estimated useful lives, ranging from 4 to 40 years.
- Investments. Investments consist of the Company's 50-percent interest in a joint-venture partnership accounted for under the equity method and other investments.
- Share and Per Share Amounts. All common share and per share amounts have been restated to give effect to the five-for-four stock split and the four-for-three stock split effected in the form of stock dividends in June 1990 and June 1989, respectively, and the 5 percent stock dividend in November 1991 (except for the Statements of Stockholders' Equity). Common equivalent shares outstanding include amounts for options outstanding and, for the period ended 31 December 1989, probable future stock issuances for a past acquisition (subsequently issued in 1990).
- Reclassifications. Certain prior-year amounts have been reclassified to conform with the 1991 financial statement presentation.

2. Inventories:

Inventories as of 31 December 1991 and 1990 comprised the following (dollars in thousands):

Inventories, at first-in, first-out (FIFO) cost:	1991	1990
Raw materials	$7,324	$7,982
Work in progress	3,653	3,310
Finished goods	9,687	10,703
	20,664	21,995

Less amount to state inventories at LIFO cost	(2,330)	(3,181)
Inventories, at LIFO cost:	$18,334	$18,814

3. Property, Plant and Equipment:

Property, plant and equipment as of 31 December 1991 and 1990 comprised the following (dollars in thousands):

	1991	1990
Land	$1,838	$1,799
Buildings and improvements	16,452	16,707
Machinery and equipment	67,153	68,341
Automobiles under capitalized leases	1,244	1,459
Construction in progress	5,580	10,952
	92,267	99,258
Less accumulated depreciation and amortization	(31,380)	(33,987)
	$60,887	$65,271

Depreciation expense from continuing operations was $7,445,000 in 1991, $6,254,000 in 1990, and $5,463,000 in 1989.

4. Goodwill and Other Intangible Assets:

Goodwill and other intangible assets as of 31 December 1991 and 1990 comprised the following (dollars in thousands):

	1991	1990
Goodwill	$33,418	$ 21,840
Other intangible assets	7,369	6,917
	40,787	28,757
Less accumulated amortization	(4,053)	(2,545)
	$36,734	$ 26,212

Amortization expense from continuing operations was $1,615,000 in 1991, $1,300,000 in 1990, and $977,000 in 1989.

5. Accounts Payable and Accrued Liabilities:

Accounts payable and accrued liabilities as of 31 December 1991 and 1990 comprised the following (dollars in thousands):

	1991	1990
Accounts payable:		
Trade and other payables	$11,357	$ 8,517
Bank overdraft for outstanding checks, net of cash in banks	2,415	3,773
	$13,772	$12,290
Accrued liabilities:		
Salary and other compensation	3,015	2,397
Other	9,154	5,439
	$12,169	$ 7,836

6. Long-term Debt:

Long-term debt as of 31 December 1991 and 1990 comprised the following (dollars in thousands):

	1991	1990
Unsecured senior promissory notes, interest at 9.33 percent to 12 percent, due in installments through September 2001.	$26,475	$26,945
Revenue bonds, interest at floating rates less than prime, due in quarterly installments through April 2004, $1,091 of which are secured by certain plant and equipment.	6,711	7,060
Unsecured credit agreement notes, interest not to exceed prime.	7,466	1,774
Urban Development Action Grant, interest at 9 percent, due in quarterly installments through January 2001, with a subordinated security interest in certain plant and equipment.	893	952
Installment notes, interest at prime to 14 percent, due in monthly installments through January 1994, secured by certain plant and equipment.	750	797
Capital lease obligations, interest at 9 percent to 14 percent.	1,210	1,066
	43,505	38,594
Less current maturities.	(1,749)	(1,700)
	$41,756	$36,894

Future maturities of long-term debt (excluding capital lease obligations) as of 31 December 1991 were as follows: $1,110,000 in 1992; $1,151,000 in 1993; $5,751,000 in 1994; $4,343,000 in 1995; $4,359,000 in 1996; and $25,581,000 thereafter.

In the third quarter of 1990, the Company issued $20,000,000 of senior unsecured promissory notes at interest rates of 9.33 percent to 9.63 percent, due in varying annual installments beginning 1 September 1995 through 1 September 2001. The borrowings were used to repay term loans of $6,000,000 that were used in the second quarter of 1990 to finance the purchase of Ariston, Inc., and to refinance certain Ariston debt. The remainder of the borrowings were used to repay moneys borrowed on the unsecured long-term credit agreements maintained by the Company.

The Company maintains unsecured long-term credit agreements providing for loans up to $50,000,000, with $7,466,000 outstanding as of 31 December 1991. Interest rates do not exceed prime. On 1 January 1994, borrowings then outstanding under the credit notes may be converted to 8-year term notes, at interest rates up to 1 percent over prime, and would be due in quarterly installments beginning upon conversion.

The senior promissory notes, long-term credit agreements, and revenue bond agreements contain certain covenants that require the Company to limit total borrowings to certain percentages of total capitalization and limit senior and secured debt to certain percentages of total capitalization. As of 31 December 1991, the covenants restrict dividend payments to a maximum of $3,500,000 and restrict investments in businesses without the Company retaining controlling interest and certain other investments not related to the Company's business to $5,390,000. Other covenants place restrictions on the Company as to borrowings, asset disposals, mergers, leases, guarantees, and liens.

The Company has short-term committed lines of credit totaling $6,000,000 provided by two principal lenders. As of 31 December 1991, there were no borrowings under these short-term lines of credit. Interest rates do not exceed prime.

7. Leases:

The Company has capital leases that expire through 1994. The Company is obligated under operating leases for certain administrative offices and manufacturing facilities expiring through 2001. Future minimum lease payments under capital and operating leases with noncancelable terms in excess of one year as of 31 December 1991 were as follows (dollars in thousands):

	Capital Lease Obligations	Operating Leases
1992	$713	$1,807
1993	446	1,565
1994	126	1,412
1995		1,213
1996		1,070
Thereafter		2,341
Total minimum payments	1,285	$9,408
Less estimated executory costs and amounts representing interest	(75)	
Net present value	$1,210	

Certain operating leases provide renewal options for up to ten additional years. Rental expense from continuing operations was $2,663,000 in 1991, $2,138,000 in 1990, and $1,722,000 in 1989.

8. Employee Benefit Plans:

The Company has a contributory employee thrift plan covering substantially all employees. Employee contributions to the plan may be invested in one or more of four funds. Company matching contributions to the plan are invested in Engraph, Inc., common stock and are based upon the earnings of the Company. As of 31 December 1991, the plan held 873,691 shares of Engraph, Inc., common stock. During 1989, the thrift plan was amended and restated in conjunction with the termination of the defined benefit plan discussed below to provide an additional annual employer contribution equal to a percentage of each employee's annual compensation. The Company incurred expense from continuing operations of $1,399,000 in 1991, $1,607,000 in 1990, and $1,649,000 in 1989 under this plan.

The Company had a noncontributory-defined benefit pension plan that was terminated as of 30 June 1989. Participants in the plan became fully vested at that date, and in May 1990 substantially all of the assets of the plan were distributed out of the plan to the participants either in the form of annuity contracts or transfers to the Company's defined contribution plan. The Company realized no material gain or loss upon termination of the plan; pension expense from continuing operations was $89,000 in 1989.

The Financial Accounting Standards Board has issued Statement of Financial Accounting Standards No. 106, Employers' Accounting for Post Retirement Benefits other than Pensions" (SFAS 106). The Company does not offer its employees postretirement benefits; therefore, SFAS 106 had no impact on the Company's financial statements.

9. Stock Options:

The Company's stock option plans allow the granting of up to 2,506,028 qualified or nonqualified options to employees for the right, when exercisable, to purchase shares of the Company's common stock at their fair market value at date of grant. One-fifth of the granted options may be exercised one year after the date of grant, with an additional one-fifth exercisable each year thereafter. Options that expire or are canceled prior to exercise are added to the shares available for future grants.

A summary of stock option activity is as follows:

	Options	Option Price Per Share
Outstanding, 31 December 1988	1,136,208	$2.42 to $ 6.22
Granted	199,047	$6.71 to $10.67
Exercised	(151,206)	$2.42 to $4.88
Canceled	(47,034)	$2.85 to $6.22
Outstanding, 31 December 1989	1,137,015	$2.85 to $10.67
Granted	203,175	$5.83 to $5.83
Exercised	(173,894)	$2.85 to $6.22
Canceled	(42,664)	$3.91 to $8.76
Outstanding, 31 December 1990	1,123,632	$2.85 to $10.67
Granted	246,075	$8.10 to $9.25
Exercised	(264,112)	$2.85 to $8.76
Canceled	(114,095)	$3.91 to $10.67
Outstanding, 31 December 1991	991,500	$2.85 to $10.67
Exercisable, 31 December 1991	394,740	$2.85 to $8.76

10. Common Stock:

The Company has a dividend reinvestment plan whereby stockholders may purchase shares of the Company's common stock at market prices through cash dividends and through cash contributions up to $5,000 per quarter. Shares issued under this plan were 33,046 in 1991; 43,141 in 1990; and 39,334 in 1989.

The Company has agreements with certain groups of stockholders that grant them the right, through years varying from 1995 to 2002, to require the Company (or its designee) to purchase up to 10 percent of the shares initially covered by such agreement in any year and, in certain cases, an additional 10 percent in any two nonconsecutive years, at a purchase price based on the average stock price for the 30 days preceding the purchase. The Company has the right of first refusal on any shares offered for sale by these stockholders. The Company or third party designees obtained 435,467 of these shares in 1991; 443,580 shares in 1990, and 337,667 shares in 1989; leaving 3,604,569 shares remaining under these agreements as of 31 December 1991.

In September 1988, the Company adopted a Stockholder Rights Plan and pursuant thereto declared a dividend of one right for each outstanding share of common stock. When exercisable, each right will entitle its holder to buy one-hundredth of a share of Series A Participating Preferred Stock at a price of $50 per right. The rights will become exercisable if a person or group acquires 20 percent of the Company's common stock or makes an offer to acquire 20 percent or more of the Company's common stock. If the Company is merged with an entity that previously acquired 20 percent or more of the Company's common stock (the "Acquiring Stockholder"), each right will entitle the holder thereof, other than the Acquiring Stockholder, to purchase $100 worth of the surviving company's common stock, based on the market price at that time, for $50. Even if there is not a merger, under certain circumstances, each right will entitle the holder thereof, other than the Acquiring Stockholder, to purchase from the Company $100 worth of the Company's common stock, based on the market price at the time, for $50. The rights may be redeemed by the Company at a price of $.01 per right. If not previously redeemed, the rights will expire on 12 September 1998. At 31 December 1991, a total of 200,000 shares of authorized Series A Participating Preferred Stock, $1 par value per share, was reserved for the above purposes.

11. Income Taxes:

The components of the provision for income taxes are as follows (dollars in thousands):

	1991	1990	1989
Current Federal income taxes	$5,170	$3,493	$3,904
Current state income taxes	975	449	584
Deferred income taxes	(543)	266	600
	$5,602	$4,208	$5,088

A reconciliation of the provision for income taxes from the federal statutory rate to the effective rate as reflected in the financial statements for each of the years presented is as follows:

	1991	1990	1989
Federal statutory tax rate	34.0%	34.0%	34.0%
State income taxes, net	4.8	4.0	4.5
Goodwill	2.0	1.6	1.0
Other	1.1	(2.1)	(0.3)
	41.9%	37.5%	39.2%

The deferred provision for income taxes for each of the years presented in the financial statements comprises the following (dollars in thousands):

	1991	1990	1989
Depreciation	$24	$1,022	$1,067
Compensation timing differences	(35)	(111)	(195)
Pension accruals	72	(194)	(74)
Inventory valuations	(302)	(552)	(46)
Tax under (over) book gain on disposition of assets	288	(11)	32
Allowance for doubtful accounts	(143)	140	(210)
Other	(447)	(28)	26
	$ (543)	$ 266	$ 600

Discussion of the effect on the Company's financial position from the adoption of the Statement of Financial Accounting Standards No. 109, "Accounting for Income Taxes," is included in Management's Discussion and Analysis.

12. Acquisitions:

On 22 February 1991, the Company acquired all of the issued and outstanding shares of common stock of Graphic Resources, Inc., a Kentucky corporation. The transaction was accounted for as a purchase with the results of Graphic Resources, Inc., included with those of the Company beginning 23 February 1991. The negotiated purchase price was $11,614,000 in cash. Graphic Resources, Inc., is a leading producer of printed pressure-sensitive roll labels and folded and multilayer coupons.

In June 1990, the Company acquired substantially all of the property, rights, and assets of Ariston Incorporated, pursuant to the terms and conditions contained in the Asset Purchase Agreement among the Company, Ariston Incorporated, and its former owners. The transaction has been accounted for as a purchase, with the results of Ariston Incorporated included with those of the Company beginning 4 June 1990. The negotiated purchase price was (i) $3,760,000 in cash, (ii) $1,662,500 payable no later than 6 June 1992, and (iii) a contingent amount of up to $4,837,500 payable in cash dependent on the future earnings of the acquired business. Ariston Incorporated is a producer of screen-printed identification materials and specializes in producing high-quality pictorial graphics.

On 31 January 1989, the Company acquired substantially all of the property, rights, and assets employed in, and associated with, the Patton Division of Afford Industries, Inc., an indirect, wholly owned subsidiary of Kane Industries, Inc. The transaction was accounted for as a purchase with the results of the Patton Division included with those of the Company beginning 1 January 1989. The negotiated purchase price for the assets of the Patton Division was $23,000,000 and was paid in cash. Concurrently, Afford paid to the Company $800,000 as payment for certain air pollution abatement equipment required to bring the manufacturing facilities, transferred as part of the purchased assets, into compliance with applicable laws and regulations. The net amount ($22,200,000) of the consideration given in exchange for the purchased assets ($23,000,000) and the consideration received for the air pollution abatement equipment was allocated among the purchased assets and assumed liabilities. Patton manufactures and distributes specialty labels of various types, and its specialized labeling machinery and its principal manufacturing facilities are located in New Jersey.

13. Purchase Commitments:

The Company has committed to purchase miscellaneous manufacturing equipment. As of 31 December 1991, the Company has signed contracts requiring remaining future payments of $691,000 once the machinery is delivered and installed according to the terms of the contracts.

14. Business Segment:

The Company operates as a single-segment business providing printed packaging and product identification materials. No customer accounted for 10 percent or more of net sales during 1991, 1990, or 1989.

15. Discontinued Operation:

On 15 March 1991, the Board of Directors approved the sale of the Company's Package Products Flexible division ("Flexible"). On 18 April 1991, the Company sold Flexible to Gravure International Corporation. The selling price, or transaction expenses, approximated book value. The Company received $9,200,000 in cash and a five-year note for approximately $3,711,000.

Net assets of Flexible, included in the accompanying balance sheets, are as follows (dollars in thousands):

	1990
Current assets	$ 5,819
Property, plant and equipment, net	9,532
Other assets	39
Total liabilities	(2,196)
Net assets of discontinued operation	$13,194

The financial statements reflect the operating results of Flexible separately from continuing operations. The prior year's Consolidated Statements of Income and related footnotes have been appropriately restated. Revenues applicable to Flexible were $8,169,000, $32,420,000, and $36,072,000 for the years ended 31 December 1991, 1990, and 1989, respectively.

Report of Independent Public Accountants

To the Stockholders of Engraph, Inc.:

We have audited the accompanying consolidated balance sheets of Engraph, Inc. (a Delaware corporation) and Subsidiaries as of 31 December 1991 and 1990 and the related consolidated statements of income, stockholders' equity, and cash flows for each of the three years in the period ended 31 December 1991. These financial statements are the responsibility of the Company's management. Our responsibility is to express an opinion on these financial statements based on our audits.

We conducted our audits in accordance with generally accepted auditing standards. Those standards require that we plan and perform the audit to obtain reasonable assurance about whether the financial statements are free of material misstatement. An audit includes examining, on a test basis, evidence supporting the amounts and disclosures in the financial statements. An audit also includes assessing the accounting principles used and significant estimates made by management, as well as evaluating overall financial statement presentation. We believe that our audits provide a reasonable basis for our opinion.

In our opinion, the consolidated financial statements referred to above present fairly, in all material respects, the financial position of Engraph, Inc., and subsidiaries as of 31 December 1991 and 1990, and the results of their operations and their cash flows for each of the three years in the period ended 31 December 1991 in conformity with generally accepted accounting principles.

Arthur Anderson & Co.

Atlanta, Georgia
12 February 1992

Industry Information

An established method of looking at a company is to compare it with others in the same industry through the use of Robert Morris Associates annual *Statement Studies,* which organizes Standard Industrial Classification (SIC) code and industry comparison data.

The astute analyst will read the Robert Morris Associates' disclaimer statement:

> RMA cautions that the *Studies* be regarded only as a general guideline and not as an absolute industry norm. This is due to limited samples within categories, the categorization of companies by their primary Standard Industrial Classification (SIC) number only, and different methods of operations by companies within the same industry. For these reasons, RMA recommends that the figures be used only as general guidelines in addition to other methods of financial analysis.

Engraph is a very interesting company in that there is not a specific SIC code to address all its business lines. SIC codes are useful in that they enable the analyst to compare a company with others in the same industry. However, in today's world, companies are frequently more complex than in the past. Corporations often comprise many divisions that bridge different industries, or technology is changing so rapidly that a company does not easily fit into an established niche.

The industry classification that most nearly fits Engraph is SIC No. 2759, Manufacturers—Commercial Printing, Letterpress & Screen. The data are as follows:

MANUFACTURERS—COMMERCIAL PRINTING, LETTERPRESS & SCREEN SIC #2769

Type of Statement		*Current Data Sorted By Sales*											
Unqualified		*1*		*6*		*3*		*12*		*11*		*9*
Qualified						*1*		*1*				
Reviewed		*8*		*23*		*11*		*15*		*8*		*1*
Compiled		*30*		*48*		*11*		*6*		*1*		*1*
Other		*15*		*10*		*3*		*6*		*7*		
		110 statements (6/30-9/30/89)				*138 statements (10/1/89-3/31/90)*						
		0-1MM		*1-3MM*		*3-5MM*		*5-10MM*		*10-25MM*		*25MM+*
NO. OF STATEMENTS		*54*		*87*		*29*		*40*		*27*		*11*
ASSETS		%		%		%		%		%		%
Cash & Equivalents		8.4		10.7		6.1		5.1		6.3		13.1
Trade Receivables - (net)		29.4		30.9		34.3		32.4		31.7		23.2
Inventory		12.4		11.5		16.2		17.2		16.6		15.2
All Other Current		1.9		1.4		1.6		0.9		2.1		1.0
Total Current		52.1		54.6		58.3		55.7		56.7		52.4
Fixed Assets (net)		36.6		39.1		32.3		37.5		34.4		33.8
Intangibles (net)		2.5		0.9		1.4		0.4		3.8		2.7
Other Noncurrent		8.8		54.0		8.0		6.4		5.1		11.1
Total		100.0		100.0		100.0		100.0		100.0		100.0
LIABILITIES												
Notes Payable-Short Term		9.3		6.7		9.8		8.3		8.5		0.2
Cur. Mat.-L/T/D		5.5		6.2		7.2		4.7		5.7		1.7
Trade Payables		15.0		13.3		12.0		14.8		12.5		9.9
Income Taxes Payable		1.3		1.1		0.7		0.3		0.4		1.5
All Other Current		9.5		6.5		10.1		11.0		10.0		7.9
Total Current		40.6		33.9		40.2		39.2		37.2		20.8
Long-Term Debt		27.2		26.4		17.9		18.6		23.1		17.9
Deferred Taxes		0.1		0.4		0.7		1.2		0.8		1.4
All Other Noncurrent		0.6		3.4		1.2		3.2		4.8		3.2
Net Worth		31.5		36.0		40.0		37.9		34.0		56.6
Total Liabilities & Net Worth		100.0		100.0		100.0		100.0		100.0		100.0
INCOME DATA												
Net Sales		100.0		100.0		100.0		100.0		100.0		100.0
Gross Profit		47.4		38.8		37.6		27.7		28.5		28.4
Operating Expenses		41.3		34.0		33.3		23.3		23.5		19.7
Operating Profit		6.1		4.8		4.3		4.4		5.0		8.7
All Other Expenses (net)		1.5		1.4		0.8		1.5		2.3		0.6
Profit Before Taxes		4.6		3.4		3.5		2.9		2.6		8.1
RATIOS												
		2.4		2.4		2.4		1.9		1.9		3.9
Current		1.5		1.7		1.4		1.4		1.6		1.9
		0.8		1.2		1.0		1.1		1.3		1.7
		1.8		1.7		1.6		1.3		1.5		2.2
Quick		1.0		1.3		0.9		0.9		1.2		1.6
		0.6		0.9		0.7		0.7		0.7		1.1
	28	13.0	37	9.8	37	9.8	38	9.5	41	8.9	44	8.3
Sales/Receivables	42	8.7	46	7.9	51	7.2	47	7.8	63	6.9	46	8.0
	57	6.4	56	6.5	64	5.7	60	6.1	70	5.2	62	5.9
	13	27.4	11	33.3	16	23.5	24	15.0	19	19.7	26	13.8
Cost of Sales/Inventory	26	14.8	26	14.3	29	12.8	33	11.0	32	11.5	29	12.8
	42	8.7	46	8.2	49	7.4	55	6.6	51	7.1	83	4.4
	13	29.0	18	20.2	18	20.2	18	20.7	15	23.9	20	18.0
Cost of Sales/Payable	32	11.4	28	13.0	26	14.1	28	13.1	22	16.3	25	14.6
	64	5.7	61	7.1	44	8.3	40	9.1	40	9.1	31	11.7
		8.3		6.4		6.8		7.9		6.9		3.2
Sales/Working Capital		17.6		11.2		20.0		15.6		9.9		7.0
		-29.2		34.7		137.8		81.2		21.1		11.9
		5.5		4.7		6.0		5.7		5.3		
EBIT/Interest	(51)	2.2	(81)	2.3	(27)	3.1	(39)	2.4	(23)	2.6		
		1.0		1.3		1.3		1.4		0.9		
		4.6		4.8		5.4		5.7		5.5		
Net Profit + Depr., Dep.,	(21)	1.3	(50)	2.1	(21)	2.1	(29)	2.2	(18)	2.3		
Amort./Cur. Mat. L/T/D		0.4		1.5		1.2		1.4		0.8		

	0.5	0.6	0.4	0.6	0.7	0.4
Fixed/Worth	1.1	1.1	0.9	1.1	0.9	0.5
	3.6	2.3	2.0	1.8	2.8	0.8
	0.9	0.9	0.8	0.8	1.1	0.3
Debt/Worth	2.4	1.9	1.7	2.0	1.9	0.7
	6.8	3.4	4.0	3.6	5.6	1.4
	50.5	36.1	32.5	31.0	35.6	31.4
% Profit Before Taxes/ Tangible Net Worth	(46) 27.0	(83) 16.0	(28) 15.9	(39) 17.1	(23) 18.2	(10) 26.2
	5.9	4.0	3.6	7.8	10.1	13.5
	24.0	10.7	14.3	11.3	14.1	14.9
% Profit Before Taxes/ Total Assets	7.4	6.3	6.6	5.4	9.1	12.7
	0.2	1.7	0.8	2.1	-0.1	6.0
	15.5	10.4	11.7	12.6	10.8	7.7
Sales/Net Fixed Assets	6.9	6.4	7.6	6.2	6.7	5.0
	3.8	3.5	5.5	3.5	4.6	3.0
	3.2	2.9	3.0	3.2	2.6	2.2
Sales/Total Assets	2.6	2.3	2.4	2.3	2.2	1.8
	1.7	1.8	1.9	1.7	1.7	1.4
	2.3	2.5	2.5	1.3	2.2	1.9
% Depr.. DAD., Amort../ Sales	(47) 4.3	(80) 4.0	(28) 3.2	(36) 2.7	(25) 3.8	3.1
	6.3	6.2	4.3	4.2	4.7	4.8
	7.1	3.9	3.9	2.5		
% Officer's Comp/Sales	(34) 9.4	(52) 5.9	(17) 5.9	(11) 3.5		
	10.9	8.3	8.2	4.6		
Net Sales ($)	32585M	160834M	111535M	293029M	379810M	909503M
Total Assets ($)	14544M	76379M	48725M	145648M	196262M	552183M

Questions about Engraph

1. How would you determine the legal structure of Engraph?
2. What effect could Engraph's size and legal structure have on its financing needs?
3. How would you describe the business operation of Engraph?
4. What is Engraph's industry?
5. What kind of operating cash flow cycle might you expect to see with Engraph, and how might this differ from its accounting for income?
6. Is Engraph's balance sheet typical of a manufacturer?

The Balance Sheet

LEARNING OBJECTIVES

After studying this chapter, you will be able to

- understand both the overall structure of and the individual accounts on a balance sheet,
- evaluate asset accounts in terms of quality, liquidity, and potential collateral for loans,
- explain the various methods for depreciating fixed assets,
- evaluate each liability account in terms of its repayment requirements, and
- distinguish different types of debt and their effect on the probability of loan repayment.

INTRODUCTION

The balance sheet provides a financial picture of a company at a given time. It categorizes all of a company's resources as assets, liabilities, and owners' equity. The company uses its assets, including facilities and equipment, to manufacture or purchase products for inventory that, when sold, converts to cash or creates accounts receivable. A company's assets are financed by the company's liabilities (also called debt) and owners' equity (also called net worth or, simply, equity).

The basic structure of the balance sheet is represented by the simple equation

$$\text{Assets} = \text{Liabilities} + \text{Equity}.$$

This equation helps the credit analyst understand each business' constantly occurring changes in financial structure. Since equations must always be in balance, a change on one side must be offset by an equal change on the same or other side to maintain the balance. For example, an increase in assets (whether fixed assets or inventory) must be balanced by a decrease in another asset account (such as accounts receivable) or an increase in liabilities (such as bank debt) or equity. Thus, a company can only obtain assets by liquidating other assets, creating new liabilities, or raising additional equity. Liabilities can be paid by liquidating assets or by increasing other liabilities or equity. Any combination of increasing or decreasing assets, liabilities, and equity can complete a transaction, provided the equation remains in balance.

This book reviews the balance sheet before the income statement and the statement of cash flow for two reasons:

- The balance sheet is traditionally the financial statement that bankers focus on. As is discussed later, some bankers think that this focus supports lending based too much on *collateral,* physical assets which may be sold to repay the loan if the business venture fails. Furthermore, if many current assets and few current liabilities along with low debt relative to equity characterize a borrower's balance sheet, management's character and abilities are less likely to be tested; thus, the banker may take a more relaxed view of the company's creditworthiness.
- Placing the income statement review in the next chapter leads us more directly to the cash flow analysis presented in chapter 5, and we feel that for most firms—especially growing ones—cash flow analysis is key to making a sound loan.

The balance sheet review consists of evaluating each asset account in terms of its value and liquidity (capacity for being quickly converted into cash at or near market value). In general, high liquidity reduces the risk of *insolvency,* the inability to pay bills as they come due. Thus, each asset is considered to be potential collateral in a lending situation. Each liability account is evaluated in terms of its repayment requirements and the expected sources of repayment. Equity may be evaluated in terms of a future source of cash through sales of stock.

Finally, the chapter discusses how to use trend analysis to evaluate major changes in a company's balance sheet over time to determine the company's strengths and weaknesses, the effectiveness of its managerial strategies, and its responsiveness to general market trends.

ADDITIONAL ANALYTICAL ISSUES

The asset and liability structure of a company's balance sheet depends on the numerous industry factors discussed in chapter 2. In reviewing a balance sheet, the credit analyst should recognize that the type of business, the industry, and the company's managerial style each affects the distribution of assets, liabilities, and equity in characteristic ways. These same factors, as well as the conditions in the company's markets, the stage in the company's development, its management's financing philosophy, and the availability of financing—debt and equity—also affect the company's balance sheet structure.

Financial Policies

A company's objectives and managerial decisions affect the company's balance sheet mix. Generally, a company's financial policies can be characterized as *conservative* or *aggressive*. Even companies within the same industry can have quite different balance sheet characteristics if their basic managerial policies differ. Companies with conservative financial philosophies tend to emphasize short accounts-receivable terms, low inventories, surplus cash, and marketable securities balances as well as little debt as a source of financing, even if these policies reduce sales somewhat.

Avoidance of risk-taking generally results in a balance sheet in which equity predominates over debt—a condition approved of by lenders. Conservative managers usually place less reliance on trade credit and take very strict control of their accounts receivable rather than extend payment terms as a marketing tool to encourage sales. Since conservative management places most of its emphasis on equity, the company's growth is limited by the availability of internally generated equity (through retaining profits) and selling new common stock.

A more-aggressive financial philosophy would emphasize enhancing returns on equity by increasing the amount of debt rather than equity since stockholders usually expect a higher return in line with the higher risk they take. Also, the more assertive policy would encourage sales by extending payment terms, maintaining lots of inventory in order to more promptly respond to customer orders, and purchasing the latest in fixed assets to permit growth. The resulting balance sheet would probably show higher debt, lower equity, and greater investments in accounts receivable, inventory, and fixed assets.

Less-stringent credit requirements and more-liberal credit terms invite a significant increase in accounts receivable. A management team that emphasizes the importance of never losing a possible sale must also maintain a heavy inventory. Such policies require financing, which often is accomplished with liabilities rather than with equity because most companies do not generate profits quickly enough to pay for the assets that rapid growth requires. In general, new and smaller businesses take a more aggressive stance because of their limited access to equity.

Working Investment Analysis

One way to determine a company's management philosophy is to analyze its current assets and liabilities. Working investment analysis focuses on the current assets of a company and how their growth is financed as sales grow. It also provides a quick means of projecting the financing required when a company's current assets increase to support its growth in sales.

As a company's sales grow, the base level of its current assets (cash, accounts receivable, and inventory) normally grows proportionately. Sometimes it is said that sales growth causes *spontaneous growth* in current asset accounts. Accounts payable and accruals also evidence spontaneous growth as materials and labor provided by suppliers increase. Therefore, the increase in current liabilities provides some financing for the growing accounts receivable and inventory levels; however, that portion of current assets not supported by the company's increasing payables and accruals must be financed by other sources, specifically borrowings or retained earnings. This assumes that the company has not already earmarked its profits to reduce existing debt or to purchase capital equipment and that the profits are available to support the increased working investment requirements.

If the company exhibits growth in current asset accounts that is proportionally greater than the increase in sales, management is exhibiting an aggressive approach. This approach will require more financing than the conservative one and is discussed more in depth in the first section of chapter 9.

Leverage Analysis

An example of the increasing use of debt financing by corporations can be found in a comparison of *leverage* ratios from 30 years ago with the same ratios now. At the Provident Tradesmen's Bank in Philadelphia in the 1960s, a customer with a balance sheet exhibiting a ratio of total debt to net worth in excess of 1:1 was not welcome as a prospective borrower. Recently, according to Standard & Poor's, the liabilities-to-net worth ratio is less than 1:1 only for the average industrial company rated AAA and AA (extremely high ratings). In fact, single B rated firms, similar to the typical bank customer, have an average debt-to-worth ratio of 2.4:1.

Most banks today would consider a single B rated firm to be a reasonable credit. A problematic explanation for the difference between the 1960s and now is that banks have relaxed their leverage standards, especially with regard to the debt-to-worth ratio. A better explanation is that banks now rely less on this common leverage relationship and more on cash flow, discussed in chapter 5. Nevertheless, understanding the limitations and risks imposed on a firm by its debt in relation to its equity is an important goal of financial statement analysis. Review of the balance sheet should include this thorough examination of debt.

CONCEPT OF THE SPREADSHEET

Most frequently, financial statement analysis begins with scrutinizing each account on the audited statements and placing the information into a format used for all credit analysis within the bank—the *spreadsheet*. The advantages of using spreadsheets include ease of dealing with rounded and common-sized numbers (defined in the introduction to the comparative analysis section later in this chapter), consistent treatment of accounts for all borrowers, and ease of spotting trends.

If possible, refer to your own bank's spreadsheet format. If you wish to use the worksheets in this book, the first one, dealing with the balance sheet, is found in Exhibit 3.1. It may be a good exercise for you to obtain a financial statement and a blank copy of the spreadsheet you will be using and try to follow along as you read the following section. The case study at the end of the chapter will require this.

GAAP Account Revaluation

The financial statements provided to the analyst by a prospective borrower do not necessarily show the only possible picture of the firm's financial condition. Why is this so? The firm's accountants create the financial statements for all the stakeholders: owners, managers, employees, customers, and lenders—and each of these has very different purposes for reviewing the statements. Moreover, for obvious reasons, a public firm's management will want to make the financial statements make its efforts for the year look as good as possible.

Further, the firm's accountants, even if independent, are not preoccupied with the lender's concerns. Generally accepted accounting principles (GAAP) require accountants to use the concept of *going concern* to value assets. Going

Exhibit 3.1 Balance Sheet: Spreadsheet Form

Company Name:
Balance Sheet Date:
Rounded to:

ASSETS	$	%	$	%	$	%
1 Cash						
2 Marketable Securities						
3 Accounts Receivable - Trade						
4 Inventories: Raw Materials						
5 Inventories: Work in Process						
6 Inventories: Finished Goods						
7 Subtotal Inventories						
8 Prepaid Expenses						
9 Other Current						
10 **Total Current Assets**						
11 Property, Plant & Equipment						
12 Capital Leased Equipment						
13 Operating Leased Equipment						
14 (Less Depreciation)						
15 Subtotal Net Prop, Plant & Equip.						
16 Investments and Advances						
17 Long Term Marketable Securities						
18 Affiliate & Sundry Receivables						
19 Net Assets/Discont. Operations						
20 Other Noncurrent Assets						
21 Intangibles (Patents & Rights)						
22 Goodwill (Resulting from Mergers)						
23 **Total Fixed Assets**						
24 **TOTAL ASSETS**						
LIABILITIES						
25 Notes Payable						
26 Accounts Payable - Trade						
27 Taxes and Accrued Expenses						
28 Other Current						
29 Cur. Portion L-T Debt (Operating)						
30 **Total Current Operating Liabs.**						
31 Cur. Portion L-T Debt (Remaining)						
32 Deferred or Unearned Income						
33 Long Term Debt - Unsecured						
34 Long Term Debt - Secured						
35 Capital Lease Obligations						
36 Present Value of Operating Leases						
37 Other Noncurrent Liabilities						
38 **Total Senior Term Debt**						
39 Subordinated Debt						
40 Unfunded Pension Obligations						
41 Deferred Taxes (Debt Portion)						
42 **TOTAL LIABILITIES**						
EQUITY						
43 Deferred Taxes (Equity Part)						
44 Minority Interest						
45 Preferred Stock						
46 Common Stock						
47 Retained Earnings						
48 (Treasure Stock & Other Red.)						
49 **Net Worth**						
50 **TOTAL FOOTINGS**						

concern means that GAAP do not require accountants to determine the market value of the assets, but they do require accountants to keep the original cost (unless it has declined) *capitalized* on the balance sheet for future expensing on the income statement. That is, in the case of fixed assets, the balance sheet becomes somewhat of a repository of historical values, less depreciation or amortization of the expense onto the income statement. Therefore, one of the basic instincts of the lender, that the balance sheet represents actual value (liquidation or market), is contrary to the accountant's intent.

From an economic or financial point of view, assets are investments in the sense that they are expected to produce future revenue streams. Assets can become obsolete and unable to produce revenue despite their apparent physical strengths and capabilities. Assets also may retain substantial value in the face of depreciation being taken over many years, based upon a pessimistic estimate of the original useful life by the management. The analyst must consider unexpected variations in an asset's future revenue stream when determining what value to place on the spreadsheet.

Thus, to successfully determine the debt capacity of a prospective borrower, an analyst must be prepared to disassemble the financial statements—even certified ones—that the borrower supplied. The objective is to calculate the collateral value of the firm in case it fails and its assets have to be sold to satisfy the liabilities.

The following chapters explain how to calculate the cash-flow-generating capacity of a firm, assuming the most likely course, that management succeeds sufficiently in its goals to enable the firm to repay its debts and remain a functioning unit.

Financial statement analysts debate the merit of revaluing the accounting statements, especially since much of the industry data and the firm's own prior-year information, which is used for comparison, is not so adjusted. Before it was recently acquired, a major New York bank prepared a special computer software program to create spreadsheets for analysts working on public corporations. When any analyst typed the stock "call" letters into a terminal, the software automatically used the regularly updated information filed with the Securities and Exchange Commission to spread the financial statement. While the last line of the computer printout advised the analyst to obtain the financial statement and examine the footnotes carefully before proceeding with analysis, the preprinted computerized form predisposed everyone to look at alterations as having lesser validity than the computerized balance sheet and income statement SEC numbers.

A former lending officer of this institution expressed disapproval. He was concerned about the acuteness with which the credit officers examined the comments within the credit write-up. This officer also felt that using the footnoted information to adjust the financial statements would give the bank's officers an advantage in detecting companies that would not be able to repay their loans.

Rules

The following are basic rules for developing a spreadsheet:

1. *Round off numbers to four or five digits.* This practice makes the spreadsheet easier to read. For instance, if financial statement entries are in millions, round them to thousands for the spreadsheet. If financial statement entries are in thousands, round everything to hundreds for the spreadsheet. The spreadsheet allows the analyst to review several years of financial performance at once; thus, it is important to simplify the presentation. For example, if sales are $11,234,565, show $11,235 with the label "000s omitted" at the top of the spreadsheet.

2. *Spread annual statements and interim statements separately.* Interim statements should be compared only with interim statements of the same date from previous years if the business experiences seasonality in its sales or production. If regular quarterly or monthly statements are available, the analyst should create multiple spreadsheets that contain fiscal years, first quarters, second quarters, third quarters, and fourth quarters.

3. *Read the CPA's opinion and the footnotes before beginning the analysis.* Since the first footnote generally details the basic conventions used to construct the financial statements, it is essential that it be read before spreading the statement. Some footnotes contain information that does not show up anywhere on the balance sheet, income statement, statement of cash flows, or reconciliation of equity. The information may include executory and contingency commitments, information about potential lawsuits, warranties, and events that are to take place after the statement date.

   Most significantly, however, the auditors use footnotes to describe some of the alternative presentation formats, which provides cogent information for analysts who wish to improve their review process. The footnotes are frequently the main platform of the auditors, their primary chance to speak about decisions management made in preparing its financial statements. A careful reading of the footnotes allows the analyst to make judicious adjustments to the spreadsheet from the management's organized financials and to accomplish his or her mission.

4. *Consider the effects of inflation.* The use of inflation-adjusted accounting to improve the proper recording of assets and income is now quite difficult since Statement of Financial Accounting Standards (SFAS) No. 33, "Financial Reporting and Changing Prices," has been made voluntary. Since GAAP no longer require that current cost information be included in the footnotes, obtain independent third-party appraisals that provide realizable (generally market) as well as liquidation (sometimes called auction) values. It is important to consider the

issues that gave rise to SFAS No. 33 (to be discussed later in this chapter) because inflation-adjusted accounting is useful in reviewing a company's long-range performance and identifying collateral value.

5. *Examine intangibles.* Intangibles must be identified, researched, and evaluated. As you progress through the financial statements, it will become evident that it is worthwhile to spend more time on certain entries: the highest asset-risk categories are goodwill and deferred charges. These entries will be discussed in greater detail later on in this chapter.

ANALYSIS OF ASSET ACCOUNTS

Even large banks have few borrowers that merit unsecured loans. While some lenders believe that dependable and stable cash flow is the key to determining debt repayment capacity, other lenders evaluate assets in terms of their value as collateral because that provides a "back door" out of the transaction if the cash flow analysis should prove inaccurate. In contrast to this idea, one of the basic principles guiding accountants is the concept of the going concern, mentioned above.

From the collateral viewpoint, assets should be reviewed in terms of their marketability (ability to add to the firm's liquidity). An important part of reliability of collateral value is an item's *fungibility,* that is, its usefulness to others. As an example, a corporate jet aircraft may be of limited use to a real estate developer in the event of a recession in that industry; nevertheless, an oil company may be able to use it unless there is a nation-wide recession. Nearly everything has some fungibility. For example, a ship's value could fall drastically during a recession in international trade, but something could be recovered since it may still be cut up for scrap steel.

Another principal factor in analyzing value is *liquidity.* This concept measures how quickly an asset can be converted into cash *at or near its market value.* Assets on the balance sheet are presented in order of their liquidity:

- Accounts receivable, which merely need to be collected;
- Inventory, which needs to be sold and then collected; and
- Fixed assets, which need to be used with raw materials and labor to create something useful which then needs to be sold and the money collected.

Finally, a review of assets should also determine the following:

- Whether the assets are unencumbered (not specifically pledged to other lenders). Although liens do not affect asset quality, they do affect a lender's ability to have recourse to the asset if necessary.

- How fast the asset may lose value through wear and tear and obsolescence.
- The controllability of the asset—whether it can be easily moved or hidden by a difficult borrower.
- Whether there is any environmental or other regulatory risk that a lender would have to take into account in seizing the asset.

The following sections survey traditional assets in both the current (converting to cash in less than one year) and fixed (long-term) categories.

Current Assets

Current assets are commonly defined as assets that will be converted to cash by normal operations of the firm within a period not to exceed one year. This definition came from the agricultural background of a one-year operating cycle. That is, from seed to cultivation to harvest to sale, most growing of crops takes place in a one-year cycle. This cycle distinguishes these one-year assets from those, like the barn and plow, that obviously hung around for far longer. In this accounting model of the world, horses were inventory only to horse dealers; common farmers would carry their horses as fixed assets.

A topical controversy in the accounting field is, how current is current? For example, tobacco growers/processors/companies are permitted to carry tobacco as current inventory, though tobacco remains in process for periods substantially in excess of one year. Liquor producers are another example. Because one-year period has many exceptions, when studying certain industries, analysts should be on the lookout for assets that do not meet the criterion.

Current assets are discussed below as they are shown on the balance sheet, in order of their fungibility and liquidity—cash first, followed by marketable securities, accounts receivable, inventory, and prepaid expenses.

Cash

In keeping with the priority of liquidity, cash is listed first on the balance sheet. Companies can hold cash in various forms, some of which are restricted for special purposes. For example, some companies may keep only a small amount of petty cash on the premises to take care of small disbursements that cannot be paid by check or credit card. Retailers require more cash to be on hand for making change; therefore, their high cash position may not be an advantage.

Cash is most frequently represented by deposits in checking accounts that are available for use in a company's operations or in temporary interest-bearing investments. In analyzing a company's cash account, the availability of the cash is the most important consideration. For example, restrictions may apply if interest-bearing deposits are pledged against debt. Thus, if a company pledges its accounts, the cash becomes unavailable for daily operations. Compensating balances, which may be required for support of bank credit facilities, may also be unavailable for operations.

A company with foreign bank accounts may find that other governments make it difficult to transfer deposits to domestic operations. Moreover, deposits of foreign currency are subject to exchange fluctuations, and funds borrowed for construction purposes may be restricted. In assessing the assets available to a business, carry as a noncurrent asset cash that is not readily available. The amount of time that elapses between the disbursement and collection of cash (for example, between purchasing inventory or paying expenses and collecting accounts receivable) helps determine a company's cash requirements. The analysis of this particular issue is the entire subject of chapter 7. In summary, low or restricted cash balances increase the risk of insolvency, the inability to pay bills as they come due.

Marketable Securities

The second category of assets on a balance sheet is *marketable securities*. Companies often invest their excess cash temporarily in certificates of deposit, bankers' acceptances, U.S. government securities, or high-grade corporate commercial paper. These investments earn income in the form of interest until cash is needed in the business. Analysts should carefully analyze the current value of a company's marketable securities account as well as its types of investments and their relative liquidity. To have the full confidence of the analyst, these securities should

- be readily marketable,
- have a short term to maturity, and
- pose no risk of losing principal.

Other securities do not meet these criteria. If management claims to have temporary investments in securities, even including stock traded on a major stock exchange, stocks that are not actively traded, stocks in closely held corporations, and stocks held in affiliates, these investments are classified as marketable securities by accountants. For the credit analyst, they should be classified as "other assets" and carried noncurrent for the following reasons:

- Stocks are subject to wide swings in value.
- Stocks may be being held to further the investment interests of management; they could end up as the first step in an acquisition and otherwise be indicative of long-term interests.
- Stocks represent ownership interest in corporations, not in assets. In case of a problem, stock owners receive proceeds only after all creditors are satisfied.

These stocks should not be carried as current marketable securities on the balance sheet. However, unless it is large, this account is normally not a significant consideration in financial statement analysis.

Accounts Receivable

When a company sells merchandise or services on credit, it provides payment terms that allow the purchaser to pay within a specified time and may offer a discount as incentive for early payment. Credit sales are shown as *accounts receivable* on the balance sheet until they are collected. Other receivables, such as those created by credit extended to company officers, employees, or affiliates and by sales of other assets, should not be included in this account, which is reserved for trade accounts receivable.

Both the size and quality of this balance sheet account are of prime interest. The size of a company's accounts receivable is influenced by

- the amount of credit sales,
- the company's credit terms and collection policies, and the
- customers' payment habits.

The more liberal the credit terms offered, the larger the accounts receivable will be. For example, suppose a company's sales total $30,000 per month, its terms are net 30 (that is, payment is required in 30 days), and all its customers pay within the established time frame. The company's accounts receivable will never exceed $30,000. However, if the company were to extend terms to 60 days, its accounts receivable could easily double to $60,000. Increasing terms always increases the likelihood of loss because of the possibility of unexpected events occurring. For the same reason, lax collection practices tend to result in delayed or lost payments. In the last example, if the company ignored overdue accounts and allowed customers to pay in 90 days rather than within the stipulated 60-day terms, its accounts receivable could increase by another $30,000 to $90,000. Liberal extension of credit to noncreditworthy customers or lax collection policies can undermine the quality of a company's accounts receivable.

A lagging economy can also result in slowed payments on accounts receivable. When an overall downturn in economic activity occurs, companies generally earn less profit and their liquidity is reduced. A chain reaction of slowed payments results as companies, paid more slowly by their own customers, in turn slow their payments to creditors. Since a company's liquidity is reduced when its receivables convert to cash less readily, less cash is generated for the business's operations.

If accounts receivable have increased rapidly, the income statement should be examined to see whether there has been a corresponding increase in sales. If not, the increase in receivables may indicate credit terms are being extended to stimulate sales.

From the lender's standpoint, accounts receivable normally represent a good source of collateral because they generally are more liquid than the inventory which they replace. With a large customer base, the repayment risk is spread out. And a company's credit terms give an idea of the approximate time before accounts receivable convert into cash. Accounts receivable also represent good collateral because they can be collected to repay debt.

Access to an *aging-of-accounts-receivable* statement makes it easier to evaluate receivables. Studying this statement is a means of determining the punctuality of a company's accounts in relation to the credit terms allowed, the success of the company's collection efforts, and the overall quality of the accounts receivable. The company should be able to supply a statement showing the aging of each accounts receivable, both individually and by category. This information is important because the older the receivable, the less likely it is to be paid.

Exhibit 3.2 shows that 75 percent of the receivables are current (that is, are not delinquent) and 89 percent are less than 30 days past due. It is difficult to tell whether this represents a good collection effort without knowing Sherwin Clock Company's credit terms and something about the customers who are delinquent.

The credit analyst can also use the accounts receivable aging statement to identify any concentration of accounts receivable in one or a few accounts.

Aging of Accounts Receivable

Exhibit 3.2

Sherwin Clock Company
Accounts Receivable Aging

			Delinquent			
Customer Name	*Total*	*Current*	*1–30 Days*	*31–60 Days*	*61–90 Days*	*Over 90 Days*
C. Kennedy	$ 10,000	$10,000	—	—	—	—
M. Fernandez	14,000	—	$14,000	—	—	—
T. Puckorius	15,000	10,000	—	$5,000	—	—
A. McMeen	21,710	21,710	—	—	—	—
T. Carlin	13,500	13,500	—	—	—	—
T. Martin	14,790	14,790	—	—	—	—
F. Serpa	11,000	5,000	—	—	—	$6,000
Total	$100,000	$75,000	$14,000	$5,000	0	$6,000
Percentage	100%	75%	14%	5%	0%	6%

Such concentration usually means increased repayment risk, although this depends on the quality of the customer representing the concentration.

Companies should age their accounts periodically to monitor the quality of their receivables over time and to spot current repayment trends. In many service industries, the accounts receivable should be broken out into (1) completed work and (2) work in process. For example, a CPA firm may list accounts receivable for audits in process as well as those that are completed. Analyzing several different agings of receivables for the same company enables the analyst to detect whether the past-due receivables have become more current. If the trend is negative, the analyst determines the causes and investigates what actions management has taken to reverse the slowing trend.

Accounts Receivable Loss Reserve

Some amount of accounts receivable will usually remain uncollected and, therefore, constitute a loss or bad debt. A company prepares for this by calculating the percentage of bad debt over recent years and creating a reserve that is deducted from its accounts receivable. The company increases this reserve by regularly expensing for bad debts through the income statement. When an account becomes uncollectible, it is charged against the *accounts receivable loss reserve* instead of directly to the income statement, cushioning the income statement from a sudden loss resulting solely from poor credit judgment.

In assessing a company's accounts receivable, an analyst determines the adequacy of a company's bad-debt reserve. If credit term policies do not change, the reserve should be a set percentage of the company's receivables. Thus, in normal sales growth, as accounts receivable increase, the reserve should increase proportionally. If the reserve has not, the analyst can make an adjustment by charging both the accounts receivable and the retained earnings account for the difference—to keep the balance sheet balanced.

If the quality of the company's accounts receivable deteriorates, say, because of a change toward more-aggressive financial policies, the reserve should also be increased. For example, if losses have historically been 1 percent of average accounts receivable, the reserve should represent at least 1 percent of average receivables. If losses in a particular year begin to escalate and this higher level is expected to continue, then the company should increase the amount expensed on the income statement for bad debts.

Notes Receivable

A *note receivable* is an outstanding note with a specific repayment agreement. Notes receivable are not a normal part of the operations of most businesses, and thus usually do not constitute a significant asset account. However, some businesses accept notes for the sale of merchandise. For instance, a heavy-equipment dealer may accept notes with extended payment terms for the sale of large pieces of equipment.

If a note is not due within 12 months, then only the maturities due in the next 12 months are included under the company's current assets. The remaining maturities are carried on the balance sheet as noncurrent assets.

An evaluation of the quality of any notes begins with their payment status. If a customer took the note out to pay a past-due accounts receivable, for example, then a collection problem already exists and the note may be of questionable value. The company's liquidity is reduced if it cannot collect the note on a timely basis. If the company's notes receivable start to become a significant account, the analyst should investigate the company's credit policies.

The next step is to evaluate any built-in interest rate charged to the customer. Since GAAP assume that the rate being charged corresponds to the market rate, only a sharp deviation will raise a warning. The problem with this limited concern for the note-receivable rate of interest is that a rate lower than market can reduce the value of this asset to the firm. For example, consider the automobile companies that offer 2.5 percent annual rate of financing on a five-year car loan in order to induce potential purchasers. Clearly, the purchaser sees this as an inducement for the same reason the lender would find the value of the note compromised below the face value. In effect, the automobile manufacturer is giving a discount to the buyer and also reducing the value of the note. By the way, in this case at least, the firms have had to account for these notes at a discount from face value.

Companies can also assign notes as collateral. However, before a bank accepts notes as collateral, it obtains financial information about the debtor to determine whether the note will be paid within its specified terms.

Inventory

Finished Goods Inventory

Finished goods are salable merchandise. For the retailer or wholesaler, finished goods have been purchased for resale and constitute the vast bulk of the inventory. For a manufacturing company, the *finished goods inventory* includes any finished products not yet sold, but it is primarily made up of the raw materials used in the manufacturing process and the work-in-process inventories discussed immediately below. For service companies, consumable supplies used in the business of providing a service are considered inventory, but are not salable directly, so would be considered raw materials even though they would be finished goods for a retailer. For example, replacement tires kept on hand by a trucking company would be classified as raw materials inventory.

For a retailer or wholesaler, the risk that the finished goods inventory will not sell is primarily related to the style sensitivity of the merchandise. A manufacturer's finished inventory is subject to this same risk. Therefore, an analyst should assess a company's inventory account in terms of the present and future marketability of its inventory. Some kinds of merchandise have predictable and long-term marketability. For example, undergarments are staple items that tend to hold their value because they are a basic clothing item subject to continuous consumer demand. If, however, a company's inventory consists of trendy video games that are subject to obsolescence, a sudden drop in market demand could render the inventory valueless. In evaluating a company's inventory account, determine if it includes obsolete inventory that failed to meet market demand. If so, the value of the company's inventory may be overstated. Obsolete inventory does not represent liquidity for the company nor good collateral value for a lender to liquidate to repay debt.

Whenever management decides to compete more aggressively by keeping inventory stock high, it takes the risk that the demand for the product will suddenly drop. Sometimes companies keep large inventories because obtaining supplies is difficult or entails lengthy waits before delivery, as is the case with orders from overseas.

Raw Materials Inventory

In addition to finished goods inventory, manufacturers typically hold some *raw materials* inventory to be used in the manufacturing process. Analysts evaluate these inventory accounts on the same basis as they do finished goods—that is, in terms of their marketability. The end use of raw materials determines their marketability. If the raw materials have multiple uses and could be liquidated by being sold to various manufacturing industries, their marketability is much better than that of a raw material used in a single manufacturing process.

A large raw materials inventory account can result from speculation in inventory. A company may try to hedge on prices by buying inventory in bulk at a low price in the hope of selling it later at a higher price or avoiding having to purchase it a higher price in the future. If the price of the goods decreases unexpectedly instead of increasing, a large loss may result. Often, companies are not in a position to hold onto excess inventory because they need liquidity. Moreover, holding onto inventory can be expensive, especially during periods of high interest rates, if bank financing is required.

Work in Process

This inventory is the most problematic from the lender's viewpoint; it may be very hard to salvage in case of a liquidation. The amount of *work in process* inventory depends primarily on the length of the production process. If the production process is short, then the value of the company's work in process will be small in relation to its raw materials and finished goods inventories.

However, if the process is complex, as in manufacturing large or heavy equipment, then a more significant proportion of a company's assets may be tied up in work in process.

Partially completed products not only require additional investment before they reach the value of finished goods, but also usually have a market value that is less than the invested costs. Therefore, the lender should assign a low value, if any, to work-in-process inventory for loan collateral purposes.

A company that makes customized products on order usually has a large work-in-process inventory and no finished goods inventory since its products are delivered to the buyer immediately upon completion. Because the general marketability of custom-made products is very low, a manufacturer should require substantial deposits or progress payments while manufacturing the products in order to reduce the risk of custom orders not being accepted. Custom-made inventory usually has little collateral value in the eyes of a credit analyst.

Inventory Valuation Method

The convention used to account for inventory is different from the idea that each piece of inventory is actually tracked by the accounting system. The choice of the accounting convention is also important to determining the collateral value. There are two basic methods of valuing inventory: last-in, first-out (LIFO) and first-in, first-out (FIFO). LIFO charges to expenses the most recent, last-in, cost of inventory because the firm will have to replace the used inventory at current value cost. (Remember, the actual physical inventory is not an issue in the choice of an accounting convention.) Unfortunately, a by-product of this method is to account for the inventory on the balance sheet at older prices.

FIFO expenses the old inventory cost first; this method places the current value of inventory on the balance sheet. If the firm uses LIFO to value inventory, the analyst should look at the footnote on inventory, which will give the difference between the FIFO and LIFO valuations. Add this difference, known as the LIFO reserve, to the balance sheet LIFO value in the spreadsheet and also add the difference between FIFO and LIFO amounts to retained earnings to balance the statement. This way, the current costs of the inventory value will be identified. The situation is made somewhat complicated over time by inflation and growing inventories, and this issue is discussed further in the chapters on the income statement and on ratio analysis (chapters 4 and 6). Average cost is another option that produces values between LIFO and FIFO.

Prepaid Expenses

Other outlays of funds that have neither produced benefits nor been expensed on the income statement are capitalized into *prepaid expenses*. Examples of prepaid expenses include insurance premiums paid annually and lease rentals paid in advance. Prepaid expenses probably provide little liquidity, although they do provide a future reduction in current cash outlays.

Carrying the prepaid expenses in the current side of the balance sheet is probably best; unfortunately, many companies combine prepaid expenses with current receivables due from officers and affiliates, which are not very liquid. Thus, as a practical matter, the combined account is almost always carried noncurrent, unless the analyst is able to separate the accounts.

Other Current Assets

Other current assets is usually an insignificant account. For example, an analyst would list an income tax refund due in this account on the spreadsheet. As mentioned above, stock securities, which management may have listed in the marketable securities account, may be carried here if management intends them to be temporary investments only.

Cash-value life insurance, which represents cash deposits built up in a whole-life insurance policy, is another item that might show up in the other current assets account. A company can use this available cash in the business if the cash value is unencumbered by a loan from the insurance company or other financial institution.

The insurance policy's real liquidity depends on the death of the insured. The analyst must determine who is insured and the face value of the policies. The lender should also evaluate the adequacy of the insurance coverage in terms of the importance of the insured persons to the company and the liabilities that would need to be paid from the proceeds of the insurance policy.

Noncurrent Assets

The assets described up to this point are all classified as current assets. Noncurrent assets, in contrast, are not expected to convert to cash within 12 months. The principal category of noncurrent assets is fixed assets, plant and equipment. Other noncurrent assets are loans due from company officers and affiliates, investments in other companies, deferred charges, and intangible assets.

Fixed Assets' Cost Basis

Fixed assets include equipment, buildings, vehicles, tools, computers, office equipment, leasehold improvements, and furniture—that is, any items of a fairly permanent nature that are required for the normal conduct of a business. The fixed-asset account may be highly significant or small, depending on the type of business. The valuation of fixed assets is an important consideration in analyzing this account.

Financial statements prepared in accordance with GAAP report the value of fixed assets at *book value*. Book value is predicated on accounting conventions that carry assets' values based on their original *historical cost* (the purchase price paid by the company) minus allowable depreciation to date. Unfortunately, however, historically based book values may be of little worth to lenders. Lenders are concerned primarily with liquidation value—the amount that a company or creditor could realize if it had to dispose of the assets quickly. Most assets have substantially less value in liquidation than their market value, which is defined as the price a company could reasonably expect to receive for an asset sold in the open market under normal economic conditions. Thus the liquidation value of assets may be either more or less than their book value.

The credit analyst should also assess the capacity, efficiency, and specialization of a company's fixed assets. Capacity is defined in terms of how much additional sales volume a company's existing fixed assets can support. For example, if a company produces $1 million in sales using one 8-hour work shift, it should have the capacity to produce $3 million in sales using three 8-hour shifts. However, if management expects sales to increase above $3 million, the company will probably need additional capacity and equipment.

A company's efficiency depends on the cost-effectiveness of the equipment it uses. More-efficient equipment may or may not reduce the cost of manufacturing products or providing services to a point that replacing existing equipment is cost-effective. However, as less-efficient equipment nears the end of its economic life, it may pay to replace it with state-of-the-art equipment. Old equipment can become technologically obsolete because of new production methods or because more-advanced equipment comes on the market. A company with inefficient equipment and the resultant higher costs may become less competitive in its pricing, resulting in a decline in sales.

Specialized equipment may have a lower resale value than more-commonly used equipment. The marketability of a company's fixed assets, rather than their book value (cost minus depreciation), determines their value as collateral. Thus multi-use fixed assets have higher collateral value than single-purpose fixed assets, the actual value of which could be less than their cost or book value. For example, when a company incurs a large cost preparing a building to accept a highly specialized piece of equipment, it increases the cost (book value) of the building. However, a prospective buyer who plans to use the building for a different purpose will not want to pay extra for these added features.

Any costs of improving a leased building—such as carpeting, special lighting, general renovations, and decorating—are not expensed on the income statement, but are capitalized onto the balance sheet as fixed assets and depreciated. However, these types of fixed assets, called leasehold improvements, usually stay with the building and become the property of the building's owner should the company ever move to a new location. For this reason, banks give leasehold improvements little or no value as collateral. It is not unusual for leasehold improvements to constitute the major category of fixed assets for certain types of service companies.

Capital leases of equipment, as defined by SFAS No. 13, are considered a fixed asset and are capitalized on the balance sheet. However, since the company does not legally own the equipment, this type of fixed asset has no liquidation value. When making a lending decision, an analyst must find out about any leased assets in the fixed asset account. They are usually listed in a footnote with details on leases. The auditor will indicate a value based upon taking a present value of the future contracted-for lease payments, limited by the original cost of the equipment.

If there is no footnote on leases, a value can usually be approximated by referring to the long-term debt footnote, where the debt associated with these capital leases is identified and, if material, quantified. At the inception of a capital lease, the amount incorporated into the debt section is usually a good estimate of the purchase price of the equipment. Eventually, the firm accounts for the "debt" by amortizing it over the life of the lease. Unfortunately, for lenders, the amortization does not match the depreciation taken against equipment. Nevertheless, the remaining debt shown is usually the best available approximation of the value of the equipment.

One of the best solutions is for the analyst to look to outside independent appraisers who have achieved credibility in identifying the proper value range of an asset. If the borrower has completed a recent appraisal of its physical assets, this can be an excellent starting point. Other options include

- randomly verifying the values presented by calling firms in the same industry;
- using appraisers identified by insurance companies in claims of losses on similar types of equipment (while few bank employees are qualified for such work, there are qualified appraisers in every field from intellectual copyrights to real estate), and

- referring to used-equipment value books such as the *Green Guide*, a construction equipment valuation book published by Commerce Clearing House.

It is important for the analyst to explain to the appraiser precisely what type of valuation is sought. Whether the appraiser should consider the possibilities of a depression as severe as the one in the 1930s depends on the polices of the bank. Remind the appraiser that present boom or recession times may not extend to the full term of the loan, and that the term of the loan is the real issue.

Depreciation Methods for Fixed Assets

With the exception of land, fixed assets are assumed to lose their economic value over time—for financial statement analysis as well as for GAAP and IRS reporting. A fixed asset is initially valued at cost,limited by fair market value, when it is purchased. Each year thereafter it is *depreciated*—that is, partially expensed on the income statement and valued at a progressively lower amount (called *book value*) on the balance sheet. Finally, it is considered either to be without value or to have reached a *salvage* value below which it cannot fall. This reflects the fact that most fixed assets eventually wear out and must be replaced. However, there are various ways of figuring depreciation, and the same company may figure depreciation differently for financial reporting purposes and for tax purposes.

Straight-line depreciation is calculated by dividing the cost of a fixed asset by its initially estimated useful economic life and recording that amount on the financial statements each year. Exhibit 3.3 shows this calculation on a fixed asset costing $10,000 and having a useful life of five years. The annual depreciation expense, which is recognized on the company's income statement as an operating expense, and the value of the asset are reduced to zero over a five-year period.

Straight-Line Depreciation

Exhibit 3.3

Cost of asset: $10,000
Useful life: 5 years
Depreciation rate: $10,000/5 years; $2,000 (20%) per year

End of Year	*Depreciation Expense*	*Book Value of Asset*
1	$ 2,000	$8,000
2	2,000	6,000
3	2,000	4,000
4	2,000	2,000
5	2,000	-0-
	$10,000	

Some firms try to set a salvage value for a piece of equipment before calculating the annual depreciation under the straight-line method. Because current tax law does not require salvage, some firms have dropped the practice and assume that the salvage will be of nominal value. If both the tax valuation and the book valuations are wrong, if in fact the equipment is worth a considerable amount more than was expected, a windfall profit will occur upon disposal.

Since depreciation is a noncash yet tax-deductible expense, it could be a tax advantage to write off the value of an asset as quickly as possible, assuming that the company has taxable income or that it can carry back the current-year losses to the previous year's taxable income and receive a refund. Because of this possibility, the Internal Revenue Service has published guidelines for how quickly companies can depreciate fixed assets for tax purposes. The current rules were created by the Tax Reform Act of 1986 and are called MACRS, short for *modified accelerated cost recovery system*. MACRS allows more cost recovery in the earlier years of the recovery period, which is why it is called *accelerated cost recovery*. There are now seven classes of property, each with different allowable recovery periods, as shown in Exhibit 3.4.

Exhibit 3.4

Accelerated Cost Recovery

Class (Years)	*Declining Balance Percentage*
3	200
5	200
7	200
10	200
20	150
27.5	straight-line
31.5	straight-line

The depreciable percentage of the cost of most equipment assets is now either 200 percent or 150 percent of the straight-line percentage for the respective periods. This accelerated write-off percentage is calculated on the declining balance of the cost of an asset as each year's depreciation is deducted. This is done until the straight-line depreciation amount for the declining balance over the remaining years of the recovery period exceeds the MACRS amount. Then the straight-line amount can be used to complete the write-off. The last two recovery classes (primarily real estate) are required to use the straight-line method only.

The process is further complicated because depreciation taken the first year may be constrained by either the half-year convention or the mid-quarter convention, depending upon when the company took equipment deliveries during the year. The untaken portion (in percentage terms) of the first-year depreciation must be taken in an additional period added to the class life, which is illustrated in Exhibit 3.5 for typical equipment lives of 3 to 10 years.

Exhibit 3.5

MACRS Depreciation Table
Revised 1987

Year	*3 Years*	*5 Years*	*7 Years*	*10 Years*
1	33.33%	20.00%	14.29%	10.00%
2	44.45%	32.00%	24.49%	18.00%
3	14.81%	19.20%	17.49%	14.40%
4	7.41%	11.52%	12.49%	11.52%
5	0.00%	11.52%	8.93%	9.22%
6	0.00%	5.76%	8.92%	7.37%
7	0.00%	0.00%	8.93%	6.55%
8	0.00%	0.00%	4.46%	6.55%
9	0.00%	0.00%	0.00%	6.56%
10	0.00%	0.00%	0.00%	6.55%
11	0.00%	0.00%	0.00%	3.28%
	100.00%	100.00%	100.00%	100.00%

Using MACRS results in a lower taxable income and, hence, lower taxes. However, the straight-line depreciation method is frequently used for financial reporting purposes because it reduces income less than the alternative accelerated method does, and public firms, at least, wish to show higher income.

GAAP are concerned that using accelerated depreciation methods for tax purposes and the straight-line method for financial reporting purposes may distort income reporting in the present. Theoretically, MACRS would initially produce low taxes, but may end up giving the firm higher taxable income in the future if the firm did not continue to purchase equipment and, thus, ran out of depreciation expense. In order to prevent this occurrence, GAAP require the creation of a reserve for deferred taxes, offsetting the actual tax savings. The reserve appears on the balance sheet between liabilities and equity; this is discussed below in the liabilities section.

Nondepreciable Fixed Assets

Land is one fixed asset that does not depreciate on the balance sheet. If used in the normal course of operations, land is considered a fixed asset; otherwise, it is considered an investment. Since land is valued at cost on the company's balance sheet, its appreciation can represent hidden value. The same is true of buildings that accountants wish to depreciate on the financial statements, but may actually appreciate in value over time.

Due From Officers or Partners

This noncurrent asset account represents a company loan to one of its officers or owners. Although they are usually shown as accounts receivable on financial statements, such loans often do not represent a liquid asset convertible to cash and available for business operations. Company officers normally pay the company last because they control the company. Therefore, all such loans are spread in the noncurrent asset category and not in current accounts receivable.

The credit analyst should also determine why the loan was made and the prospects for repayment. For example, an officer may have taken a loan from the company in lieu of a salary or bonus. This loan is, in effect, an expense not recognized by the company, thus improving its profitability. Moreover, the company officer need not claim the loan as income, thus avoiding additional personal taxes, assuming the loan does not stay on the books too long. An officer may even purchase stock in the company through the use of a note; this is a sham, creating an asset account as an offset to an equity account. Valid loans to company officers should be examined closely by the lender to determine whether the officer has sufficient personal liquidity to repay this receivable.

Due From Affiliated Concerns

Affiliated companies are those related by common ownership, either one owning the other or both companies owned by the same individual or other company. *Amounts due from affiliates,* like those due from officers or partners, are usually disclosed as accounts receivable on the company's financial statements. However, this receivable is frequently nonliquid because of the nature of the affiliation and the absence of pressure to pay such debts. Therefore, an analyst should consider it as a noncurrent asset and also determine its purpose. For example, the analyst should find out if

- ❐ normal sales exist between the companies, if
- ❐ one company has lent money to the other one, and if
- ❐ the affiliate has the ability to repay the receivable, regardless of the reason behind the account.

If a company wants to borrow money from the bank in order to lend it to an affiliated company, obtain financial statements on the affiliate as well as on the company in order to evaluate its ability to back up repayment. Extensive intercompany borrowings or investments bear watching, particularly in a closely held company where the distinction between the owner's and the company's finances may be blurred.

Investments in Affiliates

When one company owns less than 20 percent of another, the *affiliate* status of the two companies is not necessarily recognized. Ownership of debt or equity may be carried in the long-term marketable securities account. From an analysis viewpoint, it would be desirable to know the extent of management's involvement in the investment. If a substantial block of assets appears in the marketable securities account, the analyst should be stimulated to question the possibility of external involvement, consolidation, or de facto affiliation.

Ownership of from 20 percent up to 50 percent of the common stock of another company normally requires the *equity method of accounting* for the investment. This method reflects the original amount of investment in the affiliate in addition to the owner's accumulated share in the earnings or losses of the affiliate since the investment was made. Any dividends that have been received are deducted from the investment. Thus, this account represents the net historical book value of the investment. Any earnings or dividends will show up as other income on the income statement. Unfortunately, accounting for an affiliate in this manner can disguise how much the other firm can loose, because the investment cannot be reduced below zero.

Since the most important issue is control or influence by management, GAAP require consolidation if management controls the company or owns 50 percent or more of the company. Therefore, the analyst must always be alert to the possibility that management is using GAAP for its own best interests.

Consider this example from research and development. On the one hand, if a firm wished to do research on a particular product, initial expenditures would be charged to the income statement as expenses in the period in which they were incurred. On the other hand, if the firm contracted with an outside party to do the work, neither firm would have to take the expenditures as expense until the contract was complete. Therefore, the originating firm could set up a less-than-50-percent-owned affiliate, contract with it for the research, capitalize the expenditures (remember that this means to place the expenditures on the balance sheet as an asset at cost), and even carry the investment in the affiliate firm on an equity basis.

As a result, the firm would avoid GAAP's immediate expensing requirement for research as well as limit losses on the research project to the amount of its investment in the affiliate firm (since the equity method requires that losses be recognized proportionately only to the extent of the initial investment cost). The final irony in this construction is that the less-than-50-percent-ownership requirement could be fabricated by having the originating firm put up all the money and the research staff be awarded the balance of stock as a reward for hard work. For the analyst, this entire GAAP accounting construction could be misleading.

Deferred Charges

Deferred charges usually represent services that have already been performed and on which payment has been made, carried in accounts payable, or accrued. However, even though there is little or no possibility of refund, these expenditures have been capitalized and not yet expensed. This happens because GAAP's accrual accounting wishes to match the outlay's expense to the future anticipated benefit. An obvious example would be a fee paid to a banker for committing to a three-year revolving loan. Such a commitment would provide value to the firm over the entire three years and perhaps should be expensed (charged against income) over the three years.

The above examples show that the nature of deferred charges is different from that of prepaid expenses. For prepaid expenses, either the services have not been performed or the products have not been delivered. Prepaid expenses are more like a deposit, since cash has been paid out against the benefits of future services or products. Moreover, prepaids are usually refundable if the service or product is not used, and carrying the value on the balance sheet evidences that. This is clearly not the case in deferred expenses, where the outlay is irreversible and the service or product has been received. As a result, the company's balance sheet overstates its assets and equity when these deferred expenses are incurred but not expensed.

Some companies show their start-up expenses as deferred charges because they will result in future sales benefits. However, from a liquidation viewpoint, the value of start-up expenses is questionable. Developmental expenses related to real estate, such as architectural fees and surveys, are usually carried as deferred charges. Whether this account represents value in liquidation or liquidity for operations depends upon the company's prior track record. If the firm has consistently performed, capitalizing developmental expenditures to better match them with the revenues produced is good practice. Such expenditures may represent an intangible (see below) that could be sold to another firm. Thus, an analyst should thoroughly investigate any sizable amount in the deferred charges account.

Deferred Taxes (as an Asset)

When deferred taxes appear on the balance sheet as an asset, it is because of GAAP's attempt to eliminate the differences between tax and GAAP depreciation accounting. According to the latest rules (SFAS No. 109), losses in operations can create future tax benefits that are shown as assets. This has no effect on the company's operations except to reduce GAAP's provision for taxes. Therefore, these losses should be directly offset against deferred taxes on the liability side of the balance sheet. (The deferred tax issue is discussed at the end of this chapter.)

Intangibles

Intangibles is one of the most misunderstood and maligned accounts on the balance sheet. It is standard procedure to categorize the whole account as a nonentity on bank spreadsheets, with the resulting reduction of the net worth accounts creating a new one called *tangible net worth*. Deducting the intangibles from the book net worth to produce tangible net worth compounds the problem of calculating net worth on the basis of assets at historical cost. This procedure springs from an era when banks financed primarily manufacturing firms that owned substantial long-lived physical assets. Today, due to the rapid pace of technological advancement, physical assets can lose their value more quickly than in the past. Meanwhile, intangible assets, covering everything from intellectual copyrights to a favorable long-term lease contract, can have significant value. Therefore, disregarding the intangibles account can obscure important information about the company, its operations, and its real value in liquidation.

The failure of *Cue Magazine* illustrates how important intangibles can be. When *Cue Magazine*, a "what's playing around town" periodical, went into bankruptcy, its primary salable asset was an intangible—the costs that it had incurred to acquire its subscribers. Because it felt that it catered to a similar audience, *New York Magazine* paid millions of dollars for *Cue*'s subscription list so that it could enlarge its own list. However, an intangible cannot appear on the balance sheet unless cash or other good and valuable consideration has been given. Thus, curiously enough, while it could not exist on *Cue*'s balance sheet, it legitimately appeared on *New York*'s.

To proceed in a proper evaluation, an analyst must find out what items are included in the intangibles account, including patents, trademarks, or operating rights. *Patents* give a company the exclusive right to manufacture a product. The intangibles account reflects only the purchase price of the patent or the legal cost of recording internally developed patents, although the value of a patent for a highly successful product will be far greater than these costs. A *trademark* represents the registered name of a product or service. Trademarks can be bought and sold or used in exchange for royalty payments. Again, the balance sheet account reflects only the purchase price or legal cost of recording the trademark, although the current value of a trademark may be far greater.

Operating rights, special rights granted by government regulatory agencies, are required in certain industries. For example, telephone companies, airlines, and television stations all must obtain operating rights for their areas of business. Because companies can sell or lease these rights, the rights often represent a far greater value to a company than is shown on the balance sheet. The balance sheet value of this right may also be understated in terms of its liquidating value.

Many service companies have a substantial part of their net worth tied up in intangibles, and routine removal will not accomplish much toward the objective of determining what these assets will bring in liquidation. Instead, the analyst should put forth at least an equal effort in evaluating these assets as in evaluating the physical kinds of inventory mentioned above.

Another intangible that frequently shows up on balance sheets is called *goodwill*, an accounting term used for capitalizing acquisitions when the price paid to purchase another company exceeds the market value of its physical assets. Goodwill represents payment in consideration of the acquired company's established customer base, reputation, and future earnings potential. Again, traditional credit theory discards the possibility of evaluating such a figure.

The Phillip Morris Corporation provides an illustrative example of how current credit theory evaluates goodwill. Philip Morris acquired General Foods in 1985. On Phillip Morris's balance sheet at the end of 1985, goodwill totaled $4.5 billion. If this figure had been subtracted from its net worth, Phillip Morris's net worth would have fallen to $280 million and its debt-to-worth ratio would have become more than 45 to 1. Obviously, the lenders that financed this acquisition evaluated this goodwill favorably and did not remove it from the balance sheet of Phillip Morris. They may have estimated the future revenue stream (in other words, cash flow) that could be derived from this goodwill. That is one approach to evaluating any intangible—just as it is in a correct evaluation of any asset.

In theory, the amount a company pays in excess of book value when acquiring another firm should lose value over time because the new owners will make their own imprint on the acquired firm. Therefore, GAAP generally require amortization, or gradual expensing over many years, of goodwill and most other intangibles over no more than forty years. However, management may be given leeway for intangibles that are less than 10 percent of a company's total assets. The IRS takes the opposite approach and does not permit any expensing of goodwill until the actual asset acquired is sold again!

Today's analyst will eliminate many favorable lending opportunities unless he or she makes the effort to evaluate intangibles. A good source of additional information is *Valuation of Intellectual Property and Intangible Assets* by Gordon V. Smith and Russell L. Parr and other books on similar topics.

Other Noncurrent Assets

Assets that do not fit into any other category are valued at cost, although they may have significant market value. Some of the same concerns expressed above should be considered by the analyst studying other noncurrent assets.

REVIEW OF LIABILITIES AND NET WORTH ACCOUNTS

Now look at the other side of the Assets = Liabilities + Net worth equation. Unlike assets, which can fluctuate in market value, most liabilities are fixed in their obligation to pay and eventually must be paid at that value, with few exceptions. Finance people consider assets to be the tools with which a business entity functions, whereas liabilities and net worth represent sources of cash to purchase those assets. While these same people frequently refer to the entire right side of the balance sheet as equities, in this book the words *liabilities* and *debt* are used for claims having a fixed repayment schedule and, usually, an interest payment. Also, in this book the terms *net worth* and *equity* are used to mean claims that have no repayment schedule or an annual payment schedule that is implemented at the discretion of management, as in the case of common stock, or is dependant on the information reported in the income statement, as in the case of preferred stock. Preferred stock, seen in this light, is like a cross between debt and equity: it is usually entitled to a set dividend per year, but the entitlement is limited to the firm's profits.

From the lender's perspective, the less debt the better, because the lender obtains no benefit from greater returns on equity stimulated by low-cost debt. Further, more debt, with its fixed repayment schedules, can threaten the survival of the company if profits or cash flow dwindle.

An analyst should evaluate a company's liabilities in terms of their repayment requirements, their continued availability as a source of financing for the company, and their anticipated sources of repayment. Liabilities should also be evaluated in terms of their present and future interest cost to the company and the assets that may secure them. Short-term or revolving debt is normally incurred to finance current assets that grow with sales (such as accounts receivable and inventory), whereas fixed-amortization, long-term loans are normally used to finance fixed assets that lose value over the amortization schedule. This *matching maturities* concept is important for debt capacity evaluation.

In summary, during the review of any liability, the analyst should determine to whom the money is owed, why it was borrowed, its repayment terms, whether assets have been pledged, and whether any restrictive loan agreements are in force.

Current Liabilities

Current liabilities are subject to the same questions raised before concerning how current is current? The issue here is tied to the cash generating cycle of the firm, which is dealt with in chapter 7, the cash budget. A company normally pays its current liabilities (or short-term debt) when current assets are converted to cash.

A company's current liabilities may include notes payable to banks, commercial paper, accounts payable, accruals, loan repayments to analysts or affiliates, and current-year income taxes. Thus, this area is more important for short-term loan analysis than for long-term loan analysis. The liquidity of the borrower's assets and the relationship between assets and current liabilities may change significantly over a long period. To pay short-term liabilities, however, the firm will need to have sufficient cash on hand or convert assets to cash quickly enough to pay the current liabilities as they come due. Thus, review of the timing of a liability's repayment terms is the essence of debt evaluation.

From the loan applicant's viewpoint, the level of current liabilities, and especially their relationship to current assets, is a sensitive point because borrowers know that bank analysis frequently focuses on it. Therefore, borrowers take care to arrange the fiscal year end to occur at a time when short-term financing needs will be the lowest. Think about suggesting to Macy's executives that they close the financial statements on November 30. At that time of year, most of the retailer's assets are invested in inventory; the retailer is just beginning to enter its busiest season, when 35 percent of its total sales occur in just 30 days. Thus, short-term borrowings are bound to be high as the firm strains to provide the supply and variety of merchandise demanded by its customers. Liquidity will look very low.

Before charge accounts were common, retail stores frequently made their fiscal year-end report on January 31 (after an "inventory reduction sale"). However, now that charge accounts are common, if stores chose that alternative, their receivables would be unacceptably high. Therefore, most retail stores currently release year-end statements either at June 30 or July 31. These dates allow the stores to collect most of their accounts receivable from their Christmas selling season and also to have low inventories (because July is in their slowest quarter). The absence of accounts receivable and inventory permits the stores to use their cash to pay down liabilities and present a financial statement that looks better than one with assets and liabilities high relative to equity.

Notes Payable to Banks

Notes payable to banks frequently represent the short-term financing of a company's current assets (accounts receivable and inventory). A company with seasonal financing needs may have a seasonal line of credit. For example, a retail company may use a bank loan to increase its inventory prior to Christmas. As the company sells its inventory, it creates accounts receivable or cash. When these accounts are collected or cash sales accumulate, the bank loan is repaid. Therefore, short-term bank debt may fluctuate, depending on when in the cash conversion cycle a company prepares its balance sheet. Further, most lending institutions expect that during the slow part of the year the borrower will evidence its nonseasonal self-sufficiency by paying back all lines of credit. This period is called a *clean-up period*.

If a company's bank debt represents a seasonal or revolving line of credit, the analyst must determine its terms, including payout requirements, if applicable. Since the company may have loans from more than one bank, the evaluation should cover the purpose, expiration date, interest rate, and security pledged on each credit line. The evaluation should also assess the adequacy of these lines of credit for the company's needs. A company may have *asset-based financing*, which is a term for loans secured by certain assets. Asset-based financing is usually maintained at a set percentage level in relation to the assets financed.

Current corporate finance theory attempts to quantify the obvious tendency for firms that are rapidly growing and are not seasonable to require permanent increases in inventories and accounts receivable. Such firms do not earn sufficient profits to cover their growth requirements. These types of issues are addressed in more depth in the chapters on ratios and cash budgets.

While some institutions have funded this requirement for inventories and accounts receivable with long-term debt, thereby matching long-term funding with long-term needs, this may not be the best solution. A problem occurs because long-term loans usually have a built-in amortization rate, and this rate may not be consistent with the rate of profits or cash flow needed to repay the loan, just as mentioned in the last paragraph. Further, inventories and accounts receivable needs may continue to grow. While lines of credit at one time were considered synonymous with seasonal borrowing, today banks offer a line of credit to support accounts receivable where no clean-up period is expected and repayment at year end is expected to come from renewal of the credit line or other refinancing. (Sometimes this type of loan is called a one-year revolving credit.)

Ultimately, slowed growth and profits over a period of time should result in less use of the credit line and a gradual lowering of the credit-line amount each time it comes up for renewal. A credit line typically has one year or less maturity, is secured by accounts receivable at a minimum, and typically provides advances made against a borrowing base. While this is technically a mismatch of financing—short-term financing for a long-term need—banks prefer the control that a one-year commitment provides, given that the companies using this type of service tend to be undercapitalized.

Commercial Paper

Commercial paper usually represents unsecured short-term borrowings from investors for up to 270 days in amounts of $100,000 or more. This form of financing is usually only available to well-regarded companies with an established credit rating (as conferred by such investment services as Moody's Investors Service or Standard & Poor's). Another alternative is that a bank may issue a letter of credit to back the commercial paper issue of smaller firms that cannot obtain such a rating. In any case, the credit rating agencies always require open bank credit lines to back up outstanding commercial paper.

The incentive to use commercial paper, as mentioned in chapter 1, is that firms usually pay lower interest rates than bank prime rates for commercial paper.

From a legal viewpoint, commercial paper includes all publicly issued debt, and an analyst may occasionally note this account title in the long-term section of the liabilities. Accountants usually do not make mistakes on debt maturities, so in this event it is safe to assume that the legal definition is being used in contrast to the financial one.

Notes Payable To Others

Notes payable to others include any amounts borrowed from creditors other than banks and investors in commercial paper. An analyst should determine the identity of such creditors, including the reasons for creating the note, its terms, and the security pledged. Because such notes may represent a significantly past-due trade account, existence of this account on the balance sheet should signal caution.

Accounts Payable

Trade *accounts payable* represent normal credit extended by suppliers for purchases of inventory and services. Trade accounts payable owed by one company are shown as accounts receivable on its creditors' financial statements. Find out the normal credit terms and then make a judgment about whether the borrower is showing the ability to take advantage of discounts, which may work out to be a high effective rate of interest.

Accounts payable represent a permanent source of "interest free" funding for the company because, as the company pays its accounts, financing always remains available for new purchases. If, however, a company does not pay its accounts on a timely basis, its suppliers may refuse to extend it credit for new purchases. The company then either has to pay cash or finds itself without a source of inventory to continue its operations. Stretching the amount of time between making purchases and paying for them is referred to as "riding the trade" and could indicate mismanagement or inadequate liquidity. Chapter 6 covers accounts payable analysis in more detail.

Due to Affiliates

Any amounts owed to company officers, partners, or other owners as well as debts owed to affiliated companies are properly carried as current liabilities, regardless of their stated term. This is prudent since management controls repayment and could pay such debts at will. Analysts need to determine how this liability to officers or affiliated companies arose and its terms.

As stated above, for tax reasons, company owners may lend cash to the company rather than invest in additional stock as equity. This type of debt should normally be subordinated to bank debt.

Accruals

Accruals represent unpaid costs that the company has expensed through the income statement. These expenses usually are those paid at regular intervals, such as salaries and wages, utilities, and withholding taxes. For example, if a balance sheet is prepared in the middle of a pay period, the wages owed as of that date are shown as an accrual.

An analyst should look for significant amounts in this account. If a comparative analysis reveals any unusual buildup, a liquidity crisis could be in the making. Accruals of prior quarters' withholding taxes are especially crucial because of potential Internal Revenue Service priority to a company's assets. Most banks do not lend money to companies with delinquent tax liabilities.

Current Maturities of Long-term Debt

Current maturities of long-term debt represent the principal portion of installment payments on long-term debt due (annually, quarterly, or monthly) over the next 12 months. Unlike other current liabilities, which depend on the conversion of current assets for repayment, these current maturities are usually paid from a company's net cash flow. The analysis of this concept appears in chapter 5.

The analytical problem with this account is that some firms have cash flow or net cash conversion cycles shorter than one year. This means that all of the other current asset and liability accounts, mentioned above, will likely be of shorter maturity than this account. In the case of a food service company, for example, the cycle could be as short as a week. Comparing the current maturities of long-term debt for a whole year to those shorter accounts may be misleading with regard to the liquidity problems of the firm.

Analysis of amortizing debt should include identification of its terms, conditions, security, and to whom it is owed. Some loans are structured so that no principal repayments are made until the end when the entire balance of the loan becomes due. An analyst must be alert to any such "bullet" loans or other "balloon" payments (substantial and irregular principal repayments) in this account since they may require refinancing. If refinancing is likely to be needed, the lender needs to determine the likelihood of such refinancing being available.

Income Taxes Payable

Income taxes payable represents the actual tax liability due, probably by the next tax payment date. The tax liability shown in this account seldom matches the income tax expense from the income statement for two reasons.

First, companies pay estimated income tax for the current year on a quarterly basis. Thus the year-end tax liability is far less than the total tax liability. In fact, any taxes owed for previous quarters should put the credit analyst on notice for potential IRS liens.

Second, the income-taxes-payable account does not include any of the noncurrent deferred taxes (refer to "Depreciation Methods for Fixed Assets," above) that may be recorded on the income statement—as provision for taxes—but are not due since they are only a theoretical liability for a future period. Taxes due on a deferred basis are recorded as a reserve item. (See "Deferred Income Taxes" in the section on quasi net worth.)

Other Current Liabilities

Other current liabilities are usually insignificant in relation to total current liabilities. This account is usually made up of reductions to asset accounts as deferred or unearned income, unfilled subscriptions, or deposits of some kind. For example, if a company manufactures custom-made or high-priced products, it may require deposits before processing or shipping orders. Such deposits, which are classified as a current liability, can be an important source of financing for these firms.

Any firm that operates under contracts and calculates its income on the percentage-of-completion basis, like a construction firm, may have *deferred income*. Under percentage-of-completion accounting, profits in excess of the originally budgeted amount are not recognized until the contract is completed. This can be an especially harsh treatment for firms doing business with governmental bodies that traditionally are slow to officially approve the completion of the contract. In some of these cases, a cash payment may even have been made, but the income cannot be recognized. Assuming the contract is completed without unexpected mishap, this liability will actually become part of net worth.

In liquidation, customer deposits can also affect the value of inventory, especially if the deposits were for inventory in stock and a security interest was granted to the depositor. Cash held for year-end disbursement to a profit-sharing plan would also be reported in this account.

Long-term Liabilities

Long-term debt represents liabilities with maturities in excess of 12 months. It is usually used to finance land, buildings, and equipment and occasionally to allow permanent increases in inventory levels and accounts receivable. Concerning the latter, see the comments in "Notes Payable to Banks" above. Purchasing another company or buying back a firm's stock off the market may also be financed with long-term debt.

Previous distinctions between long-term debt (with maturities over five years) and intermediate-term debt (with maturities of more than one year but less than five years) are combined on the balance sheet. Distinguishing between them is less valuable today because the variety of long-term amortization terms available makes the detailed study of these terms, while a more-complex process, more indicative of debt capacity than merely determining the final maturity date. For example, traditional long-term debt did not amortize over its term; today this debt would be called a *bullet loan* because it comes due all at once. Many publicly issued bonds are structured in this fashion. Naturally, the strong firm that arranges such debt will refinance it a couple of years before its maturity. The analytical problem is that the strength of the firm or of the market may not permit such a refinancing and bring on a catastrophic crisis.

Except for the top-rated public firms, some *amortization*—repayment of a portion of the debt before maturity—of long-term debt principal over the course of its maturity is almost always required. This amortization schedule is of prime analytical importance. The analyst should prepare an independent schedule of the principal repayments required by the reported debt. The resulting schedule should confirm that the repayments are within the company's normal net cash flow expectations. If they are not within cash flow expectations in any future years (frequently the amortization requirements are shown only for five years into the future), discussions about refinancing should begin immediately.

Repayment of longer-term liabilities normally comes from net cash flow and not just from the conversion of current assets to cash. Therefore, a company's long-term debt burden must be analyzed in relation to future net cash flow, to be discussed in chapter 5. Again, debt analysis should cover the terms, purpose, interest rate, and security pledged for all outstanding loans.

Long-term Debt Covenants and Security

When a business incurs long-term debt, it usually enters into a loan agreement, which an analyst should obtain. It will detail such provisions as terms and conditions of repayment, including default provisions. The analyst must determine whether other creditors have restricted the company from incurring the proposed debt or placed other restrictions on the firm, such as meeting certain ratio requirements. If the firm is near any of the limits stated in the loan agreement—in the *covenants*—then negotiations with that lending institution should begin with the object of obtaining a waiver of this restriction. Alternatively, the company may offer a plan to allow it to properly maintain its required ratios.

The balance sheet or loan agreement may also distinguish between secured and unsecured debt. A secured loan is one against which an asset has been pledged in case of default on the loan. If the current lending institution is not the party secured, efforts may be made to join the other lending institution in a joint security agreement. Otherwise, the asset's pledged status should be noted on the spreadsheet.

Occasionally, the borrower may sign a lending agreement covenant which stipulates that it will not pledge its assets to any other party. This is called a *negative pledge.* Falling short of actually pledging collateral, this technique gives the borrower greater freedom in disposing of or selling the asset without requiring individual releases from the lender. The lender is protected because, assuming the covenant is properly recorded under the Uniform Commercial Code, no other lender can presume to take a lien on anything that it does not directly finance. Indeed, if another lender does not file on directly financed assets within 10 days of delivery, the "spreading nonlien" takes precedence. If such a negative pledge already exists with another institution, then the analyst should be aware that these assets would not be available to pledge and would be valuable only to the general creditor pool in a bankruptcy.

Leases & Other Off-Balance-Sheet Liabilities

Perhaps the most problematic change for financial statement analysts in the past 20 years has been the increasing use of *off-balance-sheet financing* by corporations. Three major factors are behind this increase:

- acquisition or creation of captive finance and real estate subsidiaries,
- acquisition of less than a 50-percent interest in or joint venturing of affiliates, and
- growth of the equipment leasing industry.

With the implementation of Statement of Financial Accounting Standards (SFAS) No. 89, captive "other purpose" subsidiaries were eliminated as a form of off-balance-sheet financing as of December 1988. A company, however, can still form up to a 50-percent-owned joint venture with another party and account for it on an equity basis, ignoring the debt the subsidiary itself accumulates since the parent company does not hold a majority interest. Thus, unconsolidated affiliates of companies can still be a source of off-balance-sheet financing.

Operating leases of equipment and real estate (under SFAS No. 13) are popular with highly leveraged companies like transportation firms and retailers because they may be long-term commitments that are not identified on the balance sheet. They allow for substantial off-balance-sheet financing because SFAS No. 13 considers them to be executory agreements signed in the ordinary course of business instead of liabilities. Financial statement analysts should expect off-balance-sheet financing to increase.

The credit analyst's responsibility includes calculating the extent of the fixed commitments which firms have off the balance sheet and understanding lease repayment terms and purposes. Thus, analysts should examine closely each element of a firm's funding structure, as detailed in the footnotes, rather than just transfer numbers from the balance sheet to the spreadsheet.

If a firm appears to have substantial off-balance-sheet commitments, then estimates of the potential impact of these commitments must be made.

Experts in the field may be consulted, or books like *Equipment Leasing Guide for Lessees* by Albert R. McMeen may provide assistance.

Subordinated Debt

Subordinated debt is a junior liability (usually held by company officers or affiliated companies) that can only be repaid when specified debt obligations—the terms of the subordination agreement—have been met.

Entrepreneurs frequently lend funds to their companies, rather than finance solely with equity, because for tax purposes subordinated debt pays interest, which firms can deduct as an expense. In contrast, no deduction may be taken for dividends paid to common stockholders. From the bank's point of view, these liabilities are the equivalent of equity. For example, a bank may extend a loan to a company only on the condition that any debt held by the owner or other stockholders be subordinated to the bank debt. If debt is subordinated to the bank, the bank should hold the original agreement and notes and thoroughly understand their terms.

On the other hand, the company may have publicly issued convertible subordinated debt; naturally, having physical possession of the debentures, as noted above, would not be practical. Since the intention of the investor in convertible subordinated debt may be to eventually convert the debt obligation to stock if the firm does well, the concept just established in regard to having to repay the value of debt is abandoned. In the case where the subordinated debt holders may be presumed to intend to convert their debt to stock, the bank may wish to treat the debt as equity. This would be particularly likely if the stock price rises above the conversion price on the debt.

While the holders of this security will be junior to the bank that is a senior lender, subordinated debentures have certain entitlements to interest payments. Therefore, the analyst may want to look at whether these entitlements would have a deleterious effect on cash flow. For most cases, this aspect of subordinated debt forces analysts to retain the debt character of this account because it is entitled to interest payments—and conceivably principal payments—no matter what the profits are.

Contingent Liabilities

Contingent liabilities can pose a significant threat to the viability of a company's operation. A prime example of contingent liabilities causing problems is the potentially ruinous asbestos liability faced by Johns-Manville Corporation. After the company filed for protection under the bankruptcy statutes, its shareholders lost their investment in favor of plaintiffs in asbestos legal suits.

The fact that the creditors were relatively protected by this bankruptcy agreement demonstrates that senior creditors have an advantage.

Another category of contingent liabilities includes contracts undertakings, such as guarantees, contractual commitments, and letters of credit. In the ordinary course of business, these are frequently referred to as executory agreements or contracts. (Operating lease agreements are a special case of this type of contract and were discussed above.) It is clear that these legal commitments can bankrupt a firm; here are some examples:

- For a construction firm, legal commitments could arise from a simple error in estimating costs on a particular job.
- For an importer, the signing of a letter of credit to import materials commits payment whether the products shipped were the correct ones, were salable, or were otherwise usable.
- To enable a supplier to obtain credit, large purchasers occasionally guarantee the obligations of the smaller supplier to assist the latter to obtain needed working capital. Paying in advance would use up cash, but also would be reflected on the balance sheet, while the contingency is not.
- In a joint venture, a parent company, but less-than- 50-percent owner, may provide an earnings maintenance agreement for creditors, but avoid the appearance of any notation on its own balance sheet, since these agreements are considered contingent.

The analytical problem is that contingent liabilities are not placed on the balance sheet because no specific amount can be feasibly estimated. Nevertheless, careful reading of any contingency footnotes is still important. Moreover, credit analysts must stay abreast of news events concerning their borrowers, their borrower's customers and suppliers, the relevant industries, and any pending government regulations or public policy issues that might affect a borrower. If a nonofficial estimate of the liability can be obtained, it probably should be viewed cautiously.

Quasi Net Worth

Quasi net worth includes accounts that fall on the right-hand side of the balance sheet but are not clearly debt or equity because the issue of committed annual payments and repayment dates are difficult to determine. In certain cases GAAP have set up equity accounts that are segregated from net worth for specific purposes, like foreign subsidiary currency revaluation reserves. Frequently, these accounts are created to inform the reader of the complexity of the company's operations, not to imply that funds are owed to some other entity.

The analyst needs to closely examine these quasi net worth accounts to determine independently whether they may interfere with the firm's debt repayment capacity. If they do interfere, then these accounts should be spread as debt, even though they may not be debt in the strict sense. Likewise, if these accounts do not interfere, then they should be considered equity. This may have a significant impact on ratios that reference net worth, which are covered in chapter 6.

Reserves

A business's *equity reserves* represent a liability that will become due sometime in the future. Although they, like contingent liabilities, are not a formal debt currently owed to a creditor, their cost has been estimated by some method approved by GAAP and recognized on the balance sheet as a liability that will theoretically become due sometime in the future. For example, losses on bad accounts receivable that have not yet been recognized are estimated into a bad-debt reserve. Expensing through the income statement creates and adds to the reserve; when the cost is actually realized, the reserve should be large enough that additional expensing will not be required and current income will not be distorted.

Another example of using reserves, one that is currently newsworthy, is for corporations to discontinue operations or offer substantial severance payments to encourage reduction of their staff. A reserve for discontinued operations can be created if a manufacturer plans to discontinue a product line, especially if equipment and other assets are unusable in its other processes and the company has to liquidate the equipment for less than its book value. This liquidation may create a loss in an amount that the company can reasonably estimate and recognize in advance. The company can expense the difference between the book value of the equipment and the actual selling price through the income statement and create the reserve.

When it actually liquidates the asset, the company charges any loss to the reserve rather than to its income statement. Although the reserve does not represent a liability actually owed, the fixed assets must be spread so that they are reduced in value by at least the reserve amount. The fixed assets are then worth less than accounting book value for collateral purposes. In the case of severance reserves, the outlay will have to actually be paid in cash, but the reserve should be present for only a short time.

Deferred Income Taxes

Deferred income tax liability, the most common reserve item, is usually created to reconcile discrepancies arising from the use of different fixed asset depreciation methods for tax purposes and for financial reporting purposes, as mentioned above in the discussion of fixed assets. Many companies depreciate fixed assets faster for tax purposes than for financial reporting purposes, although, over the long term, both methods result in the expensing of 100 percent of the cost of the fixed asset. From GAAP's viewpoint, it is better to even out the reported profits after taxes than to show the actual cash that flows to the government. This is not necessarily the financial analyst's position.

To achieve the objective of evening out the reported income, GAAP record an "extra" tax liability incurred by reporting the straight-line rather than the accelerated depreciation method for financial reporting purposes. Since it is not paid out in cash, it is segregated from the normal net worth accounts and carried as a reserve for deferred taxes. Assume, for example, that a company shows $10,000 net profit before tax on its income statement. (See Exhibit 3.6.) Included in its GAAP expenses are $2,000 of depreciation on a $10,000 depreciable asset, figured using the straight-line depreciation method. However, for tax purposes, the company uses the accelerated depreciation method which, as shown by Exhibits 3.4 and 3.5, enables the company to depreciate the asset far more quickly in the early years. Thus, depreciation for tax purposes is $3,200 for the second year, and taxable income becomes $1,200 less than in the GAAP statement reflecting the additional depreciation, or $8,800. The resulting tax (at a 34 percent rate) is $3,400 for GAAP purposes, but only $2,992 is actually payable on its income tax return.

The $408 difference between the $3,400 tax liability reported on the income statement and the $2,992 tax liability reported on the company's tax return would be recorded on the company's balance sheet as a reserve for deferred income taxes. In the second year the deferred tax account would increase by $408 and GAAP income reporting would show that the provision for taxes was at 34 percent of the straight-line depreciation calculated income.

In the fourth year, the MACRS depreciation has declined below that of the straight-line method; now the GAAP income stays the same, while the deferred tax account is charged for the additional $288 in taxes required by the IRS method.

Exhibit 3.6

Deferred Tax Account Posting

Income Statement

	Year #2		Year #4	
Items	*GAAP*	*IRS*	*GAAP*	*IRS*
Sales	$100,000	$100,000	$100,000	$100,000
Cost of Goods Sold	75,000	75,000	75,000	75,000
Depreciation	2,000	3,200	2,000	1,152
Operating Profits	23,000	21,800	23,000	23,848
Other Expense	13,000	13,000	13,000	13,000
Net Income Before Tax	10,000	8,800	10,000	10,848
Tax @ 34%	3,400	2,992	3,400	3,688
Net Income After Tax	6,600	5,808	6,600	7,160
To (From) Deferred Tax Account		$408		$288

In contrast to the above, as long as the value of the company's fixed assets continues to increase, the reserve remains stable or increases as additional depreciation is figured on an accelerated basis. Thus this tax liability can be deferred indefinitely, unless there is a substantial drop in the company's fixed asset purchases. The latter could easily occur in the case of a smaller firm that had just built a new plant filled with new equipment. The firm is unlikely to purchase additional equipment in the immediate future; its large increases in depreciation from the new fixed assets will initially increase its deferred income taxes, and then the lack of new purchases will not add to it. In this case, the deferred tax account serves a justifiable purpose in smoothing income over the life of the equipment.

Because most firms purchase equipment evenly over many years, there is some controversy as to whether to reflect this account as a liability or as equity or as neither, especially when calculating ratios (discussed in chapter 6). Since no interest payments are required and the date of repayment is not known, this account lacks the specific aspects of a liability; thus, it may be considered equity from a lender's viewpoint. If the analyst has information about the future investment plans of the firm, a more judicious decision may be made from this specific information.

In the case of a substantial drop in asset purchases, the reserve may convert to a current liability (income tax debt) requiring payment in the current year; however, the lenders may not care because a company going through such a contraction probably would not request new loans, but would have cash available to repay existing loans.

Minority Interest

Minority interest occurs only when the reporting company owns more than 50 percent of another firm and consolidation is required, but the reporting company owns less than 100 percent of the affiliate. When a parent company consolidates the subsidiary into its financial statements (that is, it shows all of the assets, liabilities, and net worth for both firms), then the minority interest not owned by the parent company's shareholders must be segregated from the claims represented as common stock to the parent company. This quasi equity is not considered a debt, but represents equity claims of common shareholders of the subsidiary. Therefore, an analyst must not use this account in calculating leverage for the company, but carry it in the net worth section.

The existence of this account indicates that some of the assets on the financial statement are not owned directly by the parent company. Indeed, the parent company is merely an owner of stock in the subsidiary. Therefore, in the event of a problem in the parent company, the entire asset base represented by the subsidiary might not be available to help alleviate the problem. Indeed, the minority interest may be only the proverbial tip of the iceberg.

For example, in the bankruptcy of the Penn Central Railroad, several subsidiaries, including Buckeye Pipeline, had significant liquidity and, had they not had outside shareholders and independent loan covenants against "up streaming" funds to the parent, they could have helped overcome the insolvency. If minority interest is of significant size, the indications are that the parent firm is only a stock investor, a holding company; this is an inappropriate borrower. Banks should only lend to operating companies if the loan is conceptually supported by operations of the firm rather than by the assignment of specific collateral.

Net Worth

The difference between a company's total assets and its total liabilities is its equity, or *net worth* (also called owners' equity or shareholders' equity). The amount of equity represents the cushion available to a lender in liquidating assets to repay liabilities. Equity or net worth may consist of capital stock, paid-in surplus, retained earnings, and treasury stock. Net worth is calculated as the sum of the first three components less the fourth component (treasury stock).

A company's liabilities to its creditors do not shrink if asset values are reduced. Therefore, to obtain a true picture of the relationship between a company's debt and equity, compare the revalued assets to its liabilities. (The issues of goodwill and other intangibles have already been discussed.)

Analysts also take into consideration a company's investment in nonproductive assets, such as automobiles, boats, planes, and so on that may have been purchased for the pleasure of the company's owners. The true relationship between equity and debt can be determined when equity has been adjusted for these weak asset values. Then net worth gives the lender a closer picture of a company's financial cushion in the face of shrinkage in its asset values.

Stockholders, like creditors, have a claim against the assets of a company. However, stockholders can make their claims only after all the company's creditors have been paid. Stockholders must absorb any shrinkage in a company's asset values, and they take the most risk in financing a company.

The more-recent concerns for this section are stocks that have aspects of debt, given certain circumstances or occurrences. The best-known example is employee stock ownership plans (ESOPs). In these plans, the firm loans money to the employees to buy stock in the firm. Only as the employees pay off the loans does the equity created by this transaction have any meaning in financial statement analysis. Depending on the particular ESOP agreement, substantially predicated on tax advantages to the company and the employees, there may be little equity cushion in these firms. Determining the nature of some of these stock hybrids is more important than a detailed reconciling of the net worth section. Any listing of multiple classes of stock deserves legal attention to determine the various rights and triggers that may accompany each class.

Stock (Common Stock, Par Value, and Preferred Stock)

Capital stock includes the minimum legal value of the company's outstanding shares of stock, usually called par value. Par value—usually 1 dollar—is an arbitrary value established when a company authorizes shares to be issued. Common stock entitles the holder to vote at shareholders' meetings and provides potential income to the investor through declared dividends and appreciation in value. Dividends are declared at management's discretion.

Paid-in surplus represents additional equity generated when the company sells stock because the stock's price is usually more than the par value. Although a company increases the balances in this account when first issuing stock for cash, paid-in surplus also results when stock is issued in exchange for a note receivable, in a stock dividend, or for an asset invested in the company. If the company accepts an asset in exchange for stock, determine how the company established value for the asset, which now appears on the left side of the balance sheet.

Preferred stock often does not entail voting rights, but dividends accrue at a set rate (which is fixed at the time of issuance). However, unless it has a net profit or common stock dividends have been declared, the company may not have to pay the set rate. In liquidation, preferred stockholders also have preference ahead of common stockholders to the company's assets. The lack of mandatory annual cash payments removes the debt aspect from preferred stock, which also departs from debt in that it may not have to be redeemed at par value unless management so wishes. It could be mentioned that preferred stock is frequently held by other corporations as an investment since intercorporate dividends are partially exempted from income taxes.

Retained Earnings

Retained earnings represent the amount of net profit after tax that is kept in the company as a source of financing. Most companies retain some of their earnings to reduce their dependence on outside capital markets. Many firms pay dividends to their owners (the stockholders) because market experts tell them that this is a way of retaining a possible source of financing through new stock issues. Paying out a high portion of earnings in dividends, however, provides less support for future growth of the firm, given the high cost of common stock issuance and the requirements of most lenders that the equity base remain proportionate to the debt level.

Treasury Stock

Treasury stock consists of stock that was issued and later repurchased by the company. Thus it represents a reduction in equity. The value of treasury stock is subtracted from the other accounts that constitute a company's net worth.

Reconciliation of Net Worth

GAAP require a detailed reconciliation of net worth as a part of the financial statement presentation. If the statements are unaudited, the analyst should prepare a reconciliation showing any changes in the equity accounts (net worth) from the last statement. A company's net worth increases as after-tax profits are added to retained earnings. Increases may also result from new equity investments involving the sale of additional stock to shareholders. Additionally, a company's equity accounts may increase as a result of extraordinary credits to retained earnings not related to the company's operations, such as the life insurance proceeds from a deceased officer, a donation of assets to the company, changes in the conversion values of international operations, and changes in the recording of pension obligations and deferred taxes.

Sometimes a company's equity accounts may decrease. For example, equity will decrease if there is a net operating loss after taxes or if earnings are paid out as dividends to stockholders. Decreased equity may also result from the repurchase of outstanding shares of stock as treasury stock and from extraordinary charges to retained earnings not related to the company's operations, such as asset value loss due to uninsured or partially insured accidents or thefts.

An analyst should review changes to a company's equity accounts and direct specific questions to the company's management. It should be remembered that the source of entries to these accounts are the income statement, covered in the next chapter, and stock transactions.

INTRODUCTION TO COMPARATIVE ANALYSIS

Comparative analysis allows the analyst to get a sense of how a firm is positioned relative to its previous situation and to other comparable firms. This includes internal comparisons of a company's current and previous balance sheets (generally called trend analysis) and external comparisons of the company's results with those of other companies or with industry averages. However, because a company's balance sheet represents its financial condition at a given point in time, an analyst needs to make sure that balance sheet comparisons are meaningful.

While it is difficult to state here with certainty how to decide if the balance sheet comparisons are meaningful, it is possible to suggest certain steps to take. The seasonality of a firm's operations may be taken into account when doing trend analysis. Further, making intercompany comparisons requires thought about relevant dates, the size of firm, the breadth of the industry classification, and so on. It is not possible to categorically rule out using older industry data or observing trends at different month ends or quarters ends. Generally, similar year ends may be used without much questioning, but even this would be inappropriate if, for example, the economy had plunged into a recession in the current year; its behavior in the last recession may be the better comparison.

Trend Analysis

In spreading the company's balance sheet accounts, the analyst normally calculates the *common-size* ratios in the column with the percentage at the top, as shown in Exhibit 3.1. To common-size means to reduce the raw dollar amounts to percentages, so that each balance sheet account is shown as a percentage of total assets. The credit analyst can thus evaluate each account in absolute dollar terms and also in terms of the relative distribution of assets and their financing sources: liabilities and equity. These comparisons can help the analyst pinpoint changes that need to be further explained by the company's management. For example, if a company's balance sheet shows increased current assets (inventory and accounts receivable) without sales growth to justify it, the analyst would seek further explanation.

Trend analysis compares balance sheet accounts from period to period in terms of increases and decreases both in absolute dollars and in percentages of the total. However, only balance sheets prepared at the same phase of the cash conversion cycle allow a meaningful comparison of all accounts. For toy manufacturers, this would be on the same day for consecutive years; for tissue paper makers, a shorter period might be acceptable.

It is important for an analyst to remember that a particular percentage change may not reflect a change in that account, but changes in other accounts. For example, a decline in the cash percentage of total assets may be a result of purchasing a new plant and selling an old, depreciated one, while cash balances have not risen proportionately. Chapter 6 provides a more detailed discussion of the analysis of balance sheets using ratio analysis. Since balance sheet accounts also reflect anticipated or actual sales, comparative analyses of income statements and balance sheets should be done concurrently.

Intra-industry Comparisons

Besides comparing current balance sheet accounts with a company's past statements, analysts also compare the company's balance sheet to those of other similar companies in the same industry and to statistics covering many other firms in the same industry. Internal comparisons may show an improving situation, while external comparisons may show the company's performance to be relatively poor by industry standards.

For example, assume that a company's inventory decreased by 25 percent compared to the previous year as the result of a more-efficient inventory control system. But if the industry's average inventory decreased by 50 percent overall, the company did not perform as efficiently as other companies in the industry. Such *intra-industry comparisons* permit credit analysts to rate a company's performance as average, favorable, or unfavorable.

As mentioned previously, Robert Morris Associates publishes industry averages that are very useful in this regard. A sample of a Robert Morris Associates *Annual Statement Studies* is presented and explained in the chapter on ratios.

SUMMARY OF IMPORTANT CONCEPTS

Gaining a thorough understanding of a company's balance sheet is the first step in a financial statement analysis. By knowing the type of company, its industry, and its general managerial policies, the credit analyst should have a general idea of what the company's balance sheet will look like. By reviewing asset values, liability repayment terms, and the relationship between debt and equity, credit analysts can better predict the consequences of having to liquidate a substantial borrower that has failed.

An evaluation of each asset account in terms of value and liquidity—the ability to convert an asset to cash quickly at or near market values—assists the credit analyst in determining the company's debt repayment capability and the need for collateral to secure debt. Furthermore, an evaluation of each liability account helps determine the current repayment requirements of the company in relation to its possible new financing requirements. An evaluation of a company's liabilities in relation to its equity accounts enables the credit analyst to compare the bank's overall risk as a creditor with the risk faced by an investor.

Recognize that, whereas the value of assets fluctuates (which means their book values do not represent real values), the value of liabilities usually does not fluctuate as much. Equity is important, then, for two reasons. First, the more equity there is, the more owners will work diligently to protect that equity and repay the company's liabilities. Second, equity represents the cushion between a company's asset book values and its liabilities.

Greater uncertainty in the value of assets may require a larger cushion to protect liabilities. Nevertheless, absolutist statements about leverage need to be tempered with references to cash flow and assessment of risk in the business's operations. It is clear that high leverage works for firms with highly stable cash flows, like public utilities. This issue is addressed in the next two chapters to ensure that all credit risk issues are understood.

Once an analyst has analyzed and spread a company's individual balance sheet accounts, the lender can begin making comparisons with the company's past balance sheets. Analyze both absolute changes in dollars and percentage changes in the distribution of assets, liabilities, and equity. Also do a comparative analysis of the company's balance sheet accounts and trends over time with those of other companies.

EXERCISES

Important Terms to Define

insolvency
aggressive financial policy
leverage
going concern
collateral
liquidity
marketable securities
accounts receivable aging
note receivable
work in process
prepaid expenses
fixed assets
Green Guide
accelerated cost recovery
equity method of accounting
intangibles
trademark
goodwill
net worth
current liabilities
asset based financing
commercial paper
accruals
income taxes payable
bullet loan
covenants
subordinated debt
equity reserves
minority interest

retained earnings
comparative analysis
intra-industry comparisons
conservative financial policy
spontaneous growth
spreadsheet
capitalized
fungibility
current assets
accounts receivable loss reserve
finished goods inventory
raw materials inventory
inventory valuation method
other current assets
historical cost
depreciation
amounts due from affiliates
deferred charges
patents
operating rights
current liabilities
matching maturities
notes payable to banks
clean-up period
accounts payable
current maturities of long-term debt
deferred income
amortization

off-balance-sheet financing
contingent liabilities
deferred income tax
net worth
treasury stock
trend analysis

Dependable Doors Case Study

1. Looking at the balance sheet, evaluate the management philosophy of Dependable Doors (hint—make sure you consider working investment).
2. From a collateral point of view, how marketable are the assets of Dependable Doors?
3. Spread and common-size the balance sheet.
4. How does the balance sheet of Dependable Doors compare to RMA industry statistics?
5. As a lender, how do you feel about the trends in Dependable Door's balance sheet?
6. Do the notes to the financial statement provide any information that can be of assistance in an examination of the balance sheet?

The answers to the Dependable Doors questions appear in the appendix.

Engraph Case Study

1. Spread Engraph's balance sheet.
2. Common-size the numbers on the balance sheet that you have just spread.
3. Using the balance sheet, evaluate the financial management philosophy of Engraph (hint—make sure you consider working investment).
4. From a collateral point of view, how marketable and liquid are the assets of Engraph?
5. How can you tell which method of inventory valuation Engraph is using? What effect does it have on ending inventory?
6. On the company's balance sheet, how can deferred taxes be both an asset and a liability?

The Income Statement

LEARNING OBJECTIVES

After studying this chapter, you will be able to

- identify the basic components of an income statement,
- spread and common-size an income statement,
- apply the concepts of comparison and trend analysis to the income statement,
- differentiate between those expenses that are included in cost of goods sold, those that are included as operating expenses, and those that are nonoperating (other income and expense) on an income statement,
- explain the distinctions between different operating strategies, based upon market conditions,
- explain the difference between LIFO and FIFO and how the inventory valuation method affects a company's profitability, and
- explain how income serves as one of the principal components of cash available for debt repayment and as an indication of continuing operating viability.

INTRODUCTION

The *income statement*, also called a profit and loss statement or earnings statement, is an accounting statement that uses accrual concepts to match a company's revenues with its expenses over a stated period of time, as long as a year. Because income statements are a gauge of a company's ability to use its resources to generate wealth, commercial credit analysts rely on the income statement as one of the principal tools for evaluating a company's long-range viability.

Income statement examination consists of two basic analyses: revenues and expenses. Companies are profitable when their revenues exceed the expenses incurred in generating revenues. Profits do not equal cash, which is the account through which all debt must be paid off. However, a company's profitability is a primary component of the cash available to repay debt and a major factor in the lender's decision to extend credit.

The framework for income statement review also requires an understanding of the company's markets. To do that, an analyst must identify both internal and external factors—that is, factors that the company can control and those over which it has no control—that contribute to the demand for a firm's particular products or services. The industry material is more fully covered in chapter 2. Operating distinctions among different firms are enlarged upon here only as they relate directly to the concept of short-term asset conversion.

Before analyzing a company's income statement, an analyst should remember to consider such factors as

- the methods the company uses to recognize revenue and expenses,
- who prepared the statements,
- whether the statements are fiscal year or interim statements, the context of the business in which the company is engaged, and
- the characteristics of the market in which the company operates (as discussed in detail in chapter 2).

When *common-sizing* an income statement, all accounts are shown as a percentage of sales.

The Spreadsheet

Financial statement analysis begins with scrutinizing each account on the audited statements and placing the information into a format used for all credit analysis within the bank: the *spreadsheet*. You are encouraged to refer to your own bank's spreadsheet format, if possible. If you wish to use the worksheets in this book, the second one, dealing with the income statement, is found as Exhibit 4.1. It may be a good exercise for you to go back to the beginning of chapter 3 and review the concepts and rules about spreading a financial statement. The case at the end of the chapter uses this information.

Exhibit 4.1

Company Name:
Statement Dates:
Rounded to:

INCOME STATEMENT	$	%	$	%	$	%
1 **Net Sales (Revenues)**						
2 Cost of Goods Sold (Less Dep.)						
3 Depreciation Expense						
4 **Gross Profit**						
5 Selling Expense						
6 General & Admin. Expense						
7 Officers' Compensation						
8 Other Operating Expenses						
9 **Operating Income**						
10 Other Nonoperating Income						
11 (Interest Expense)						
12 Interest Income						
13 (Other Nonoperating Expense)						
14 (Plant Closings $ Writedowns)						
15 Earnings on Equity Investments						
16 **Profit Before Tax**						
17 Income Tax						
18 **Income from Continuing Operations**						
19 Net Profit from Discount Operations						
20 Gain (Loss) on Sale of Operations						
21 **Income (Loss) before Extraord. Income**						
22 Extraordinary Income (Loss)						
23 **Net Profit**						
CASH FLOW STATEMENT						
24 Net Income From Contin. Operations						
25 Depreciation & Amortization						
26 Change in Deferred Taxes						
27 Adj. to Reconcile Net Income						
28 **Funds Flow from Operations**						
29 (Increase in Accounts Rec.)						
30 (Increase in Inv. & Other Cur. Assets						
31 Increase in Accounts Payable						
32 Increase in Accruals & Other Cur. Liabs.						
33 **Net Cash Provided by Operations**						
34 Fixed Asset Sales						
35 (Net Capital Expenditures)						
36 (Purchase of Companies/Assets)						
37 **Funds After Investments**						
38 Increase in Long-Term Debt						
39 Issuance (Purchase) Own Stock						
40 (Dividends)						
41 **Net Change in Cash and Equiv.**						

NOTES:
1. **Positive Number = a Source of Cash, and a Negative number = a Use of Cash**
2. **You may have only enough information to just complete the current year cash flow**

Period of Income Statement

An income statement covering a year is called an *annual statement*. Income statements prepared for periods of less than 12 months are called *interim statements*. While some businesses experience a production cycle of greater than one year, they still have to prepare income statements every 12 months to meet requirements of most lenders and the Internal Revenue Service. The most-common interim periods are semiannual, quarterly, and monthly. Year-to-date figures compiled at the end of any month during the year can also serve as interim statements. Therefore, the time represented by an interim statement can be from 1 to 11 months. Generally, lenders require prospective borrowers to submit annual income statements for at least 2 or 3 years as well as current interims if the annual statements are over 4 months old. Of course, lenders definitely prefer audited statements, as discussed in chapter 3.

Accrual Accounting and Revenue/Expense Matching

Most financial statements are prepared on an *accrual basis* rather than a cash basis. Thus, revenues (used interchangeably with sales) are recognized when sales are made, not when payment is received, and expenses are recognized when they are incurred, not when payment is made. Moreover, different expenses are recognized in distinct time periods. Expenses that relate directly to sales—called *cost of goods sold* on the income statement—are not recognized until the inventory item or service is sold. Consequently, a buildup in inventory (for a wholesaler or retailer) or in raw materials, work-in-process, or unsold finished goods (for a manufacturer) does not affect a company's profits since inventory expenditures are capitalized on the balance sheet and expenses are recognized only when matched to the revenues they help produce. Further, expenses related to the purchase of fixed assets such as equipment are not recognized at the time of the purchase or even upon delivery of the equipment. Instead, expenses derived from fixed assets are recognized over a period equal to their expected use by the firm.

Accrual-basis accounting also allows other operating expenses to be recognized more immediately in the period in which they are incurred, but paid for in a prior or a subsequent period. If an item is paid for in one period and recorded as an expense in a later period, the item is likewise capitalized—carried as an asset, a deferred charge, or a prepaid expense—on the balance sheet. If, however, expenses are recognized before they are paid, they are frequently carried in the liabilities or equity section, possibly as accruals or reserve accounts. These accounts are discussed more fully in chapter 3.

Example Used in the Chapter

Exhibit 4.2 shows an income statement for Bud's Sporting Goods, a retailer of weight-lifting equipment, athletic shoes, and uniforms. This income statement, which includes comparative data for three years, is used in examples throughout this chapter. Refer to this exhibit when prompted in the text.

Example Income Statement

Exhibit 4.2

Bud's Sporting Goods
Income Statement for the Years Ending June 30, 1989-1991
(Dollars in 000s)

	1989	*1990*	*1991*
Sales	$350.0	$400.0	$450.0
Cost of goods sold	190.0	209.0	225.0
Gross profit	160.0	191.0	225.0
Operating expenses	147.0	160.0	171.0
Operating profit	13.0	31.0	54.0
Other income	—	—	4.0
Other expenses	5.0	5.0	5.0
Interest expense	– –	10.0	10.0
Profit before tax	8.0	16.0	35.0
Income taxes @ 34%	2.7	5.4	11.9
Net profit after tax	5.3	10.6	23.1

REVENUE ANALYSIS

Aside from the fact that the level of sales does not depend on the amount of cash taken in because most companies offer sales on credit, from GAAP's viewpoint *sales* can only be recognized on the income statement when delivery of the product or service occurs. Since common law regards delivery of a product or service as equivalent to passage of title, it stands to reason that if the seller no longer owns the goods, the buyer does and a sale has taken place.

One analytical problem is that handing over the merchandise at a retail store, like Bud's Sporting Goods, clearly fulfills the delivery requirement, but in some other cases it is difficult to discern when delivery occurs. For example, a health club provides membership services over a period of time, but GAAP allow the income recognition to take place as soon as the member signs a contract. (Given the lack of concern for actual cash receipts, it does not matter if the contract calls for the member to make payments over the term of the membership.) This approach is based upon the idea that no particular expenses are incurred as a result of signing up one new member; no delivery takes place other than already having the club available to serve the member. Given the typical court's unwillingness to enforce the payment terms of the contract, because of the often hard-sell tactics of health clubs, the otherwise convenient understanding of the term *sale* is less than clear. Especially for certain industries, like health clubs, the analyst will want to make some effort at assuring him- or herself that delivery really has occurred and even go the extra step to be reasonably sure that payment will indeed be forthcoming before accepting the sale number.

Additional problems can limit an analyst's hope that the sales numbers really indicate successfully completed transactions. Consumer rights legislation, for example, has made it difficult for a manufacturer to avoid responsibility for a product's safety even when it operates in accordance with the expectations of the marketplace, which is sometimes called fit for a particular purpose. While the seller's warranty used to be considered an after-thought contingency account on the balance sheet, the present-day analyst cannot regard it so lightly. The current competitive environment has encouraged manufacturers and others to offer trial periods and money-back guarantees on products. Courts take a stern view of efforts by firms to oversell their products. In some cases, firms have lost both the right to a payment and the right to have the product returned to them. Firms rely more on their reputation in a market congested with products, and they will consider taking back products from the distribution channel or giving account receivable credits if questions about their quality of pricing competitiveness arise.

Another factor is that not all sales result in full payment. Discounts, allowances, and returns must be deducted from gross sales. In some industries, it is common to offer discounts for large volumes of purchases. *Allowances* result when customers are compensated for faulty goods by receiving credit on future bills. *Returns* result when merchandise is returned and the bill is canceled. Increasing allowances and returns can be an indicator of a decline in the quality of a firm's products or services.

Net sales, the first entry on most income statements, is calculated as follows:

Net sales = Gross sales – (Sales discounts + Sales returns + Allowances).

EXPENSE ANALYSIS

After studying the revenues shown on the income statement, the analyst's next step is to study the corresponding expenses incurred. The ultimate goal, of course, is to assess the company's past profitability and to be able to make an educated guess concerning the company's future profitability. Meanwhile, the current goal is to determine the veracity of the expense amounts.

The examination of expenses in relation to revenues begins with a consideration of the company's cost of goods sold and a review of gross profit margins and then entails a detailed analysis of its operating expenses.

Cost of Goods Sold

The second entry on the income statement is *cost of goods sold*. Whenever a product is manufactured or sold, certain direct costs are incurred. These direct costs, called cost of goods sold, include the expenses of production (the cost of materials, labor, and manufacturing overhead) in a manufacturing company. For a wholesale or retail company, cost of goods sold equals the cost of purchased inventory. A service company's product manufacturing cost is minimal, for example, the paper and binders that public accountants produce for their clients, and its income statements do not calculate a cost of goods sold. For another example, if Bud's Sporting Goods purchases golf balls at a cost of $2.00 and resells them for $3.00, the cost of goods sold is $2.00. The $1.00 markup represents the gross profit margin resulting from the sale of each weight.

Calculating Cost of Goods Sold

The cost of goods sold is based on the many products purchased or manufactured during a business's operating cycle or interim period and available for sale. However, these costs are not recognized until the company sells its inventory. Therefore, to calculate the cost of goods for the products that were sold, a company's beginning and ending inventory are taken into consideration.

The cost of goods sold for a wholesaler or retailer is calculated by adding the company's inventory purchases to the beginning inventory for the period and then subtracting the ending inventory. This gives the cost of the merchandise sold (or lost or stolen) during the period. The basic formula then for calculating the cost of goods sold for a retailer or a wholesaler is this:

Cost of goods sold = Beginning inventory + Net cost of purchases – Ending inventory.

The net cost of purchases includes shipping costs and can be further refined by subtracting any volume discounts, returns, and allowances on purchased goods. This is shown by the following formulas:

Net cost of purchases = Net purchases + Transportation costs.

Net purchases = Purchases – Purchase discounts + Purchase returns and allowances.

Exhibit 4.3 shows the calculation of cost of goods sold for Bud's Sporting Goods for 1988. No labor or overhead expenses are allocated to the inventory since a retailer adds no value to the inventory. The inventory handling expenses—such as the wholesaler's labor, delivery, and warehousing costs—are not included in the cost of goods sold, but are included on the income statement as operating expenses.

Cost of Goods Sold - Retail

Exhibit 4.3

Bud's Sporting Goods
Cost of Goods Sold
Dollars in 000s

	1989	*1990*	*1991*
Beginning Inventory	10.0	20.0	35.0
Purchases	85.0	175.0	257.0
Cost of goods available for sale	95.0	195.0	292.0
Ending Inventory	20.0	35.0	42.0
Cost of goods sold	75.0	160.0	250.0

For a manufacturer, the cost of goods calculation is more complex because three types of inventory must be distinguished: raw materials, work in process, and finished goods. Moreover, manufacturing expenses (direct labor costs and certain overhead expenses) must be added in to determine the true cost of the finished products. Again, these costs are recognized as expenses only when the company sells its inventory, which means that beginning and ending inventory amounts must be considered.

Labor costs comprise the wages paid to production workers. Manufacturing *overhead* expenses are usually allocated according to a percentage method of space allocation. For example, if 60 percent of a manufacturer's facilities are used in the manufacturing process, then 60 percent of the total utilities, rent, general managerial expenses, and building depreciation (a noncash expense) would be allocated to manufacturing overhead. Finally, equipment depreciation is also allocated on some basis, either by time or hours used, predicated on the original useful-life estimate of management. Thus, for a manufacturer, the formula looks like this:

Cost of goods sold = Beginning inventory + Purchased materials + Direct labor + Overhead expense + Depreciation – Ending inventory.

The analysis of a manufacturer's cost of goods sold must include not only pricing considerations, but also an evaluation of the company's cost controls. A manufacturer's efficiency in controlling productivity (manufacturing as much product as possible from a given amount of labor and related overhead expenses) is critical.

Determining Physical Inventory

Inventory is a key component in the cost of goods sold for all companies. For some retailers, a *perpetual inventory* system keeps a daily count of inventory for accounting purposes. When a business sells an item, it immediately deducts that item's cost from the inventory account. Companies usually use this system for very expensive or large inventory items that do not sell quickly.

Thus automobile dealers, heavy equipment dealers, and jewelers have traditionally used a perpetual inventory system; only the auditors physically sample the inventory.

For most firms the perpetual inventory method is impractical because of the large number of low-value parts in inventory. They use a *periodic method* of inventory instead. Even with computers at check-out counters, errors in posting, damage, waste, and pilferage require taking a physical count of inventory on a scheduled basis to get a better estimate of what is there. Especially for service firms, low-cost inventory items are expensed upon receipt—no one wants to count paper clips. Since inventory counts are normally taken once a year, or at the end of an operating cycle, interim statements are usually based on estimates of inventory. A physical count may seem to ensure an accurate accounting of inventory values, but the analytical problem is much more difficult.

Financial statements show the dollar value of physical assets. This dollar value is an estimate based upon the cost of a number of inventory items arriving at the firm over a period of time, with prices subject to different levels of inflation. Therefore, most firms use an estimating convention to identify the value of inventory. As used here, the term *convention* is not a political gathering but an agreed upon method of doing something.

Inventory Value Conventions

The two most popular conventions are known as last-in, first-out (LIFO) and first-in, first-out (FIFO). ***FIFO*** uses the cost associated with the oldest remaining unit in inventory to determine the expense taken into the income statement. The FIFO method is based on an inherently logical assumption that most firms use up old inventory (that is, first-purchased inventory) first, thereby preventing inventory from becoming stale.

Unfortunately, the FIFO method also assumes that the currency used to set inventory value is stable from one statement period to the next. In times of changing inflation rates, FIFO charges to expense the older inventory, which usually happens to be valued at lower costs, resulting in a balance sheet that contains inventory valued at current cost, as discussed in chapter 3. The result for the income statement is twofold: the statement's cost-of-goods-sold entry shows lower costs than will be required for the business to replace the old inventory and continue in business, but the statement shows a higher profit. This type of profit is called *inventory holding gains profit* since it derives from the holding of inventory and not from the operating skills of management.

In contrast, ***LIFO*** uses the cost associated with the last—the newest—unit of inventory purchased to determine the expense charged in the income statement when any unit is sold. Therefore, ending inventory is valued at old rather than recent prices. In inflationary periods characterized by rising prices, this valuation method causes the ending inventory item in the cost-of-goods formula to be lower relative to the purchases indicated. Unfortunately, then, the balance sheet contains old-cost inventory, but the income statement contains the more-recent and higher costs, in turn producing lower gross profits. The good point is that the higher cost-of-goods-sold value under LIFO is more in line with the replacement inventory costs the firm will face to stay in business.

Exhibit 4.4 illustrates how the LIFO and FIFO methods of inventory valuation could affect Bud's Sporting Goods' gross profits. From the initial year of 1989, sales increase as a result of both inflation and Bud's ability to increase the difference between his costs and the prices he charges the public, the gross margin. Furthermore, as sales go up, inventories in unit numbers stay the same, but the cost of purchases increases at the rate of inflation. Therefore, if the cost of those inventories is increasing at the same rate as inflation, then FIFO will show a higher and higher inventory value at the end of each period, while LIFO will keep showing the original inventory value as the ending inventory position.

One result of this is that FIFO income is always higher than LIFO income during inflationary times. Another result is that FIFO income changes dramatically from period to period, depending on the inflation rate. From 1989 to 1990, FIFO income jumped 23.13 percent during a 10 percent inflation rate; then, the FIFO income fell to a 15.66 percent increase when the inflation rate fell to 5 percent. In view of the lack of change in inventory values, the change in LIFO income demonstrates the true rate of profit growth, 9.38 percent in 1990 (19.38 percent minus the inflation rate of 10 percent) and 12.57 percent in 1991 (17.57 percent minus the inflation rate of 5 percent). It would have been impossible to detect this fact if Bud's Sporting Goods had been using FIFO.

Bud's Sporting Goods Inventory

Exhibit 4.4

Bud's Sporting Goods
LIFO Versus FIFO Income Recognition
(Dollars in 000s)

	1989 Base Period	*1990 10% Inflation FIFO*	*1990 10% Inflation LIFO*	*1991 5% Inflation FIFO*	*1991 5% Inflation LIFO*
Sales	$350	$400	$400	$450	$450
Beginning Inventory	60	60	60	66	60
Purchases	190	209	209	225	225
Ending Inventory	60	66	60	69	60
Cost of Goods Sold	190	203	209	222	225
Gross Profit	160	197	191	228	225
Change in Gross Profit		**23.13%**	**19.38%**	**15.66%**	**17.57%**

Although excess FIFO inventory profits are an illusion (since they must be used to replenish the inventory at higher costs), real income taxes have to be paid on them. Therefore, if the analyst believes that cash flow—rather than just profits—is an important variable, the LIFO convention method, which results in lower profits, is preferable to FIFO during periods of changing inflation.

A *LIFO windfall* can occur when a company sells more than it purchases. As a company reduces older inventory valued at lower prices, inventory profits are created when the lower-priced inventory is expensed through cost of goods sold, the very event that was occurring over time using FIFO. Thus, FIFO produces these *inventory holding gains* over time while LIFO avoids them as long as inventory is not declining, the typical situation.

The *average inventory* accounting convention is a third method that is becoming more popular with the advent of computerized inventories. Firms that have fluctuating inventory levels would be better advised to use average inventory accounting because it combines some of both other methods, reducing the inventory holding gains of FIFO and limiting the gains possible in a LIFO windfall. The problem with this method is primarily the complexity of keeping track of the average price when inventory is used daily and, possibly, arrives daily.

Overhead Expense

Overhead expense is the other item requiring some examination. First, it includes depreciation. Second, it includes such items as maintenance that management can easily stall or increase to smooth the variations in income from period to period. Concerning the smoothing variables, maintenance can be cut back in a high volume or competitive time. Most of the time this cutback will not seriously harm the future operations of the firm, unless it is prolonged. Indeed, purchase of lower-quality raw materials would be much more likely to be noticed by customers.

The effect smoothing has on profits could lull an unwary analyst into thinking things are better than they are. This is an example of the need for frequent inspections of business plants and offices; if the analyst is inexperienced, specialized firms can be contracted to perform inspections on a regular basis to verify that operations have not changed and submit written reports of their findings.

Depreciation is at once more difficult than overhead expense to verify and less important for purposes of analysis. Since it is a noncash charge, depreciation is actually of less concern because it does not affect cash flow. On the other hand, its affect on profits can be quite dramatic. The analytical problem emanates from the selection of estimated useful life discussed in chapter 3. Briefly, management can select a life that is conservatively short, thereby lowering profits, or aggressively long, thereby increasing profits. The results may even be changed later, as happened with Bethlehem Steel. Bethlehem Steel announced in the fall of 1987 that it was extending the estimated useful lives of much of its plant and equipment from a modest 12 years to a more liberal 18 years. It not only created earnings in the current year, but, by restatement, changed the prior year's loss to a profit! Although this dramatically improved the firm's income statement, the resulting change in depreciation was probably in the wrong direction from an analytical viewpoint. Regardless whether Bethlehem Steel took the correct route, it would have been useful for the analyst to know the useful-life estimates employed by the competitors in the industry.

Gross Profit and Gross Margin

The cost of goods sold is often expressed as a percentage of total sales. The difference between this percentage and 100 percent is the *gross profit margin*. Gross profit represents a company's profitability based only on its sales compared to its cost of goods sold. For a retailer or wholesaler, gross profit reflects the markup applied to the company's purchases as reflected in its selling price. For a manufacturer, gross profit represents the value added to the raw materials or parts in the manufacturing process. Gross profit is calculated using the following formula:

Net sales – Cost of goods sold = Gross profit.

The gross margin represents the percentage of each dollar of sales that is available to cover the company's other operating expenses. Although the concept is a simple one, its application in the actual operation of a business can be difficult. For instance, most companies sell several products, each of which may have a different cost of goods sold percentage and gross margin. These percentages may vary not only for different products, but also for the same products over time, depending on the competition and general market conditions. Therefore, the analyst only knows how the firm's products are doing on average.

Some believe that analysts should thoroughly investigate the performance of specific products or parts of a firm's operations. Others are not so sure that profit margin analysis is fundamental. This second position states that firms should be free to change *margin strategies* by switching from being high-margin, quality producers to being low-margin, quantity producers if the market is developing in that direction. Moreover, it seems likely that most analysts are unable to determine which of the following firms is riskier:

- A retailer has six stores, three of which are quite profitable and three of which are losing money, with the overall average a relatively low profit margin.
- A retailer has six stores, all of which are marginally profitable, with the overall average a relatively low profit margin.

Only by knowing more about the business than the management itself knows could an analyst reach a conclusion that would be more correct than that reached by management.

The primary idea is that stability and repeatability, issues of quality of earnings, are the most important issues to correlate. For example, if a company does not raise its prices as fast as its costs increase, or if it cuts prices in the face of stable supply costs (to meet competition), the cost of goods sold will increase as a percentage of sales, creating a situation of steadily eroding gross margins. Nevertheless, if sales increase as gross margin decreases, the gross profit will remain stable even though the sales level needed to cover the same level of operating expenses increases.

Sometimes a company with stable operating costs may even initiate a price decrease and accept a lower gross margin in hopes of generating enough additional sales to increase the absolute level of gross profit. Companies continually look for the optimum price—one that the market will support, yet will maximize gross profit on a given sales volume.

Again, the credit analyst can perform the same types of examination with gross profits and gross margins as performed previously for sales. That is, the lender can look at trends over time, industry comparisons, and breakdowns of profitability by product line and location. For example, by common-sizing the income statements for Bud's Sporting Goods as shown in Exhibit 4.5, it becomes clear that at the same time that its sales were increasing, the company's gross profit margin was growing—from 46 percent in 1989 to 50 percent in 1991. Clearly, this is the best possibility.

Common-Sizing and Gross Profit

Exhibit 4.5

Bud's Sporting Goods
Common-Sizing and Gross Profit
For Years Ending June 30
(Dollars in 000s)

	1989	*%*	*1990*	*%*	*1991*	*%*
Sales	$350.0	100%	$400.0	100%	$450.0	100%
Cost of goods sold	190.0	54%	209.0	52%	225.0	50%
Gross profit	160.0	46%	191.0	48%	225.0	50%

Conversly, deterioration in a firm's profit margin concurrent with sales that are remaining level or are slowly growing or declining means greater risk to the lender since profits will probably decline. Only if sales were increasing could an analyst assume that the firm is changing its *strategy* to a high volume, low margin one. Thus, while higher total sales must be achieved to cover the same level of operating expenses, it is impossible to say whether striving for high volume, low margin is a riskier strategy without knowing a great deal about the business and the markets it serves.

Other Operating Expenses

Operating expenses are those incurred by a company in the normal course of conducting its business, other than the just-mentioned expenses of purchasing inventory and direct manufacturing expenses (which constitute cost of goods sold). These operating expenses are often categorized on the income statement as officers' salaries, selling expenses, and general and administrative expenses. The latter is a catchall category including everything from salaries of office staff to postage stamps.

Officers' salaries + Selling expenses + General
and administrative expenses = Operating expenses.

(Note that factory workers' wages are included in cost of goods sold, while management's salaries are considered an operating expense.)

As mentioned previously, manufacturing firms normally allocate a portion of the company's total overhead and administrative costs to cost of goods sold and the remainder of those costs to operating expenses. Retailers and service firms keep all these expenses in operating expenses. The credit analyst may find that a manufacturer has changed the allocation of certain manufacturing costs from cost of goods sold to operating expenses, or vice versa, thus distorting trend comparisons between costs of goods sold and operating expenses. In such cases, the analyst must be cautious about evaluating large swings in gross profit margins, either positive or negative, until a detailed review of the company's expense allocations is made.

If it is available, a detailed breakdown of operating expenses is very useful in analyzing a company's operating expenses. Exhibit 4.6 presents such a breakdown for Bud's Sporting Goods. Ideally, operating costs will be shown for two or more years. These costs can be further categorized for in-depth analysis as *controllable costs* and noncontrollable costs. Controllable costs—which include such items as bonuses, profit-sharing contributions, and a company's travel and entertainment budget—are prone to excessive spending. These types of expenses can escalate because they directly benefit the persons controlling them, the managers. For example, charging excessive rental or lease payments to the company for facilities owned by parties related to the owners or managers of the company is a violation of the firm's financial integrity. If the owner or managers hire family members, the analyst should determine that they make a meaningful contribution to the company's operations.

Noncontrollable costs include utility payments, office salaries, and long-term lease obligations—all the necessary costs of doing business that cannot easily

Exhibit 4.6

Bud's Sporting Goods
Operating Expense Comparisons
For 1989-1991

	1989 Amount	*% of Sales*	*1990 Amount*	*% of Sales*	*1991 Amount*	*% of Sales*
Sales	$350,000	100.0%	$400,000	100.0%	$450,000	100.0%
Operating Expense						
Salaries officers	20,000	5.7%	25,000	6.3%	25,000	5.6%
Salaries other	40,000	11.4%	45,000	11.3%	47,600	10.6%
Payroll taxes	4,500	1.3%	6,000	1.5%	6,200	1.4%
Rent	24,000	6.9%	24,000	6.0%	24,000	5.3%
Auto leasing	10,000	2.9%	10,000	2.5%	9,000	2.0%
Insurance	5,000	1.4%	6,000	1.5%	6,300	1.4%
Repairs and maintenance	2,600	0.7%	3,000	0.8%	2,700	0.6%
Telephone	4,000	1.1%	3,500	0.9%	4,000	0.9%
Travel and entertainment	10,000	2.9%	12,500	3.1%	15,000	3.3%
Profit sharing	5,000	1.4%	7,000	1.8%	12,450	2.8%
Legal	1,000	0.3%	1,000	0.3%	1,350	0.3%
Accounting	2,400	0.7%	3,000	0.8%	3,150	0.7%
Advertising	17,000	4.9%	12,000	3.0%	12,000	2.7%
Depreciation	1,500	0.4%	2,000	0.5%	2,250	0.5%
Total	**$147,000**	**42.0%**	**$160,000**	**40.0%**	**$171,000**	**38.0%**

be changed by management. For example, once an equipment lease is signed, that expense cannot be altered, at least in the near term.

Identifying noncontrollable expenses and controllable expenses, especially in a small, privately held company, helps the credit analyst identify the costs that must be met if the company is to remain in business as opposed to those that could possibly be reduced to improve profitability. Presumably, if management has shown consistent and effective restraint over its controllable expenses in the past, it is likely to continue doing so during a debt repayment period.

Bad debts (such as uncollectible accounts receivable) are classified as an operating expense—a necessary cost of doing business. To provide for losses, companies establish reserves based on actual and projected losses as a percentage of sales. GAAP regulate the methods by which this sales percentage is devised. The amount is then regularly recognized as an expense each period, which maintains the reserve at the required level. The reserve appears on the balance sheet as allowance for bad debts, as discussed in chapter 3. Credit analysts should evaluate the adequacy of the company's method of recognizing bad debts.

While depreciation of plant and equipment is primarily charged to cost of goods sold for a manufacturer, depreciation of equipment used by the sales and administrative sides of all firms is considered as an other operating expense. Retailers charge all their depreciation to operating expenses since they use their equipment for either sales or administration.

Another type of noncash expense is amortization—the recognition of a deferred charge or intangible as an expense over some extended period. Generally, it can be assumed that management is taking as little of amortization as possible, since this expense has no effect on income taxes and just reduces accounting income. Moreover, this noncash expense has no effect on cash flow and is generally a small value.

Operating Expense Analysis

Another way to evaluate a company's effectiveness of control is to look at operating expenses as a percentage of sales. When sales increase faster than operating expenses, the expenses-to-sales ratio decreases, thus showing good expense control. Consistency should also be analyzed by comparing a company's expenses in relation to sales over time. In addition, comparing a company's operating costs-to-sales ratio with that of similar companies or with an industry average may be instructive.

Applying these concepts in an analysis of the operating expenses of Bud's Sporting Goods produces the conclusions shown in Exhibit 4.6.

Rent

Rental expense on Bud's Sporting Goods' facilities is $2,000 per month, and has remained unchanged for three years. The sales growth during that period indicates an increasingly efficient use of the facilities. Because commercial rents are usually based on a long-term lease, a business's rent may not increase or decrease, at least in the short run, with changes in sales volume. Nevertheless, many modern retail store leases are based on a percentage of sales, especially if the establishment is in a shopping mall. If a retailer's lease is approaching its end, the lender needs to be sensitive to the possibility that a renewed lease might increase the rent so much as to threaten the retailer's very existence.

Salaries and Profit Sharing

Bud's Sporting Goods has one owner and hires a number of employees, mainly salesclerks. The owner's salary increased and then decreased slightly as a percent of sales, a favorable trend. There do not appear to be any excessive salaries or unproductive salary expenses for family members.

However, the auto-leasing expense appears to be additional compensation to the owner and family members. Moreover, the profit-sharing contribution is a major expense for this company and has increased sharply. Since the owner has complete control over profit sharing and could use it to benefit himself or the store's employees, the credit analyst should determine the owner's plans for profit-sharing contributions in the future.

Travel and Entertainment

This is one the of the few expense categories that has consistently increased as a percentage of sales. In fact, while sales have increased by 29 percent in a two-year period, travel and entertainment expenses have increased by 50 percent. This trend is cause for the analyst to investigate whether these expense increases are justified or whether they include significant unproductive personal expenses.

Other Operating Expenses

The remaining expenses (all of which come under the category of general and administrative expenses) appear to be reasonable and controlled. As sales volume increased, these expenses increased less rapidly; thus they decreased as a percentage of sales. A greater test of expense control is required when the sales volume decreases. Evidence of such control is shown when expenses decrease at least at the same rate as sales decrease.

Operating Profit

Operating profit represents the profit from the basic operation of the company—that is, manufacturing or acquiring products and then selling them. Thus, operating profit is a key figure in analyzing how efficiently and consistently management has used the company's resources in its primary operations to generate profits.

An operating loss results if a company's expenses exceed its gross profit. Operating profit is calculated as follows:

Gross profit – Operating expenses = Operating profit or loss.

Many analysts believe that the key point with operating profits is that they can be used to compare firms regardless of their financial choices and other indirectly related activities.

OTHER INCOME AND EXPENSE ANALYSIS

Some companies have income other than sales and expenses other than those included in cost of goods sold or operating expenses. After evaluating the operating profit of the company, an analyst should look at the income and expense items that lie outside the normal operations of a business to see if they significantly affect the overall net profitability of the company and whether the probability exists of these items consistently recurring.

Operating profit + Other income – Other expenses – Interest expense = Net profit before tax.

Other Income

Other income is income generated outside the normal operating activities of the company. This income does not result from sales of the company's products or services, but from some peripheral activity. For example, a company may generate other income by renting its excess facilities or equipment to another company. Interest income, profit on the sale of fixed assets, dividend income, and discounts earned are other examples of nonoperating income. Some companies have a dependable source of other income that should be analyzed as a recurring income source. Typical sources of other income include the following:

Rental Income

Rental income is often generated from excess building facilities or equipment. A company with excess capacity that it can rent or lease without interrupting the efficient flow of its operation is wise to do so. The analyst needs to consider whether the income will be a continuing income source or whether the company will soon need to use the space or equipment itself.

Interest Income

Interest income can be generated from excess cash invested in savings deposits or from other investments, such as a loan to another company. If such investments recur, the level of market interest rates will affect the level of income generated.

Profit on the Sale of Fixed Assets

A company can generate additional income by selling its excess fixed assets at a profit. For instance, after upgrading its fixed assets with more-efficient equipment, a company may want to sell its used equipment. A profit results when the sale price exceeds the net book value of the asset sold. This net value is the asset's cost less accumulated depreciation. For example, in 1986 Bud's Sporting Goods sold some equipment for a net profit of $4,000, which is shown as other income on its income statement (Exhibit 4.2).

Dividend Income

Many companies own stock in related operating companies or in publicly traded companies. Any dividends received constitute a source of nonoperating income. Because dividends are based on the profitable operation of another company, without independent evaluation, the analyst may not assume they constitute a dependable source of income in the future.

Discounts Earned

Suppliers often offer cash discounts for prompt payment of money owed. This can benefit companies having the ability to generate cash on a timely basis to meet their maturing obligations, although the level of discounts offered by suppliers is a factor over which the company has little control. While any discounts earned by the company should be included as nonoperating income, or other income, some firms just deduct it from cost of goods sold.

Other Expenses

A company may have *nonoperating expenses* as well as nonoperating income. Such expenses might include interest expense (often shown as a separate item), loss on a sale of fixed assets, loss on a sale of stock or discontinued operations, and discounts allowed.

Loss on the Sale of Fixed Assets

If a company sells any of its fixed assets for below book value, the loss associated with the sale is recognized as a nonoperating expense. When such losses show up on the income statement, an analyst needs to determine if additional losses are to be expected. Additional losses are more likely if the company has consistently underestimated depreciation on the used equipment by overestimating its useful life; they are unlikely if a sudden jump in technology has rendered just a few assets obsolete.

Loss on the Sale of Stock or Discontinued Operations

Stocks held as a current asset are valued at market value at the time the balance sheet is dated, and the loss is posted directly to the income statement. Stocks held for the long term need not affect the income statement, even if their value is increasing or dropping. Any losses result in a direct deduction to net worth until a sale of the asset brings the loss to the income statement. The analyst may want to follow up on such losses with requests for detailed information on the remaining stocks held by the firm and its investment intentions.

A company may also choose to discontinue some of its operations. This usually occurs when certain undertakings have not been as profitable as management would like and the assets can be more efficiently used in some other area of the business. When it decides to discontinue an operation, a company usually establishes a reserve on the balance sheet by estimating what losses will occur in liquidating the related assets and contracts. The analytical problem is to determine whether the company will face additional losses in the future—something that may not be within even management's purview.

Discounts Allowed

A company may allow discounts on prompt payment of its customer accounts, just as it can earn discounts by promptly paying its own suppliers. The resulting expense depends on the level of discounts allowed and the customers' response to it. A company that needs to generate cash quickly may do so by allowing excessive discounts. Thus, an analyst must scrutinize the company's plans for future discounting to determine the probable cost. Some firms hide the extent to which they are offering discounts by netting them against sales and just reporting net sales on the income statement.

Interest Expense

The cost of borrowing money depends both on the company's overall level of borrowing and whether debt is at a fixed or floating rate; in the latter case, the market interest rate at any particular time can be consequential. Therefore, interest expense can fluctuate dramatically, depending on the company's borrowing requirements and interest rates.

Interest expense is rarely a deciding factor in the success or failure of a firm because it usually amounts to only a small fraction of revenues or of major expenses like cost of goods sold. However, when making a new loan, the lender should consider the increased interest expense and its effect on the company's profits.

Income Taxes

Provision for income taxes is deducted from a company's profit figures to get to net profit after tax. If the financial statements are prepared using generally accepted accounting principles (GAAP), the provision for taxes shown on the income statement and the actual cash taxes paid or payable usually differ. This issue was discussed in chapter 3 under the deferred tax account.

Because many factors affect the amount of taxes reported on the income statement, making useful comparisons between companies is difficult. Review of a company's ability to manage its tax burden and to project the impact of taxes on future profitability requires a detailed understanding of many complex tax issues, but foremost among them is a review of the cash taxes paid. The major difference between the provision for taxes and the cash taxes paid usually results from the firm's using different depreciation methods for tax purposes than for GAAP purposes. The cash taxes paid figure can be crudely derived by deducting the deferred taxes add-back from the statement of cash flows (discussed in the next chapter) or, if that statement is missing, by calculating the difference between the deferred tax accounts in the most recent comparable balance sheet periods.

Tax expense is one item that should be looked at as a percentage of profit before tax as well as a percentage of sales. The computation of the *cash-paid tax rate* provides a starting point for investigation. Some analysts would like to refer to this percentage as the *effective tax rate*, but GAAP mandate that the word *effective* be used for the tax percentage as dictated by the IRS, reduced only for items like investment tax credits (ITC) or credits for foreign income taxes paid. The cash-paid tax rate percentage is more useful for trend analysis than the provision for taxes percentage is, but it is advantageous to know if this expense was affected by a one-time occurrence in analyzing historical profitability since this ratio is frequently used to validate projected tax expense.

Finally, management occasionally invests in tax shelters. These investments are structured so that the tax deductions resulting from them are greater than the taxable income generated by them. Therefore, the deductions in excess of the taxable income cause a deferment of taxes on other activities. While this sounds attractive, the tax shelter investments occasionally are highly risky ventures, like financing a movie. The firm might lose its entire investment; thus, in the end the tax shelter may not produce much overall benefit for the firm. Finding such an investment in a business firm would not be a plus on the credit side.

Net Profit After Tax Analysis

After deducting corporate income taxes, *net profit after tax*—the bottom line—remains. Tracing the trend in net profits over a period of years provides insight into the consistency with which management has operated the company in the past, giving some basis for assessing the likely future profitability of the business. A company's profit record should also be compared with that of similar businesses and with industry averages. This comparison can help the credit analyst put the company's results in perspective.

Net profit before tax – Provision for income taxes = Net profit after tax.

S corporations were discussed in chapter 2. These companies, like partnerships (or sole proprietorships), are taxed to their owners. Unfortunately, this circumstance renders comparing corporations after taxes less valid. The analyst must make sure that companies under comparison are in the same tax status.

Management's Articulation of Its Strategy

Critical to the analysis of the income statement is determining management's *strategy*. Previously mentioned are the distinctions between

- aggressive versus conservative management of working capital strategies, and
- high volume, low price versus high price, low volume sales strategies.

Current analytical theory holds that these strategies are not inherently better or worse, because the industry and market conditions in which a firm finds itself may require a particular strategy for success. If a recession occurs, even a conservative management will wish to increase its credit terms to accommodate its better customers and maintain sales. It is important to distinguish this use of credit from the groundless granting of extended credit terms to untried customers for the purpose of maintaining rapid growth in sales. This reference of strategies to market connections is distinct from traditional analysis, which believes that conservative management strategies are always the best.

A supporter of the current theory is Clyde P. Stickney in his highly regarded book *Financial Statement Analysis: A Strategic Perspective*. Dismissing traditional theory, which disparages the low margin, high volume plan, he says management must stay alert for the need to change strategy in the future. The crux for management is to determine which strategy is required to survive and thrive given current market conditions, and then to implement that strategy.

In any case, many analysts believe that the purpose of statement analysis is to judge management's performance and abilities. Comparing the performance shown in the income statement with management's strategy as revealed through interviews or letters to stockholders can validate management or raise troubling doubts about its intentions.

Rather than analyzing details of products and markets, determining the adaptability and stability of management is key to identifying levels of risk in a proposed loan. Therefore, to get insights into management's strategy and experience, the loan officer needs to ask management questions that elicit discussions of how it conquered previous hard times, the primary threat to debt repayment. If management has never had or dealt with hard times, the firm is risky, no matter what its present strategy.

Sales Comparative Analysis

To put in perspective the revenue figure shown on an income statement, compare current sales with sales in previous periods and with competitors' sales growth. A company's annual sales figures are easier to evaluate when they are compared with previous years' sales and with sales of other companies in the same industry over the same period—the meaning of trend analysis. This comparison may indicate increasing, stagnant, or erratic sales behavior. Level or increasing sales and proportionate profits is key to favorable lending decisions. Comparing sales data for Bud's Sporting Goods (Exhibit 4.7) shows that the company's sales increased 14.3 percent in 1990 and 12.5 percent in 1991. Moreover, Bud's profits are rising more than proportionately, indicating an improvement in its ability to repay debt.

Change in Sales

Exhibit 4.7

Bud's Sporting Goods
Change in Sales
For Years Ending June 30
(Dollars in 000s)

	1989	*1990*		*1991*	
	Amount	*Amount*	*% Change*	*Amount*	*% Change*
Sales	$350.0	$400.0	14.3%	$450.0	12.5%
Net profit after tax	$5.3	$10.6	100%	$23.1	117.9%

Besides making internal comparisons, compare a company's sales growth with those of comparable companies. Compared to its performance in previous periods, a company's current performance may show an improvement. Yet when compared with the performance of the industry as a whole, the company's current performance may be subpar. For example, a company that has increased its sales by 20 percent in a year's time looks good until the analyst learns that the market grew by 50 percent. In this case, a market study might yield information about specific competitors that would help the credit analyst understand the cause of the company's relatively poor performance.

Seasons and Cyclical Factors

When making either internal or external sales comparisons, an analyst should use income statements covering comparable periods because *seasonality* and other *cyclical factors* may cause wide variations in sales from period to period. For example, it serves no purpose to compare revenues for a three-month period during the peak of a company's selling season with sales for a three-month period at the low point of the company's seasonal cycle. However, the key issue is peak versus low point, not any particular months of the year. A construction firm in the South with business year round could not be compared with another firm in the North that only had business during the summer months.

Similarly, for a company in a *cyclical* industry, comparisons of one company's sales trends with those of other companies may be very misleading if different time periods are compared. In an economic downturn, sales figures of a cyclical company would be expected to be lower than in prosperous years. Similarly, such a company's sales should show dramatic increases as the economy emerges from a recession. Thus it may be difficult to assess the performance of a cyclical company except by using annual statements of similar time periods to compare its performance with that of its competitors.

Market Share

Market share is a measurement of an individual firm's percentage of the total market for a particular product or service. Frequently, the geographic breadth of the market in question is given to further specify the context. For example, an analyst might talk about the market for automobiles in a local city or the whole metropolitan area. Knowledge of the market for a particular company is helpful to an analyst because it indicates the firm's success or its power to affect the market either through superior quality of product (or service), design, price, or consumer loyalty or through some incidence of monopoly.

The analyst's goal is to determine whether a change in a company's sales figures reflects a change in the overall market for the company's products or in the company's individual market share. In a rapidly growing market, for instance, a company's sales might increase while, at the same time, its market share decreases; thus, its increased sales might not be that positive. In a market with little or no growth, a company's sales growth may be entirely the result of increased market share, a plus resulting from good management decisions or other indicators of the successful matching of the company's products or services to its target market.

The extent of market control is critical to bond analysts at Standard & Poor's. They see lack of market share as added risk; if a firm has financial problems, but has a significant share for its market, changes in ratings are slowed and vice versa. Once established, consumer loyalty is difficult to change, and owning market share has helped many firms experiencing problems to get the breathing space they need to correct them. For example, a falling market share in the growing personal computer market eventually spelled trouble for even giant IBM, causing the firm to restructure and lay off 100,000 employees in 1992. (IBM's share contracted from 60 percent in 1987 to 28 percent in 1992.) Standard & Poor's cut the firm's bond rating, even though IBM's market share in traditional market of mainframe computers remained high. Unfortunately, that market was contracting and becoming more price conscious, and management was initially slow in adjusting to the changing market conditions.

Cost of Goods Sold Comparative Analysis

From the discussion above, it is apparent that to compare cost of goods sold (or profit margins) a credit analyst needs to know what inventory valuation method a company uses and also that comparisons of companies using different valuation methods may be misleading. Since a change in valuation method can significantly affect the cost of goods sold and gross margin percentages, an analyst must be alert to a change in inventory valuation method and take it into account when analyzing a significant improvement or deterioration in the cost of goods sold as a percentage of total sales.

As long as a company consistently uses the same valuation method over successive operating periods, improvement or deterioration in the company's profit margin can be a meaningful indication of the company's performance. Nevertheless, the use of FIFO in a firm with stable or growing inventories indicates that management is artificially boosting profits in inflationary times. In view of the higher taxes being paid, this practice is detrimental to the company's shareholders and creditors. In the long run, because of the higher taxes being paid, the creditor is being harmed because there is less of an equity cushion.

The conflict between the two methods opens the door to converting between the two to get more comparable figures. Consider the possibilities. GAAP require the company to provide in the footnotes information concerning the LIFO reserve so that the balance sheet may be updated with more current costs of the remaining inventory. This is done because LIFO charges current costs to the income statement—the proper approach to reflect current income unaffected by inventory holding gains.

With two years of GAAP financial statements, it is possible to combine the effects of the LIFO reporting and convert it to FIFO. Unfortunately, there is no information available to convert from FIFO to LIFO, the convention that reports income with greater consistency in times of changing inflation rates. Thus, converting LIFO to FIFO is not recommended, even if doing so would make comparing one firm to another one easier. Instead, when reviewing a firm that uses LIFO, the analyst should find a comparable firm that uses LIFO, because this convention is the better estimator of the current cost of goods sold.

SUMMARY OF IMPORTANT CONCEPTS

The income statement is of key importance in any examination because it shows sales, which are the basis of a company's existence, and profits, which determine a company's long-term viability. Spreading and common-sizing a company's past income statements facilitates comparisons over time and with industry averages. All income statement accounts are shown as a percentage of sales. Before beginning an in-depth review of a company's revenues and expenses, the analyst should already have a good understanding of the type of business in which the company is engaged and the marketplace, including sensitivity to economic cycles, seasonality, and product life cycles.

Income statement analysis begins with revenue analysis. This entails comparisons of a company's sales over time, of its sales with those of competitors, and of its current revenue projections with those previously submitted to the lender.

Expense analysis, the next step, involves assessing two basic categories of expenses—cost of goods sold and operating expenses. The cost of goods sold consists of inventory purchases for a wholesaler or retailer and of expenses for raw materials, direct labor, and certain manufacturing, depreciation and overhead for a manufacturer. In analyzing a company's cost of goods sold, consider how the company counts its inventory (perpetual versus periodic inventory systems) and how it evaluates the inventory (FIFO versus LIFO methods). The calculation of cost of goods sold enables the lender to calculate the company's gross profit margin, a key figure in assessing the company's efficiency and consistency of operation.

Next look at the company's operating expenses—including officers' salaries, selling expenses, and general and administrative expenses—to see whether any expenses appear excessive and to capture trends over time by comparing changes in sales to changes in expenses. The lender will also analyze a company's expenses in terms of controllable versus noncontrollable costs. Once changes are isolated, the lender must seek explanations for the changes.

Then look at any nonoperating income and expense items that are unrelated to the company's basic operations to determine whether any significant amounts are likely to be recurring or nonrecurring. Interest expense, often shown separately on the income statement, is an expense to which the lender should pay particular attention. Finally, analyze the company's income tax expense and its after-tax profits.

Income statement examination provides the credit analyst with a basic understanding of a company's operating performance and management's operating strategies (generating sales, pricing its products or services, controlling expenses, and, most importantly, making a profit), which, in turn, assists in the next step of the financial statement analysis—gaining an understanding of the company's cash flow, as shown by the statement of cash flow, reviewed in the next chapter.

Important Terms to Define

income statement
interim statements
market share
common-sizing
allowances
cyclical factors
perpetual inventory
LIFO
LIFO windfall
average inventory
inventory holding gains
strategy
controllable costs
other income
provision for income taxes
annual statements
spreadsheet
accrual
seasonality
returns
cost of goods sold
periodic method
FIFO
inventory holding gains profit
overhead expense
gross profit margin
operating expenses
operating profit

Dependable Doors Case Study

1. Spread and common-size the income statement numbers.
2. Do a three-year trend analysis on the income statement.
3. Does the company have sufficient profitability to service its debt?
4. How does Dependable Doors compare to the industry with respect to its income statement?
5. Do the notes to the financial statement provide any information that can be useful in an examination of the income statement?

The answers to the Dependable Doors questions appear in the appendix.

Engraph Case Study

1. Spread and common-size the income statement numbers.
2. Do a three-year trend analysis on the income statement.
3. Demonstrate the difference in profitability for Engraph using the LIFO versus the FIFO method of inventory valuation.
4. Does the company have sufficient profitability to service its long-term debt?

The Cash Flow Statement

LEARNING OBJECTIVES

After studying this chapter, you will be able to

- prepare a derived sources and uses of cash statement,
- explain why sources and uses of cash always equal each other,
- use a statement of cash flows in financial statement analysis,
- identify the questions a statement of cash flows should answer, and
- derive the capacity of the firm to repay debt.

INTRODUCTION

The *statement of cash flows* and its predecessors have had many names and have been presented in many different formats. The history of this financial statement is relatively new, and its structure and format are still under discussion and subject to change. The most recent version approved by generally accepted accounting principles (GAAP) is the Statement of Financial Accounting Standards (SFAS) No. 95, published in November 1987 by the Financial Accounting Standards Board (FASB). FASB is one of two authorities of GAAP, the other being the Securities and Exchange Commission (SEC).

A controversy is underway between public accountants and financial analysts to produce a statement that will provide real insight into the cash flows of a firm. The impetus for this statement is that accrual accounting's focus on net income has gradually directed itself toward common stock evaluation and away from determining debt repayment capacity—which is of most interest to lenders. Lenders have gradually developed their own presentation, and the latest generation of this effort is the statement of cash flows.

Before GAAP became a provider of the statement of cash flows, lenders worked out a rudimentary statement of cash flows known as the *sources and uses of cash statement*, the sources and applications of cash statement, or other names, usually substituting the word *funds* for *cash*. Whatever the format, the statement's purpose was to determine a company's capacity to generate cash internally and, thereby, to identify its capacity for repaying debt.

The *statement of cash flows* considers all the economic resources available to a company. It presents the flow of cash resulting from how a company's management has deployed economic resources over a given period, usually a year, and it allows the lender to evaluate managerial decisions regarding cash. Similar to the way the income statement identifies the flow of revenues and expenses to income, the statement of cash flows determines the total resources employed, how they became available, and how efficiently they were used.

Loan officers have said, "Loans are paid off with profits." Why should analysts not look to net income for debt repayment capacity? Because the accountant's interest has diverged from the analyst's interest. The accountant's interest is to derive wealth generation and identify long-term viability on the income statement. The analyst's concern is for the firm to evidence sufficient ability to produce cash to enable it to repay debt and to invest in new equipment as well as in current assets to support growth and stay solvent. Some of these problems are reviewed in chapter 4:

- ❒ Accrual accounting accepts as revenues the delivery of products or services in exchange for increases in accounts receivable rather than for received cash.

- Accrual accounting accepts the storing of cash outlays for inventories and labor in the inventory account as well as for plant and equipment assets in the fixed asset accounts. Moreover, other cash outlays for services with benefits anticipated to extend into the future are also held as assets on the balance sheet rather than expensed.
- There are charges to the income statement for expenses that did not incur any outlay of cash (or incurred less cash outlay), including (1) depreciation—the amortization of plant and equipment expense over its useful life—(2) provision for taxes, avoiding the impact on cash taxes payable because of modified accelerated cost recovery, and (3) amortization of capitalized assets that incurred their cash outlays in the past.

The goal of this chapter is to show how understanding cash flows can help the lender better predict whether the firm seeking a loan has the capacity to repay debt. First, the chapter looks at how to prepare a rudimentary cash flow statement, the sources and uses statement; later the chapter explains how to use the statement of cash flows in financial statement analysis.

SIGNIFICANCE OF THE STATEMENT OF CASH FLOWS

The primary goal of a company's managers is to increase sales and reduce costs. Along with supervision of marketing and production come administration of accounts receivable policy, inventory controls (and expansion), accounts payable policy, and sources of short-term financing. Credit policies may be liberalized, resulting in increases in accounts receivable, and abundant inventory may be kept on hand to support consumer demand. Accounts payable policies focus on improving supplier relations and, possibly, on obtaining discounts for prompt payment. Almost every decision management makes involves the use of cash funds, including decisions about

- capital investment outlays (both for maintaining the level of productive capacity and improving it),
- permanent increases to working capital caused by growth (expansion entails increases in accounts receivable and inventory),
- research and development expenses (matching revenues may not be forthcoming for a significant time), and
- debt servicing and repayment capacity (identifying sustainable rates of growth without changing relative debt levels, and also distinguishing recurring income and cash flow to allow paying bills as they come due).

With these issues in mind, SFAS No. 95 chose the following three subdivisions for this most recent presentation of the statement of cash flows. Following each subdivision are the questions that should be answered by it.

Exhibit 5.1

SFAS No. 95 Subdivisions

Statement of Cash Flows Subdivision	*Questions This Section Should Answer:*
1 **Operating**—measures the cash generated by the current operating cycle including short-term changes in current accounts requiring cash.	How is the company's growth or lack of growth affecting its operating cash needs? Are working capital assets being used to fund long-term assets or pay off long-term debt?
2 **Investment**—measures long-term increases in fixed assets, other long-term investments and proceeds from disposing of these assets.	Is production capacity expanding and at what rate?
3 **Financing**—Measures cash flows from debt, its repayment, proceeds from and payments to shareholders.	How fast can the company grow from internally generated cash? Is the capital structure of long-term debt and equity improving or deteriorating? How much outside funding is needed? How is the company financing its activities? Is cash flow substantial enough to repay long-term debt maturities or is old debt being merely refunded? What funding needs can be anticipated?

Cash Flows from Operations (Netted for Changes in Current Accounts)

Cash flows from operations is the first category on the statement of cash flows. It looks at cash coming into the organization through sales and receivables. Next it looks at cash being consumed in paying for supplies and services. Finally, it derives a net cash from operations value, which theoretically represents the sum total that management can use for the next two areas, investments and financing.

Calculations

Specifically, SFAS No. 95 includes in this area

- activities "normally involved in producing and delivering goods and services," including primarily the collection of accounts receivable and both short- and long-term notes receivable from customers,
- cash expenditures for acquiring materials and making payments to employees for services, including net payments to accounts payable,
- interest expense (in contrast with the income statement presentation, which shows interest expense as a nonoperating expense), and
- extraordinary items, including lawsuit settlements and insurance claims—an unfortunate addition because it disturbs the identification of the recurring cash flows in which lenders are primarily interested. Consequently, the credit analyst must adjust the subtotals in the statement of cash flows to determine the firm's recurring capability of repaying debt.

Funds from Operations

In contrast to including all changes to the current accounts in this subtotal, an argument may be made that a subtotal should be taken before those changes. This subtotal would include net income plus depreciation and other noncash charges, excluding changes in the current asset and current liability accounts. This subtotal is called *funds from operations* and was shown in the previous GAAP- required statement of changes in financial condition. The argument for taking this subtotal is based on the hypothesis that, regardless of the spontaneous tendency for these accounts to grow when sales grow, competent managers have control over their receivables, inventories, and payables policies.

This argument came under serious attack because the management of the Chrysler Corporation lost control of its inventories and receivables in 1978. If such a large company could not control inventories, how could others? However, it turned out that, as a result of near bankruptcy, Chrysler's board of directors made Lee Iacocca chairman. In turn he fired many of the top financial managers, a consequence of their incompetence—they *should* have had control over current assets, and funds from operations *should* be a valid subtotal.This subtotal—without changes in current accounts—was the first subtotal in the statement of changes in financial position, the predecessor to the statement of cash flow. Much debt-related research has been done on the value of funds from operations in predicting debt repayment capacity. It is used in the spreadsheet for the statement of cash flows and in the next chapter on ratios.

Cash Flows from Investing Activities (Sometimes Called Net Free Cash)

The second category on the statement of cash flows, *cash flows from investing activities*, includes cash flows arising from any sale or acquisition of fixed assets. According to SFAS No. 95, cash flows from investing activities includes "making and collecting loans and acquiring and disposing of debt or equity instruments and property, plant and equipment and other productive assets . . . held for or used in the production of goods or services by the enterprise (other than materials that are part of the enterprise's inventory)."

Calculations

Specifically, SFAS No. 95 includes in this area

- cash receipts from collections or sales of loans, debt or equity instruments of other entities, and returns of investment in those instruments;
- cash disbursements for loans and for payments to acquire debt or equity of other entities; and
- payments at the time of purchase or soon before or after purchase to acquire property, plant and equipment, and other productive assets.

Net Free Cash Flow

Some analysts believe that, rather than the cash flow from operations subtotal, mentioned above, the full inclusion of net capital expenditures is a better measure of operating cash flow. This subtotal, called net free cash flow, is based upon the concept that a firm has to replace its equipment as it wears out, and that frequently these purchases are committed so far in advance that short-term changing of them is not practical. The subtotal of this section is called net free cash because the remainder is what is normally available for providing returns to lenders (interest and principal payments) and stockholders (dividends).

In contrast, an argument can be made that the purpose of this section is solely to determine whether and by how much the enterprise is changing its production capabilities. Further, some evidence indicates that competent management can, in stressful times, postpone its capital expenditures.

Cash Flows from Financing Activities

Perhaps *cash flows from financing activities* is the section to which the lender is most drawn. Here the inflows and outflows of cash from and to owners and lenders are recorded. This flow of cash includes

- proceeds of equity issues or of bonds, mortgages, notes, and other short- or long-term borrowings and

- payments to owners, including dividends, and principal repayments to lenders.

Net Cash Flow

The result of all these classifications is a number that reconciles with the change in the cash and short-term marketable securities from one period to the next on the balance sheet.

DERIVED STATEMENT OF SOURCES AND USES PREPARATION

If the analyst does not receive a certified financial statement from the prospective borrower, it is possible that a statement of cash flows will not be automatically provided. To many analysts, a statement of cash flows is essential for valid financial statement analysis. If repeated requests do not produce a statement of cash flows, as a last recourse the analyst can prepare a simplified, rough statement from information contained in the income statement and balance sheet, including the footnotes.

There are serious drawbacks to this derived statement, frequently called a *statement of sources and uses*. It is important for an analyst to resist the temptation to consider this statement to be a superb alternative to the statement of cash flows because, without information directly from the firm, the analyst's calculations will result only in an approximation and should be viewed in that context, with caution.

The process of creating a statement of sources and uses entails categorizing all of the differences between the balance sheet accounts from one year to the next and the flows indicated on the income statement as sources or uses of cash. A completed statement of sources and uses must balance—thus the basic equation is

Sources of cash = Uses of cash.

Identifying Sources and Uses

The first step in creating a statement of sources and uses is to categorize changes in a company's balance sheet accounts as sources and uses of cash. For example, if a firm reduces the credit terms it offers to customers and, as a consequence, reduces its accounts receivable, it has saved cash. This is evident because the firm's customers have to pay the firm cash sooner than they otherwise would have. Thus, a reduction in an asset account (such as accounts receivable) constitutes a source of cash, while an increase in an asset account constitutes a use of cash.

IMP.

Any increase in liabilities (such as bank debt) constitutes a source of cash, while a decrease in liabilities constitutes a use of cash. This is evident, for example, in that borrowing money (increasing liabilities) from a bank generates cash for the firm. Similarly, any increase in equity (such as selling new stock) constitutes a source of cash, while a decrease in equity constitutes a use of cash. Exhibit 5.2 classifies how increases and decreases in assets, liabilities, and equity may be understood in terms of sources and uses of cash.

Exhibit 5.2

Balance Sheet Changes

Sources of Funds: Examples	*Uses of Funds: Examples*
Increase in assets—a reduction in accounts receivable.	**Increase in assets**—an increase in inventory or a purchase of fixed assets.
Increase in equity—increases in the reserve for deferred taxes.	**Decrease in equity**—the payment of dividends.
Increase in liabilities—an increase in accounts payable or in long-term debt.	**Decrease in liabilities**—a reduction in bank debt.

Preparing a Sources and Uses Statement

Net Changes to the Balance Sheet

This section illustrates the steps in preparing a statement of sources and uses. It begins by comparing a company's two most-recent fiscal-year balance sheets and labeling each change in the asset, liability, and net worth accounts as a source or use of cash. Exhibit 5.3 shows a comparative balance sheet for the Garcia-Duran Design Company as of 31 December 1990 and 1991.

In the change column, show the net difference between the value of each account as of those two dates and also the direction of change. Each change should be labeled as a source or use of cash (based on the information in Exhibit 5.2). Because the change column reflects the net result of all cash flows through a balance sheet account during the course of a year, the source or use designation represents the net change in the account for the period. For example, Garcia-Duran's cash balance declined from $31,000 at the end of 1990 to $12,000 at the end of 1991, a decrease of $19,000. This decrease in an asset account represents a source of additional cash to the company. The $163,000 increase in accounts receivable (from $543,000 to $706,000) constitutes an increase in assets and, therefore, a use of cash. The increase in inventory is designated a use of cash for the same reason.

The increases in the liability accounts—notes payable to banks, accounts payable, and accruals—should all be labeled as sources of cash. The decreases in liability accounts, such as the $1,000 decrease in long-term debt, should be

Exhibit 5.3

Garcia-Duran Design Company
Presentation of Net Changes
Balance Sheets for December 31
(in thousands of dollars)

	1990	*1991*	*Change*	*Type*
Assets				
Cash	31	12	19	Source
Accounts receivable—net	543	706	163	Use
Inventory	400	525	125	Use
Total current assets	974	1,243		
Property, plant and equipment	180	179	1	Source
Reserve for depreciation	89	99	10	Source
Fixed assets—net	91	80		
Investments in affiliates	29	35	6	Use
Other assets	11	12	1	Use
Total noncurrent assets	131	127		
Total assets	1,105	1,370		
Liabilities				
Notes payable to banks	230	410	180	Source
Accounts payable	237	290	53	Source
Accruals	30	42	12	Source
Current-year income taxes	8	5	3	Use
Total current liabilities	505	747		
Long-term debt	26	25	1	Use
Subordinated debt	101	101		
Total long-term debt	127	126		
Total debt	632	873		
Reserve for deferred income taxes	129	147	18	Source
Net Worth				
Preferred stock	9	9		
Common stock and paid-in surplus	105	105		
Retained earnings	261	267	6	Source
Less: Treasury stock	(31)	(31)		
Net worth	344	350		
Total liabilities and net worth	1,105	1,370		

labeled a use of cash. Similarly, the $6,000 increase in retained earnings shown in the net worth section of the balance sheet should be labeled a source of cash. Since there were no net changes in some of the company's accounts—for example, subordinated debt and most of the components of net worth—no net flow of cash occurred, and no source or use of cash was created in these accounts.

The next step is to verify that the sum of all sources of cash equals the sum of all uses of cash. If total sources and uses of cash do not tally, a calculation error has been made.

Incorporating into the Sources and Uses Income Statement Items

Net changes in balance sheet accounts actually conceal some cash flows; for example, the increase in retained earnings is a result of profits as well as of any dividends paid. Certain other information needed to construct a more complete sources and uses statement can be picked up from the income statement, including net profit after tax, dividends, depreciation, and purchase or sale of fixed assets. A comparative income statement for Garcia-Duran for 1990 and 1991 is shown as Exhibit 5.4.

Exhibit 5.4

Comparative Income Statement

Garcia-Duran Design Company
Income Statement
for the Years Ended December 31
(in thousands of dollars)

	1990	*1991*
Net sales	1,648	2,142
Cost of goods sold	1,125	1,500
Gross profit	523	642
Total operating expense	444	577
Operating profit	79	65
Other income	6	8
Other expense	21	30
Profit before tax	64	43
Income tax	26	16
Net profit after tax	38	27

In the case of Garcia-Duran, 1991 shows net profit after tax of $27,000 (a source of cash). To reconcile the net profit after tax with the change in retained earnings previously identified, dividends can be derived by using the following calculation:

Dividends = Beginning retained earnings + Net income after taxes – Ending retained earnings.

Since net worth increased by only $6,000 when earnings were $27,000, dividends in the amount of $21,000 are derived for Garcia-Duran. Frequently, in the absence of a statement of cash flows, a firm's income statement does not break out the depreciation amount; this makes it is necessary to attempt to separate depreciation from the change in net fixed assets shown on the balance sheet. To illustrate, suppose a company both purchased a $10,000 piece of machinery and expensed a total of $10,000 in depreciation for the year on all its fixed assets. The fixed asset account net of depreciation, as shown in a comparison of balance sheet accounts, would remain unchanged since the $10,000 source of cash attributable to depreciation would in effect cancel out the $10,000 use of cash created by the purchase of the new machine. The change in fixed assets is calculated as follows:

Net purchase (or sale) of fixed assets = Ending net fixed assets – Beginning net fixed assets + Derived depreciation.

In the case of Garcia-Duran, the balance sheet comparison (Exhibit 5.3) shows a decrease in net fixed assets of $11,000 during 1991. Depreciation is derived by looking at the reserve for depreciation increase by $10,000 in 1991. By treating depreciation as a separate source of cash, the actual decrease to fixed assets during 1991 is seen to be only $1,000 ($80,000 – $91,000 + $10,000).

Of course this formula does not take into account the possibility that Garcia-Duran may have sold a large block of fixed assets and purchased just $1,000 less than it sold, the indicated net change in fixed assets account after depreciation.

In addition to these dividend and fixed asset calculations, additional trouble spots are likely to surface during preparation of the sources and uses statement, particularly with stock transactions and long-term debt and current maturities of long-term debt:

- Stock Transactions—Calculate the change in net worth with profit/loss and dividends, using the formula above. If the equation does not balance, stock was bought or sold.
- Long-term Debt and Current Maturities of Long-term Debt—Add the change in both categories together and show as one financing flow.

Summary

Since these transactions that affect two fixed asset accounts are not recorded in a statement like the income statement, which records all of the transactions into the accounts receivable account (because they also represent sales), the lender's analysis is very likely missing information by not having Garcia-Duran supply a statement of cash flows. This illustrates the critical problem for the analyst who tries to calculate the cash flow from net numbers: the compensating flows that cancel each other out tell less than the whole story. Exhibit 5.5 is a sources and uses statement prepared on the basis of the above calculations. The next section incorporates a full explanation of the Garcia-Duran statement of cash flows.

Sources and Uses Statement

Exhibit 5.5

Garcia-Duran Design Company
Sum of Sources and Uses of Funds
for the Year Ended December 31
(in thousands of dollars)

Source of Funds		*Use of Funds*	
Net income	27	Dividends	21
Cash	19	Accounts receivable—net	163
Fixed assets sale	1	Inventory	125
Notes payable to banks	180	Investments in affiliates	6
Accounts payable	53	Other assets	1
Accruals	12	Current-year income taxes	3
Reserve for deferred taxes	18	Long-term debt	1
Depreciation	10		
Total sources	320	Total uses	320

CASH FLOW ANALYSIS—SFAS NO. 95

The statement of sources and uses of cash contains much valuable information, and it can enable the credit analyst to identify, quantify, and evaluate what sources of cash a company has and what uses the company makes of that cash. What that information implies about the company's present condition and future viability is less certain. Financial analysts believe this uncertainty results from the

- lack of gross flows to accounts in the presentation and the
- lack of structure in organizing the flows.

While the presentations of nonaccrual flows discussed above had been in use by analysts for many years, the Financial Accounting Standards Board (FASB), primarily at the request of lenders, determined to improve upon the calculation and presentation of the information. From 1981 throught 1986, FASB issued preliminary papers (called Exposure Drafts) discussing the concepts for the present standard.

Direct vs. Indirect Presentation

Despite many areas of agreement, some problems appeared to be difficult to solve, including the major one of deciding which cash flows to report gross and which ones to report net. For example, reporting gross flows of all of the transactions in a money market account would not add useful information for the analyst. On the other hand, just reporting the net purchases of plant and equipment could obscure substantive changes in the composition of the firm's fixed assets. This dialogue is characterized as the *direct method* (reporting most flows on a gross basis) versus the *indirect method* (reporting most flows on a net basis). For nonfinancial firms, the direct method was favored by the commercial banks surveyed by the FASB circulation memorandum, although the nonfinancial firms themselves did not wish to report in that method.

In the Statement of Financial Accounting Standards, the debate was expressed as follows:

> 107. The principal advantage of the *direct method* is that it shows operating cash receipts and payments. Knowledge of the specific sources of operating cash receipts and the purposes for which operating cash payments were made in past periods may be useful in estimating future operating cash flows. The relative amounts of major classes of revenues and expenses and their relationship to other items in the financial statements are presumed to be more useful than information only about their arithmetic sum—net income—in assessing enterprise performance. Likewise, amounts of major classes of operating cash receipts and payments presumably would be more useful than information only about their arithmetic sum—net cash flow from operating activities—in assessing an enterprise's ability to generate sufficient cash from operating activities to pay its debt, to reinvest in its operations, and to make distributions to its owners.
>
> 108. The principal advantage of the *indirect method* is that it focuses on the differences between net income and net cash flow from operating activities. Concepts Statement 1, paragraph 43, states that:
>
>> *The primary focus of financial reporting is information about an enterprise's performance provided by measures of earnings [comprehensive income] and its components. Investors, creditors, and others who are concerned with assessing the prospects for enterprise net cash inflows are especially interested in that information. Their interest in an enterprise's future cash flows . . . leads primarily to an interest in information about its earnings [comprehensive income] rather than information directly about its cash flows. Financial statements that show only cash receipts and payments during a short period, such as a year, cannot adequately indicate whether or not an enterprise's performance is successful.*
>
> Some investors and creditors may assess future cash flows in part by first estimating future income based in part on reports of past income and then converting those future income estimates to estimates of future cash flows by allowing for leads and lags between cash flows and income. Information about similar leads and lags in the past are likely to be helpful in that process.

Identifying differences between income items and related cash flows also can assist investors who want to identify the differences between enterprises in the measurement and recognition of noncash items that affect income.

109. Many providers of financial statements have said that it would be costly for their companies to report gross operating cash receipts and payments. They said that they do not presently collect information in a manner that will allow them to determine amounts such as cash received from customers or cash paid to suppliers directly from their accounting systems.

110. The Exposure Draft said that the Board recognized the advantages of both approaches and concluded that neither method provided benefits sufficient to justify requiring one and prohibiting the other. Enterprises therefore would have been permitted to use either method.

111. A majority of respondents to the Exposure Draft asked the Board to require use of the direct method. Those respondents, most of whom were commercial lenders, generally said that amounts of operating cash receipts and payments are particularly important in assessing an enterprise's external borrowing needs and its ability to repay borrowings. They indicated that creditors are more exposed to fluctuations in net cash flow from operating activities than to fluctuations in net income and that information on the amounts of operating cash receipts and payments is important in assessing those fluctuations in net cash flow from operating activities. They also pointed out that the direct method is more consistent with the objective of a statement of cash flows—to provide information about cash receipts and cash payments—than the indirect method, which does not report operating cash receipts and payments.

118. The Board believes that many enterprises may well be able to determine amounts of operating cash receipts and payments at the minimum level of detail that this Statement encourages . . . indirectly at reasonable cost by the procedure discussed in the foregoing paragraphs. But few, if any, companies have experimented with that procedure, and the degree of difficulty encountered in applying it undoubtedly would vary depending on the nature of an enterprise's operations and the features of its current accounting system.

Conclusion on Reporting Net Cash Flow from Operating Activities

119. The Board believes that both the direct and the indirect methods provide potentially important information. The more

comprehensive and presumably more useful approach would be to use the direct method in the statement of cash flows and to provide a reconciliation of net income and net cash flow from operating activities in a separate schedule—thereby reaping the benefits of both methods while maintaining the focus of the statement of cash flows on cash receipts and payments. This Statement therefore encourages enterprises to follow that approach. *But most providers and users of financial statements have little or no experience and only limited familiarity with the direct method, while both have extensive experience with the indirect method. Not only are there questions about the ability of enterprises to determine gross amounts of operating cash receipts and payments, as already discussed, but also little information is available on which specific categories of operating cash receipts and payments would be most meaningful.*

(The italic emphasis has been added throughout.)

A GAAP-prescribed statement of cash flows is shown in Exhibit 5.6; this is the indirect method, starting as it does with net income. The indirect method is now used by the majority of companies, primarily because it is less difficult and costly to prepare. The direct method, in comparison, begins with the total cash received from clients and others in exchange for goods and services delivered and continues with total cash expenditures to suppliers and others for materials and labor provided, but otherwise is relatively similar to the indirect method in appearance.

Many credit analysts now accept the indirect method as extremely useful; it is easier to understand than looking at all of the gross flows, given lenders' backgrounds and history of working largely with net flows.

Categorizing Sources and Uses

While the argument will continue about whether to select the direct or indirect method, SFAS No. 95 makes clear another possible improvement in understanding statements of cash flows: categorizing them as operating, investment, and financing cash flows. For example, depreciation is shown as an *operating inflow,* which indicates management's control of the operating cycle, and an increase in fixed assets is shown as an *investment outflow.* This is probably the most important aspect of SFAS No. 95.

Adequacy of Operating Cash Flows

The first category of cash flows includes those cash flows involved in or resulting from the daily operations of the business—activities such as purchasing inventory, manufacturing, selling products or providing services, and collecting receivables. The initial step in cash flow examination is to analyze these operating cash flows. This entails comparing the magnitude of the cash generated from the company's profitable operation (net income plus depreciation plus any other noncash charges) with the funding needs associated with that operation (such as increased accounts receivable and inventory). The key areas for the lender to analyze in operations are quality of earnings, management of current assets, and management of current liabilities.

Quality of Earnings

Assessing the consistency and reliability of the company's reported profits is important because their usefulness as a measure of cash flow depends upon their derivation as well as upon the accounting methods used to report them. For example, if a company's profits in a given year include a gain from the sale and leaseback of its own physical facilities, that portion of its earning stream will not be duplicated in future years. Therefore, the correct entry is net profits from continuing operations and before extraordinary items, not just net profits.

Management of Current Assets

If the statement of cash flows reveals that current assets have grown (a use of cash), an analyst should investigate whether this growth is in proportion to the growth of the revenue stream or whether it suggests a managerial problem or perhaps simply a change in strategy. If the company's current assets have decreased for the period (a source of cash), determine whether that decrease reflects a decrease in the level of revenues or a conscious management decision to change the way the company manages that asset category.

If the company has changed its management of the asset category, consider whether the company can sustain that change. If not, the funding represents a temporary measure that will have to be reversed in the future and will thus create an additional need for cash. If the decrease in assets resulted from a loss of revenues, it is likely not to be repeated since accounts receivable cannot continually be a source of cash unless the company is liquidating.

Management of Current Liabilities

If the statement of cash flows shows that accounts payable or other accruals have grown (a source of cash), determine whether that growth is in response to increased sales or whether the company has been slow in paying its trade debt. The latter situation may suggest that the company will face a need for cash in the near future. If payables are shrinking (a use of cash), determine whether this is in response to a decrease in sales or to a reversal of trade credit policy.

Appropriateness of Investment Cash Flows

The second category of cash flows includes flows of cash that relate to the acquisition or sale of fixed assets and other investments. These cash flows are considered discretionary because a company's management may postpone or cancel fixed asset purchases and investments. Naturally, the decrease in fixed assets could come about because depreciation has been accounted for and no new assets have been purchased to replace those theoretically wearing out. This could raise several questions:

- Since no new purchases have been made, is the firm now overfatiguing existing equipment? Worn equipment could reduce the volume and quality of the firm's products.
- Does the nonreplacement of equipment indicate that other costs (like labor) are going to rise in the future to compensate for the equipment's declining capabilities?
- Has recently purchased equipment produced such economies and increased capacity so much that future asset purchases will be less expensive and increase the firm's asset-use efficiency?
- Does the decline represent the elimination of surplus assets—or the disposition of assets that are critical to the operation of the company? Although elimination of surplus assets is appropriate, it typically represents only a one-time or occasional source of cash. The disposition of critical assets may severely diminish the company's ability to operate and, thus, may hinder the company's ability to create cash from operations to fund growth and to repay debt.
- Investment cash flows may also reflect such financial maneuvers as the aforementioned sale and leaseback of a major facility. Although this is a legitimate maneuver on the company's part, the credit analyst should appreciate that it is a one-time source of cash and that it creates a future cash requirement in the form of lease payments.

An increase in fixed assets (a use of cash) raises other questions, including:

- Are the acquisitions to replace worn-out assets? If so, are the new assets more expensive than the old ones?
- If new assets are more expensive than the old ones, is this a harbinger of continuing purchases of expensive replacement assets, which could severely reduce profits (due to the higher depreciation) and necessitate higher debt to pay for the assets?
- Has the firm chosen an appropriate source of cash to pay for the purchase?

Proper Structuring of Financing Cash Flows

This category includes those flows of cash that directly relate to the external financing of the business, whether involving debt instruments or equity contributions, such as payment of dividends. Financing flows is the last part of the cash flow analysis. An increase in a company's common stock and in paid-in capital accounts (reflecting the sale of additional stock) is welcome because it diminishes the company's financial leverage and thus the risk involved in lending. Unfortunately, sales of capital stock have become infrequent. The retention of earnings has become the primary cause of equity growth. Therefore, the company's *dividend policy* is important to examine, not only since payment of dividends diminishes the amount of cash flow available to repay loans and fund growth, but also because it reduces the equity. Thus, an analyst needs to compare dividends to the magnitude of the company's operating flows and to the debt and growth requirements that could otherwise have been funded.

The categorization of cash flows used here highlights the importance of notes payable to banks by including this account as a financing flow rather than as an operating flow despite its short-term nature. This serves to highlight one of the most prevalent problems with the financing structure of many companies—the funding of long-term, fixed-asset requirements with short-term debt. When confronted with this situation, an analyst should ask what change in the method of operation, in the level of fixed assets, or in financing will result in this short-term financing being repaid by its maturity date.

One-year credit lines or revolving debt, mentioned previously, is an especially appropriate method for growing companies to finance "permanent" increases in working capital. From an analytical standpoint, the primary consideration is whether the timing of converting revolving debt to term payout coincides with the timing of the company's operating cycle and, therefore, its repayment ability. Clearly, at the annual renewal date, the one-year credit lines are to be reviewed closely with the firm for future expansion plans and for the adequacy of the loss reserves for the accounts that they finance.

With long-term debt, consider whether the amortization requirement matches the company's ability to generate cash from its operating cycle. In this regard, be aware not only of immediate amortization requirements, but also of any future changes in that schedule.

Adequacy of Operating Cash Flows

The statement of cash flows for 1991 (Exhibit 5.6) shows that Garcia-Duran generated a cash flow of $27,000 in the form of profit from its operations and noncash charges of $10,000 in depreciation and $18,000 in the increase in the deferred-tax account. The analyst might question the adequacy of profits, since the 1990 and 1991 income statements (shown in Exhibit 5.4) reveal that the company made approximately 29 percent less income on 30 percent more revenue in 1990.

Statement of Cash Flows

Exhibit 5.6

Garcia-Duran Design Company
Statement of Cash Flows
for the Years Ended December 31
(in thousands of dollars)

	1990	1991
Operating Cash Flows		
Net profit after tax	38	27
Depreciation	12	10
Increase in reserve for deferred taxes	6	18
Subtotal Funds from Operations	56	55
Increase in accounts payable	42	53
Increase in accruals	4	12
Increase in accounts receivable	[66]	[163]
Increase in inventory	[101]	[125]
Decrease in current-year income taxes	[1]	[3]
Net cash flows from operations	[66]	[171]
Investment Cash Flows		
Decrease in fixed assets		1
Decrease in other assets	1	
Increase in fixed assets	[26]	
Increase in investments in affiliates		[6]
Increase in other assets		[1]
Net investment outflows	[25]	[6]
Financing Cash Flows		
Increase in notes payable to banks	94	180
Cash dividends paid	[21]	[21]
Decrease in long-term debt	[1]	[1]
Net financing inflows	72	158
Net decrease in cash	[19]	[19]

Note: Uses are in brackets and Sources are positive numbers.

Calculating the funds from operations (before changes in current accounts), the total equals $55,000 in 1991 and $56,000 in 1990. Something happened to the depreciation for tax purposes, or some other transaction took place to allow the firm to defer more taxes than the drop in income would indicate. Overall, funds flow from operations has been stable, and this would appear good if not for the 30 percent increase in sales and the needed resources required to support that growth.

The change in the current accounts for Garcia-Duran reveals increases in accounts payable and accruals, which supply additional cash flow and appear consistent with the company's revenue growth. On the outflow side, the increases in accounts receivable and inventory far outweigh the inflows. Again, the increases in current asset accounts seem to be consistent and justified since they climbed just 30 percent, which is in line with sales growth. Up to this point, it seems that Garcia-Duran's ability to generate cash flow from operations (or even funds flow) has been outstripped by the growth in working capital associated with an increase in revenues.

While some analysts believe that negative operating flows always reflect pricing, product, or operations control problems, other analysts believe that growth in sales is usually the cause. The problem is compounded by the declining profit margins that are frequently experienced along with growth.

Appropriateness of Investment Cash Flows

Garcia-Duran's outflows were further increased by a $6,000 investment in an affiliate and only very slightly offset by a $1,000 decrease in fixed assets. The analyst might question the prudence of the advance to an affiliate. Moreover, last year's $26,000 increase in fixed assets has not been repeated; with sales rising so dramatically, the analyst might consider whether this rise can continue for another year. While it does not appear that fixed assets are a major part of the Garcia-Duran production process, a decline in fixed assets in the face of growing sales is extremely unusual.

If fixed assets are required in the future, the additional question arises as to the capacity for repayment. The investment flow area focuses on the issues of growth and the capability of the company to sustain growth without additional equity capital, an issue discussed more fully in chapter 9.

Proper Structuring of Financing Cash Flows

The financing cash flows section reveals that the $180,000 in short-term borrowing provided most of the cash requirements for the firm. The analyst should question the structure and purpose of this debt. If it is the type of revolving funding mentioned in chapter 3, and if it is provided by banks that are knowledgeable of Garcia-Duran's customer base and are agreeable to supporting its sales expansion, then there is little cause for alarm.

Since the financing inflow was inadequate to fund all of the operating account growth of $288,000, the company reduced its cash balance by $19,000 and used suppliers to fund $65,000. Questions about the continued possibility of using these routes should be asked. Clearly, a recommendation would be for the company to arrange for financing at a higher level than the 63 percent indicated (180,000 ÷ 288,000) or to slow growth.

In the financing cash flows section, paying $21,000 in cash dividends at a time of rapid expansion seems contrary to good financial management. The operating cash shortfall was exacerbated by the fact that the company's entire $27,000 in profits went either to the owners or was invested in an affiliated company.

Conclusion

The credit analyst at this point should have five concerns:

1. The company's profitability has declined during its growth period, which has decreased its capacity to fund its operations.
2. The working capital requirements associated with the company's growth are substantial in relation to the amount of profit created. However, they do relate to the increased level of operations.
3. A large portion of the profits was either paid out to the owners or invested in affiliated companies. Moreover, profits are not being maintained at levels proportionate to sales. These are not positive developments.
4. The operating shortfalls, which appear to be permanent or long-term in nature, were funded with short-term debt and a reduction in cash balances. Be concerned about the company's likely inability to reduce that short-term debt within a short period. Thus, look at the company's present banking arrangements for reassurance that they are properly documented for continued growth.
5. The company's statement of cash flows evidence that, when growth of inventory and accounts receivable do not require new funds, and when capital expenditures are not high, sufficient cash is available to repay long-term debt amortization.

Tentative conclusions such as these can frequently be verified or contradicted by analyzing cash flows over more than two years. Thus, the lender will next look at the cash flow figures for Garcia-Duran Design Company for past years.

Garcia-Duran has borrowed through short-term loans to fund operating assets to support a rapid increase in sales. Assuming this rapid growth in sales continues, and assuming the company's profitability does not improve greatly, Garcia-Duran's need for debt will continue to increase. The fact that the cash used to support operating assets exceeds the cash provided by ongoing operations raises the question of the structure of the debt—that is, of how and when the bank is to be repaid.

An analyst should also take a closer look at the company's use of its operating cash to see, for example, whether its accounts receivable and inventory relative to sales could be reduced. The lender might also conclude that the payment of dividends at this point should be reduced or eliminated since operating earnings are proving insufficient to support both the growth of the company and the payment of dividends. Finally, the analyst must question whether an equity contribution would be appropriate to supplement the financing inflows provided by short-term bank debt.

SUMMARY OF IMPORTANT CONCEPTS

The statement of cash flows is an important analytical tool that enables the credit analyst to determine how a company obtains and uses its economic resources. By creating a structured report showing the inflows and outflows of cash associated with the operating, investing, and financing activities of a company, the credit analyst can answer such questions as those suggested at the front of the chapter.

Deriving a statement of sources and uses of cash starts with two balance sheets, which are point-in-time statements reflecting the company's financial status at the beginning and end of the year. Besides the changes in balance sheet accounts (each of which reflects either a source or a use of cash), additional cash flow information (net profit, depreciation, and dividends paid) can be estimated from the income statement or the footnotes. In constructing a statement of sources and uses of cash, remember that all sources of cash must equal all uses of cash.

A lender's analysis of a company's statement of cash flows focuses on an assessment of the adequacy of the company's operating cash flows, the appropriateness of its investment cash flows, and the proper structuring of its financing cash flows. Tentative conclusions can often be verified or contradicted by doing a comparative analysis using the prior year's statement of cash flows. For example, when analyzing a growing, profitable company, many credit analysts immediately assume the company is healthy (which, in most cases, is true). Yet rapid growth, even when it is profitable, can lead to insolvency because the company's requirements for working capital may exceed its internal funding capability—and the need for outside financing may outstrip the company's borrowing capacity. While various types of cash flows with differing names are in use, the advantage of the statement of cash flows presented in the text is that it clearly identifies the

inflows and outflows of cash and categorizes them according to how they actually occur in the business—that is, a company has a current operating cycle (operating cash flows), makes long-term expansion decisions (investment cash flows), and then finances the actions taken (financing cash flows).

A major drawback of financial statement analysis based on the use of a statement of cash flows is that some flows of cash can be subject to varying interpretations; it is important that any conclusions be substantiated. As is true of any analytical tool, cash flow review will not provide a total answer to a loan question, but it comes closer to the goal than any of the other tools thus far reviewed.

EXERCISES

Important Terms To Define

- statement of cash flows
- funds from operations
- cash flows from financing activities
- sources of cash
- direct method of the statement of cash flows
- cash flows from operations
- cash flows from investing activities
- statement of sources and uses
- uses of cash
- indirect method of the statement of cash flows
- dividend policy

Dependable Doors Case Study

1. Using Dependable Doors' statement of cash flows, analyze the company's cash flows from operating activities for 1990 and 1991.
2. Does Dependable Doors have sufficient cash from operations in 1990 and 1991 to service its debt?
3. Compare the traditional method of calculating cash flow with the statement of cash flows for both 1990 and 1991.
4. Analyze Dependable Doors's cash flow from investing activities.
5. Analyze Dependable Doors's cash flow from financing activities in 1990 and 1991.
6. Analyze the dividends payments on the statement of cash flows with changes in the equity accounts on the balance sheet. What do you think happened between 1990 and 1991?

The answers to the Dependable Doors Case Study questions appear in the appendix.

Engraph Case Study

1. Using Engraph's consolidated statements of cash flows, analyze the company's cash flows from operating activities.
2. Does Engraph have sufficient cash from continuing operating activities to pay interest and principal on it's debt obligations?
3. Using Engraph's consolidated statements of cash flows, analyze the company's cash flows from investing activities.
4. Using Engraph's consolidated statements of cash flows, analyze the company's cash flows from financing activities.

Ratios

LEARNING OBJECTIVES

After studying this chapter, you will be able to

- calculate key financial ratios,
- explain what the ratios mean and how they are used in financial statement analysis,
- identify the three main ratio analysis groups and their subcategories—liquidity, with subcategories for liquidation and activity; leverage, with subcategories for liquidation and coverage; and profitability—and the various ratios that fit into each category,
- use financial ratios to compare a company's performance with that of the industry,
- explain why ratios must be used with caution, and
- avoid "elevator analysis" and instead offer possibilities in a report of trend and comparative analysis as to the cause of ratios being out of alignment.

INTRODUCTION

Ratios are among the most well-known and widely used financial statement analysis tools. Ratios allow the study of relationships among various components of a set of financial statements by putting information in a manageable form. Because ratios serve as comparative tools, the analyst can measure a company's performance over time (trend analysis) and compare it with that of its competitors or industry benchmarks (comparative analysis).

Ratios are perhaps the most overrated and the most widely misused of financial statement analysis tools as well. Although easily calculated, ratios can be very misleading. They should be used as a measuring device that leads to asking instructive questions and as building blocks in the construction of a company's total financial picture. They should *never* be used as the primary basis for approving a loan or, for that matter, rejecting a loan.

The figures used in calculating ratios come from the income statement, the balance sheet, and the statement of cash flows. Thus, ratio analysis is really an extension of the analytical techniques discussed in the preceding chapters.

This chapter explains the arithmetic computation and meaning of three key categories of financial ratios—liquidity (both liquidation and activity types), leverage (both liquidation and coverage types), and profitability. It also discusses how ratios are selected and used to spot significant trends and to compare a company's performance in key areas with that of other companies in its industry.

USES AND LIMITATIONS OF RATIOS

Ratios show the relative size of things. In financial statement analysis, ratios help the loan officer measure relationships or proportions between various accounts included in a company's financial statements. For example, a ratio will clearly show that the relationship between $112 of assets and $224 of liabilities is the same as the relationship between $54,743,952 of assets and $109,487,904 of liabilities. Moreover, ratios are usually expressed in their most simplified form. The ratio of both of the above, for example, would be 1:2, a relationship quickly and easily figured in the first relationship, but more difficult to see in the second.

Relationship

Since a ratio can be calculated using any two numbers, be aware that the analytical significance of a ratio depends upon there being a meaningful relationship between the accounts being compared. For example, because the relationship between a company's income and its interest expense has meaning, the times-interest-earned ratio is significant. The ratio of inventory to deferred taxes, however, is not significant because no meaningful relationship exists between the two accounts.

The interrelationships of different ratios are also important to the examination. Ratios can have offsetting or balancing influences on each other. For example, high leverage, demonstrated by the debt-to-worth ratio, may be offset by the high debt service coverage ratio because of high cash flow. More of these relationships are pointed out in the discussion below.

When writing an analysis, the loan officer must relate the ratio to some business cause; it is incorrect merely to convert the number from a table of ratios to a sentence in prose. *Elevator analysis* refers to the practice of identifying that the ratio (or any financial statement account, for that matter) went up or down in a particular year from the last, without adding an explanation. In this book, discussions of the individual ratios endeavor to relate the result of a ratio to its possible causes. While indicating causes may appear to be idle speculation, it will raise more analytical questions to be asked of the prospective borrower, one of the chief purposes of a financial statement review.

Comparability

The quality of the numbers used to calculate a ratio also affects the significance of a ratio. Meaningful ratio analysis depends not only on the accuracy of the computations used in deriving a financial statement, but also on the consistency of the numbers in terms of the underlying accounting methods of the companies being compared. For example, any intercompany comparisons of ratios involving assets must take into consideration the many different valuation methods that may have been used:

- The valuation of inventory on the balance sheet, which can differ dramatically depending on whether the company employs the first-in, first-out (FIFO) or the last-in, first-out (LIFO) method. Therefore, an effort should be made to adjust the balance sheet of companies that use LIFO to current cost via the LIFO reserve footnote, as noted in chapter 3.
- The valuation of accounts receivable, which depends on the company's policy for determining the reserve for bad debts.
- The valuation of fixed assets, which will be affected by whether the company uses straight-line or accelerated depreciation. In addition, some balance sheets may include significantly undervalued fixed assets, such as land that has been held for a considerable length of time or a heavily depreciated plant.

Also recognize that any management decision that influences the valuation of a balance sheet item also affects the income statement. A lower valuation of inventory resulting from the use of LIFO in times of rising prices, the establishment of a larger bad-debt reserve, and the use of accelerated depreciation to more rapidly write off depreciable assets, all have the additional effects of reducing a company's net profit. This, in turn, affects any ratio involving net profit, such as the return on assets or return on sales.

When performing a trend analysis comparing ratios for a single company over time, the particular accounting policies used in preparing the statements are less important as long as they are consistently applied. However, when making industry-wide comparisons, try to find companies that use the same accounting procedures and apply them consistently. Even if this cannot be done, industry comparisons have some validity since ratios are not intended to be absolute indicators, but rather relative indicators that may point up areas for further study or inquiry.

Industry Sources and Limitations

Useful sources of industry information include the Robert Morris Associates (RMA) *Annual Statement Studies* and the Dun & Bradstreet (D&B) *Key Business Ratios*. Care must be taken when using such sources, however, since generally the industry figures available for comparison will be a year behind the statements available for the company being analyzed. With particular industries and some undiversified geographic regions subject to economic swings, it may be difficult to draw meaningful comparisons using year-old data.

Another drawback to using industry comparisons is that some diversified companies consolidate their various lines of business into a single financial statement, making accurate comparisons very difficult. This text stresses throughout that no single financial technique yields a complete financial picture of a company. This is especially true of ratios. They are relative measures that have significance only in relation to other reference points or benchmarks.

Summary

Ratio analysis is usually most useful when

- ❐ comparing a company's past financial performance with its current performance,
- ❐ analyzing projected financial statements, and
- ❐ making industry comparisons, such as with a specific group of companies in the same industry.

For analytical purposes, ratios generally can be grouped into three main categories, with two having subcategories; each category represents an aspect of a company's financial well-being. The main categories are liquidity, with subcategories for liquidation and activity; leverage, with subcategories for liquidation and coverage; and profitability. In practice, analysts normally do not calculate every ratio, but may select one or two ratios from each category to begin a review and then select additional ratios as deemed appropriate to help interpret and complete the analytical picture. Experienced loan officers may use additional ratios not included in this chapter.

In the following sections, each of the categories of ratios is discussed in turn. In the examples, the calculation of ratios is based on financial statements for the Carroll Company, a retail department store. Exhibit 6.1 is a common-sized comparative (four-year) balance sheet for the company, while Exhibit 6.2, (p. 194) shows the company's income statement results for the same four years.

Carroll Company's Common-Sized Comparative Balance Sheet

Exhibit 6.1

Carroll Company
Balance Sheet
for the Years Ending January 31
(in thousands of dollars)

	1988	*%*	*1989*	*%*	*1990*	*%*	*1991*	*%*
Assets								
Cash and marketable securities	241	5.0	300	5.3	213	3.5	115	1.7
Accounts receivable—net	43	0.9	76	1.3	80	1.3	90	1.3
Inventory	2,376	49.1	2,746	48.7	2,846	46.6	3,135	47.0
Current assets	2,660	55.0	3,122	55.3	3,139	51.4	3,340	50.1
Fixed assets—net	1,942	40.1	2,234	39.6	2,601	42.6	2,876	43.1
Other assets	235	4.9	286	5.1	362	5.9	457	6.8
Noncurrent assets	2,177	45.0	2,520	44.7	2,963	48.6	3,333	49.9
Total assets	4,837	100.0	5,642	100.0	6,102	100.0	6,673	100.0
Liabilities and Net Worth								
Notes payable to banks	—	0.0	186	3.3	—	0.0	168	2.5
Accounts payable—trade	936	19.4	1,058	18.8	1,060	17.4	1,253	18.8
Accruals	405	8.4	485	8.6	550	9.0	499	7.5
Current maturities long-term debt	48	1.0	53	0.9	59	1.0	64	1.0
Current debt	1,389	28.7	1,782	31.6	1,669	27.4	1,984	29.7
Long-term debt—secured	1,503	31.1	1,632	28.9	2,037	33.4	2,167	32.5
Total debt	2,892	59.8	3,414	60.5	3,706	60.7	4,151	62.2
Deferred income taxes	29	0.6	43	0.8	51	0.8	64	1.0
Capital stock—common	122	2.5	123	2.2	124	2.0	124	1.9
Paid-in surplus	230	4.8	243	4.3	254	4.2	264	4.0
Retained earnings	1,564	32.3	1,819	32.2	1,967	32.2	2,070	31.0
Net worth	1,916	39.6	2,185	38.7	2,345	38.4	2,458	36.8
Total liabilities and net worth	4,837	100.0	5,642	100.0	6,102	100.0	6,673	100.0

Liquidity Ratios (Liquidation Type)

In finance, liquidity means the ability to convert an asset to cash quickly without the loss of market value. For a firm to have high liquidity it must have the ability to maintain a good relationship between the conversion of current (short-term) assets and the maturity of current liabilities. Because maturing obligations must generally be paid in cash, the examination of liquidity focuses on the availability of cash or the company's ability to generate cash by converting its assets into cash without a significant loss in value.

Liquidation herein refers to the tendency of lenders to consider the liquidation of the firm in order to recover the principal. It frequently carries with it the idea of assets being auctioned at less than their fair market value because of the urgency in the recovery process and the involuntary aspect of the sale for the owner. Ratios generally associated with liquidation are balance-sheet oriented and do not look at the dynamic quality of the income statement or statement of cash flows because the assumption is that the firm has failed and liquidation is the only alternative left to the lender to recover principal.

Liquidation ratios have rules of thumb attached to them based upon the idea that in liquidation the auction or fast-sale value will be approximately half the market value. This is based on historical precedent: When United Merchants and Manufacturers, once the largest manufacturer of clothing in the United States, went bankrupt in 1979, the inventory of its large men's store chain, Robert Hall Clothes, was sold off for forty-seven cents on the dollar—including the racks. That was not forty-seven cents on the dollar of retail value, but forty-seven cents on the dollar of cost: the capitalized expenditures to generate finished goods inventory on the books of United Merchants and Manufacturers. Currently, these 50-percent rules of thumb may be either inadequate or overindulgent. The real liquidation values are a result of the type of industry, the state of the economy, and the skill of managers in purchasing and adding value to develop their inventories and other assets.

Legitimate levels of current assets required to meet short-term obligations are directly related to the risk and fluctuations involved in a company's short-term stream of funds flows. For example, a manufacturer whose sales cannot be predicted with reasonable accuracy needs more current assets to ensure it will be able to meet its obligations. Alternatively, a utility company that can accurately forecast the demand for power and thus has a steady and predictable level of operating cash inflow needs a lower level of current assets.

A company's need for financial flexibility also affects its desired level of liquidity. For example, both a company that wants to be able to rapidly deliver inventory when customers make occasional large purchases and a company that wants to quickly increase advertising outlays in response to competitive demands need higher liquidity. The amount of prearranged outside funding to be made available to a company on demand—like a line

of credit or revolving credit—may also affect the company's need for liquidity.

A company is illiquid if it is in danger of being unable to meet its current financial obligations. This may be a temporary, self-correcting problem, or it may be a symptom of more serious and permanent problems in a company's operation. Illiquidity typically results from a combination of several situations.

First, the company may have its funds tied up in illiquid assets—that is, assets that the company cannot quickly convert to cash. A company that invests its money in a new factory, for example, cannot readily liquidate the factory to obtain needed cash if the factory itself does not generate sufficient cash.

Second, the company may have funded its operation improperly. For example, the business may have taken on too much debt given its ability to generate cash to pay interest and principal, or the schedule for repaying its financial obligations may not match the timing of its cash generation.

Third, the company may be losing money in its operation. In other words, a business that is spending more money than it takes in cannot generate sufficient cash to meet its obligations.

Fourth, the company's current financial obligations may have grown faster than its ability to generate cash. This situation often occurs when the company is experiencing growth.

Depending on the reasons for and the magnitude of a company's illiquidity, the results can range from simple inconvenience to impending disaster. Illiquidity might merely result in having to forgo discounts offered by creditors for exceptionally prompt payment. Or it might result in a need to borrow money from its bank. On a more serious note, illiquidity might damage a company's credit rating. Or the company might have to pass up additional business because of its inability to handle its existing financial obligations. Most seriously, the company may have to liquidate its operating assets, which can impair its future ability to generate cash through operations.

Some credit analysts think of liquidation-type ratios as adequate for defining liquidity because these ratios show the margin of current assets to current liabilities that should result from a total liquidation of the company's accounts. The following are some examples of liquidation-type ratios:

Current Ratio

Two *liquidity (liquidation type)* ratios commonly used to get a rough indication of liquidity are the current ratio and the quick ratio. The *current ratio*—so called because it compares a company's current assets to its current liabilities—compares the absolute quantity of the company's current assets to its current liabilities at a certain point in time. In other words, it shows the amount of cushion provided by a company's current assets relative to its current liabilities.

A ratio of 2 to 1 (or 2:1, or simply 2) of current assets to current liabilities has historically been the accepted standard for the current ratio. This is based on the 50-percent rule of thumb of liquidation just mentioned. That is, if assets fall in value by 50 percent, then the remaining value will be sufficient to repay current liabilities assuming the ratio was 2 to 1 before the liquidation.

The need for a high liquidity cushion and, thus, a high current ratio varies among industries and also depends on such factors as the composition and quality of the company's current assets. The most important factor is the quality of the receivables and the near-term maturity of the current liabilities. For example, consider a farmer who borrows money in the spring to pay for fertilizer and seed with the intention of repaying the loan after the harvest in October. Reviewing the May statement without this knowledge of when and how the farmer intends to repay would show a poor current ratio; but since the maturity of the current liability is after harvest, the current ratio should not be alarming. Generally, the higher the current ratio, the more comfortable is the cushion against the effects of reduced inventory values, uncollected receivables, and unanticipated cash needs. However, a large current ratio may signify idle cash, too much inventory, or a slow collection of accounts receivable.

The current ratio is calculated using the following formula:

$$\frac{\text{Current assets}}{\text{Current liabilities}} = \text{Current ratio}$$

A look at the 1991 figures on the Carroll Company's balance sheet (Exhibit 6.1) shows the company's current assets at $3,340 and its current liabilities (or debt) at $1,984. (Dollar amounts in this chapter are in thousands of dollars to correspond with the amounts in the exhibits.) Using the formula above, the Carroll Company's current ratio can be calculated as follows:

$$\text{Current ratio} = \frac{3{,}340}{1{,}984} = 1.68{:}1$$

The Carroll Company's current ratio of 1.68:1 means that, for every dollar of current debt, the Carroll Company has $1.68 of current assets. Thus the value of the Carroll Company's current assets could shrink as much as 40 percent (.68/1.68) without impairing the company's ability to pay its creditors through the liquidation of its current assets.

The current ratio is not an absolute measure of debt-paying ability since in its normal operations the company will never fully liquidate its current assets.

Moreover, the current ratio does not measure the quality of the current assets, but only their existence. Some analysts believe that the pitfalls of relying on the current ratio require severe warnings about previous misguided trust by well-intentioned lenders.

Quick Ratio

The *quick ratio* (also called the acid-test ratio) is a more stringent measure of liquidity than the current ratio because it includes only the most theoretically liquid current assets—it assumes that accounts receivable are more liquid than the remaining current assets. The company's inventory and other current assets are eliminated from current assets for this calculation, leaving only cash, marketable securities, and accounts receivable—those assets that a company should be able to convert to cash quickly to pay obligations. The quick ratio is calculated using the following formula:

$$\text{Quick ratio} = \frac{\text{Cash + Marketable securities + Accounts receivable}}{\text{Current liabilities}}$$

The Carroll Company's 1991 balance sheet shows the company's cash and marketable securities at $115, its accounts receivable at $90, and its current liabilities (the same figure used in the current ratio) at $1,984. Using the formula above, the Carroll Company's quick ratio can be calculated as follows:

$$\text{Quick ratio} = \frac{115 + 90}{1{,}984} = 0.10{:}1$$

Historically, a quick ratio of 1:1 has been accepted as an indication of good liquidity. Thus the Carroll Company's quick ratio of 0.10:1, which means the company has only 10 cents of very liquid assets available for each $1 of current debt, is low by the standard for most industries. However, retailers typically have low quick ratios because they have low accounts receivable, thanks to widespread use of credit cards, and most cash is quickly reinvested in inventory.

Liquidity Ratios (Activity Type)

Unlike the previous liquidation ratios, which use elements only from the balance sheet, the following *liquidity (activity type) ratios* use a mix of income statement and balance sheet variables. They may be better indicators of liquidity since they attempt to ascertain the quality of the underlying asset. The faster a business can process its inventory and accounts receivable, the higher that asset is in quality.

Activity ratios give further insights into how efficiently a company uses its assets. Generally, these ratios compare the company's sales to the three major trading accounts—accounts receivable, inventory, and accounts payable. The ratios measure how frequently the company turns over these accounts—that is, how long it takes for accounts receivable to be collected, inventory to be sold, and accounts payable to be paid.

Exhibit 6.2

Carroll Company's Income Statement

Carrol Company
Income Statement
for Years Ending January 31
(in thousands of dollars)

	1988	%	1989	%	1990	%	1991	%
Net sales	11,696	100	12,731	100	14,204	100	16,527	100
Cost of goods sold	8,566	73	9,283	73	10,417	73	12,360	75
Gross profit/revenues	3,130	27	3,448	27	3,787	27	4,167	25
Total operating expenses	2,503	21	2,839	22	3,326	24	3,810	23
Operating profit	627	6	609	5	461	3	357	2
Other income	151	1	190	1	208	1	246	1
Interest expense	142	1	171	1	227	1	276	1
Profit before tax	636	6	628	5	442	3	327	2
Income taxes	292	3	270	2	181	1	107	1
Net profit after tax	344	3	358	3	261	2	220	1
Notes:								
Dividends	88		103		113		117	
Depreciation	146		166		198		230	

Accounts Receivable Turnover Ratio

The relationship between accounts receivable and sales can be expressed in either of two ways. The first gives the number of times during the year that the average accounts receivable is collected. The *accounts receivables turnover* ratio is calculated as follows:

$$\text{Receivables turnover ratio} = \frac{\text{Credit sales}}{\text{Average accounts receivables}}$$

The second method gives the average number of days that uncollected sales are outstanding (sometimes called DSO) in the company's accounts receivables. Also known as the *average collection period* (ACP), it is calculated by taking the turnover ratio and dividing that result into the 365 days in a year as follows:

$$\text{Average colletion period} = \frac{365}{\text{Receivable turnover ratio}}$$

Presented together the entire formula is:

$$\text{Average collection period} = \frac{365}{\text{Credit sales} \,/\, \text{Average accounts receivable}}$$

The little extra work of converting a receivables turnover ratio into days will be more than repaid by the added meaning that expressing the relationship in this way provides. For example, a slowing in a company's average collection period from 37 days to 44 days is much easier to grasp than a decline in receivables turnover from 9.9 to 8.3 times per year. The conversion to days also makes it easier to compare a company's actual accounts receivable turnover with the credit terms it offers.

The *average collection period* shows the average number of days it takes for a company to collect on credit sales to its customers. Since this will vary greatly for different types of companies, it is important to make comparisons with similar companies or to look at trends over time. Ideally this ratio is calculated using the average of monthly or quarterly credit sales that gave rise to the level of receivables shown on the balance sheet. Because the company's statements do not distinguish between the company's credit sales and cash sales, and because cash sales are often insignificant amounts, total sales are typically used.

An analyst should make every effort to obtain the monthly or quarterly sales and receivables levels to confirm that the cash sales are indeed minimal. If such detailed information is not available, then alternative information about the seasonality of the firm needs to be obtained. Otherwise, the year-end balance sheet may not be at all representative of the average year, a problem mentioned in chapter 3 concerning Macy's year end. In the absence of any of this information, the ratio can be forced by using the average of the beginning and ending receivables and the aggregate sales level for the entire period.

If any significant deviation in the collection period shows up from the trend or comparative analysis, discuss it with a company representative. Also compare the company's average collection period to the collection terms allowed by the company to determine whether its collection of receivables is in line with its credit policy. The Carroll Company's balance sheet shows accounts receivables for fiscal year-end 1990 and 1991 at $80 and $90, respectively. The average of these two figures is taken, or the ending accounts receivable can be substituted. Since credit sales are not shown separately, the company's total sales for 1991 ($16,527) is used. The resulting calculation is as follows:

$$\text{Average collection period} = \frac{365}{16{,}527 \,/\, \frac{80+90}{2}} = 1.88 \text{ days}$$

The Carroll Company's average collection period is slightly less than two days, indicating almost no receivables, as would be expected for a retailer accepting payment in cash, checks, or bank credit cards.

This ratio has more meaning for a company with significant credit sales or with an ability to isolate credit sales from cash sales.

Inventory Turnover Ratio

The *inventory turnover* and *days in inventory* ratios show how often the inventory is turned or sold to generate the current sales volume. Inventory turnover measures the company's purchasing, selling, and manufacturing efficiency, but it is meaningful only in relation to the company's past performance and to the performance of similar companies in the same industry.

Cost of goods sold is used instead of sales in this formula since it shows the cost to the company of inventory sold during the year. For a manufacturer, cost of goods sold also includes overhead and manufacturing costs, and it is desirable that these (rather than just purchases) be included because the processing time and costs (adding value) are part of the item the analyst is trying to identify.

$$\text{Inventory turnover ratio} = \frac{\text{Cost of goods sold}}{\text{Average inventories}}$$

The days in inventory looks very much like the aging collections period and is calculated the same way, by dividing the days in the year by the turnover ratio:

$$\text{Average days in inventory} = \frac{365}{\text{Inventory turnover}}$$

Presented together the entire formula is:

$$\text{Average days in inventory} = \frac{365}{\text{Cost of goods sold} \,/\, \text{Average inventories}}$$

The Carroll Company's balance sheet shows inventory for fiscal year end 1990 and 1991 at $2,846 and $3,135. The two inventory figures are averaged (or ending inventory may be substituted for average inventory). The resulting figure is divided by the cost of goods sold for 1991, shown on the income statement as $12,360. Thus, Carroll Company's days in inventory is calculated as follows:

$$\text{Average days in inventory} = \frac{365}{12{,}360 \Big/ \frac{2{,}846 + 3{,}135}{2}} = 88.31 \text{ days}$$

The Carroll Company's days in inventory during 1991 was about 88 days. This means that if sales were to continue at the current level, the company could theoretically liquidate its entire inventory in 88 days.

Because detailed inventory information is rarely available and because a company may stock various types of inventory at widely varying levels, this ratio is only an approximation.

In addition, the accuracy of the calculation is affected by many differences in the numbers that make up the denominator. For example, the use of LIFO or FIFO in valuing inventory also affects the result and may mean that days in inventory are not comparable among companies. This supports the revision to the spreadsheet, mentioned in chapter 3, incorporating the LIFO reserve from the footnote into the inventory value. Otherwise, the ratio only allows for company trend comparisons. A change in this ratio, while not conclusive in itself, may raise questions that will lead to a better understanding of the company's inventory strategy or problems. For example, a trend of increasing days in inventory may indicate obsolescence of inventory. Although the ratio itself does not tell the lender if any inventory is obsolete or the mix of the inventory, it may signal the lender to ask these questions.

Accounts Payable Turnover Ratio

The *accounts payable turnover*, or days payable, ratio measures how promptly the company pays its trade accounts. This ratio will vary notably for different industries since standard credit terms vary greatly. Be alert to any significant changes in this ratio since

- ❒ a significant decrease could simply mean the company is taking advantage of discounts offered for early payment, but it could also indicate that suppliers are withdrawing trade credit, and
- ❒ a significant lengthening of the payables turnover could reflect the fact that suppliers have granted the company additional trade credit or longer terms, or it could reflect cash flow problems that are delaying payments to suppliers.

This ratio is also subject to inaccuracies because, while it should relate purchases to payables, purchase figures are frequently unavailable. Consequently, the cost of goods sold is substituted for purchases even though, for a manufacturer, this includes certain overhead accounts as well as direct labor. For this reason, the ratio is best used as an approximation in comparing similar companies or in trend analysis. The average accounts payable turnover is calculated using the following formula:

$$\text{Accounts payable turnover} = \text{Cost of goods sold} \Big/ \text{Average payables}$$

The average days payable formula is also similar to those previously used:

$$\text{Average days payables} = \frac{365}{\text{Payables turnover}}$$

Accounts payable as of fiscal year end 1990 and 1991, taken from the Carroll Company's balance sheet, list as $1,060 and $1,253, respectively. The average of these two payable figures is used, but ending accounts payable may be substituted. Since purchases are unavailable for Carroll Company, the cost of goods sold for fiscal year 1991 ($12,360) is taken from the income statement. Thus, the company's days payable ratio is calculated as follows:

$$\text{Average days payables} = \frac{365}{12{,}360 \Big/ \frac{1{,}060 + 1{,}253}{2}} = 34.15 \text{ days}$$

The days payable ratio shows that Carroll Company pays its creditors, on the average, in 34 days. This should be quite accurate since as a retailer the Carroll Company's cost of goods sold should equal its purchases unless the company is increasing the inventory level. If greater accuracy is desired, especially in the case of a manufacturer, the credit analyst can request an aging of payables from management.

Dollar Impact on Financing from Activity Ratios

In addition to reviewing the number of times per year and the days turn of the current asset and liability accounts, also examine the dollar changes taking place. Because they lend dollars, bankers must know how much is represented in dollars to measure the amount of credit needed. Further, this concept is related to the operating cycle of the firm—processing raw materials or purchased goods, adding value for resale, and collecting the cash from the sales.

The length of the operating cycle will directly influence the firm's financing needs if sales grow in the future. When the accounts receivable changes from 37 to 44 days, the firm's cash cycle is delayed not just by 7 days, but also by 7 days times the dollar sales per day. In the Carroll Company case, annual sales are $16,527; daily sales are that amount divided by 365.

$$\$16{,}527 / 365 = \$45$$

This means that the firm will have a daily dollar delay of $45 times 7 days, or $315 in cash shortage.

A similar calculation should be made for inventory and accounts payable, but for these multiply the days turnover times the daily level of cost of goods sold.

Leverage Ratios (Liquidation Type)

Leverage in financial statement analysis measures the relative levels of financial risk borne by the creditors and the shareholders of a business—risk inherent in the fixed payment requirements of debt. Thus, *leverage (liquidation type) ratios* provide a view of how much protection the company's assets provide for a creditor's debt, since assets must be financed either by owners' equity (net worth) or creditors' liabilities or debt.

Like liquidity (liquidation type) ratios, leverage ratios show the hypothetical margin of protection provided by assets relative to a corresponding group of liabilities if the firm is liquidated. The higher the proportion of borrowed funds to owner-contributed funds, the greater the assumed risk to lenders. These ratios could also be interpreted to show how much the assets could contract, should liquidation occur, without harming the creditor. Two leverage (liquidation type) ratios used in financial statement analysis are the debt-to-worth ratio and the debt-to-capitalization ratio.

A possible side issue here is the definition of net worth. As previously discussed, the convenience of simply deducting intangibles from net worth to derive tangible net worth has been abused. An alternate approach is to carefully evaluate the intangible *and* the tangible assets and use the most reliable data available to derive the net worth of a firm. These ratios are intended to assess liquidation scenarios, and they should be pragmatic, not just handy historical costs.

Debt-to-Worth Ratio

The *debt-to-worth* (or *debt-to-equity*) *ratio* indicates how well the shareholders' investment in the company provides a cushion for asset shrinkage. It also attempts to measure how much the shareholders have at risk versus how much the creditors have at risk and, thus, examines the company's capital structure.

Like the current ratio, the debt-to-worth ratio measures a company's ability to liquidate its assets in order to satisfy debt. This ratio enables the analyst to gauge how much a company can reduce the valuation of its assets before its creditors sustain a loss. Typical debt-to-worth ratios vary greatly for different industries. The debt-to-worth ratio is calculated using the following formula:

$$\text{Debt-to-worth ratio} = \frac{\text{Total liabilities}}{\text{Net worth}}$$

In calculating the debt-to-worth ratio, the analyst should not include the company's long-term deferred income tax liability, if any, as a liability because, as explained in chapter 3, the reserve for deferred income taxes can normally be deferred indefinitely. On the other hand, no matter how likely the firm is to continue building its deferred tax account, it is still considered optimistic to add the deferred tax account to the net worth value for the denominator. Nevertheless, in the event of a liquidation it is unlikely that the IRS would expect to collect any of the deferred tax account. The deferred tax account would have become a true equity account, taking the full reduction for the decline in asset prior to the creditors having to suffer.

The Carroll Company's balance sheet shows its total debt (as of year end 1991) at $4,151 and its net worth at $2,458. Since the presentation does not include the company's reserve for deferred taxes (which is relatively minor), and there do not appear to be any intangibles, the Carroll Company's debt-to-worth ratio calculation below would be easily calculated:

$$\text{Debt-to-worth ratio} = \frac{4{,}151}{2{,}458} = 1.69{:}1$$

The Carroll Company's debt-to-worth ratio of 1.69:1 indicates that creditors have 1.69 times as much invested in the company as do the shareholders—as measured by the book value of the assets. The relative value of the shareholders' and creditors' risk could be different from what the debt-to-worth ratio shows if the market, or liquidation, value of the assets differs significantly from their book value.

Debt-to-Capitalization Ratio (Sometimes Called Funded Debt-to-Net Worth)

Used primarily by bond rating agencies, like Standard & Poor's, the *debt-to-capitalization* ratio is based on an assessment of the permanent capital of a company—that is, its long-term debt and net worth. This ratio shows what percentage of the company's permanent capital is financed with debt as opposed to shareholders' investment.

The debt-to-capitalization ratio ignores short-term debt that is tied to the financing of inventories and accounts receivable, which is either seasonal or of relatively short duration and, conceptually, is repaid by current asset turnover or a seasonal decrease in business activity. This ratio suggests to what extent the company is relying on long-term debt and lease obligations for financing assets and the resulting need of profitable operations to support this leverage. The debt-to-capitalization ratio is calculated using the following formula:

$$\text{Debt-to-capitalization ratio} = \frac{\text{Long-term debt}}{\text{Long-term debt} + \text{Net worth}}$$

If a company has on its balance sheet capitalized lease obligations that are not already included as part of its long-term debt, these obligations should be added to long-term debt both in the numerator and denominator of this equation. The Carroll Company's 1991 balance sheet shows long-term debt at $2,167 (a figure that includes capitalized lease obligations) and net worth at $2,458. Thus, the company's debt-to-capitalization ratio is calculated as follows:

$$\text{Debt-to-capitalization ratio} = \frac{2{,}167}{2{,}167 + 2{,}458} = 0.47{:}1$$

The Carroll Company's debt-to-capitalization ratio of 0.47:1 indicates that the company's long-term creditors supply just under half of its permanent capital.

This ratio is primarily used for comparison of companies in the same industry.

Leverage Ratios (Coverage Type)

Coverage ratios are another type of leverage ratios commonly used in financial statement analysis. They measure the extent to which a company's fixed charges from debt obligations are met or exceeded by the flow of funds from the company's operations. Obviously, a company's ability to cover principal and interest payments is a key indicator of financial health that is of crucial concern to lenders.

While a detailed examination of cash flows entails the preparation of a statement of cash flows (as discussed in detail in chapter 5), coverage ratios are most frequently calculated using the funds flow concept. Funds flow is cash flows before changes in current accounts have been considered. Basically, funds flow is net profit plus any noncash charges such as depreciation and changes in the deferred tax account. Nevertheless, coverage ratios can be calculated using SFAS No. 95's net cash flow from operations, as long as it is used consistently in trend and comparative analysis.

In contrast to liquidation type ratios, both of which assess the lender's margin of comfort in the event of liquidation, coverage type ratios indicate the funds (or cash) flow margin of comfort while regarding the company as a going concern. Funds (or cash) flow to current maturities, times interest earned, and dividend payout are common coverage ratios.

Highly leveraged firms are more vulnerable to an economic downturn because the fixed payments of debt may conflict with reduced cash flow from falling sales. These ratios are useful because the company's cash flow from operations generally pays for the company's term debt and lease obligations

Funds (Cash) Flow-to-Current Maturities of Long-term Debt Ratio

The *funds (cash) flow-to-current maturities of long-term debt ratio* shows what proportion of a company's funds (cash) flow will be needed to pay the principal due on long-term debt in the coming year. This ratio serves as a fairly reliable indicator of a company's future performance, provided profitability and funds (cash) flow are expected to remain the same or increase. The lower the ratio, the smaller the margin of safety. Clearly, if a company's funds (cash) flow-to-current maturities ratio falls below 1:1, it is not generating enough cash to repay its fixed obligations and will have to borrow in the coming year to meet these obligations.

Current GAAP add the current amount of any capitalized lease obligations to current maturities. Some lenders are also concerned with recurring payouts of dividends to owners of small businesses, particularly S corporations. These analysts would subtract dividends from the numerator. However, since dividends are normally a discretionary outflow, and since the wise lender will restrict dividend payouts in earnings periods where they are not the proper response, the ratio has been calculated as follows:

$$\text{Funds (cash) flow to current maturities} = \frac{\text{Profit after taxes} + \text{Depreciation} + \text{Other noncash charges}}{\text{Current maturities of long-term debt}}$$

The Carroll Company's income statement shows that after-tax profits and depreciation for 1991 are $220 and $230, respectively. No noncash expense other than depreciation is shown. The Carroll Company's balance sheet shows current maturities of long-term debt for 1991 at $64. Therefore, the company's 1991 funds (cash) flow-to-current maturities long-term debt ratio is calculated as follows:

$$\text{Funds (cash) flow to current maturities} = \frac{220 + 230}{64} = 7.03{:}1$$

The company's ratio of more than 7:1 indicates that funds (cash) flow could decrease by more than 85 percent while still allowing the business to pay its current maturities.

An argument can be made that this calculation of the ratio can be misleading because funds flow ignores the changes in the current accounts. It does not address the cash flow required to fund the increased operating assets associated with growth in sales. The counter argument, as discussed in chapter 5, is that company management can change or control *working capital* policy in tight times. Nevertheless, if the analyst wants to take the more pessimistic approach, the net cash flows from operations can be used.

Unfortunately, when full-year figures are used, the funds (cash) flow-to-current maturities long-term debt ratio does not take into consideration the timing of a company's cash flow, which could affect the company's ability to repay debt as it comes due. A cash budget (see chapter 7) indicates the timing of a company's ability to pay debt as it comes due. Nevertheless, the ratio is a good general measure to use, especially when doing a trend analysis of a company's earnings over several years.

Times-Interest-Earned Ratio

The *times-interest-earned ratio*, another measure of the coverage type used principally by the public bond rating agencies, shows what proportion of a company's earnings is needed to pay interest on its debt. The principal reason for this focus on interest expense by the rating agencies is that, traditionally, public bonds did not require amortization of any kind. In the case of bonds issued by highly rated firms, the firms would issue new bonds with the express purpose of paying off the old bond a couple of years prior to its maturity; therefore, the only analytical problem was assuring analysts that interest expense could be paid on time.

Although this ratio suffers from drawbacks, it provides a valuable picture of the extent to which earnings are penalized to pay the financing costs of the company and the potential impact of an increase in interest rates on the company's cash flow. A ratio of greater than 1 is almost mandatory, since a lower ratio would indicate a company's earnings are insufficient to cover the interest on its debt. This ratio is calculated as follows:

$$\text{Times-interest-earned ratio} = \frac{\text{Profit before tax} + \text{Interest expense}}{\text{Interest expense}}$$

The Carroll Company's income statement shows profits before tax for 1991 at $327 and interest expense at $276. Thus, the 1991 times-interest-earned ratio for the Carroll Company is calculated as follows:

$$\text{Times-interest-earned ratio} = \frac{327 + 276}{276} = 2.18{:}1$$

With a times-interest-earned ratio of 2.18:1, the Carroll Company's interest expense could more than double before the company at its current level of earnings would be unable to pay its interest from profits.

Because the times-interest-earned ratio fails to consider cash flow for funding the company's operating assets or the principal portion of debt maturities, it is less important in an environment where most debt is amortizing before maturity.

Dividend Payout Ratio

The *dividend payout ratio* shows what percentage of profit after tax a company pays to shareholders in the form of dividends. These funds thereby become unavailable for other uses, such as to support asset growth and to fund current maturities of long-term debt. The dividend payout ratio, which can help explain trends in equity growth and leverage, is calculated as follows:

$$\text{Dividend payout ratio} = \frac{\text{Cash dividends paid}}{\text{Profit after tax}}$$

Carroll Company paid $117 in cash dividends and earned $220 in profit after tax for 1991. Consequently, its dividend payout ratio is calculated as follows:

$$\text{Dividend payout ratio} = \frac{117}{220} = 53\%$$

A dividend payout ratio of 53 percent indicates that the company pays slightly more than half its earnings to shareholders in the form of dividends.

Credit analysts are unable to assess the level without comparing it to past trends, other firms in the same industry, and management growth plans. These dividend issues are addressed in more detail in the analysis section of this chapter.

Enhanced-Fixed-Charges-Payout Ratio

Designating individual ratios as particularly useful may cause analysts to rely on them beyond all reasonable logic. The important point to keep in mind is that ratios are primarily intended as tools for trend and intraindustry comparative analysis. Nevertheless, if an analyst must concentrate on a single ratio, a strong argument can be made that the ratio should be funds or cash flow focused and should use variables from all three financial statements: the income statement, the balance sheet, and the statement of cash flows.

The *enhanced-fixed-charges-payout* ratio presented here is a variant on the Securities and Exchange Commission (SEC) fixed-charges coverage ratio required to be reported by public companies. In addition to the fixed-charges coverage ratio, this ratio takes into account other required loan principal repayments as well as lease rentals. Further, it ignores the problem of spontaneously increasing net working capital needs by taking the less pessimistic approach of not taking into effect the changes in current accounts and by using the funds from operations concept rather than the net cash from operations procedure. This means that the calculation also leaves no room for any discretionary expenditures or dividends.

This enhanced-fixed-charges-payout ratio calculates the relationship between

- all of the cash made available from operations (excluding spontaneous increases in net current assets) plus any discretionary cash and
- all loan principal and interest charges (including lease rentals).

The following is the suggested form of the enhanced-fixed-charges-payout ratio:

$$\frac{\text{Profits after taxes} + \text{Depreciation} + \text{Other noncash charges} + \text{Interest expense} + \text{Lease rentals}}{\text{Current portion long-term debt} + \text{Interest expense} + \text{Lease rentals}}$$

This ratio must be at a minimum computation of 1:1 or greater to give any level of comfort. Any results lower than this require additional financing just to meet presently contracted for payments, a hazardous position indeed.

Profitability Ratios

Profitability is somewhat less important than cash flow because it implies that a company has long-term viability rather than the ability to repay debt. The examination of a company's profitability usually relates the company's profits to various other standards, such as the level of sales, assets, and equity. Taken together, they give a good indication of a company's ability to survive and continue to attract new equity or debt funding in the future.

As discussed in chapter 4, the common-sizing of an income statement (in which each account is shown as a percentage of sales) produces several useful ratios, including gross profit margin, which was discussed in relation to income statement analysis. Not discussed in any detail was the net profit margin—also called return on sales—perhaps the most frequently used measure of profitability. However, since the true measure of profitability is the efficient use of assets and the return on the shareholders' equity, the amount of assets required to support a given level of sales and the amount of equity required to support that level of assets are also important measures of the overall profitability of the company.

Consider, for example, Company X and Company Y. On the same level of sales, Company X makes $5,000 profit while Company Y makes $10,000 profit. It would appear on the surface that Company Y is more profitable. Suppose, however, that Company Y required $50,000 in assets to support its sales, while Company X required only $15,000 in assets to support the same level of sales. Company X, then, made more profits per dollar of assets employed than did Company Y. The two companies might also require different levels of shareholders' investment to support a given level of assets.

Thus, an analyst should consider several variables when assessing a company's profitability.

Return-on-Sales Ratio (Sometimes called Net Profit Margin)

The *return-on-sales ratio* (or net profit margin) simply measures the extent to which a company's revenues exceed all of its expenses—that is, how much profit the company earns on each dollar of sales. There is no benchmark figure that a lender looks for since return on sales will vary greatly with the industry. However, a company with highly volatile sales should have a higher return on sales than a company with predictable profits over the years. In addition, the level of assets and equity required to generate a specified sales level should also be taken into consideration in determining a satisfactory return on sales. The return-on-sales ratio, or net margin, is calculated as follows:

$$\text{Return-on-sales ratio} = \frac{\text{Net profit}}{\text{Sales}}$$

Continuing with the example, the Carroll Company's income statement shows net profit at $220 and sales at $16,527 for 1991. Thus, the company's return-on-sales ratio is calculated as follows:

$$\text{Retun-on-sales ratio} = \frac{220}{16{,}527} = 1.33\%$$

This return-on-sales ratio shows that the company earned $1.33 for each $100 of sales. In other words, 1.33 percent of each sales dollar remains after accounting for all expenses.

However, dividends paid to shareholders further reduce the amount that can be added to equity. The return-on-sales ratio is useful in comparing companies within the same industry and in analyzing the trend in the relationship between a company's profits and sales over several years.

The ratio also indicates how much cost of goods sold and operating expenses can change without adversely affecting profits.

In this case, if Carroll's product costs and operating expenses (such as rent and salaries) were to increase by 1.33 percent divided by the quantity 1 minus the tax rate, the company would become unprofitable. Therefore, the company must increase the prices of its products and control its expenses more efficiently.

$$1.33\% / (1 - 34\%) = 2.02\%$$

The taxes must be removed from the increase, since expenses are tax deductible. The profitability indicated above implies that taxes had already been deducted.

Asset Turnover Ratio

The *asset turnover ratio* measures how efficiently a company uses its assets by showing how many dollars of sales are generated by each dollar of assets. When comparing the asset turnover ratios of various companies, remember that the ratio is calculated using the book value of assets (which may not reflect the true value of assets). For example, a fully depreciated loom in a textile mill may produce just as many yards of cloth of the same quality as a new loom. Yet its effect will be to increase the company's asset turnover ratio by decreasing the book value of assets used in the calculation.

This means that the asset turnover ratio for companies with older equipment will tend to be higher than for companies with newer equipment.

The asset turnover ratio is calculated using the following formula:

$$\text{Asset turnover ratio} = \frac{\text{Sales}}{\text{Average assets}}$$

The Carroll Company's income statement shows sales of $16,527 for 1991. Its assets as of fiscal year end 1991 and 1990 list as $6,102 and $6,673 on the balance sheet. These asset figures may be averaged, or ending assets may be substituted for average assets. Thus, the Carroll Company's asset turnover ratio for 1991 is calculated as follows:

$$\text{Asset turnover ratio} = \frac{16{,}527}{(6{,}102 + 6{,}637)/2} = 2.59 \text{ times}$$

The asset turnover ratio shows that the Carroll Company generates $2.59 of revenues for every $1.00 of assets employed.

Again, this ratio is used primarily to compare a company to its industry peers.

Return-on-Assets Ratio

The *return-on-assets* (ROA) ratio measures the profitability of a company in terms of how efficiently it uses its assets. It is basically a comparison of net profit to total assets. This ratio is frequently calculated incorrectly by not taking into account the variations in profit caused by different levels of interest expense. Conceptually, interest expense is part of the company's return on assets (after cost of goods sold, operating expenses, and so on), but it is that part of the return that goes to lenders rather than shareholders. Failure to include the interest expense in the return on assets calculation of a highly leveraged company will by itself cause the return on assets to be lower than for a firm which has little debt, obscuring the calculation of how efficiently the respective managements use the assets.

A more-precise calculation results when the numerator is fine-tuned by adding interest expense to net profit and then subtracting the tax benefit of interest expense. Calculated in this way, the ratio eliminates the effect of leverage on the return because it treats all returns as returns on equity, on which taxes have been paid. Average total assets is the preferred denominator, although, for simplicity's sake, many analysts use ending assets rather than average assets. While somewhat less accurate, this practice is generally accepted.

The return-on-assets ratio is calculated, then, as follows:

$$\text{Return-on-assets ratio} = \frac{\text{Net profit} + \text{Interest expense} - \text{Tax benefit of interest expense}}{\text{Average total assets}}$$

Carroll Company's income statement shows net profit at $220 and interest expense at $276 for 1991. The tax benefit of interest expense equals the interest expense multiplied by the company's tax rate. The tax rate may be found by dividing the provision for income taxes (as shown on the income statement) by profit before tax, which in this case comes to 33 percent (107 ÷ 327).

The company's balance sheet provides the information needed to calculate average total assets. The total assets as of the end of the 1991 fiscal year are listed as $6,673 compared with the previous year-end assets of $6,102. Average total assets is obtained by summing both amounts and dividing by 2. Thus, the Carroll Company's 1991 return-on-assets ratio is calculated as follows:

$$\text{ROA} = \frac{220 + 276 - (0.33 \times 276)}{(6{,}102 + 6{,}673)/2} = 6.34\%$$

Carroll Company's return on assets is 6.34 percent, or about 6 cents on every dollar of sales—a number that is meaningful only when it is compared to the ROA of previous years or of other companies in the industry.

When applying it, remember that this ratio may be misleading if the company has significant fixed assets, such as land, that are undervalued on the balance sheet. Another problem can occur because the income information is generated from a period that spans the two or more points-in-time of asset information; thus, imbalances may occur due to timing differences. For example, if a manufacturing company spent much of the year building a new manufacturing facility that did not begin production until the end of the year, the facility's impact as an asset in the denominator of the ratio will be far greater than its profit-generating impact in the numerator.

Return-on-Equity Ratio

Another measure of profitability is the *return-on-equity* (ROE) ratio, which measures the efficiency with which a company uses its stockholders' equity (without, however, taking into account the risk of the company's capital structure or business activities). Again, the credit analyst may substitute ending net worth for average net worth in the calculation with only a modest impairment of the ratio's accuracy. The return-on-equity ratio is calculated as follows:

$$\text{Return-on-equity ratio} = \frac{\text{Net profit}}{\text{Average net worth}}$$

This ratio is not adjusted for interest expense because it examines the return to shareholders *after debt expense is paid.*

The Carroll Company's 1991 income statement shows a net profit of $220, while the balance sheet lists the company's net worth for fiscal year end 1990 and 1991 as $2,345 and $2,458, respectively. The sum of these two figures is averaged to obtain the denominator for the equation. The company's return-on-equity ratio is calculated as follows:

$$\text{ROE ratio} = \frac{220}{(2{,}345 + 2{,}458)/2} = 9.16\%$$

The Carroll Company's return-on-equity ratio is 9.16 percent. Depending on what alternative investments are available, this return may not provide a good, short-run incentive for investors to invest their capital in Carroll Company's stock. However, a one-year return-on-equity of 9.16 percent may not be indicative of return on equity in future years.

If management is making efficient use of the company's assets (that is, if the company has an adequate return on assets), a low return-on-equity ratio may result from excessive equity relative to debt which, from a shareholder's point of view, suggests inefficient use of equity or insufficient financial leverage. A high return-on-equity ratio may not be entirely laudatory, however, because it could indicate too little equity, which is usually associated with high financial leverage. This is another instance where the credit analyst might draw erroneous conclusions by looking at a ratio outside of a comparative context.

ROBERT MORRIS RATIO STUDIES

Robert Morris Associates (RMA) is the national association for bank loan and credit officers. It has over 15,000 associate members. Each year RMA requests that members complete a limited-detail statement spreadsheet, by SIC code, sales and asset sizes, for companies to which the banks lend. RMA then computes common-sizes and other ratios for each company (over 100,000) and calculates the averages by asset and sales sizes for six different sizes of firms as show in Exhibit 6.3:

Exhibit 6.3

RMA Ratio Categories

Asset Categories	*Sales Categories*
0-500,000	0-1,000,000
500,000-2,000,000	1-3,000,000
2-10,000,000	3-5,000,000
10-50,000,000	5-10,000,000
50-100,000,000	12-25,000,000
100-250,000,000	25,000,000 and over

Two examples of portions of pages from the RMA *Annual Statement Studies* book [1990] are presented in the Dependable Doors and Engraph case studies at the end of chapter 2. You may wish to look at them again; they are on page 57 through page 84. Exhibit 6.4 is part of the RMA statement for the asset-size categories for Retailers - Department Stores, SIC No. 5311. This particular statement resembles the Carroll Company's industry. The following analysis uses information from this example, which shows only the middle four categories.

Regarding the use of these calculations, Robert Morris Associates makes the following disclaimer statement:

> RMA cautions that the *Studies* be regarded only as a general guideline and not as an absolute industry norm. This is due to limited samples within categories, the categorization of companies by their primary Standard Industrial Classification (SIC) number only, and different methods of operations by companies within the same industry. For these reasons, RMA recommends that the figures be used only as general guidelines in addition to other methods of financial analysis.

As Exhibit 6.4 shows, RMA occasionally does not get data from a sufficient number of companies (more than ten) to produce statistically significant averages. Therefore, cells for those companies are left blank, although the companies are included in the comparative historical data columns, which are not shown in this exhibit.[1]

1. The comparative historical data columns present five-year historical comparisons. Because they contain unweighted averages of all financial statements' results, the numbers in these columns are not particularly reliable for intercompany comparisons. For instance, the net sales and total assets in the largest two categories are usually many times the total sales of the firms in the smallest category. Since the comparative historical data columns average all firms together, the number of firms is what matters. The smaller categories usually have many more entries than the larger ones; thus, the smaller categories of firms contribute much more to the average than do the larger firms, making comparison of any

The RMA Common-Sizes

The top-most portion of the RMA statement lists the type and number of statements incorporated into each category. Next is a straightforward common-size analysis of the balance sheet. Assets are listed as a percentage of total assets; liabilities and net worth are listed as a percentage of total liabilities and net worth. Users select the relationships they wish to scrutinize. The RMA spread's account breakdown is so abbreviated, compared to the usual multiple page spreadsheet used by lenders, that the analyst may have to respread the subject firm's financials in order to make an item-by-item comparison.

By comparing the individual companies, you are studying with the specific sheet in the Robert Morris book, it should be easy to detect which balance sheet or income statement items are out of line. In many industries, the smaller firms are less profitable because their owners frequently pay themselves relatively large salaries or other fringe benefits to reduce income. Otherwise the owners would subject themselves to double taxation. (That is, the firm would have to pay taxes on net profits, and the owners would have to pay taxes on dividend income.)

Smaller companies also typically have older, more fully depreciated equipment. This can be verified by looking at the common-size percent. Larger businesses often find they can achieve real productivity gains with newer equipment. Consequently, the common-size analysis will show a higher percentage of total assets invested in fixed assets.

Another feature more commonly related to size than to different industries is the percentage of long-term debt relative to trade debt. Most small businesses depend much more on trade credit and, compared to larger competitors, do not have significant long-term financing from outside lenders.

RMA Ratios

The bottom two thirds of the RMA statement consists of a list of ratios. Three values are presented for each ratio. The middle number is the median (middle) score of all companies individually. The top number is the median score for the better half of all companies. The lower number is the median for the worse half. These three medians give rise to four quartiles. The first quartile of firms has ratios appearing entirely above the top number; firms in the second quartile have ratios that appear between the top and middle

---

single firm with the "all" column less useful. Therefore, these columns should be avoided for comparing individual firms. Instead, the comparative history data columns should be used only to look at trends within the industry as a whole, not to identify a specific comparison date.

number; the ratios of firms in the third quartile appear between the middle and lower number; the fourth-quartile firms have ratios that appear below the lowest number. This means that only 50 percent of the companies have ratios that are between the top and bottom numbers. Many analysts refer to the quartile position of the subject firm in their credit analysis reports.

RMA arranges all ratio calculations so that the quartiles accurately position the best firms in the top quartile and vice versa. For example, in the current ratio, quick ratio, accounts receivable turnover, and inventory turnover, the higher the ratio, the better the quality. Therefore, the highest values are the top numbers. In sales as a percentage of working capital the lower the ratio,

Robert Morris Associates

Exhibit 6.4

RETAILERS - DEPARTMENT STORES SIC #5311

Current Data Sorted By Sales				*Type of Statement*
3	17	39	15	*Unqualified*
1		3		*Qualified*
4	11	5		*Reviewed*
11	14	2	1	*Compiled*
12	9	7	2	*Other*
127 statements (10/1/89-3/31/90)		*29 statements (6/30-9/30/89)*		
500M-2MM	*2MM-10MM*	*10-50MM*	*50-100MM*	***Asset Size***
31	*51*	*56*	*18*	*NO. OF STATEMENTS*
%	%	%	%	**ASSETS**
5.7	6.9	7.3	4.6	Cash & Equivalents
16.3	20.3	20.9	16.8	Trade Receivables -(net)
53.1	48.7	36.0	33.9	Inventory
2.0	1.0	2.4	3.0	All Other Current
77.1	76.8	66.5	58.3	Total Current
15.8	16.2	26.9	30.2	Fixed Assets (net)
0.2	0.3	1.1	2.5	Intangibles (net)
6.9	6.8	5.5	8.9	All Other Noncurrent
100.0	100.0	100.0	100.0	Total
				LIABILITIES
11.1	7.8	5.6	3.4	Notes Payable-Short Term
2.7	2.0	2.3	3.0	Cur. Mat.-L/T/D
11.1	13.1	13.4	12.0	Trade Payables
0.6	0.9	1.9	1.8	Income Taxes Payable
6.0	9.6	9.6	11.8	All Other Current
31.5	33.5	32.9	32.1	Total Current
22.7	13.4	22.3	27.9	Long-Term Debt
0.6	0.9	2.2	1.8	Deferred Taxes
1.7	2.7	2.2	4.9	All Other Noncurrent
43.5	49.5	40.4	33.4	Net Worth
100.0	100.0	100.0	100.0	Total Liabilities & Net Worth
				INCOME DATA
100.0	100.0	100.0	100.0	Net Sales
36.4	34.4	34.5	35.0	Gross Profit
34.5	33.5	31.9	31.0	Operating Expenses
1.9	0.8	2.6	3.9	Operating Profit
0.5	0.7	0.1	1.0	All Other Expenses (net)
1.5	1.5	2.8	2.9	Profit Before Taxes

								RATIOS
	4.9		3.6		2.7		2.6	
	2.9		2.6		2.2		2.0	Current
	2.1		1.8		1.7		1.3	
	1.9		1.5		1.5		1.4	
(30.0)	0.5		0.8		1.0	**(17.0)**	0.6	Quick
	0.3		0.3		0.3		0.3	
3.0	121.5	**3.0**	143.1	**3.0**	119.6	**2.0**	153.3	
21.0	17.2	**34.0**	10.8	**46.0**	8.0	**23.0**	15.7	Sales/Receivables
62.0	5.9	**61.0**	6.0	**79.0**	4.6	**96.0**	3.8	
78.0	4.7	**83.0**	4.4	**78.0**	4.7	**91.0**	4.0	
166.0	2.2	**114.0**	3.2	**96.0**	3.8	**104.0**	3.5	Cost of Sales/Inventory
228.0	1.6	**140.0**	2.6	**114.0**	3.2	**126.0**	2.9	
9.0	41.3	**19.0**	19.3	**21.0**	17.1	**26.0**	13.8	
25.0	14.7	**27.0**	13.6	**32.0**	11.4	**40.0**	9.1	Cost of Sales/Payables
45.0	8.1	**38.0**	9.7	**44.0**	8.3	**50.0**	7.3	
	2.8		3.7		4.0		3.5	
	3.7		5.4		5.6		7.2	Sales/Working Capital
	6.4		9.5		9.1		17.2	
	3.3		9.4		5.6		3.5	
(25.0)	1.8	(48.0)	2.6	(52.0)	2.5	(15.0)	1.7	EBIT/Interest
	1.0		1.2		1.6		1.6	
			3.3		8.5		6.3	Net Profit + Depr. Dep.,
		(27.0)	1.5	(43.0)	2.8	(15.0)	2.8	Amort./Cur. Mat. L/T/D
			0.4		1.4		0.7	
	0.1		0.1		0.4		0.5	
	0.3		0.3		0.7		1.2	Fixed/Worth
	0.8		0.6		1.2		2.1	
	0.3		0.4		1.0		1.3	
	1.4		1.1		1.5		2.4	Debt/Worth
	3.0		2.1		2.3		3.7	
	18.3		24.1		22.7		18.3	
(29.0)	9.5		7.3	(55.0)	15.1	(17.0)	14.4	% Profit Before Taxes/
	2.2		0.9		4.5		9.2	Tangible Net Worth
	10.0		9.8		8.8		6.8	
	3.4		3.8		6.2		4.2	% Profit Before Taxes/
	1.0		0.6		1.9		2.8	Total Assets
	58.3		40.2		13.6		8.4	
	22.9		17.5		8.7		5.0	Sales/Net Fixed Assets
	6.3		10.0		5.3		4.5	
	2.4		3.2		2.7		2.3	
	1.8		2.5		2.1		1.7	Sales/Total Assets
	1.6		17.0		1.5		14.0	
	0.7		0.6		1.1		1.4	
(24.0)	1.1		1.1	(53.0)	1.8	(17.0)	2.1	% Depr. Dep. Amort./
	1.7		1.7		2.3		2.5	Sales
	3.5		1.6					
(12.0)	4.6	(14.0)	2.5					% Officer's Comp/Sales
	8.7		4.2					
	28816M		50784M		3322408M		248745M	Net Sales ($)
	13115M		193923M		137349M		137052M	Total Assets ($)

the more select it is. Therefore, the low values are at the top. The following information highlights the better ratios for analysis.

Liquidity (Both Liquidation and Activity Types)

The current and quick ratios, liquidation measures of liquidity, are followed by the activity focused ratios of receivables, inventory, and payables turnovers. There are two columns of ratios for the turnovers ratios. The column to the left lists the average number of days turnover per year and the other column lists the average turnover times per year.

Leverage (Both Liquidation and Coverage Types)

The fixed assets-to-worth and debt-to-worth ratios are shown as examples of the liquidation approach to leverage review. The fixed assets-to-worth ratio is useful in reviewing manufacturing and transportation industries, both of which are heavily invested in fixed assets. These ratios indicate how much the equity investment accounts for these assets. The debt-to-worth ratio is discussed above.

The *interest coverage ratio* is particularly important when reviewing firms with long-term mortgages and those with little amortizing debt. Interest coverage is followed by derived funds flow (from operations) divided by current maturities of long-term debt. While useful, this latter ratio has a slight defect in that it fails to illuminate any bulges in the long-term debt repayment schedule. Nevertheless, it is a reasonable ratio for measuring debt repayment obligations of the coming year.

Performance

The return on net worth is calculated by taking profits before taxes and dividing by tangible net worth. As mentioned, the notion of tangible net worth needs further individual investigation because some firms have undervalued assets. Moreover, because tangible net worth is smaller than total assets less liabilities, the return on net worth percentage will appear to be better than if intangibles are included. It seems incongruous to improve a return percentage artificially by eliminating intangibles.

Fortunately, an average ratio can be derived and ROE and some other useful ratios can be calculated by using the percentages in the common-size analysis along with the total sales and assets listed at the bottom of the page. For example, Exhibit 6.5 shows a sample of how the totals have been used to recalculate the return on total net worth. Refer to the third column of Exhibit 6.4.

Exhibit 6.5

Deriving ROE for Total Net Worth

Item	*Percentages*	*Raw Numbers*
Net Sales	100.0 (given)	3,322,408 (given)
Profit Before Taxes	2.8 (given)	**93,027 (2.8% x 3,322,408)**
Total Assets	100.0 (given)	1,373,491 (given)
Total Net Worth	53.5 (given)	**734,818 (53.5% x 1,373,491)**

Now divide 93,027 by 734,818 to obtain profit before taxes as a percent of total net worth, which is 12.7 percent. This answer, as expected, is lower than the 15.1 percent median given on the RMA page for return on tangible net worth because intangibles are no longer being removed, reducing the total assets and artificially increasing the ROA. (While the average could be naturally lower than the median, it could also be higher; the point is still valid.)

The next ratio listed is profit before taxes-to-total assets. While accurate for comparable calculations, this ratio is not an accurate calculation of return on assets. As discussed above, this formulation of ROA sharply penalizes firms that have significant debt in their capital structures. Unfortunately, interest expense is not reported separately on RMA sheets so, in this case, the ratio cannot be adjusted.

The last two performance ratios are sales-to-net fixed assets (fixed asset turnover) and sales-to-total assets (total asset turnover). These ratios have earned a reputation for being good industry benchmarks since the treasury division of the E.I. Du Pont de Nemours & Co., Inc., popularized them for interdivisional analysis. If a subject firm is significantly above or below industry averages in these ratios, it may be evidence of either strikingly superior management or serious problems ahead.

EXAMPLE OF RATIO ANALYSIS

After calculating the three major categories of ratios—liquidity (liquidation and activity types); leverage (liquidation and coverage types); and profitability—the analysis can begin.

In the case of the Carroll Company, the ratios calculated will first be compared with ratios calculated for the industry, as shown in the Robert Morris Associates *Annual Statement Studies* of the retail department store industry discussed above in the section on comparative analysis. Since Carroll's total assets in the latest year are between $1 and $10 million, the industry comparisons will come from the second column of the RMA statement shown as Exhibit 6.4. Since the RMA statement does not have all of the ratios used in this book, some ratios may be derived. The ratios provided by RMA but not developed in this book are ignored.

Next, Carroll Company's own ratios will be compared with its own showing in previous years (trend analysis). With regard to the trend analysis, all the ratios will be compared, but those that appear to be significant to the examination of the Carroll Company will be emphasized.

Liquidity and Current Asset Management Analysis

Comparative Analysis

Ratio	*Carroll 1991*	*Higher*	*Median*	*Lower*
Current Ratio	1.7	3.6	2.6	1.3
Quick Ratio	.08	1.5	.8	.3

Carroll Company's current ratio appears in the 3rd quartile, between the median and the beginning of the lower median. The ratio of 1.3 times suggests that in liquidation the Carroll Company's current assets—after receiving a 50-percent auction price—would not be enough to pay its current liabilities. Moreover, its quick ratio puts it in the bottom, or lowest quartile, since it is below the lower median. An experienced credit analyst would recognize that the median of Carroll's quick ratio is low by most standards. However, this ratio is not very significant for retailers since inventory (which is included in the current ratio, but not in the quick ratio) comprises the primary type of current asset for all three companies included in the RMA statement. Moreover, their level of receivables is small because retailers primarily deal in cash or bank credit cards

The credit analyst could conclude that the Carroll Company's current position is not too out of line with that of other companies in the industry. A low quick ratio may be less risky for a retailer than for a manufacturer. Because it is all finished goods, a retailer's inventory can be converted to cash relatively quickly in contrast to, for example, a real estate developer's inventory of homes built on speculation. In this latter case, work-in-progress inventories would predominate.

Nevertheless, some analysts believe the contrary about merchandisers of all types. This opinion expresses the concern that merchandisers sometimes buy unfashionable or obsolete inventories and cannot resell them at a price that even covers their costs. From this viewpoint, merchandisers put lenders more at risk, something clearly indicated by the low quick ratio exhibited here.

It is difficult to be conclusive about any ratio, since the primary purpose of a ratio is to red flag problem areas. This controversy is a clear example of the need to understand the business firm and its industry, since contrary opinions could be expressed about the same set of figures.

Trend Analysis

Carroll Ratio	*1989*	*1990*	*1991*
Current Ratio	1.8	1.9	1.7
Quick Ratio	.2	.18	.1

The Carroll Company's current ratio increased from 1.8 in January 1989 to 1.9 in 1990 and then dropped to 1.7 in 1991. However, an examination of the Carroll Company's balance sheets shows that long-term debt increased by about $400,000 during fiscal 1991. This reduced the company's need for short-term borrowings to support its asset base, thus improving its current ratio for 1991. If the company had had no additional long-term debt, the current ratio for both 1989 and 1990 would have been even lower.

From fiscal year end 1989 to 1990, the Carroll Company's quick ratio dropped from 0.2 to 0.1, reflecting a lowered cash balance and higher debt. This could be the result of a more-aggressive cash management program, a cash flow problem, or a temporary decrease in cash.

Leverage and Debt Management Analysis

Comparative Analysis

Ratio	*Carroll 1991*	*Higher*	*Median*	*Lower*
Debt to worth	1.7	.4	1.1	2.1
Debt to capitalization	.4		.2	
Times Interest Earned	2.2	9.4	2.6	1.2
Funds Flow/CPLTD	7.23	3.3	1.5	.4
Dividend Payout Ratio	53%	N/A	N/A	N/A

The Carroll Company's debt-to-worth ratio of 1.7 indicates that in a liquidation, where 50-percent markdowns are the rule of thumb, there would be insufficient assets to repay creditors. Moreover, the ratio is below the median for its industry.

The Carroll Company's debt-to-worth ratio of 1.7 means that the company's creditors have 1.7 times as much value entrusted to the company as the shareholders have. This is considerably less than the median position in its size range in the retail industry and would also be low for a manufacturing company.

Unfortunately, the RMA book does not calculate the debt-to-capitalization ratio; therefore, it has been derived, as follows:

Items from Common-Size Table	*Industry (2-10 MM asset size)*
Long-term Debt	13.4 (given)
Deferred Taxes	.9 (given)
All Other Noncurrent	2.7 (given)
New Worth	49.5 (given)
Total Capitalization	66.5 (derived)
Long-Debt/Total Capitalization	.2 (derived)

The Carroll Company's debt-to-capitalization ratio is substantially above the industry average. One possible explanation may be that the company has the use of a long-term debt facility, such as a revolving credit line, that extends over several years. That arrangement would enable the company to borrow and repay under the credit facility as if it were a short-term line of credit. Thus, the company would gain the flexibility of short-term access to funds while its balance sheet would reflect the funds as long-term debt, thereby increasing the debt-to-capitalization ratio above that of its peers.

Turning to the coverage ratios, an examination of the times-interest-earned ratio for the industry shows the Carroll Company to be slightly lower than the median position. This may indicate that the company is slightly more highly leveraged than other companies and thus carries a higher level of interest-bearing debt (a hypothesis also supported by the high debt-to-worth ratio). After studying both the times-interest-earned and the debt-to-worth ratios, the loan officer might conclude that the Carroll Company lags in the industry. However, the loan officer should exercise caution in reaching such a conclusion since other factors, such as the cost of debt, can also affect the ratio results.

A look at the funds flow-to-current maturities ratio shows the Carroll Company leading the rest of its industry segment by a large margin. The firm appears to have extremely long terms on its outstanding long-term debt, since only 3 percent of it is maturing next year—giving the debt a 33-year maturity! Because such long terms are not available in the debt markets, this information warns the loan officer that the firm has a nonamortizing debt that will mature all at once (a bullet loan). If the loan's maturity date is close at hand or within the maturity date of any long-term debt under consideration, the analyst should discuss with the company its plans for the disposition of the cash necessary to replace this large debt.

The Carroll Company's dividend payout ratio of 53 percent appears to be impeding its equity growth during a time when the analysis indicates that equity growth is most needed. However, because payout ratios for the other two businesses in the RMA sample are not available, it is difficult to quantify the comparison. In addition, dividend payout ratios are only one of many ways that owners can take funds out of a firm. An analyst should also look for excessive officer/owner salaries and fringe benefits, renting fixed assets from owners, and so on.

Trend Analysis

Calculations of the debt-to-worth and debt-to-capitalization ratios for the Carroll Company for the past three years yield the following results:

Carroll Ratio	*1989*	*1990*	*1991*
Debt to worth	1.6	1.6	1.7
Debt to Capitalization	.4	.5	.5
Times Interest Earned	4.7	3.0	2.2
Funds flow/CPLTD	7.9	5.9	5.2
Dividend payout ratio	29%	43%	53%

The increasing debt-to-worth ratio suggests that the Carroll Company's retained earnings are insufficient to fund its balance-sheet growth in the same proportions as it had in former years. Although this situation could have resulted from a conscious managerial decision to use the company's leverage more aggressively, a review of Carroll Company's after-tax profits for fiscal years 1989, 1990, and 1991 ($358,000, $261,000, and $220,000) and its dividend policy (a dividend payout ratio of 29 percent, 43 percent, and 53 percent) would appear to support the conclusion that the problem stemmed from insufficient retained earnings.

To stabilize its debt-to-worth ratio, the Carroll Company could slow its asset growth relative to its equity growth or increase its equity more rapidly relative to its asset growth. The company could control its asset growth either through more-efficient use of assets or through slower growth in revenues and number of business locations, thus reducing the need for operating assets. The company could also increase its equity growth through higher earnings, lower dividends, or additional equity contributions.

The growth in the Carroll Company's debt-to-capitalization ratio from 0.4 to 0.5 is not large enough to be considered significant. Nevertheless, the growth does show that the company's funded permanent debt has grown faster than its equity.

For the last three years, the Carroll Company has experienced a deterioration in each of its coverage ratios. While the company's 1991 times-interest-earned ratio of 2.2 and its 1991 funds flow-to-current maturities ratio of 5.2 remain in the acceptable range, the deterioration should prompt the loan officer to further explore this area.

Of additional concern is the dividend payout ratio, which has increased from 29 percent to 53 percent. During the same period that the Carroll Company's cash dividends increased, its after-tax profit declined. Analysts should also look out for publicly held companies that have decided to support their stock price and provide a stable and dependable dividend stream or to buy stock in the market to increase the price in order to provide short-term satisfaction to their shareholders, perhaps to the detriment of the long-term health of the company.

Profitability Analysis

Comparative Analysis

Ratio	Carroll 1991	Higher	Median	Lower
Return on Sales	1.3		1.3	
Return on Assets	6.3	9.8	3.8	.6
Return on Equity	9.2		7.9*	

*Derived using the method as demonstrated above.

The lower-than-median return on sales shows that Carroll receives less profit for each dollar of sales than does the industry, which indicates that its sales strategy is to have higher volume at lower margins. Its higher-than-median return on assets indicates that it uses its assets more efficiently than others in its industry to produce profits. Perhaps it does not decorate its stores as much as its competition does. In terms of shareholders' return, the Carroll Company's return-on-equity ratio is also excellent, surpassing the derived industry median.

Trend Analysis

A review of the Carroll Company's profitability ratios shows a continuing decline in its operating performance:

Carroll Ratio	1989	1990	1991
Return on Sales	2.8	1.8	1.3
Return on Assets	8.7	6.7	6.3
Return on Equity	17.5	11.5	9.2

In two years, the Carroll Company's profitability declined from 2.8 percent to 1.3 percent, its return on assets declined from 8.7 percent to 6.3 percent, and its return on equity declined from 17.5 percent to 9.2 percent. All three return indicators remain at the median or above median for the industry, and this should provide some reassurance. However, the decline itself indicates a significant shift in strategy toward a high-volume, low-margin expansion. This alone is enough to encourage the analyst to conduct an in-depth review to determine the reason for the company's decline.

The low return on sales may signify stiff competition, lack of expense control, or both. The low return on assets is again from a poor sales-to-assets ratio (reflected in the activity ratios) and the low return on sales. A review of the Carroll Company's management policies is definitely in order.

SUMMARY OF IMPORTANT CONCEPTS

While it is easy to calculate an impressive array of them, ratios are not meaningful in and of themselves and can lead to erroneous conclusions if they are not analyzed in a broad context rather than in isolation. Ratio analysis is only one part of the total financial statement analysis of a company and should not in itself lead to any lending decisions.

Ratios do, however, assist in converting a company's financial information into a meaningful analytical format. Ratios are particularly useful in facilitating comparisons of companies of varying size, particularly among companies in the same industry. They also facilitate trend analysis, which entails looking at a company's ratios over a period of two or more years. The most widely used ratios help in analyzing a company's liquidity (both liquidation and activity), leverage (both liquidation and coverage), and profitability.

The liquidity ratios (liquidation type)—current ratio and quick ratio—measure a company's financial strength in liquidation. These ratios are based on the assumption that all assets will be sold in a forced sale and that all liabilities will be paid. The liquidity ratios (activity type) have significant implications for the examination of going concerns because they show a company's ability to meet its current obligations and sustain operations by examining the quality—the cash conversion cycle—of current assets. The principal activity ratios compare income-statement accounts (sales, or cost of goods sold) to balance-sheet accounts to determine asset turnover, accounts receivable turnover, inventory turnover, and accounts payable turnover. These turnover ratios are often expressed in days—as in the average accounts receivable collection period, days in inventory, and days in accounts payable.

The leverage ratios (liquidation type)—the debt-to-worth and debt-to-capitalization ratios—attempt to measure the equity cushion or risk shouldered by a company's creditors in the event of a liquidation. The leverage ratios (coverage type)—times-interest-earned, cash flow-to-current maturities, and dividend payment ratios—measure the ability of a company to meet its long-term debt obligations through the flow of funds (cash) from its operations.

Profitability ratios—return on sales, return on assets, and return on equity—look at the relationship between net profit and sales, assets, and equity, respectively.

It is important to keep in mind that because financial statements may reflect different accounting methods, corporate structures, and management policies, ratio comparison is rarely exact. Therefore, view any findings as general indicators of performance rather than as absolute predictors.

EXERCISES

Important Terms to Define

- ratios
- *Annual Statement Studies*
- current ratio
- working capital
- average collection period
- days in inventory
- leverage ratios
- debt-to-capitalization ratio
- times-interest-earned ratio
- enhanced-fixed-charges-payout ratio
- return-on-sales ratio
- return-on-assets ratio
- interest coverage ratio
- funds (cash) flow-to-current maturities long-term debt ratio
- elevator analysis
- liquidity ratios
- quick ratio
- accounts receivables turnover
- inventory turnover
- accounts payable turnover debt-to-worth ratio
- coverage ratios
- dividend payout ratio
- profitability ratios
- asset turnover ratio
- return on equity ratio

Dependable Doors Case Study

1. Calculate the liquidity and activity ratios for Dependable Doors over the last three years. Calculate the activity ratios in terms of days on hand.
2. Discuss the trends in the liquidity and activity ratios in light of what has been happening with Dependable Doors over the last three years.
3. Calculate appropriate leverage ratios for Dependable Doors over the last three years and discuss their significance.
4. Calculate the coverage ratios for Dependable Doors over the last three years and comment on their significance.
5. Calculate the profitability ratios of Dependable Doors and explain the trends over the last three years.
6. How does Dependable Doors compare to industry averages? Explain any divergences from the norm.

The answers to these Dependable Doors questions appear in the appendix.

Engraph Case Study

1. Following the formulas presented in the chapter, calculate liquidity and current asset ratios for Engraph over the last two years. For receivables, inventory, and payables, calculate the ratio in terms of days on hand.
2. Discuss the significance of the liquidity and current asset ratios in light of what has been happening with Engraph over the last two years.
3. Discuss the significance of the leverage and debt management ratios in light of what has been happening with Engraph over the last two years.
4. Calculate and discuss the profitability ratios of Engraph over the last two years.

Cash Budgets

LEARNING OBJECTIVES

After studying this chapter, you will be able to

- name the primary uses of cash budgets,
- construct a cash budget,
- do an interpretive analysis of a cash budget as part of a comprehensive financial statement analysis, and
- explain why cash budgets are useful in determining seasonal and other interim funding needs.

INTRODUCTION

Cash budgets are a tool that helps forecast a company's future short-term financing needs. Chapter 5 explains that the net income reported on a company's accrual-basis income statement does not reflect the amount of cash generated. Consequently, the credit analyst trying to make a decision on a short-term loan request might have difficulty determining the borrower's ability to generate cash and repay debt.

Because it provides an estimate of a company's cash position and funding requirements for each forecast period, a cash budget is particularly useful in determining the credit needs of companies with seasonal variations in operations. The cash budget bridges the gap between statements by examining the periodic flow of cash through the company's accounts over a designated time period. Credit analysts are most interested in reviewing cash budgets for the periods between the origination and repayment of loans; companies are interested in making up cash budgets to control their monthly, weekly, or daily cash requirements. By projecting a company's schedule of receipts and disbursements on a monthly, weekly, or daily basis, an analyst can identify the cause, timing, and magnitude of a company's peak borrowing needs and its repayment capabilities.

Principles and Assumptions

Ideally, since most companies use cash budgets as a part of their own internal financial planning process, a borrower will include a cash budget in its loan application package. If the application does include a cash budget, the credit analyst may be able to get by with just a close examination of the underlying assumptions of the company's forecast. However, in most cases, the credit analyst will have to construct a cash budget, and then analyze it. In that case, the analyst must be able to take the information derived from accrual-basis financial statements and convert it to cash-basis information.

A *cash budget* looks at a company's inflows and outflows on a cash basis, rather than on an accrual basis. It takes into account the timing of these cash flows and the company's actual cash requirements. This means that while a company's income statement recognizes sales at delivery, a cash budget recognizes only collections on receivables. Thus, if a company makes credit sales on 30-day terms, a cash budget recognizes the collection of cash 30 days after the sale rather than on the day of sale.

An income statement recognizes an *expenditure* as an *expense* when a purchase is delivered or (in the case of cost of goods sold) when a sale is made. The cash budget is concerned, not with *whether* an expenditure is an expense, but *when it is paid*. If an insurance premium is paid annually, rather than being expensed evenly throughout the year, it is entered as a cash expenditure during the month it is paid.

For constructing the budget, analysts use the common-size analysis of the income statement as well as the GAAP financial statements to identify turnover ratios on receivables, inventories, and payables. Thus, one of the *prime assumptions in a cash budget* is that the past turnovers in a company's accounts receivable, inventories, and accounts payable will remain steady. An analyst must be able to rely on the relationship of a company's various current asset and liability accounts to its sales. If any changes are to be made in these relationships, as would occur in a switch in collection payment terms, the analyst needs to know of them to properly complete the budget.

A cash budget is also based on detailed cash flow information about the acquisition of capital equipment, the repayment of long-term debt, the purchase of other companies, and the selling of capital stock. The timing of such expenditures, such as when interest and principal payments on a loan come due, needs to be known at least to the month.

To summarize, cash budgets forecast a company's cash receipts and disbursements between statement dates, usually monthly. The most-common source of cash is the collection of accounts receivable, and the most-common uses of cash include payments of accounts payable (for inventories), interest, taxes, labor (payroll), and capital expenditure. A cash budget includes all of a company's anticipated cash inflows (including loan proceeds, cash sales, and the collection of accounts receivable) and all of its potential cash outflows (purchases, labor, selling expenses, interest and principal on loans, utilities, and other capital expenditures).

Use of Cash Budgets

Companies use cash budgets, quite simply, to keep their checking accounts from running out of cash. Lenders use cash budgets primarily to assure themselves that borrowers will be able to repay short-term loans. The credit analyst may want to rework the cash budget to test how unexpected changes in cash-flow assumptions could affect it. This procedure, commonly referred to as *scenario analysis*, may enable the lender to uncover financing needs not foreseen by the company.

In simplest terms, projected receipts and projected disbursements represent a company's projected cash flow, positive or negative. By evaluating the likely timing and magnitude of these cash inflows and outflows, the credit analyst can determine the company's cash needs for its operating cycle. A negative cash flow, or a positive cash flow that produces less than the company's minimum cash requirement, indicates that the company faces at least a temporary funding requirement. Thus, the cash budget allows a company's management to determine the cash implications of its plans and strategies, and it enables both management and the credit analyst to anticipate the company's financing needs and determine the company's ability to generate sufficient cash to repay a loan. A toy manufacturer, for example, must be able to forecast its cash needs from when it begins building inventory (for its major selling season in the summer) through when it collects its accounts receivables. The hope is that it can discover when its financing requirements will be the greatest. The magnitude and timing of the toy manufacturer's cash needs determine both the amount of the company's loan request and when repayment is possible.

By identifying the various components of cash flow, a cash budget also enables management to control (and the lender to scrutinize) the company's performance on an interim basis. Management can react quickly if the actual cash flow varies significantly from the expected cash budget. Management's effectiveness in dealing with any such deviations depends upon what time increment is used in preparing a cash budget (usually monthly or weekly) and how often the company's performance is reviewed. Obviously, a company can react to problems more quickly if its cash flow is monitored weekly rather than quarterly or semiannually.

When approving a short-term loan request, the loan officer must have strong confidence in the company's cash budgets. This confidence results directly from how well management has performed against its previous plans and how dependable the company's cash flows have been in the past. A cash budget shows absolute cash needs; however, because the budget is only a forecast and a single short-term event could delay a receipt of cash, the lender should be ready to finance more than the budget estimates.

Format of a Cash Budget

Ideally, the prospective commercial borrower will have provided the bank with a detailed cash budget categorized as to cash inflows (receipts) and outflows (disbursements). With the cash budget in hand, the analyst's job is to check the timing and magnitude of the company's projected cash flows in the light of other available financial information. The review that precedes the preparation or interpretation of a cash budget takes into consideration all the information gathered, including income tax information. The assumptions behind the projections, however, are really the critical part of the cash budget.

Whether constructing a cash budget or simply reviewing an existing one, an analyst must identify

- all the aspects of the company's operation that influence incoming and outgoing cash (for example, the percentage of a company's sales that are credit sales),
- the timing and amount of the company's cash sales revenues, credit sales, and conversion of accounts receivable to cash inflows,
- the company's receivables turnover compared with its established credit terms,

- the suppliers' credit terms and the company's payment practices with respect to purchased materials,
- the magnitude and timing of the company's direct labor and overhead costs and of its various operating expenditures, including its general and administrative expenses and selling expenses, and
- nonoperating expenditures (dividend payment policies, loan repayment schedules, and interest payments).

Principal Variables

The specific format that companies use for their monthly cash budgets varies. A typical format, modeled after one published by the Small Business Administration (SBA), shown as Exhibit 7.1, includes the following elements:

1. Cash on hand at the beginning of each period.
2. Cash receipts, including cash sales, collections of accounts receivable, and other cash proceeds.
3. Total cash receipts.
4. Total cash available (projected cash on hand plus projected cash receipts).
5. *Operating cash paid out*, including inventory purchases, wages, payroll expenses, outside services, supplies, repairs and maintenance, advertising, transportation, accounting, legal, rent, telephone, utilities, insurance, and interest.
6. *Nonexpense cash flows*, including capital expenditures; stockholder and long-term debt transactions, including loan principal payments, capital expenditures, and withdrawals; and so on.
7. Total cash paid out.
8. Cash position (total cash available minus projected cash outflow).
9. Minimum ending cash (the amount required for ongoing operations).
10. *Additional funding requirement* (the amount needed to bring the company's cash position up to its minimum cash requirement). Negative funding requirements indicate amounts available for repayment of previous funding needs.

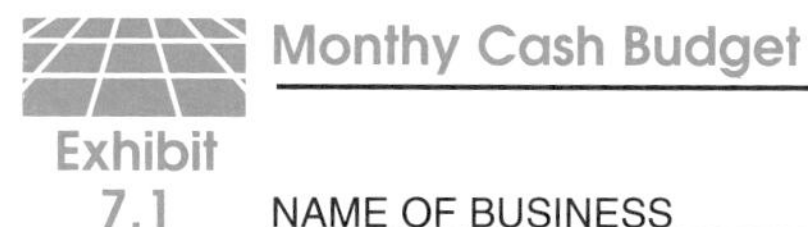

Monthy Cash Budget

Exhibit 7.1

NAME OF BUSINESS

Shaded lines are informational and not added into totals.					
MONTH	Prior Jan.	Feb.	Mar	Apr.	May
1. CASH ON HAND (Less any borrowings)					
2. CASH RECEIPTS					
(a) Total Sales					
(b) Cash Sales					
(c) Credit Sales					
(d) Collections from Credit Accounts					
(e) Other Proceeds: Sale of Assets, and so on					
3. TOTAL CASH RECEIPTS (2b+2d+2e=3)					
4. TOTAL CASH AVAILABLE (1+3)					
5. CASH PAID OUT					
(a) Purchases (Orders)					
(b) Purchases (Cash Payment)					
(c) Gross Wages (Excludes withdrawals)					
(d) Payroll Expenses (Taxes, etc.)					
(e) Outside Services					
(f) Supplies (Office and operating)					
(g) Repairs and Maintenance					
(h) Advertising					
(i) Car, Delivery, and Travel					
(j) Accounting and Legal					
(k) Rent					
(l) Telephone					
(m) Utilities					
(n) Insurance					
(o) Interest					
(p) Income Taxes					
(q) Miscellaneous (Unspecified)					
(r) Subtotal Expenses					
(s) Loan Principal Payment					
(t) Capital Expenditures					
(u) Owner's Withdrawal or Dividends					
6. TOTAL CASH PAID OUT					
7. CASH POSITION (4 minus 6)					
(a) Minimum Cash Required					
(b) Loan Required to Reach Cash Required					
(c) Excess Cash to Repay Loan					
ESSENTIAL OPERATING DATA					
A. Accounts Receivable (End of Month)					
B. Bad Debt (End of month)					
C. Inventory on Hand (End of month)					
D. Accounts Payable (End of month)					
E. Depreciation					

EXAMPLE OF CASH BUDGET IDENTIFYING SEASONAL FINANCING NEEDS

For a company with *seasonal sales,* the cash budget is a critical tool of financial statement analysis. Seasonal financing requirements arise in response to increases in a company's inventory and accounts receivable associated with periodic peaks in sales, production, or purchasing. Such an interim need may not be apparent from a company's year-end financial statements since a true short-term need will be self-liquidating—that is, the assets being financed will convert to cash to repay debt.

SBA FORM 1100

June	July	Aug.	Sep.	Oct.	Nov.	Dec.	Jan.	Total
								N/A
								N/A
								N/A
								N/A
								N/A

The company should be able to pay the interim loan during the course of an operating cycle—that is, the period during which cash converts into inventory, then into receivables, and then, through the collection of receivables, back to cash. If the company cannot pay back its interim loan by converting its assets into cash during the operating cycle, its borrowing need is not short term. Since seasonal borrowing is self-liquidating, the company does not have to be profitable to repay the debt, provided its cash flow is not negative.

The monthly cash budget is an excellent tool for identifying the cause, timing, and magnitude of a company's peak borrowing needs during interim periods between fiscal year-end statements. By determining the company's period of peak borrowing needs, the credit analyst can better evaluate the bank's potential exposure to loan loss.

The amount and quality of the company's assets (usually current) that are available to secure indebtedness or to convert into cash can be determined by abstracting the accumulating inventories through the peak period. The cash budget will indicate to the lender whether borrowing is needed to support accounts receivable or inventory. This is consequential to the lender because each asset has a different amount of risk associated with it. The application of cash budget analysis to seasonal working-capital needs is illustrated in the following example of a variety store called the Grab Bag.

Basic Subtotals of the Cash Budget

The simplified income statement and the balance sheet used to construct the Grab Bag's cash budget are shown in Exhibit 7.2. Exhibit 7.3 shows the cash budget resulting from these assumptions.

Cash on Hand

The first step in filling in the cash budget is to show the amount of *cash on hand* at the beginning of the year (Exhibit 7.3; line 1). For cash budget purposes, both cash and marketable securities are considered to be cash. The cash budget for Grab Bag begins with the ending cash from its previous year ($22,000) as the amount of cash on hand in February 1991. Thereafter, the cash on hand at the beginning of each month is reduced (increased) by the repayments (borrowings) necessary to maintain the minimum cash required position (line 7(a)) at the end of the preceding month.

Cash Receipts

For informational and computational purposes, the first entry in the *cash receipts* section is cash sales. Next is credit sales, which are normally categorized separately to allow computing some delay for collections from accounts receivable, which appears on line 2(d). Finally, there are other cash receipts, which could be from nonoperating activities such as interest on certificates of deposit.

The manager of Grab Bag has reported that sales are highly seasonal, with only 7 percent of the company's yearly total occurring in each month from January through October (for a sum of 70 percent), with jumps to 10 percent in November and 20 percent in December. Total sales for the 1991 fiscal year (which begins in February 1990 and ends in January 1991) are expected to be the same as last year, $1,200,000.

The company must provide to the analyst the division between its cash and credit sales. Grab Bag has reported that half its sales are cash and half are on

Exhibit 7.2

Grab Bag Variety Store, Inc.
Financial Statements for Year Ending January 31, 1991
(Dollars in 000s)

Income Statement	*1991*	*Common-Sized*
Sales	$1,200.0	100.0%
Purchases	$540.0	45.0%
Gross Profit	$660.0	55.0%
Wages	$90.0	7.5%
Payroll Taxes	$13.5	1.1%
Outside Services	$15.0	1.3%
Office Supplies	$4.4	0.4%
Repairs and Maintenance	$17.0	1.4%
Advertising	$60.0	5.0%
Transportation	$10.0	0.8%
Accounting and Legal	$12.0	1.0%
Rent	$280.0	23.3%
Telephone	$2.4	0.2%
Utilities	$7.2	0.6%
Insurance	$7.5	0.6%
Depreciation	$14.6	1.2%
Interest	$15.0	1.3%
Total Operating Expenses	$548.5	45.7%
Net Profit Before Taxes	$111.5	9.3%
Taxes	$42.4	3.5%
Net Profit After Taxes	$69.1	5.8%

Balance Sheet	*1991*
Assets	
Cash in Bank	$22.0
Accounts Receivable	$50.0
Inventories	$160.0
Current Assets	$232.0
Equipment	$175.0
Total Assets	$407.0
Liabilities	
Accounts Payable	$45.0
Current Portion L-T D	$25.0
Current Liabilities	$70.0
Long-term Debt	$125.0
Net Worth	$212.0
Total Liabilities & Equity	$407.0
Nonexpense Cash Flow Items:	
Planned Capital Expenditures	$40.0
Owner Withdrawals	$35.0
Minimum Cash Required	$50.0

Monthly Cash Budget Exercise

Exhibit 7.3

NAME OF BUSINESS: Grab Bag Variety Store

Shaded lines are informational and not added into totals. MONTH	Prior Jan.	Feb.	Mar	Apr.	May
1. CASH ON HAND (Less any borrowings)	$22.0	$108.1	$112.0	$120.1	$124.0
2. CASH RECEIPTS					
(a) Total Sales	$84.0	$84.0	$84.0	$84.0	$84.0
(b) Cash Sales	$42.0	$42.0	$42.0	$42.0	$42.0
(c) Credit Sales	$42.0	$42.0	$42.0	$42.0	$42.0
(d) Collections from Credit Accounts	$120.0	$42.0	$42.0	$42.0	$42.0
(e) Other Proceeds: Sale of Assets, and so on					
3. TOTAL CASH RECEIPTS (2b+2d+2e=3)	$162.0	$84.0	$84.0	$84.0	$84.0
4. TOTAL CASH AVAILABLE (Before cash out)(1+3)	$184.0	$192.1	$196.0	$204.1	$208.0
5. CASH PAID OUT					
(a) Purchases (Orders)	$37.8	$37.8	$37.8	$37.8	$37.8
(b) Purchases (Cash Payment)	$37.8	$37.8	$37.8	$37.8	$37.8
(c) Gross Wages (Excludes withdrawals)	$6.3	$6.3	$6.3	$6.3	$6.3
(d) Payroll Expenses (Taxes, etc.)	$0.9	$0.9	$0.9	$0.9	$0.9
(e) Outside Services	$1.1	$1.1	$1.1	$1.1	$1.1
(f) Supplies (Office and operating)	$0.4	$0.4	$0.4	$0.4	$0.4
(g) Repairs and Maintenance	$1.4	$1.4	$1.4	$1.4	$1.4
(h) Advertising	$4.2	$4.2	$4.2	$4.2	$4.2
(i) Car, Delivery, and Travel	$0.7	$0.7	$0.7	$0.7	$0.7
(j) Accounting and Legal	$1.0	$1.0	$1.0	$1.0	$1.0
(k) Rent	$19.6	$19.6	$19.6	$19.6	$19.6
(l) Telephone	$0.2	$0.2	$0.2	$0.2	$0.2
(m) Utilities	$0.5	$0.5	$0.5	$0.5	$0.5
(n) Insurance	$0.6	$0.6	$0.6	$0.6	$0.6
(o) Interest	$1.3	$1.3	$1.3	$1.3	$1.3
(p) Income Taxes					$10.6
(q) Miscellaneous (Unspecified)					
(r) Subtotal Expenses	$75.9	$75.9	$75.9	$75.9	$86.5
(s) Loan Principal Payment		$4.2		$4.2	
(t) Capital Expenditures					
(u) Owner's Withdrawal or Dividends					
6. TOTAL CASH PAID OUT	$75.9	$80.1	$75.9	$80.1	$86.5
7. CASH POSITION (4 minus 6)	$108.1	$112.0	$120.1	$124.0	$121.5
(a) Minimum Cash Required	$50.0	$50.0	$50.0	$50.0	$50.0
(b) Loan Required to Reach Cash Required	$0.0	$0.0	$0.0	$0.0	$0.0
(c) Excess Cash to Repay Loan	$58.1	$62.0	$70.1	$74.0	$71.5
ESSENTIAL OPERATING DATA					
A. Accounts Receivable (End of Month)	$50.0	$50.0	$50.0	$50.0	$50.0
B. Bad Debt (End of month)					
C. Inventory on Hand (End of month)	$160.0	$160.0	$160.0	$160.0	$160.0
D. Accounts Payable (End of month)	$45.0	$45.0	$45.0	$45.0	$45.0
E. Depreciation	$1.2	$1.2	$1.2	$1.2	$1.2

30-day terms. The company's December's sales of $240,000 show up on the cash budget as $120,000 in cash receipts in December; the credit sales of $120,000 are collected in January. There are no other cash proceeds received by Grab Bag.

Following the above principle, Grab Bag's sales for each month would be evenly split between lines 2(b) and 2(c) on Exhibit 7.3. Unfortunately, payment for purchases made on 30-day terms is not always received on time. The analyst must verify the firm's performance by checking the turnover in its accounts receivable. To calculate the turnover, divide the $50,000 in accounts receivable into $600,000 credit sales (50 percent). The turnover is 12 times, confirming the number supplied by Grab Bag.

June	July	Aug.	Sep.	Oct.	Nov.	Dec.	Jan.	Total
$121.5	$85.5	$83.0	$70.7	$8.6	$1.9	$13.7	$51.5	N/A
$84.0	$84.0	$84.0	$84.0	$84.0	$120.0	$240.0	$84.0	$1,200.0
$42.0	$42.0	$42.0	$42.0	$42.0	$60.0	$120.0	$42.0	$600.0
$42.0	$42.0	$42.0	$42.0	$42.0	$60.0	$120.0	$42.0	$600.0
$42.0	$42.0	$42.0	$42.0	$42.0	$42.0	$60.0	$120.0	$600.0
								$0.0
$84.0	$84.0	$84.0	$84.0	$84.0	$102.0	$180.0	$162.0	$1,200.0
$205.5	$169.5	$167.0	$154.7	$92.6	$103.9	$193.7	$213.5	N/A
$37.8	$54.0	$108.0	$37.8	$37.8	$37.8	$37.8	$37.8	$540.0
$37.8	$37.8	$54.0	$108.0	$37.8	$37.8	$37.8	$37.8	$540.0
$6.3	$6.3	$6.3	$6.3	$6.3	$9.0	$18.0	$6.3	$90.0
$0.9	$0.9	$0.9	$0.9	$0.9	$1.3	$2.6	$0.9	$13.2
$1.1	$1.1	$1.1	$1.1	$1.1	$1.6	$3.1	$1.1	$15.6
$0.4	$0.4	$0.4	$0.4	$0.4	$0.4	$0.4	$0.4	$4.4
$1.4	$1.4	$1.4	$1.4	$1.4	$1.4	$1.4	$1.4	$17.0
$4.2	$4.2	$4.2	$4.2	$4.2	$6.0	$12.0	$4.2	$60.0
$0.7	$0.7	$0.7	$0.7	$0.7	$1.0	$1.9	$0.7	$9.6
$1.0	$1.0	$1.0	$1.0	$1.0	$1.0	$1.0	$1.0	$12.0
$19.6	$19.6	$19.6	$19.6	$19.6	$28.0	$55.9	$19.6	$279.6
$0.2	$0.2	$0.2	$0.2	$0.2	$0.2	$0.5	$0.2	$2.4
$0.5	$0.5	$0.5	$0.5	$0.5	$0.7	$1.4	$0.5	$7.2
$0.6	$0.6	$0.6	$0.6	$0.6	$0.6	$0.6	$0.6	$7.5
$1.3	$1.3	$1.3	$1.3	$1.3	$1.3	$1.3	$1.3	$15.0
	$10.6			$10.6			$10.6	$42.4
								$0.0
$75.9	$86.5	$92.1	$146.1	$86.5	$90.2	$138.0	$86.5	$1,115.9
$4.2		$4.2		$4.2		$4.2		$25.2
$40.0								$40.0
							$35.0	$35.0
$120.1	$86.5	$96.3	$146.1	$90.7	$90.2	$142.2	$121.5	$1,216.1
$85.5	$83.0	$70.7	$8.6	$1.9	$13.7	$51.5	$92.0	$92.0
$50.0	$50.0	$50.0	$50.0	$50.0	$50.0	$50.0	$50.0	N/A
$0.0	$0.0	$0.0	$41.4	$48.1	$36.3	$0.0	$0.0	N/A
$35.5	$33.0	$20.7	$0.0	$0.0	$0.0	$1.5	$42.0	N/A
$50.0	$50.0	$50.0	$50.0	$50.0	$68.0	$128.0	$50.0	
$160.0	$176.2	$246.4	$246.4	$246.4	$230.2	$160.0	$160.0	
$45.0	$61.2	$115.2	$45.0	$45.0	$45.0	$45.0	$45.0	
$1.2	$1.2	$1.2	$1.2	$1.2	$1.2	$1.2	$1.2	

Expenses Paid Out

The cash-paid-out figures are estimates based on the expenses calculated from the company's income statement. Exhibit 7.2 shows that the income statement has been common-sized. Again, assuming that these relationships are retained is one of the fundamental suppositions of devising a cash budget; it is wise to confirm these expectations with the firm. Expenditures might also be based on company-provided estimates, especially with regard to capital expenditures and withdrawals.

The company's cost of goods sold consists only of its purchases, according to the company. Inventory purchases are caused by anticipated sales, and the analyst normally would identify the inventory turnover to assess how far in advance of sales the purchases occur. Unfortunately, the inventory turnover calculation would be inaccurate in this seasonal case, since the inventory being looked at is for the end of January and is not what would be expected to be found at peak season in November. The analyst needs to obtain at least quarterly statements in the case of a seasonal firm.

Assume that the firm's purchases are 45 percent of sales and occur in the pattern shown in Exhibit 7.4:

Calculating Average Inventory

Exhibit 7.4

Grab Bag Variety Store
Average Inventory

Time Period	*Amount*
Quarter ending April 30	160,000
Quarter ending July 31	160,000
Quarter ending October 31	260,000
Quarter ending January 31	160,000
Average	185,000

With this information, the inventory turnover ratio can be calculated by dividing purchases by the average inventory, or 540,000 ÷ 185,000 = 2.92 times per year. This means that the firm maintains approximately 365 ÷ 2.92 = 125 days, or 4 months in inventory. Therefore, purchases should be made at the rate of 45 percent of expected sales, four months hence.

The payment for purchases occurs next. By calculating the accounts payable turnover (dividing purchases by accounts payable, or 540,000 ÷ 45,000 = 12 times), the payment history of 30 days is determined. Therefore, line 5(b) will be one month delayed from line 5(a). With regard to other expenditures, the prime question is whether they are attached to, or vary with, sales or are constant throughout the year. Of the items shown in Exhibit 7.5, it would seem reasonable for the following to be relatively constant throughout the year:

Nonseasonal Expenses

Exhibit 7.5

Grab Bag Variety Store
Nonseasonal Expenses

Item	*Amount*
Office supplies	4,400
Repairs and Maintenance	17,000
Accounting and Legal	12,000
Insurance	7,450
Interest	15,000

Therefore, divide these individual numbers by 12 and place each in the appropriate month across the budget.

With regard to the remaining expenditure items, look up the common-size column on the income statement and, for each month's entry, multiply the percentage shown times sales in that month. (Assume that the payments for these items are within the month in which they are incurred.)

The income tax area is problematic for cash-budget forecasters because income tax is a rate charged against a different result than the product of either the cash budget or even the income statement. The major, but not only, changes in the tax area are from tax depreciation (MACRS), a noncash expense, and the normal accrual-based revenues and expenses. Furthermore, taxes are paid on an estimated basis in the 4th, 6th, 9th, and 12th months of the firm's fiscal year. Therefore, while the tax is customarily calculated on the basis of the estimated total profits and paid evenly over the four months, many seasonal firms will calculate their taxable profits on a quarterly basis or base their tax payments on the previous year's income, and this complicates the forecast. For the Grab Bag example, take the $42,357 taxes reported last year, divide by 4 (resulting in $10,590), and spread the result evenly into the months of May, July, October, and January. The *nonexpense-cash-flow* categories also need to be placed on the cash budget, and the company is probably the only reliable source for this information. Assume that the Grab Bag plans to acquire $40,000 worth of new display cases in June, and that the owners intend to withdrawal $35,000 at the end of December. Further, assume that the current portion of long-term debt is repaid evenly every other month.

Cash Position

The company's cash position at the end of each month equals its total cash available (line 4 of Exhibit 7.3) minus total cash paid out (line 6). The credit analyst can see that from September to November the company's outflows exceed its inflows plus available cash.

Loan Required

During the entire fall period, the company's end-of-month cash position will be below its minimum cash requirement of $50,000, requiring it to borrow up to a peak of $48,100 to maintain its minimum, as shown in line 7(b). This amount will enable it to purchase sufficient inventory for its end-of-year sales period. It will be able to begin making substantial payments on the loan in November, and will have it completely repaid in December, according to the cash budget.

Essential Operating Data

The cash budget also includes relevant non-cash-flow information on a month-to-month basis. These accrual-basis figures—accounts receivable, inventory on hand, and so on—underlie the cash-basis figures shown in the cash budget.

COMPUTING AN EXPANSION CASH BUDGET

This section uses the Pearson Company as an example of how to show a cash budget for expansion purposes.

The Pearson Company specializes in the production of automotive and farm machinery, but it also has a secondary line of products in the oil-drilling industry. The company, in operation for about ten years, became concerned about its slow 4-percent growth rate in the past year. Sales grew steadily in 1991, if slowly, as shown in Exhibit 7.6:

Pearson Company Sales for 1991

Exhibit 7.6

Pearson Company
Actual Sales for 1991
(Dollars in 000s)

Month	Sales	Month	Sales
January	$450.1	July	$459.2
February	$451.6	August	$460.7
March	$453.1	September	$462.3
April	$454.6	October	$463.8
May	$456.2	November	$465.4
June	$457.7	December	$466.9
		Total	$5,501.60

To correct this situation, on 2 January 1992 the company requested bank financing for a new ball-bearing casting mold that costs $600,000. The Pearson Company plans to pay $100,000 down and finance the balance over five years (the depreciable life of the casting mold). The company requested a loan with a five-year, level amortization of principal plus interest. The firm felt that this purchase would raise the growth rate to a more respectable 14 percent.

The bank's examination of the Pearson Company's financial statements made the credit analyst wonder if the company might also need permanent funding or a revolving credit to support the growth in sales resulting from the addition of the casting mold. Therefore, the analyst decided to construct a new cash budget. Exhibit 7.7 summarizes the major accounts from the Pearson Company's 1991 financial statements as well as some additional cost breakdowns supplied by management. These figures provide the basis for

Exhibit 7.7

Financial Statements
Financial Statements for Year Ending December 31, 1991
(Dollars in 000s)

Income Statement	*1991*	*Common Sized*
Sales	$5,500.00	100.0%
Purchases	2,200.00	40.0%
Wages-Manufacturing	750.00	13.6%
Payroll Taxes	112.50	2.0%
Repairs and Maintenance	137.50	2.5%
Rent of Plant	650.00	11.8%
Depreciation	120.00	2.2%
Gross Profit	$1,530.00	27.8%
Salaries-Officers	$165.00	3.0%
Office Supplies	$52.50	1.0%
Advertising	$220.00	4.0%
Transportation	$57.00	1.0%
Accounting and Legal	$55.00	1.0%
Office Rent	$97.55	1.8%
Telephone	$47.50	0.9%
Utilities	$256.41	4.7%
Insurance	$94.05	1.7%
Interest	$109.99	2.0%
Total Expenses	$5,125.00	93.2%
Net Profit Before Taxes	375.00	6.8%
Taxes	145.50	2.6%
Net Profit After Taxes	$229.50	4.2%

Balance Sheet	
Assets	
Cash in Bank	$90.00
Accounts Receivable	916.00
Inventories	1,132.00
Current Assets	$2,138.00
Equipment	$822.00
Total Assets	$2,960.00
Liabilities	
Accounts Payable & Accruals	$675.00
Current Portion Long-term Debt	210.00
Current Liabilities	$885.00
Long-term Debt	$470.00
Net Worth	$1,605.00
Total Liabilities & Equity	$2,960.00
Planned Capital Expenditures	$600.00
Dividends	$120.00
Minimum Cash Required	$80.00

the construction of the company's 1992 cash budget. The 1992 monthly cash budget for the Pearson Company is shown in Exhibit 7.8. A discussion of each line of the budget follows.

Pearson Company's Monthly Cash Budget

Exhibit 7.8

NAME OF BUSINESS PEARSON COMPANY

Shaded lines are informational and not added into totals.

MONTH	Dec.	Jan	Feb	Mar	Apr	May
1.CASH ON HAND (Less any borrowings)	$90.0	$93.3	$22.6	$45.5	$65.7	$51.0
2. CASH RECEIPTS						
(a)Total Sales	$466.9	$468.5	$474.0	$479.5	$485.1	$490.7
(b)Cash Sales						
(c) Credit Sales	466.9	468.5	474.0	479.5	485.1	490.7
(d)Collections from Credit Accounts	463.8	465.4	466.9	468.5	474.0	479.5
(e)Other Proceeds: Sale of Assets, and so on		500.0				
3. TOTAL CASH RECEIPTS (2b+2d+2e=3)	$463.8	$965.4	$466.9	$468.5	$474.0	$479.5
4. TOTAL CASH AVAILABLE (Before cash out)(1+3)	$553.8	$1,058.7	$489.5	$514.0	$539.7	$530.5
5. CASH PAID OUT						
(a) Purchases (Orders)	$192.8	$195.1	$197.4	$199.7	$202.0	$204.4
(b) Purchases (Cash Payment)	185.5	186.1	192.4	194.9	197.2	199.5
(c) Gross Wages (Excludes withdrawals)	65.3	66.0	66.8	67.6	68.4	69.2
(d) Payroll Expenses (Taxes, etc.)	9.6	9.7	9.8	9.9	10.1	10.2
(e) Outside Services - Officer's Salaries	13.8	13.8	13.8	13.8	13.8	13.8
(f) Supplies (Office and operating)	4.7	4.7	4.7	4.8	4.9	4.9
(g) Repairs and Maintenance	12.0	12.1	12.3	12.4	12.6	12.7
(h) Advertising	18.7	18.7	19.0	19.2	19.4	19.6
(i) Car, Delivery, and Travel	4.7	4.7	4.7	4.8	4.9	4.9
(j) Accounting and Legal	4.6	4.6	4.6	4.6	4.6	4.6
(k) Rent	62.3	62.3	62.3	62.3	62.3	62.3
(l) Telephone	4.2	4.2	4.3	4.3	4.4	4.4
(m) Utilities	21.9	22.0	22.3	22.5	22.8	23.1
(n) Insurance	7.8	7.8	7.8	7.8	7.8	7.8
(o) Interest	9.2	12.5	12.5	12.4	12.4	12.3
(p) Income Taxes	36.4				36.4	
(q) Miscellaneous (Unspecified)						
(r) Subtotal Expenses	$460.5	$429.3	$437.2	$441.4	$481.7	$449.3
(s) Loan Principal Payment		6.8	6.9	6.9	6.9	7.0
(t) Capital Expenditures		600.0				
(u) Owner's Withdrawal or Dividends						
6. TOTAL CASH PAID OUT	$460.5	$1,036.1	$444.0	$448.3	$488.6	$456.3
7. CASH POSITION (4 minus 6)	$93.3	$22.6	$45.5	$65.7	$51.0	$74.3
(a) Minimum Cash Required		80.0	80.0	80.0	80.0	80.0
(b) Loan Required to Reach Cash Required	0.0	57.4	34.5	14.3	29.0	5.7
(c) Excess Cash to Repay Loan	93.3	0.0	0.0	0.0	0.0	0.0
ESSENTIAL OPERATING DATA						
A. Accounts Receivable (End of Month)	$50.0	$916.0	$923.0	$934.0	$945.1	$956.4
B. Bad Debt (End of month)						
C. Inventory on Hand (End of month)	160.0	1,132.0	1,145.2	1,158.6	1,172.1	1,185.8
D. Accounts Payable (End of month)	45.0	675.0	682.9	690.8	698.9	707.1
E. Depreciation	1.2	13.8	13.8	13.8	13.8	13.8

Jun	Jul	Aug	Sep	Oct	Nov	Dec	Total
$74.3	$62.6	$88.9	$116.8	$109.9	$140.9	$173.6	N/A
$496.5	$502.3	$508.1	$514.1	$520.1	$526.1	$532.3	$5,997.1
							0.0
496.5	502.3	508.1	514.1	520.1	526.1	532.3	5,997.1
485.1	490.7	496.5	502.3	508.1	514.1	520.1	5,871.1
							500.0
$485.1	$490.7	$496.5	$502.3	$508.1	$514.1	$520.1	$6,371.1
$559.3	$553.4	$585.4	$619.1	$618.0	$655.0	$693.6	N/A
$206.7	$209.2	$211.6	$214.1	$216.6	$219.1	$221.7	$2,497.4
201.8	204.2	206.6	209.0	211.4	213.9	216.4	2,433.5
70.0	70.8	71.6	72.4	73.3	74.1	75.0	779.2
10.3	10.4	10.5	10.7	10.8	10.9	11.0	124.3
13.8	13.8	13.8	13.8	13.8	13.8	13.8	165.0
5.0	5.0	5.1	5.1	5.2	5.3	5.3	60.0
12.9	13.0	13.2	13.3	13.5	13.6	13.8	118.5
19.9	20.1	20.3	20.6	20.8	21.0	21.3	239.9
5.0	5.0	5.1	5.1	5.2	5.3	5.3	60.0
4.6	4.6	4.6	4.6	4.6	4.6	4.6	55.0
62.3	62.3	62.3	62.3	62.3	62.3	62.3	747.6
4.5	4.5	4.6	4.6	4.7	4.7	4.8	54.0
23.3	23.6	23.9	24.2	24.4	24.7	25.0	281.9
7.8	7.8	7.8	7.8	7.8	7.8	7.8	94.1
12.3	12.2	12.2	12.1	12.1	12.0	12.0	146.9
36.4			36.4			36.4	145.5
							0.0
$489.7	$457.4	$461.5	$502.0	$469.9	$474.1	$514.8	$5,608.2
7.0	7.1	7.1	7.2	7.2	7.3	7.3	84.7
							600.0
						120.0	120.0
$496.7	$464.4	$468.6	$509.2	$477.1	$481.4	$642.1	$6,412.9
$62.6	$88.9	$116.8	$109.9	$140.9	$173.6	$51.5	$51.5
80.0	80.0	80.0	80.0	80.0	80.0	80.0	N/A
17.4	0.0	0.0	0.0	0.0	0.0	28.5	N/A
0.0	8.9	36.8	29.9	60.9	93.6	0.0	N/A
$967.8	$979.3	$991.0	$1,002.7	$1,014.7	$1,026.7	$1,038.9	
1,199.6	1,213.6	1,227.7	1,242.1	1,256.6	1,271.2	1,286.1	
715.3	723.6	732.1	740.6	749.3	758.0	766.9	
13.8	13.8	13.8	13.8	13.8	13.8	13.8	

Cash on Hand

From the Pearson Company's 1991 balance sheet, the cash account at year end 1991 totaled $90,000. Line 7(a) on the cash budget shows the Pearson Company's stated *minimum cash balance required* for ongoing operations to be $80,000. The cash on hand (line 1) following December 1991 shows the minimum, less any borrowing. If cash goes higher than the $80,000 at the end of any month, it is because all short-term debt has been repaid.

Cash Receipts

First, the total sales are recorded on line 2(a) of Exhibit 7.8. As summarized in Exhibit 7.9, Pearson Company projects sales for 1992 to increase at a rate of .135% per month to produce a sales schedule reaching $6,000,000, as follows:

Exhibit 7.9

Pearson Company's Projected Sales for 1992

Pearson Company
Estimated Sales for 1992
(Dollars in 000s)

Month	*Amount*	*Month*	*Amount*
January	$468.5	July	$502.3
February	$474.0	August	$508.1
March	$479.5	September	$514.1
April	$485.1	October	$520.1
May	$490.7	November	$526.1
June	496.5	December	$532.3
		Total	$5,997.3

Since all of the Pearson Company's sales are credit sales, cash sales are zero on its cash budget. To determine the collections, first look at the company's balance sheet, which shows that its accounts receivable balance at year end 1991 was $916,000. Since the company's receivables turnover rate is six times each year, an analyst would conclude that $916,000 in accounts receivable represents two months of sales. In other words, the firm receives payment two months following the sale.

Based on this conclusion, the analyst would list $465,000 (expected receipts from November 1991 sales) on the cash budget as cash receipts for January 1992, and so on. January 1992 sales of $468,500 are expected to be collected in March 1992, a pattern of deferred collections that continues for all 12 months. November and December 1992 sales are assumed to be collected the following year and do not show up on the cash budget.

The only other cash receipt shown for the company in 1992 is the $500,000 in projected long-term loan proceeds in January. Total cash receipts then equal $957,600 for January, $466,900 for February, and the amount from the above schedule (Exhibit 7.9) for each month thereafter (accounts receivable collections only).

Total Cash Available

The total cash available for the company's monthly operations, shown as line 4 of the cash budget (Exhibit 7.8), is calculated by adding required cash (less any short-term loans taken in line 7(b)) at the beginning of each month (line 1) to the total cash receipts during the month (line 3).

Cash Paid Out

The cash-paid-out figures are usually estimated expenditures based on the expenses as a percentage of sales as calculated from the company's previous income statement. The analyst might wish to receive assurance from the borrower that the new equipment and growth will not affect these cost relationships, which could go either up or down. Moreover, the analyst must analyze the expense categories to determine which of them may remain stable in the face of growing sales and which will grow in tandem with sales. Cash budget expenditures might also be based on company-provided estimates of its proposed expenditures.

Purchases Ordered

Since the analysis predicts growing sales for the Pearson Company, it is logical to assume that many of the company's costs will grow at the same 14 percent rate and remain at the same common-size percentages as they did in 1991. For purchases, this will certainly be the case. The next step, to calculate the time prior to sale that the inventory is acquired, is accomplished by reviewing the inventory turnover. Remembering that the inventory on the balance sheet represents all of the direct costs of the firm's products capitalized, the analyst next takes all the direct costs evidenced on the income statement, even the noncash expense of depreciation, to derive the cost of goods sold, which is necessary for calculating the inventory turnover.

Subtracting the gross profits from sales, an easy way to derive the cost of goods sold, leaves $3,850,000. Dividing the end-of-year inventory (average inventory would have been better in a growing firm like this) into cost of goods sold produces 3.51 times, or 104 days. Here is an example of how the cash budget model departs from reality: While some of the purchasing occurs well in advance of the three months, some occurs closer to the time of sale. Regardless, the cash budget averages all direct costs together and orders them into time periods—usually over only two time periods, in this case months three and four—that span the average acquisition instead of the many actual time periods. Therefore, it can be assumed that Pearson acquires inventory over three to four months, some of it three months in advance and the rest four months in advance. The problem is to determine how to split up the ordering between the months three and four. To calculate how far in advance the inventory is acquired *on average*, take the *longer* of the two possible periods, subtract the turnover days, and divide the result by 30 days:

(larger time period - turnover days) / 30 = (120 – 104) / 30 = 53%

The results of the formula give the percentage to multiply times the quantity for the *shorter* time period. The remainder is multiplied times the *longer* time period.

To check these calculations, multiply the 53 percent times 90 days (three months is the shorter of the two periods) for a product of 48 days; next, multiply the 47 percent times 120 days (four months is the longer of the two periods) for a product of 56 days; now add together 48 days and 56 days, which verifies the total of 104 days.

Since the method's accuracy has been confirmed, calculate the amount to be ordered in January by multiplying the purchases percentage of sales, times the 53 percent and times sales expected to occur in three months:

Purchases percentage of sales x percentage of purchases to be ordered 3 months in advance x sales 3 months hence

or

40% x 53% x $485.1 = 102.84

The remainder of the purchases for January is 47 percent times the sales expected to occur in four months:

40% x 47 % x $490.7 = 92.25

To repeat, the calculation for the shorter period uses the formula with the longer period. In other words, purchases for January are obtained by multiplying the purchases percentage times 43 percent times sales for April and adding to it the purchases percentage times 57 percent for the May sales. In this case the growth rate of 14 percent per annum is followed in the growth of the purchases.

Purchases Payments

The actual timing of a company's accounts-payable payments must also be considered when creating a cash budget. The Pearson Company's accounts-payable turnover (again using the derived cost of goods sold) shows turn-overs averaging 5.9 times, or 62 days in 1991. To calculate the amount paid in January, take the larger of the two possible periods, 90 days in this case, subtract the turnover days, then divide the result by 30 days.

(larger time period - turnover days) / 30 = 90 – 62 / 30 = 93%

To calculate the amount paid in January, multiply 93 percent times purchases occurring two months ago (November) and 7 percent times purchases occurring three months ago (October). This, then, is the amount of cash projected to be paid out for purchases in January 1991:

Purchases percentage paid in 2 months x sales 2 months prior x purchases as a percent of sales

plus

Purchases percentage paid in 3 months x sales 3 months prior x purchases as a percent of sales

or

$$(.93 \times 465.4 \times .4) + (.07 \times 463.8 \times .4) = 173.13 + 12.98 = 186.11$$

Of course, once the purchases are shown on the cash budget, the calculation may be made by multiplying the purchases percentage paid in each month times the respective purchases in the month, skipping the sales and purchases-as-a-percent-of-sales parts of the formula.

Direct Labor, Payroll Taxes, Repairs and Maintenance (parts of Cost of Goods Sold)

After considering each expenditure, the analyst has marked on Exhibit 7.10, below, whether the category varies with sales.

Expenditures Varying with Sales

Exhibit 7.10

Pearson Company
Expenditures in Relation to Sales

Expenditures	*Vary with*
Inventory purchases	sales
Wages	sales
Payroll expenses	sales
Repairs and maintenance	sales

Direct labor, payroll taxes, and repairs and maintenance all vary with sales. Like purchases, they are accounted for before gross profit on the Pearson financial statement. In this case, since they are usually considered part of cost of goods sold and are capitalized into inventory, their occurrence is calculated by using the same formulas as were used for the purchases. Note, however, that these expenses are paid in the same month in which they are incurred. This assumes that finished goods are carried in inventory for a while instead of shipped immediately.

Once their percentages have been broken out in the common-size column, multiply the percentages times the sales in the appropriate month of sales and anticipate that the outflow of cash will be within the same month:

Direct cash cost item percentage of sales x percentage of sales incurred 3 months prior to sale x sales 3 months hence

plus

Direct cash cost item percentage of sales x percentage of sales incurred 4 months prior to sale x sales 4 months hence.

For example, regarding January wages, the correct formula is

Wages common-size percentage x 3 months prior percentage of sales x sales in April

+

Wages common-size percentage x 4 months prior percentage of sales x sales in May

or

$$(.136 \times .93 \times 485.1) + (.136 \times .07 \times 490.7) = 66$$

For January rent, the correct formula is

$$(650 + 97.55) / 12 = 62.3$$

Naturally, depreciation is ignored in these calculations since it is not a cash expense.

General and Administrative Expenditures

Often a company's income statement will list the individual expense categories that constitute its general and administrative expenses, as the Pearson Company has done. These categories include such items as officers' salaries, office supplies, advertising, transportation, accounting, and so on. In the example of the Pearson Company, each of these categories has been listed separately so that a table may be constructed.

Exhibit 7.11, below, identifies which expenditures should be varied with sales and which ones (because they are stable or fixed) should merely be divided by 12 and placed on the cash budget.

Exhibit 7.11

Pearson Company
Expenditures in Relation to Sales

Expenditures	*Vary with*	*Expenditures*	*Vary with*
1. Rent of plant	stable	7. Office rent	stable
2. Salaries-officers	stable	8. Telephone	sales
3. Office supplies	sales	9. Utilities	sales
4. Advertising	sales	10. Insurance	stable
5. Transportation	sales	11. Interest	stable
6. Accounting and legal	stable	12. Income taxes	income

Expenditures that vary with sales should be incurred in the same month as the sales and paid for in that same month. There is probably no need in the general and administrative list to plan for these expenditures to take place in advance of the sales date.

Interest Expenditure

While the Pearson Company's present interest expenditure may be considered stable, the new $500,000 loan will increase interest and the cash flow required for principal repayment. Specifically, assume that the interest will be at an 8 percent rate. For this example, divide the $110,000 in initial interest by 12 months for $9,167 per month and, using an amortization table, add the interest on the 5-year amortizing note. It is likely that the interest expenditure will decline each month, a result of the current accounting treatment for interest expense. A very rough estimate could be made by multiplying the average principal by the interest rate and dividing the result by the number of times that the interest is paid each year. If they were due semiannually (rather than monthly), the interest payments would be shown as cash paid out in those months when payment fell due.

Income Taxes

As mentioned previously, income taxes are somewhat of a problem when firms prepare cash budgets. Firms having such long inventory turnover periods that they have large accrual income that differs from the income reported in their cash budget have special difficulty. It is assumed for this example that the Pearson Company will make quarterly payments equal to last year's tax bill of $145,500. This amounts to a quarterly payment of $36,375 in April, June, September, and December. In addition, the other cash outlays and payment schedules have been identified in Exhibit 7.12.

Exhibit 7.12

Pearson Company Cash Outlays and Payment Schedule

Pearson Company
Other Cash Outlays

Other Cash Outlays	*Estimated Timing*
1. Loan principal payments	CPLTD monthly on even basis
2. Capital purchases	In January
3. Dividends	End of year in December

*Current Portion Long-Term Debt

As in the case of interest expenditure, this information will affect the values placed into the cash budget. Each category of cash paid out is discussed separately below.

Loan Principal Payments

The Pearson Company's balance sheet shows current maturities of long-term debt in 1991 at $210,000 (this balance sheet was prepared before it was assumed that the company's current loan request would be approved). For cash budgeting purposes, assume that there will be level principal payments throughout the year for the existing loan, which amounts to monthly payments of about $17,500. Starting in February, payments will be made on the requested loan payments, again calculated with a loan amortization table, accounting for only the principal portion.

Capital Equipment Purchases

The company's only projected capital equipment purchase for 1991 is the casting mold scheduled to be purchased at a cost of $600,000 in January (assuming the loan request is approved).

Total Cash Paid Out

The credit analyst has now accounted for all the Pearson Company's anticipated cash expenditures for the year. The company's projected cash outlays are listed for each month on line 6 of Exhibit 7.8.

Cash Position

This line of the cash budget, calculated by subtracting total cash paid out (line 6) from total cash available (line 4), shows that the Pearson Company's cash outflows never exceed its cash inflows plus cash on hand.

Minimum Cash Required

The Pearson Company states that the minimum amount of cash it needs for ongoing operations is $80,000. This figure is entered for each month on line 7(a) since any excess cash will be used to repay the company's accumulated short-term debt.

Loan Required

This is the amount of cash the company needs to maintain its stated minimum cash position of $80,000. The amount was calculated by subtracting the company's cash position (line 7) from its minimum cash requirement (line 7(a)). It shows that the company needs to borrow $57,400 immediately to maintain its required cash position during January. Lesser amounts of cash will also be required periodically throughout the year—for example, $34,500 in February and $14,300 in March.

The cash budget shows that the Pearson Company will have to borrow through June. From then on, as the company's cash position improves, it is able to build up surplus cash until the December dividend payment. Thus, whereas a forecast balance sheet might show only the $28,000 December shortfall as the cumulative funding requirement, the cash budget shows that the funding requirement peaks at $57,400 in January.

INTERPRETATION OF THE CASH BUDGET

Continuing the Example of the Pearson Company

Although the Pearson Company does not have a seasonal sales cycle, the cash budget shows the company's borrowing need peaking at $57,400 (the funding requirement for January 1992). Recall, too, that the company's management had identified no funding need beyond the $500,000 loan for the purchase of the casting mold. This cash flow inadequacy results from the company's having to make a $100,000 cash down payment for the new piece of equipment. Thus the cash budget shows that the Pearson Company needs to borrow $57,400 immediately (over and above the $500,000 loan amount).

In situations where the required amounts are larger than the requested amounts, determine the interest cost associated with the needed short-term loan and add it to the interest already shown on the cash budget. The Pearson Company's cash budget demonstrates the timing and magnitude of the company's interim cash needs. Without the cash budget, the credit analyst might well have overlooked a significant financing requirement.

Interrelationship Between the Operating Cycle and Cash Needs

As mentioned in passing several times, the cash conversion (or operating) cycle will have much to do with a firm's needs for a cash budget. For example, a restaurant will probably not require a cash budget, because its operating cycle is so short, possibly only a week. The distinction between its accrual income and its cash income will be slight. Further, review of its monthly statements is practically mandatory for a lender because the capability of generating income can turn down so quickly.

For manufacturing firms, the long operating cycle is a problem because it requires sizable working capital. Considerable cash is essential for acquisition of raw-materials inventories, paying wages to employees to produce a product, and maintaining an inventory of finished goods to respond to customer orders in a timely manner. For these firms, cash budgets are essential.

Interrelationship Between Working Capital and Capital Expenditures

Clearly, sudden demands for growth, as in the Pearson Company example, or even replacement of capital expenditures, require careful planning. If the firm can schedule repayment of capital in accordance with the useful life of the equipment, then, at least, working capital issues can be easily addressed by carefully drawing a cash budget. One of the real dangers is using working capital for expansion, then running into trouble with increasing needs for working capital.

The issue of separating financing for permanent expansion of fixed assets from working capital needs is addressed by the cash budget. Its focus on cash flow makes it an exceptionally good demonstration of the difference between accounting for income and determining debt repayment capacity. Convincing a borrower to use this approach for its own understanding is invaluable.

Interrelationship Between the Cash Needs and Profit Margins

If a firm has a substantial profit margin, as IBM had historically, it can frequently finance most, if not all, of its working capital needs. Analysis of working capital needs requires integration of the company's ability to produce net cash flow, its capital structure—debt leverage and equity cushion—and the required speed of growth in its working capital.

Persons working in finance frequently talk about spontaneous growth in working capital needs. The thought that accounts payable may grow as rapidly as the combination of accounts receivable and inventories depends on the size of cash profit margins; if they are big enough, then it is possible, but they rarely are.

SUMMARY OF IMPORTANT CONCEPTS 

The monthly cash budget is an important tool of financial statement analysis because it helps identify the cause, timing, and magnitude of a company's peak borrowing needs during interim periods that may not show up on its financial statements. For example, financing required to purchase inventory for seasonal sales increases can be identified. In addition, the company's ability to repay the additional debt requirement will be apparent.

Cash budgets are also used to determine whether borrowing needs are truly short-term or whether they represent permanent funding needs. In self-liquidating loans, the assets being financed are converted to cash to repay the debt. In long-term loans, the debt is repaid from the net cash flow of the business. Thus a cash budget can help lenders avoid the pitfall of inadvertently lending for the short term when the borrower actually has a long-term need.

A cash budget also helps monitor a company's cash flow and can serve as an early warning signal that the company's cash flow is less than expected, which may affect its ability to repay a loan.

The timing of cash flows relative to sales and accounts receivable, inventory purchases and accounts payable, and other expenditures are crucial components of a company's cash flow and must be taken into consideration in constructing a cash budget. These and other assumptions must be in line with the company's past performance and with management's plans for the year (such as plans to make capital purchases, to tighten up the company's credit policies, or to carry more or less inventory). In addition, the lender's assumptions used in constructing the cash budget should be consistent with its review of the company's financial statements.

EXERCISES 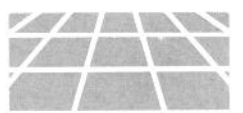

Important Terms to Define

- cash budget
- scenario analysis
- expenditure
- prime assumptions in a cash budget
- cash on hand
- cash receipts
- operating cash paid out
- nonexpense cash flows
- additional funding requirement
- seasonal sales
- minimum cash balance required
- borrowing need peaking

Dependable Doors Case Study

Review the cash budget, shown below, supplied by the management of Dependable Doors.

	Oct	Nov	Dec	Jan	Feb
Cash on Hand	548	300	300	300	300
Cash Receipts	2,080	2,081	1,100	1,500	2,200
Total Cash Available	2,628	2381	1,400	1,800	2,500
Cash Paid Out					
Purchases	1,076	631	545	545	545
Payroll	725	725	725	725	725
Manufacturing Overhead	316	505	505	505	505
SG&A Expense	380	400	400	400	400
Interest expense	93	95	94	106	116
Income Tax	0	(426)	0	190	0
Cash Dividends	0	0	36	0	0
Subtotal	2,590	1,930	2,305	2,471	2,291
Loan Principal Payments	0	0	36	0	0
Capital Purchases	15	15	15	15	15
Total Cash Paid Out	2,605	1,945	2,356	2,486	2,306
Cash Position	23	436	(956)	(686)	194
Minimum Ending Cash	300	300	300	300	300
Additional Funding Requirement (or Repayment)	277	(136)	1,256	986	106
Cumulative Funding Requirement	2,924	2,788	4,044	5,030	5,136

1. Do you detect any seasonality in the sales pattern of Dependable Doors?
2. What ramifications do Dependable Door's annual projections have on the company's projected monthly cash needs?
3. After examining the monthly cash budget submitted by Dependable Doors, do you think the company's debt is structured correctly?
4. Based upon the above, prepare your own cash budget for Dependable Doors.

Engraph Case Study

1. What ramifications does the lack of seasonality have in structuring debt repayments?
2. What events might cause the company's sales pattern to change?
3. Construct an expansion cash budget for Engraph assuming last years growth will continue.

Mar	*Apr*	*May*	*June*	*July*	*Aug*	*Sept*	*Total*
300	300	300	300	300	300	300	3,848
3,200	3,600	3,500	3,400	2,700	2,400	2,200	29,961
3,500	3,900	3,800	3,700	3,000	2,700	2,500	33,809
545		545	545	545	545	545	925
725	725	725	725	725	725	725	
505	505	505	505	505	505	505	
400	400	400	400	400	400	400	
117	110	97	85	76	72	71	
190	0	0	190	0	0	191	
36	0	0	36	0	0	36	
2,518	2,285	2,272	2,486	2,251	2,247	2,853	28,499
37	0	0	37	0	0	37	
15	15	15	15	15	15	15	
2,570	2,300	2,287	2,538	2,266	2,262	2,905	28,826
930	1,600	1,513	1,162	734	438	(405)	
300	300	300	300	300	300	300	
(630)	(1300)	(1,213)	(862)	(434)	(138)	705	
4,506	3,206	1,993	1,131	697	559	1,264	

Pro Forma Forecasting Analysis

LEARNING OBJECTIVES

After studying this chapter, you will be able to

- identify the primary uses of a pro forma forecast as a financial statement analysis tool,
- construct and analyze pro forma forecasts of income statements and balance sheets,
- identify the benefits and shortcomings of a pro forma forecast analysis, and
- explain the importance of properly interpreting pro forma forecasts.

INTRODUCTION

Most companies prepare forecast financial statements as part of their routine financial planning. *Pro forma forecast* income statements and balance sheets represent management's best guess as to how the company will perform in the coming years, taking into consideration the expected economic, competitive, and regulatory environments in which the company will operate. Lenders typically require commercial loan applicants to submit forecast financial statements showing the company's projected financial results over the term of the loan. Some lenders also request copies of forecast statements from past years so that they can compare management's past predictions with the company's actual results.

Even at their best, pro forma forecast statements have their shortcomings. No one can predict the future with certainty, and many unforeseen factors can dramatically affect a company's projected financial plans. Of course, the number of years covered in a pro forma forecast is entirely up to the analyst. Some prefer the less extensive route and forecast for only one year, feeling that the business environment is too uncertain to put any stock in a longer forecast. The following material uses this one-year forecast for convenience, but the principles expressed here may be easily extended for up to five years.

Optimism and Pessimism

Marketing-oriented people tend to view the future optimistically; they trust in their promotional capabilities. The world would be a gloomier place without them. Production-oriented people tend to view the future with pessimism. They are used to struggling with equipment and people who do not live up to their promises.

One of the analyst's first tasks in reviewing management plans is to discover whether the tilt of these plans is toward optimism or pessimism. Hastily reviewing a pessimistic set of company plans may erroneously convince the lender to avoid what might have been a profitable lending opportunity. Blindly going along with a rosy-colored set of overly optimistic plans may lead both the company and the lender down the same trail to losses.

The lender wants to consider the realistic possibilities of events happening. In other words, the lender is likely to be more successful by thinking in terms of better or worse scenarios than in terms of best or worst scenarios. The chances of being realistic in assessing plans are improved by constructing multiple-year forecasts on a computer program. A good computer program allows the analyst to change the assumptions easily to fit various scenarios and to run simulations to see the possible results of changes in important variables. Applying proper statistical analysis to these forecasts can give the analyst a specific level of confidence in the results.

Forecasting and Cash Flows

The goal of credit analysis is to predict a company's future ability to repay its debt, and identifying a firm's cash flows from operations is an important part of that analysis. As in the discussion of cash budgets (chapter 7), think about everything in relation to cash flows rather than to accrual income because it is the former that repays the debt. Financial statements will be prepared in the process, primarily to determine essential details such as how much additional working capital will be needed.

Forecasting uses conceptual and mechanical tools that make the predictions as reasonable as possible. The conceptual part of the analysis is based on analyzing the firm's past performance as evidenced by its prior financial statements, statements of cash flows, and ratio analyses. The pro forma forecast must also consider the financial consequences of management's plans and strategies—and assess their effect on the company's borrowing needs, repayment capacity, and general creditworthiness. Internal and external forces play upon these expectations.

The mechanical tools that help the analyst generate reports include the percentage-of-sales method discussed in the last chapter. The final calculation will be of cash flow surpluses and shortages, covering the firm's need for short- and long-term financing. The following chapter closely enumerates these mechanics and follows with an example case.

Framework for Analysis

The basic framework for forecasting financial statements involves paying attention to

- the company's past performance and its reliability,
- the external and internal factors that affect the company's operation, and
- the many sources of information about a company and the industry in which it operates.

An analyst who considers these elements will be able to determine not only whether a company's financial projections are technically correct, but whether they are based on reasonable assumptions.

Revaluation

An analyst reviewing a company-supplied forecast will not rely totally on the company's assumptions, but generally will introduce others that may be more realistic. (This process is similar to revaluing financial statements, covered in chapters 3 and 4.) Then the company's results and the credit analyst's results can be compared. However, the basis of both sets of projections and of the resulting analysis is the company's past financial results and its plans for sales, capital equipment, and plant expenditures for the coming years.

Besides reviewing the financial documents submitted by the company, a credit analyst may personally visit the company to meet the principals and to see the company in action. Another option is consulting with outside sources such as competitors, suppliers, customers, and trade associations.

Financial Statement Background

To ensure that the multiple-year forecast analysis is comprehensive and credible, an analyst must have on hand

- management's multiple-year forecast of sales and capital equipment expenditures,
- a complete set of income statements, balance sheets, and statements of cash flows for the past three to five years,
- the company's debt schedule,
- the company's projections for past periods,
- the company's formal business plan, and
- management's organizational diagram.

Dependability of Performance

A thorough understanding of the company, the industry, and the market helps the credit analyst judge the reliability of a company's financial projections. *Long-term forecasts* are most dependable for companies that have established consistent performance trends and closely track the industry. Much of this information will already have been derived from analyzing the company's balance sheets and income statements as well as industry trends and ratios. At this point in the review, the credit analyst should have a solid grasp of the company's operations and its past and current performance.

Doing a meaningful forecast analysis for companies with a brief record or for companies with inconsistent performance records is exceedingly difficult. One alternative is for the newer company to supply the lender with contracts concerning sales and supplies. A firm that provides products or services for a competitive market (especially a commodities market) is subject to rapid loss of market share; a young firm can gain some dependability in the lender's eye by obtaining contracts that ensure a minimum level of sales.

A firm using price- or availability-sensitive supplies, such as petrochemical compounds, can have its entire product or service process disrupted through some unforeseen event. Even well-established firms can be affected by unanticipated events. For example, the U.S. airlines were financially hurt during the period of the Desert Storm war against Iraq because the price of oil increased unexpectedly.

As mentioned earlier, obtaining a price or availability guarantee on supplies might provide some stability to a company subject to sudden changes in the supply or price of necessary supplies. Yet that option is not always available or desirable. Though well-established, the U.S. airlines were vulnerable to price increases in part because they had not accepted long-term supply contracts from producers of fuel. Their position was not unique, however. Firms frequently avoid signing contracts for selling and supplying goods and services because such contracts usually diminish profits.

Selling contracts are obtained by cutting price below the present (or expected) market price, and supply contracts are obtained by paying more than the present (or expected) market price. For example, during boom times a real estate developer knows that building on the hope that renters will be available (sometimes called *building on speculation*) will result in higher profits. Nevertheless, many bank real estate departments can attest to the additional risk undertaken by the lender that finances an uncommitted development. More conservative developers sacrifice some profits by obtaining lease commitments on structures before they obtain financing.

Time Intervals

Be sure that the time interval represented by the company's forecast statements suits the purpose and matches the repayment period for the proposed loan. For example, in projecting seasonal borrowing needs, the company should construct a cash budget as reviewed in the previous chapter.

Projections that support long-term financing requests should indicate the company's ability to repay the debt and should extend far enough into the future to reassure the credit analyst that current trends will continue. These projections should be consistent with trends established over the same period of time in the past. If they are not, the projections should present substantive explanations for the departures from the past.

External Factors

External factors affect a company's operations and thus the analysis of its forecast statements. Keep in mind how these various factors may change over time and thereby influence the company's future performance in unexpected ways. To ensure that the forecast analysis is comprehensive and credible, have on hand

- industry trends and projections, optimally including Robert Morris Associates' *Annual Statement Studies*,
- information about competitors (especially those that bank with the lender),
- current economic multiple-year forecasts relative to the industry, and
- past economic data about the borrower.

Although a company's management cannot control the *external factors* that make up the company's operating environment, it must anticipate and plan for them if the company is to reach its financial objectives. In making or analyzing projections, the company or analyst should take into consideration such major external factors as

- *the economy*—predictions as to general business conditions, interest rates, and economic fluctuations;
- *the industry*—its growth or stagnancy, the ease of entry into it, its degree of competitiveness and number of competitors, and the company's position in the industry (whether it is a leader or a marginal producer);
- *the market*—its degree of diversification (number of buyers), the cost of entry into it, the basis of competition (price, quality, technology), the competition from complementary products, and sociological trends (consumer preferences, environmental concerns, and so on;
- *government regulations*—prospects for regulatory changes (deregulation), especially with regard to environmental issues, and future vulnerability to imports or protection by import restrictions; and
- *labor*—the future availability and cost of labor; if nonunionized, prospects for unionization; if unionized, likelihood of strikes and anticipated costs of new contract negotiations.

Internal Factors

Internal factors include the human, financial, and physical resources available to the company. Company management can control these factors and use them to maximize its operational performance and to provide future direction. The major internal factors to consider are

- *management*—its experience, past performance, ability to project performance and to perform according to projections, ability to achieve objectives and to grow with the company;

- *physical plant*—its capacity, condition, efficiency compared to that of competitors, and technological sophistication;
- *financial controls*—the accounts receivable systems (approval and collection), inventory and purchasing systems, accounts payable systems, expense controls, and budgetary provisions;
- *marketing strategy*—the company's niche, marketing plan and market territory, adequacy of financial and human resources to support the plan, and distribution system; and
- *managerial reports*—the quality and adequacy of the financial and other managerial reports that are a basis for decision making.

The essence of good management is the ability to contemplate an uncertain future, to plan for that future, and to marshal the company's resources to fulfill its objectives. This requires a thorough knowledge of both the external and internal factors that affect a company and the requirements and limitations they impose.

In summary, forecast analysis enables the company's management and the bank's credit analyst to anticipate together the financial consequences of the company's plans and strategies. This should help the lender understand the company's past performance, its financial structure, and its managerial philosophy, strategy, and positioning within the industry as well as provide the basis for reasonable expectations about the company's capacity for repaying debt.

PEARSON COMPANY

The Pearson Company is a fictitious business, first described in chapter 7, that will be used again throughout this chapter to illustrate the forecasting process. The Pearson Company specializes in the production of automotive and farm machinery, but also has a secondary line of products in the oil-drilling industry. The company has been in operation for about 10 years.

On 2 January 1992, the company requested bank financing for a new ball-bearing casting mold that costs $600,000. The Pearson Company plans to pay $100,000 down and finance the balance over five years (the depreciable life of the casting mold). The company has requested a loan with a five-year level amortization of principal plus interest. While a five-year forecast should be prepared, for the example only the steps for a one-year forecast are shown.

Required Information

Management has provided the bank with three years of operating statements, past forecast statements to compare against actual results, and a forecast income statement and balance sheet. Normally, lenders request financial statement forecasts showing projections for five years when a loan with a five-year term is being requested.

The bank has provided various services to the Pearson Company for the past three years. As part of their commercial relationship, the Pearson Company provides the bank with copies of its quarterly and annual financial statements. Because of these past dealings, the credit analyst has a good feel for the company's strengths and weaknesses and knows a number of its officers. The company's borrowings traditionally have been long-term loans for the purchase of equipment; however, it has one revolving-credit, working-capital loan outstanding.

To supplement the company's financial statements, the credit analyst has also obtained industry information from the company's trade institute.

External Factors

The economy is currently strong, and all economic indicators project stability for the next two to three years. Monetary growth and inflation also appear stable for the immediate future. Industry predictions are that the value of ball- and roller-bearing shipments will increase by 5 percent in the current year to $3.95 billion in order to satisfy the expanding demand from the aircraft and automotive industries. Demand for these products by the construction, mining and oil, and farm machinery industries is also growing.

The bearing industry, after keeping price increases to a minimum during the previous several years, increased prices in 1990 and 1991 to catch up with accumulated labor and material cost increases. Price increases in 1992 are not expected because domestic companies continue to face stiff price competition from imports.

Imports of ball bearings have increased significantly each year since 1989. They continue to penetrate the high-volume, price-competitive U.S. market. Import revenues from ball and roller bearings are expected to reach 16 percent of U.S. consumption. Government regulations have little direct effect on the bearing industry, and no import protections are expected in the foreseeable future.

The Pearson Company employs unionized workers, but the union has made only reasonable demands in the past, and no work days have been lost due to union negotiations. Moreover, a contract settlement was reached in 1991, and no new negotiations are expected for the next three years.

Internal Factors

The Pearson Company's management team strongly desires to be a leader in the industry. For the last three years, the company has performed well. Now, the team wants to direct a growth-oriented company with top-of-the-line products. Management's primary weakness lies in its lack of a marketing chief; the president presently functions in that position. The Pearson Company has excellent facilities—its plant capacity is considerably greater than is required by the company's current sales level. Much of the equipment is relatively new and state-of-the-art.

An examination of the company's internal controls shows them to be adequate, but still subject to improvement. Although the Pearson Company has not had a major receivable remain unpaid in three years, many of its customers do not pay on the 30-day terms quoted.

While the company's management intends to take an aggressive position in the market, it is unwilling to erode profit margins to achieve an increased market share. Management believes in hiring top-notch salespeople and compensating them well; unproductive employees are readily let go.

Past Performance

A company's past performance is an important indicator of the predictability of the future. Thus the company's past history offers a basis on which to judge the reasonableness of the assumptions used to construct the projected statements. Exhibits 8.1 and 8.2 show the Pearson Company's common-sized income statements and balance sheets for the past three years, including the industry standard (based on the most recent RMA figures available).

Common-Sized Income Statement

Exhibit 8.1

Pearson Company
Common-sized Income Statement
for the Years Ending December 31
(in thousands of dollars)

	12/31/89	*%*	*12/31/90*	*%*	*12/31/91*	*%*	*RMA*
Net sales	4,000	100	4,800	100	5,500	100	100
Cost of goods sold	2,720	70	3,232	69	3,730	70	70
Depreciation	80		80		120		
Gross profit/revenues	1,200	30	1,488	31	1,650	30	30
Officers' salaries	120	3	144	3	165	3	
Selling expenses	160	4	192	4	220	4	
General and administrative expenses	440	11	672	14	660	12	
Total operating expenses	720	18	1,008	21	1,045	19	19
Operating profit	480	12	480	10	605	11	11
Interest expense	120	3	144	3	110	2	2
Profit before tax	360	9	336	7	495	9	9
Income taxes	144	4	134	3	192	3	
Net profit after tax	216	5	202	4	303	6	
Ratios							
Cash flow-to-current maturities	2.50		1.60		2.00		3.80
Times interest earned	4.00		3.30		5.50		4.10

Common-Sized Balance Sheet

Exhibit 8.2

Pearson Company
Balance Sheet
As of December 31
(in thousands of dollars)

	12/31/89	*%*	*12/31/90*	*%*	*12/31/91*	*%*	*RMA*
Assets							
Cash	25	1	87	3	85	3	3
Marketable securities	125	6	130	5	5		
Accounts receivable—net	548	25	727	28	916	31	28
Inventory	652	30	946	36	1,132	38	39
Other current assets							1
Current assets	1,350	62	1,890	72	2,138	72	71
Fixed assets—net	822	38	742	28	822	28	24
Noncurrent assets	822	38	742	28	822	28	29
Total assets	2,172	100	2,632	100	2,960	100	100
Liabilities and Net Worth							
Accounts payable—trade	400	18	500	19	559	19	16
Accruals	39	2	60	2	62	2	8
Current maturities—long-term debt	120	5	170	6	210	7	3
Current-year income taxes	33	2	40	2	54	2	
Other current liabilities							4
Current debt	592	27	770	29	885	30	31
Long-term debt—secured	480	22	560	21	470	16	15
Other long-term debt							1
Total long-term debt	480	22	560	21	470	16	16
Total debt	1,072	49	1,330	50	1,355	46	47
Capital stock—common	50	2	50	2	50	1	2
Retained earnings	1,050	49	1,252	48	1,555	53	51
Net worth	1,100	51	1,302	50	1,605	54	53
Total liabilities and net worth	2,172	100	2,632	100	2,960	100	100
Ratios:							
Quick/current	1.2/2.3		1.2/2.4		1.1/2.4		0.9/2.0
Debt-to-worth	0.97		1.02		0.84		0.89
Sales-to-receivables (days)	7.3 (50)		6.6 (55)		6.0 (61)		6.1
Cost of goods-to-inventory (days)	4.3 (85)		3.5 (104)		3.4 (107)		3.4
Purchases-to-payables (days)	4.9 (75)		4.6 (79)		4.8 (76)		—

Past Income Statements

The Pearson Company has had two successive years of sales increases—20 percent in 1990 and 15 percent in 1991—compared with an industry growth of only 16 percent in 1990 and projected growth of 5 percent in 1991 (actual figures not yet available). The Pearson Company is growing faster than the market.

The income statement also shows that the company's gross margin is both dependable and predictable—holding steady in the 30 percent range. Although total operating expenses have fluctuated a few points over the years, operating profits have consistently measured a very respectable 10 percent to 12 percent of sales. General and administrative expenses have ranged from 11 percent to 14 percent of sales. And although a major new company entered the market during the past 18 months, Pearson's profitability is holding well. It appears to have an established niche in the marketplace.

Past Balance Sheets

An examination of past years' balance sheets should help to create expectations for the company's future financing needs. The Pearson Company's balance sheet shows the company's financial position to be stable. Its liquidity measures—current and quick ratios of 2.4 and 1.1, respectively—are well within industry guidelines, as is its debt-to-worth ratio of 0.84.

The company sells on 30-day terms but lags in its collection efforts. Receivables are collected on the average in 61 days. However, the company's inventory turnover, at 107 days, equates to 3.4 times a year, right on industry averages.

FORECASTING THE INCOME STATEMENT

Sales

The *sales projection* is the cornerstone for the entire forecast income statement. It also affects key accounts on the forecast balance sheet. An unrealistic sales figure causes the rest of the projections to be of questionable value, since the forecast income-statement accounts are usually calculated as a percentage of sales. The sales projection also affects many balance sheet accounts, such as accounts receivable and inventory. The basis for the estimate of sales can vary. Sales can be projected on the basis of a very precise, detailed sales budget or as a percentage increase over the previous year's figures.

The Pearson Company's management has projected a 15 percent sales increase for the next five years. Thus, based on 1991 sales of $5,500,000, sales of $6,325,000 are predicted for 1992.

The credit analyst can see from the company's past forecast statements (not shown here) that its past sales projections have been unrealistically high. For example, management projected a 30 percent increase in sales for 1990 and a 25 percent increase for 1991, but actual sales increases were 20 percent and 15 percent, respectively. Moreover, although Pearson's sales growth in recent years has exceeded that of the industry, industry growth is expected to remain steady at 5 percent annually. A major new competitor has recently entered the market.

Considering an alternate scenario of slower sales growth, then, the credit analyst projects a 10 percent figure rather than the 15 percent projected by the company. Higher sales growth could push the company to reduce its prices and increase its selling expenses. Exhibit 8.3 shows the company's forecast as well as that of the bank.

Forecast Pro Forma Income Statements

Exhibit 8.3

Pearson Company
Pro Forma Income Statements
for the Year Ending December 31, 1992
(in thousands of dollars)

	Optimistic Pro Forma	%	*Pessimistic Pro Forma*	%
Net sales	6,325	100	6,050	100
Cost of goods sold	4,188	70	3,995	70
Depreciation	240		240	
Gross profit/revenues	1,897	30	1,815	30
Officers' salaries	127	2	182	3
Selling expenses	253	4	242	4
General and administrative expenses	633	10	847	14
Total operating expenses	1,013	16	1,271	21
Operating profit	885	14	545	9
Interest expense	124	2	148	2
Profit before tax	761	12	397	7
Income taxes	259	4	135	2
Net profit after tax	502	8	262	4
Ratios:				
Net profit-to-worth	26.44		14.21	
Net profit-to-total assets	15.28		7.97	
Cash flow-to-current maturities	2.39		1.62	
Times interest earned	5.04		2.77	
Dividends—common	$ 151			

Cost Of Goods Sold

The cost of goods sold usually ranks second behind sales in importance on the forecast income statement. As was discussed in chapter 4, the cost of goods sold for a manufacturer consists of the cost of raw materials, labor, and overhead (including depreciation) related to the production of inventory. It is usually calculated as a percentage of projected sales, taking into consideration both the company's past and anticipated performance. When a company must trim its selling prices to remain competitive, the cost of goods sold as a percentage of sales increases.

Check that management's projected cost of goods sold is consistent with previous years' figures. If it appears inconsistent, find out why. For example, the company may be planning to take a higher markup, to switch to lower-quality products, or to begin buying products at a discount.

The Pearson Company's cost of goods sold has held constant at just about 70 percent of sales for the past three years. Management projects cost of goods sold at 70 percent of projected sales for the following year as well.

The credit analyst believes that the company's projected cost of goods sold as a percentage of its sales is realistic since it is consistent with past performance. In addition, Robert Morris Associates' *Annual Statement Studies* shows that the company's estimate is consistent with industry averages. Thus, the credit analyst applies the same percentage to the level of sales projected by the bank.

Operating Expenses

A company's operating expenses include selling, general and administrative expenses, and officer's salaries. These expenses differ from those included in the cost of goods sold in that they are not directly related to the purchase or production of goods or services. However, they are usually the easiest expenses to get out of control if sales change rapidly. A company normally projects its operating expenses as a percentage of projected sales or as a percentage change from the previous year's operating expenses.

Selling expenses include the cost of advertising, market research, sales training, promotion, and commissions. These are expenses that management controls—that is, management can vary these expenses at its discretion as warranted by changing conditions in the marketplace. For instance, when a company introduces a new product or if it encounters increased competition in the industry, management might increase its sales commissions or promotional outlays.

General and administrative (G&A) expenses include rent, utilities, real estate, taxes, depreciation (of assets not used in production—such as administrative offices and equipment), telephones, staff and officer's salaries and benefits, travel, entertainment, and subscriptions. If the company anticipates no dramatic changes, these items can usually be calculated as a percentage of sales based on past history. When analyzing loan requests from companies with marginal repayment ability or high risk, evaluate the assumptions behind each figure in this category.

In the past, management has consistently held selling expenses to approximately 4 percent of sales and plans to do so again in the coming year. The credit analyst thinks that with a new competitor entering the market, the company might need to increase its advertising budget or pay higher commissions to remain competitive. Nevertheless, the bank accepts the company's projection of selling expenses as 4 percent of sales because this cost has been so well controlled at this level over the last three years.

Although the Pearson Company's general and administrative expenses have ranged from 11 percent to 14 percent of sales over the past three years, management anticipates reducing this category of expenses to 10 percent of sales. Specifically, management foresees lower spending for professional services, having recently decided to change attorneys and accountants because of their excessive fees. The company also anticipates more telephone sales and, hence, reduced travel expenses.

Considering an alternate scenario, the credit analyst takes a pessimistic posture and uses the company's highest general and administrative expense percentage to date—that is, 14 percent (for 1990).

Operating Profit

After the operating expenses have been subtracted from the gross revenues, the company's operating profit remains. The optimistic projection of sales and expense figures results in an operating profit of 14 percent, or $885,000; the more pessimistic projections result in an operating profit of 9 percent of sales, or $545,000. The industry average, according to RMA, is about 11 percent.

Other Income and Expense

Income statements often include other income and other expense items that do not result from the company's normal business operations. Although these accounts are normally quite small, find out what specific items are included and whether they are recurring or nonrecurring. These accounts are not usually predictable as a percentage of a company's sales. The Pearson Company has not had other income in the past and does not anticipate any in the coming year. Its only nonoperating expense is interest.

Interest expense is often listed separately on the income statement. This is usually a relatively predictable expense, because a range of interest rates can be assumed for term debt and short-term (seasonal) borrowings. It is estimated on the basis of the average amount of term and seasonal debt outstanding during the year. Some highly leveraged firms, such as transportation companies, have substantial interest charges; generally, however, a firm's interest expense is relatively unimportant compared to the cost of goods sold and operating expenses.

For the Pearson Company, although management projects no seasonal needs, averaging outstanding debt for 1989 and 1990 would be misleading because the entire loan is taken down in January. For the first year of the multiple-year forecast, the new loan would be averaged in as if it had been in existence at the beginning of the year. Further, for future years the analyst would calculate the outstandings by using amortization schedules provided by the company for the existing debt and generating a new amortization table for the new debt (Exhibit 8.4).

Amortization Table for New Debt

Exhibit 8.4

Pearson Company
Schedule of Existing Debt
As of December 31, 1992

Loan No.	*Origination Date*	*Original Amount*	*Outstanding*	*Rate*	*Principal Monthly*	*Current Maturity*	*Long-Term*
1	12/15/89	600,000	360,000	Prime + 2%	10,000	120,000	240,000
2	12/15/90	250,000	200,000	Prime + 2%	4,167	50,000	150,000
3	1/7/91	160,000	120,000	Prime + 2%	3,333	40,000	80,000
4	1/2/92	500,000	500,000	Prime + 2%	8,333	100,000	400,000
Total		1,510,000	1,180,000		25,833	310,000	870,000

Management predicts that the prime rate will average 10 percent and that it will pay two points over prime for the new loan (as it does for its current loans). Although the prime rate is currently 10 percent, management expects Congress to take action to reduce the federal deficit, which management believes will result in lower interest rates.

Considering an alternate scenario, the analyst assumes that companies are often overly optimistic that interest rates will decline and thus project interest expense that is unrealistically low. Certainly, very few companies projected the annual interest costs in the 20 percent or so range that appeared on statements composed in 1979 and 1980! A pessimistic approach would be to assume that interest rates will remain level or possibly rise one to two points during the year. The volatility of interest rates makes it especially prudent for banks to assume a pessimistic stance when performing a multiple-year forecast analysis. Thus, the credit analyst projects the company's interest expense based on a prime rate of 12 percent.

Income Taxes

Income taxes are frequently projected using current IRS income tax tables. Unfortunately, because of tax incentives associated with fiscal tax policies, this may not be a realistic assumption. Indeed, few if any growing firms are paying the current corporate tax-schedule rate. The problem is complicated because accrual accounting according to GAAP requires that the provision for taxes be at the standard rate.

Since this forecast is attempting to identify the cash flow resulting from the company's operations, accrual accounting may distort cash outflow. The projection of the balance sheet, shown as Exhibit 8.5, bases increases in the current accounts on sales changes, a reasonable assumption. Therefore, the statement of cash flows accounts for the accrual-accounting differences by adjusting net cash from operations for changes in the current accounts. Since there is no reasonable way to anticipate changes in the deferred tax account, there is no way to adjust the statement of cash flows for the different cash outflow resulting from it.

Exhibit 8.5

Pro Forma Forecast Balance Sheet

Pearson Company
Pro Forma Balance Sheets
As of December 31, 1992
(in thousands of dollars)

	Optimistic Pro Forma	%	*Pessimistic Pro Forma*	%
Assets				
Cash	101	3	97	4
Marketable securities	353	10	0	
Accounts receivable—net	866	24	1,011	27
Inventory	976	28	1,051	34
Current assets	2,296	65	2,158	65
Fixed assets—net	1,242	35	1,242	35
Total assets	3,538	100	3,400	100
Liabilities and Net Worth				
Notes payable to banks			25	4
Accounts payable—trade	402	11	328	13
Current maturities—long-term debt	310	9	310	9
Current debt	712	20	663	29
Long-term debt—secured	870	25	870	17
Total debt	1,582	45	1,533	45
Capital stock—common	50	1	50	2
Retained earnings	1,906	54	1817	53
Net worth	1,956	55	1,867	55
Total liabilities and net worth	3,538	100	3,400	100
Ratios:				
Current	3.22		3.26	
Debt-to-worth	0.81		0.82	
Sales-to-receivables (days)	7.30	50	5.98	61
Cost of goods-to-inventory (days)	4.29	85	3.80	96
Cost of goods-to-payables (days)	10.42	35	12.20	30

For assistance, review the firm's statement of cash flows. Here the prior year's change in the deferred tax account is indicated as a cash inflow. By subtracting this inflow from the provision for taxes found on the past income statement, the actual cash tax obligation is identified. This, then, should be divided by the profit before tax to estimate the *cash rate of income taxes* to be applied in the forecast.

When considering alternate scenarios, apply the cash tax rates to both different profits before taxes. This factor will tend to reduce the differences between the pessimistic and optimistic scenarios.

Income after Taxes

Except for the change in tax accounting to cash basis, the last item on the income statement is the accrual-accounting income. For an estimate of the cash to be generated by an organization, this step is but the first. Next comes forecasting the balance sheet and adding this income prediction to the statement of cash flows. Finally, the results are analyzed.

FORECASTING THE BALANCE SHEET

After analyzing and reworking the Pearson Company's forecast income statement, turn to the pro forma forecast balance sheet (Exhibit 8.5). This exhibit, like the income forecast, is a combination of an optimistic one submitted with the loan application and a more pessimistic one made up by the credit analyst. The assumptions made and conclusions reached in projecting the various income-statement accounts also affect many entries on the forecast balance sheet. Therefore, the assumptions used in composing (or critiquing) the forecast balance sheet must be consistent with those used for the income statement: a percentage of sales forecast.

Either the cash account in the assets section or the notes payable to banks account in the liabilities section of the balance sheet may be the *plug figures* used in constructing the forecast balance sheet. In other words, one of these accounts may be used to balance the statement after all the other accounts have been calculated. After the forecast balance sheet has been calculated, if assets exceed total liabilities and net worth (stockholders' equity), any difference may be shown by increasing the notes payable to banks account. However, if total liabilities and net worth exceed assets, the difference may be added to the cash account to balance the statement.

This balancing will tell if the forecast cash flows will be able to repay the debt as intended or even exceed the debt repayment goal. If cash flows are adequate for repaying the debt, the cash account will be the plug figure; if cash flows are insufficient for repaying the debt, the firm will have to borrow some additional funds to balance its obligations. For now, it is important to derive the changes on the balance sheet to determine the level of capital expenditures, long-term debt, and other current accounts. In addition, the analyst will be able to identify certain leverage and coverage ratios and test their relationship to those in the past and those within the industry.

Assets

Start to analyze the assets on the basis of the percentage-of-sales approach and make adjustments as other information from the company may suggest. For example, the company may be installing a new inventory control system, which will reduce the quantity of inventory.

The fixed asset account will normally grow in large chunks rather than smoothly with sales. This is particularly true in small firms, like the Pearson Company example, because plant and equipment comes in one size and cannot be installed one dollar at a time, unlike accounts receivable. Further, the fixed assets are wearing out constantly (with reference to depreciation). This complicates the forecast and necessitates checking fixed asset turnover rates to determine if a practical forecast has been created.

Cash and Marketable Securities

A company's minimum cash balance is usually assumed to be the cash at the latest period as a percentage of sales. (For forecast purposes, cash and marketable securities accounts are usually combined.) Therefore, the forecast will be based upon the percentage of sales approach because the firm has certain cash balances from the level of operations in check float, resulting from deposits yielded through collecting receivables and making payments to suppliers.

It is possible that additional balances may be required as compensating balances in the borrower's loan agreement. In that case, they should be added to the above calculated amount.

The Pearson Company projects a strong accumulation of cash and marketable securities. The company forecasts its minimum cash needs at 1.6 percent of sales. Management attributes its ability to live within the projected cash rate to its improved management of inventory and receivables. The credit analyst agrees with the Pearson Company's assessment of its minimum cash needs.

Accounts Receivable

Accounts receivable reflect the amount owed to the company by its customers at the end of the period covered by the forecast-income statement. To assess a company's projected accounts receivable, look at the company's past performance with respect to receivables turns—that is, its sales-to-receivables ratio, or the average collection period.

The credit analyst should also clearly understand management's sales and collection policies. Credit terms should be compared with actual collection periods to determine the effectiveness of a company's collection policies. Other than growing with sales, a company's sales posture will be the most important factor to affect accounts receivable. For example, management may try to increase sales by offering longer credit terms, by offering credit terms for products formerly sold only for cash, or by lowering prices.

Look at the accounts receivable calculation in light of trends from previous statements. For example, the Pearson Company's year end 1991 balance sheet (Exhibit 8.2) indicates receivables turning 6.0 times per year (16.67 percent of sales) or being collected every 61 days. Note the turns and the level of sales when calculating accounts receivable. From year end 1989 to year end 1991 (Exhibit 8.1), sales increased from $4,000,000 to $5,500,000, but the average collection period slowed by 11 days—from 50 days to 61 days.If the credit analyst has several months of accounts receivable agings for the most recent fiscal or interim statement dates, the agings should be used as an aid in evaluating the company's forecast balance sheet. As discussed in chapter 3, the agings reveal the actual age of receivables rather than the average collection period.

Sometimes the turn analysis alone may be misleading and fail to reveal problems with uncollectible receivables or disputed bills. By comparing several months, the credit analyst can also determine new accounts and predict collection times of existing accounts. This is especially helpful if a company has a concentration of sales to one company. The aging of accounts should be used to evaluate management's assumptions for future receivables because the aging reflects management's actual practices and success with respect to the collection of receivables.

The Pearson Company rarely has receivables outstanding over 75 days and has not charged off a major receivable in three years. Management believes that over the next five years the company will collect its receivables every 50 days, or 11 days faster than in 1991. This assumption is based on a stricter collection policy recently initiated by management, which the company hopes will help reduce its average collection period.

The bank's credit analyst decides to use a more-pessimistic average collection period in light of the increased competition in the market, which could put some pressure on the company's receivable turns. Moreover, if management follows its aggressive sales strategy, the company may need to offer more liberal sales terms to its customers. Normally, the bank could expect to see an industry average receivables turn of 6.1 times per year (as seen in the RMA data in Exhibit 8.2). However, the Pearson Company's receivables turn has slowed over the past three years from 7.3 to 6.0 (an average collection period of 61 days). Therefore, with the anticipated and continued pressure on the company's accounts receivable turns, the credit analyst projects receivable turns at the same rate as in 1991.

Inventory

The inventory account on a forecast balance sheet is usually calculated on the basis of the company's inventory turnover ratio (called cost of goods-to-inventory on the Pearson Company's balance sheet). In addition to considering past performance, inventory predictions should take into account any anticipated changes in the company's sales and purchasing policies.

Although the company's inventory turnover ratio was 3.4 (29.4 percent of cost of goods sold), or 107 days inventory for 1991, management believes that inventory will turn at 4.3 times per year (23.3 percent of cost of goods sold), or once every 85 days, in 1992. This projection is based on improved inventory control resulting from replacing its old manual inventory system with a computerized system. This was also the company's inventory turnover experience in 1989.

The credit analyst believes the company will be unable to achieve its goal with a brand-new system. Thus the credit analyst assumes that the company's inventory will turn at about 96 days, between the same rate as during the past year and the new goal.

The company's assumptions concerning its future sales strategy and working capital policies apparently affect inventory and accounts receivable turns dramatically. The company's projections require $220,000 less in working capital than does the bank's estimate.

Fixed Assets

Many companies routinely prepare a *capital expense budget*, which lists planned projects and their costs and anticipated sources of funding. If no such budget exists, management should provide a schedule of fixed assets and depreciation to the bank. This information may also be included in the notes to a company's financial statements. The fixed asset schedule should include the purchase date, useful life, cost, method of depreciation, and depreciation taken to date for each principal asset. Any projected increases in fixed assets (that is, anticipated purchases) should also be shown.

Use the company's past net sales to net fixed asset ratio as a rough measure for projecting fixed assets. This calculation divides net sales by net fixed assets (that is, the book value of assets net of accumulated depreciation). Thus it assumes that net fixed assets will increase at about the same rate as net sales. However, fully depreciated assets can distort the initial calculation of this ratio since the book value of such assets will be zero.

Since companies typically must replace their fully depreciated assets (which are carried at zero) at a much higher cost, an analyst should get an idea of the age and useful life of the company's fixed assets in order to determine its replacement needs. A plant having considerable excess capacity also distorts the ratio because the company can increase sales without a corresponding increase in fixed assets. Thus the capacity of the company's existing plant and equipment relative to projected production and space needs must be taken into consideration.

Some companies may show no fixed assets on their balance sheet (or a very small amount relative to sales), perhaps because the company leases its equipment or because the principals of the company own the fixed assets and rent them to the company.

The Pearson Company's assumptions for its fixed assets account are presented in Exhibit 8.6.

Fixed Assets Assumptions

Exhibit 8.6

Pearson Company
Fixed Assets Assumptions

Items	*Assumptions*
1. Capital purchases	After purchasing the $600,000 casting mold, to continue at the rate of $250,000 per year.
2. Depreciation	Expected to maintain itself at 10 percent of total equipment, growing at $25,000 per year as assumed above.

The information in Exhibit 8.6 appears to be consistent with the Pearson Company's projected sales growth. The schedule of depreciation and fixed assets furnished by the company (not shown) also appears reasonable to the credit analyst. Consequently, the bank accepts management's projections. Exhibit 8.7 presents a sample of the calculations for the first year.

Fixed Assets Forecast

Exhibit 8.7

Pearson Company
Fixed Assets Forecasts

Items	*Forecast*
Net fixed assets	$822
Less: Depreciation on existing equipment for	(120)
Plus: Cost of casting machine	600
Plus: Depreciation of casting machine	(60)
Net fixed assets	$1,242

Other Assets

Although the Pearson Company has no other assets, the analyst preparing a multiple-year forecast statement would consider the company's projections and historical data for any other assets shown, just as is done with the preceding categories of assets.

Liabilities and Net Worth

Having completed the review of the asset side of the company's forecast balance sheet, move next to the first item on the liability side of the balance sheet—notes payable to banks. As mentioned previously, notes payable to banks serves as a plug figure in balancing forecast statements. Thus, analyze the remainder of the forecast balance sheet accounts before calculating this figure.

Accounts Payable and Accruals

The amount of accounts payable is a function of the amount and terms of trade credit extended by suppliers and the company's actual payment practices. Accruals can be estimated along with the accounts payable as a percentage of cost of sales based on past trends. Chapter 6 discussed how to calculate a company's accounts payable turnover ratio, or days payable. Confirm the validity of the company's days payable by using a company-provided listing and aging of accounts payable, similar to the aging of accounts receivable used in verifying a company's average collection period.

It is difficult to obtain a listing of purchased raw materials to calculate a payables turnover ratio and enter it onto a balance sheet forecast. Usually the best that the analyst can do is relate the accounts payables and accruals to the cost of goods sold. While this may not be accurate at any one moment in time, it is a reasonable estimate of the working capital needed by the firm, unless the firm is seasonal. If the firm is seasonal, a more-appropriate average must be calculated, as was done in the Grab Bag example in chapter 7.

For the past three years, the Pearson Company has paid its suppliers on a 58-day basis (16.1 percent of cost of goods sold). However, in 1992, management expects to pay its suppliers more promptly at 35 days in order to take advantage of more early payment discounts.

The bank expects Pearson to pay its suppliers within 30 days, and for different reasons than company management does. Whereas company suppliers have previously allowed late payments, the credit analyst believes that the demand for raw materials has reached the point where suppliers will require that payments be made within normal 30-day terms, effective 1 January 1992.

Current Maturities of Long-term Debt

Current maturities represent the amounts of long-term debt due in the next 12 months. This figure can be calculated based on the schedule of debt included in the footnotes to a company's financial statements. Any current maturities resulting from the proposed loan should also be included. Exhibit 8.4 shows planned maturities of long-term debt for the next five years.

For cash budgeting purposes, identify the level of principal payments throughout the period of the existing loans. The amount of current maturities for the new loans should also be determined; they may be even principal payments, a custom-designed schedule, or even payment (including interest and principal, like installment loans), in which case amortization tables would be used.

Current maturities of the Pearson Company's three existing loans total $210,000 per year. The proposed additional debt of $500,000 is repayable with even principal payments over five years, which adds an additional $100,000 per year to the current maturities. Thus, projected current maturities as of year end 1992 total $310,000.

Long-term Debt

Long-term debt represents that portion of the debt schedule with maturities in excess of one year. Both the Pearson Company and the bank use the same calculation for long-term debt. On the schedule of projected debt, shown in Exhibit 8.4, all four existing loans (including the proposed loan) have maturities that extend beyond the current year. As new equipment is purchased in the future, it may also be partially financed or leased. This would be determined if the credit analyst were to complete a five-year projection. While the availability of long-term financing in the future may represent a risk, the discretionary nature of these fixed asset purchases means that plans could be canceled if the financing were not available or if sales growth was weak and additional fixed assets were not required.

Thus, the projection helps the analyst see the interrelated issues of cash requirements and inflows resulting from a company's growth and financing options. This leads towards the scenario analysis in the next section of this chapter.

Net Worth

The net worth section of the balance sheet is easily projected. Capital stock figures (for preferred and common stock) can be picked up from previous balance sheets unless additions or deletions to the stock were made in the current year. The retained earnings account is increased by the amount of projected after-tax profits from the forecast income statement less projected dividends.

The Plug Accounts

As discussed previously, the notes payable account is traditionally one of two possible plug (balancing) figures on the balance sheet. The other plug is the cash account. Thus, if assets exceed liabilities and net worth on the forecast balance sheet, the difference is added to the notes payable to banks in order to balance the statement. However, if liabilities and net worth exceed assets, the difference is added to cash in order to balance the statement.

The mere balancing of amounts into notes payables should not be considered a realistic alternative because, although this procedure accurately balances the balance sheet, the financing need may be long term rather than short term. (In addition, the interest expense on the plug has not been calculated, causing a slightly lower expense and lower need for funds.)

Do not forget that when a multiple-year forecast statement is prepared at the low point in the company's operating cycle, any need for seasonal debt to finance a seasonal buildup in receivables and inventory will not be apparent. This evidences the need in the case of companies with seasonal sales or production peaks to prepare the cash budgets discussed in chapter 7. For seasonal companies, it would be most desirable for the analyst to prepare a cash budget before preparing the long-term forecast.

Now decide what assets the bank will actually finance, how to structure the debt, and whether this reflects a long-term, permanent, or short-term borrowing need. The Pearson Company appears to need the additional debt to support the higher level of inventory and receivables that the bank projects the company will need to support its base level of sales in an increasingly competitive environment.

REVIEWING THE DIFFERENT SCENARIOS

The Pearson Company and the bank's credit analyst have composed two different sets of forecast financial statements, as seen in Exhibits 8.3 and 8.5. The bank's projections, which are more pessimistic, show the company needing considerably more cash than it has asked for. Some of the more significant changes made by the credit analyst to the Pearson Company's forecast statements include the following:

- The bank projects less in sales revenues than the company does.
- The bank projects more in general and administrative expenses than the company does.
- The bank projects significantly less cash flow compared with the company's projection because the bank projects slower inventory and receivables turnovers than management does. Thus, the credit analyst's

assumptions require the company to have a greater investment in current assets despite a lower projected sales level.

- The bank projects additional financing need to support these increased assets (accounts receivable and inventory).

Substantial differences in the assumptions made about the Pearson Company by its own management and by the credit analyst lead to significantly different projected financial results. The bank may also reach far less optimistic conclusions than management does concerning a company's financial needs, its ability to repay the proposed loan, and its overall creditworthiness. This emphasizes how important it is to thoroughly understand all the facets of the borrowing company in order to arrive at realistic assumptions and accurate projections.

PITFALLS OF FORECASTS

Forecast statements attempt to estimate a company's financial future in an uncertain environment. These uncertainties include the economy, competition, government regulations, technological change, and management's ability to perform effectively. Fortunately, while the further into the future the projection extends the greater is the uncertainty, the offset is that feedback received by management in the interim allows the plan to be changed. This leads to the option of sensitivity analysis discussed in chapter 9; sensitivity analysis can help the analyst identify which of the many assumptions are the most crucial.

Another shortcoming of forecast analysis is that it can result in overlooking the company's interim financing needs. Because the multiple-year forecast balance sheet reflects the company's financial state at a given point in time (usually the fiscal year end), it does not reveal any funding needs that might arise between fiscal year end balance sheet dates. These hidden funding needs typically involve the need for seasonal asset buildups in preparation for heavy sales periods. The use of projected monthly cash budgets to identify interim cash requirements was discussed in chapter 7.

SUMMARY OF IMPORTANT CONCEPTS

Long-term forecast analysis must be based on accurate knowledge of the company's past performance as well as knowlege of the many external and internal factors that affect the company's operations. It is particularly difficult to make accurate projections for young companies and for companies that have had erratic operating results in the past.

This type of forecast analysis enables the credit analyst to reach conclusions about a company's probable financing needs and repayment ability. However, the forecast results can only be as good as the underlying assumptions on which the projections are based. Therefore, closely examine the validity of the company's assumptions, making adjustments to the company's forecast statements as deemed necessary. In general, the credit analyst will favor more pessimistic assumptions than does company management.

The single most important element of long-term forecast financial statements is the sales projection. Without a reasonable sales figure, the entire forecast process is of questionable value. A change in sales can affect projected profits, accounts receivable, inventory, accounts payable, and the perceived borrowing needs of the company. Thus, even a small miscalculation in this key assumption can dramatically affect many areas of the forecast analysis. Therefore, the lender should use scenario analysis to understand how a 1 percent change in the net margin or a one-day change in inventory turnover will affect the various statements and the cash flow of the company.

In constructing a forecast balance sheet, assets are made to equal liabilities and net worth by using a plug figure—either cash and marketable securities (on the assets side) or notes payable to banks (on the liabilities side). This latter is not to be taken literally, however, since the company may actually need long-term rather than short-term financing.

Forecast analysis has a number of limitations, including the fact that it fails to reveal seasonal financing needs. In addition, because the future is unpredictable, all forecast projections should be tempered with appropriate conservatism.

EXERCISES

Important Terms to Define

pro forma forecast
building on speculation
internal factors
cash rate of income taxes
capital expense budget
long-term forecast
external factors
sales projection
plug figures

Dependable Doors Case Study

Background

Management provides you with the following information about its expectations for the company in 1992:

1. Sales are expected to increase 50 percent due to the anticipated recovery in the housing market, the company's geographic expansion into Texas and Canada, its sales of steel products to new markets, its full use of production facilities, and its introduction of new products.
2. The gross profit margin is going to increase to 27 percent of sales due to increasing economies of scale in the company's new production facility and the company's ability to raise prices in the upcoming boom market.
3. Selling expenses will decline to 5 percent of sales because of increasing sales volume per salesperson.
4. General and administrative expenses will decline slightly to 12 percent of sales due to increasing efficiency in the St. Louis plant.
5. Interest expense is expected to be $1,116,000. The increase is expected because of anticipated higher inventory levels, which will be funded with short-term debt.
6. Income taxes are expected to be 3 percent of sales.
7. Cash at year end 1992 is projected to be $300,000.
8. Accounts receivable days on hand are projected to be 51 days as the company improves the collection of receivables and institutes a new policy where salespeople do not get commissions on accounts that are over 60 days overdue.
9. Inventory days on hand are projected to be 81 days as the company eliminates some of the obsolete inventory at the St. Louis plant and gets its new inventory control system up and running.
10. Accounts payable days on hand are projected to be 28 days.
11. Fixed assets are not expected to grow next year. Depreciation expense is projected to be $660,000.
12. Other fixed assets are projected to remain the same as the prior year.
13. Accruals are expected to increase 33 percent over the prior year.
14. No new long-term debt is anticipated next year because the company plans to focus its attention on absorbing the St. Louis facility, increasing sales, and reducing expenses.

15. Deferred income taxes are expected to be 6 percent of total assets.
16. The capital accounts are not expected to grow next year.

Questions

1. On the basis of the financial statements and the forecasts provided by management, prepare a pro forma income statement and balance sheet for 31 October 1992.
2. How much additional borrowing requirement will Dependable Doors have if the gross margin is 25 percent?
3. Prepare another pro forma balance sheet and income statement using your own assumptions about the future for Dependable Doors.

Engraph Case Study

Background

Management of Engraph anticipates the following events in 1992:

1. Sales will only increase 5 percent due to increased competition and continued sluggishness in the economy.
2. In order to generate sales and respond to the competition, management plans to reduce prices, which will cut the company's gross margin to 25 percent.
3. Management plans to reduce some of its travel and entertainment expense as well as some of its advertising expense, which will reduce selling, general and administrative expenses to 16.5 percent of sales.
4. Other income will be about half of what it was in 1991.
5. Management does not expect to add any additional long-term debt in 1992, so interest expense is expected to decline slightly to $4,000,000 as rates in general decline.
6. The income tax and dividend rates will remain the same as last year.
7. All cash in excess of $700,000 at the end of 1992 will be used to reduce bank notes payable.
8. Receivable days will increase to 50 days on hand as management plans to offer better terms to stimulate sales.

9. Inventory will remain approximately the same in total dollar amount.
10. Accounts payable will also remain the same in total dollar amount.
11. Fixed assets will increase 3 percent, and depreciation will be approximately $32,500.
12. The company is not planning any purchases of companies or sales of divisions next year.
13. Investments will remain constant.
14. Intangibles and goodwill will both reduce 3 percent.
15. All other accounts will increase proportionally with sales.

Questions

1. On the basis of the financial statements and the forecasts provided by management, prepare a pro forma income statement and balance sheet for 31 December 1992.

Other Analytical Techniques

LEARNING OBJECTIVES

After studying this chapter, you will be able to

- analyze the effect that changes in a firm's sales levels have on working investment,
- explain and apply the concept of sustainable growth,
- explain and apply sensitivity analysis in a probability distribution of possible future outcomes in contrast to a single best guess, and
- apply industry factors in forecasting debt repayment capacity.

INTRODUCTION

The techniques of financial statement analysis presented thus far are the basic tools of the trade. This chapter introduces some more-advanced techniques, including working investment analysis, sustainable growth, sensitivity analysis, and industry factors. Although these techniques are discussed only briefly here, they are valuable to the credit analyst in refining and focusing the financial statement analysis process. This chapter should help in selecting the most appropriate advanced techniques and applying them along with the standard techniques to make sound lending decisions that benefit both the customer and the bank.

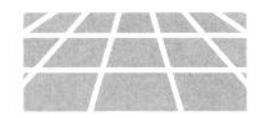

WORKING INVESTMENT ANALYSIS

Working investment analysis focuses on the current accounts of a company and how sales growth is financed. Working capital is the numerical counterpart of the percentages used in working investment analysis, which provides the credit analyst with a quick means of projecting the financing required when a company's working assets increase to support its growth in sales.

How Current Accounts Grow

As a company's sales grow, the base level of its working assets (accounts receivable and inventory) normally grows proportionately. Accounts payable and accruals, which provide the basic financing for the growing accounts receivable and inventory levels, also increase. This growth is sometimes referred to as spontaneous growth of current accounts because it is so difficult to have sales grow without, for example, growth in inventories so that there will be products to ship.

The accounts payable and accruals probably grow at as fast a rate as inventory and receivables do; however, being smaller to start with, they usually cannot support the growth in current assets by themselves. The portion of working assets that is not supported by the company's payables and accruals must be financed by debt or equity. Earlier chapters have shown that it is possible to use pro forma statements and cash budgets to project the financing required to support an increased working investment

Calculating Working Investment

Working investment analysis is a shortcut that can be used to quickly appraise the potential financial effects that the company's growth plans might have on the current accounts. This approach is especially useful for companies with a heavy investment in accounts receivable and inventory. It is not, however, intended to replace the more-accurate and detailed analytical procedures already discussed.

A company's working investment represents the difference between its working assets and its working liabilities as illustrated by the following equations:

Working assets = Accounts receivable + Inventory.

Working liabilities = Accounts payable + Accruals.

Working investment = Working assets – Working liabilities.

A company's working investment is typically expressed as a percentage of sales. Assuming that the relationship between sales and inventory, accounts receivable, and accounts payable remains fairly stable, the working investment percentage can be applied to the company's projected sales levels to determine the projected amount of working investment and the additional financing required.

The company's working investment expressed as a percentage of sales is calculated as follows:

Working investment percentage = Working investment ÷ Sales.

Working Investment Analysis: A Shortcut to Forecasting

If the company anticipates a sales increase of 20 percent in the next fiscal year (that is, total sales of $1,200,000), the additional working investment that will be required can be calculated as follows:

New working investment = Projected sales x Working investment percentage.

For example, with projected sales of $1,200,000 and a working investment percentage of 20 percent, the calculation would be

$1,200,000 x 20% = $240,000.

If the firm already has a $200,000 working investment, it will need an additional $40,000 in working investment for its projected 20 percent increase in sales.

This quick calculation of a company's projected need for working investment in support of increased sales helps the analyst compare the company's borrowing requirements with available financing alternatives. The financing alternatives are increasing bank debt, injecting equity into the company, increasing the percentage of working investment in accounts payable, or decreasing the working investment in accounts receivable and inventory.

To determine the effect of different scenarios, vary any of the assumptions used. It should be emphasized that working investment calculations cannot replace forecast statements and cash budgets; they are, however, useful in providing a rough measure that can quickly and easily predict the consequences of a company's growth or decline in sales on several key balance sheet components, especially in the short run.

SUSTAINABLE GROWTH

A company's sales growth depends on both its ability to fund increasing asset requirements and the availability of adequate equity to balance the company's increasing levels of debt. *Sustainable growth analysis* incorporates leverage, asset efficiency, profits, and dividends, allowing each to be varied to test its impact on any of the other variables. It is notably useful for long-term decision making since it adds the issue of fixed assets to the concepts developed in working investment analysis.

Basic Sustainable Growth Analysis

In basic sustainable growth analysis, when determining a company's ability to expand its sales, it is assumed that profitability, asset requirements, and dividend payout relationships with sales remain constant and that the company maintains its ratio of debt to equity at existing levels. The calculation of sustainable growth is based on two underlying assumptions:

1. For sales to increase, assets must increase; therefore, the analyst must know the rate by which assets increase for each percentage increase in sales and must assume that this rate remains constant. This implies the asset turnover ratio will be involved in the analysis.

2. Increased assets are financed by retained earnings and external debt, which remains available. (Retained earnings are net profits less dividends—both of which remain a constant historical percentage of sales and net profits, respectively) This leverage relationship, debt to equity, remains constant.

The capability of the firm to grow by retaining profits, increasing debt at its historic leverage relationship, and purchasing new assets to support the growth can be determined by using the following steps:

1. Find profits less dividends as a percentage of sales (the addition to retained earnings as a percentage of sales), identifying each year's new contribution to equity as percent of sales:

   (Profits - Dividends) ÷ Sales = Retained Profits Percentage.

2. Find the relationship of total assets to equity, which reveals the potential asset growth available based upon any growth in equity funds (assuming the debt-to-equity ratio remains constant):

Total Assets ÷ Equity = Asset Growth Supported by Retained Profits (Asset Leverage).

3. Multiply these two results by each other to get the increase in assets that will result from each year's retained profits:

   Retained profits percentage x Asset leverage = Asset Growth Supported by Profits.

4. Identify asset turnover, or sales divided by assets, which is, in effect, the percentage increase in sales permitted by a specific increase in assets:

   Sales ÷ Total assets = Asset turnover.

5. Multiply the last two numbers to get the sales growth enabled by the internally generated growth in equity funds:

Asset growth supportable by profits x Asset turnover = Sales Growth supported by Asset Growth.

To illustrate the five steps, assume that a company has $500,000 in assets, $1,000,000 in sales, equity of $250,000, a dividend payout ratio of 0, and a net profit of $20,000. The following sustainable growth results:

1. Calculate the profits less dividends as a percent of sales (retained profits percentage):

   (20,000 - 0) ÷ 1,000,000 = 2%

2. Calculate the relationship of total assets to equity (asset leverage):

   500,000 ÷ 250,000 = 2

3. Multiply the first two results to obtain asset growth supported by retained profits:

   2 x 2% = 4%

4. Calculate the asset turnover, which is sales divided by assets:

   1,000,000 ÷ 500,000 = 2

5. Multiply the third by the fourth:

   4% x 2 = 8%

Thus, for this company, given the continued constancy of asset efficiency, dividend payout, and asset leverage, the analyst could forecast that the firm can maintain sales growth at 8 percent if the rate of profits (as a percentage of sales) is 2 percent.

To identify the factor relating sales growth to percentage of profits, divide as follows:

$$0.08 \div 0.02 = 4 \text{ times.}$$

Modifying Different Variables

Generally, the real problem facing the analyst is how to validate the company's stated growth rate plan for the future. For example, assume that the above company wants a sales increase of 25 percent. The analyst knows that this is not possible, given the 8 percent sustainable growth rate indicated above.

The only alternatives are to vary one of the inputs, either the

- ❒ financial leverage (debt-to-worth ratio), the
- ❒ asset utilization (asset turnover), the
- ❒ dividend rate (dividend payout), or the
- ❒ profit rate (as a percentage of sales).

For the first variation, start by seeing how much the profit rate would have to increase to allow this kind of sales growth, assuming the other three variables are held constant:

25% (the growth rate) ÷ 4 (the factor relating growth to profits percentage, calculated above) = profits of 6.25% of sales.

The original calculation resulted in profits of 2 percent of sales.

Alternatively, the leverage could be increased. In the example, debt and equity appear to be 1:1 because, if assets are twice equity, debt is clearly being used to support half of assets. If the firm could increase the 2-times asset leverage to 3-times, debt-to-worth *in the long run* would then become 2:1. Then, the current profit margin, asset efficiency, and dividend payout would allow 12 percent growth:

2% (the profit margin from above) x 3 (the asset leverage ratio) = 6%.

6% (the asset growth supported by retained profits) x 2 (the asset turnover) = 12%.

Naturally, one year of accelerated growth would not produce such a jump in leverage. Instead, in addition to the $20,000 retained profits that are anticipated, $40,000 in debt would have to be obtained to acquire $60,000 in new assets, which by extension would allow a sales growth of $120,000, or 12 percent.

For most companies, the variable that is perhaps the most likely to change is the dividend payout ratio; however, the firm in the example pays no dividends, so changes here are not possible.

Sustainable growth incorporates assumptions about the company's total assets and debt-to-worth ratio beyond those contained in the working investment formula. These assumptions are useful for a company whose fixed assets must increase proportionally with sales, although the result will be misleading if no direct correlation exists between sales and total assets. The formulas also demonstrate the effect of growth on the company's financial leverage—which is usually one of the primary constraints on growth. Working investment and sustainable growth calculations can be used together effectively to project a company's capacity for growth and the amount of debt financing required to support that growth.

SENSITIVITY ANALYSIS

Sensitivity analysis enables the credit analyst to test the validity of financial projections, by analyzing a range of scenarios. It is readily apparent that the validity of financial projections used in long-term forecasts and cash budgets depends on the credit analyst's underlying assumptions about the company. Deriving appropriate assumptions is complicated by several factors. For example, each company has particular characteristics that contribute to its vulnerabilities. Further, projections are based on imperfect information about an uncertain future, and the combinations and permutations involved in deriving assumptions can be extensive. Although the stakes are high—both for the borrower and the lender—and despite the difficulty of accurately projecting a company's future financial stability, there is no other basis upon which loans may be committed.

Scenario Analysis

Chapters 7 and 8, about forecasting, stressed the importance of alternative projections, not just best- and worst-case options. A worst-case scenario may not be pessimistic enough, since nightmares may be the only limit to how bad things can get. Indeed, if worst-case scenarios produced acceptable financial performance, the lending decision would be easy; however, pass-book secured loans are about the only loans that can survive such a yardstick. While a lender's projections are usually based on the most-likely scenario, the analyst needs to consider alternatives beyond the worst-case scenario.

One source of alternatives is sensitivity analysis, which identifies in any forecast the variables that are most crucial to the outcome. Sensitivity analysis enables the credit analyst to change key assumptions and see how those changes might affect the company's financial results. For example, an analyst could redo the forecast and reduce management's projected sales by 20 percent. The result might help the analyst to determine how a sharp downturn in sales might affect the firm.

Identifying the key variables is a time-consuming task. The most popular technique is merely to change different variables, one at a time, in the forecast to see how much the notes payable (the plug figure) changes. For example, after calculating the change in sales growth and reviewing the impact on the forecast, the analyst would change cost of goods sold by possible percentages, identify this impact, and so on.

The key variables are the ones that change the notes payable (the plug figure) the most. For later scenario analysis, it is more fruitful to focus on these key variables. After the analyst has decided which of the variables are key, constructing pessimistic and optimistic scenarios can produce more meaningful results.

To determine a pessimistic scenario, select those factors that, based on past experience, have made the company most vulnerable. For example, companies with cyclical demands for their products typically experience a significant reduction in sales during a recession. The percentage decrease in a company's sales in past recessions could be used as the basis for a worst-case analysis. Obviously, making extensive loans to a company with numerous areas of vulnerability is risky and suggests the need for significant offsetting strengths.

An Example of Sensitivity Analysis

Exhibit 9.1 demonstrates how sensitivity analysis can be applied to working investment analysis to determine the range of possibilities between optimistic, most-likely, and pessimistic scenarios for the Duffy Paper Company. This set of scenarios was chosen because the credit analyst has concluded that the company's greatest vulnerability is the rapid growth in its working assets and the additional financing these require because of low profit margins. The key assumption of the scenarios for Duffy Paper Company, then, concerns changing the rate of sales growth and the company's ability to control working assets, liabilities, and profitability.

Scenario 1 of the exhibit presents management's projections for the company. The Duffy Paper Company has grown rapidly in recent years, with sales increases of 25 to 30 percent per year. Management anticipates a slowing of this growth accompanied by a greater emphasis on financial controls. Thus, accounts receivable and inventory turns are expected to decrease from the existing levels of 43 and 118 days, respectively. Management also predicts that accounts payable turnover will decrease to at least 45 days (probably of necessity since the industry average is 30 days).

Scenarios 2 and 3 show the range of performance the credit analyst thinks is most likely to occur, and scenario 4 presents an estimate of the pessimistic case. This latter scenario is based on accounts receivable and inventory turns remaining close to current levels while accounts payable are considerably reduced (as the result of pressure throughout the industry). The pessimistic scenario also includes substantial sales growth due to continuing market demand and very conservative estimates of profitability (a 0.75 percent profit margin compared to a current profit margin of 1.25 percent).

These four scenarios result in widely varying financing requirements—from $181,280 for scenario 1 to $307,102 for scenario 4. Since the credit analyst expects the company's performance to be in the range of scenarios 2 and 3, indicating a total financing need of $231,375 to $274,860, the analyst would examine the company's ability to handle that level of debt and the potential protection for the lender if the pessimistic scenario were to come true.

Working Investment Analysis Scenarios

Exhibit 9.1

Duffy Paper Company
Financial Projections for 1992

Items	*1 Optimistic*	*2 Most Likely*	*3*	*4 Pessimistic*
Sales	$936,000	$975,000	$1,014,000	$1,053,000
Accounts receivable	$10,000	$111,000	$125,000	$130,000
(Average collection period)	39	42	45	45
Inventory	$200,000	$220,000	$230,000	$240,000
(Days in Inventory)	111	118	118	118
Accounts Payable	$80,000	$70,000	$60,000	$50,000
(Days Payable)	45	37	31	25
Accruals	$20,000	$15,000	$10,000	$5,000
Working Investment	$200,000	$246,000	$285,000	$315,000
Net Profit	$18,720	$14,625	$10,140	$7,898
(Margin)	2.00%	1.50%	1.00%	0.75%
Financing Required	$181,280	$231,375	$274,860	$307,102

This example illustrates how to apply sensitivity analysis selectively to the key factors that affect a company's most vulnerable operating assumptions. Sensitivity analysis can help to better focus the examination and to determine the potential impacts of various analytical assumptions.

PROBABILITIES AND RELIABILITY OF FORECASTS

Statistically Quantified Risk

This section examines the idea of risk as variability and explores concepts of probability distribution curves. Persons who see risk as a qualitative expression for which precise forecasting is not possible may not be aware of the quantitative possibilities.

Everyday Forecast Risk

Consider an example in which the forecaster quantifies the risk. The man-on-the-street who hears a weather forecaster say that "there is a 60 percent chance of rain today" is hearing an example of risk being quantified. The weather forecaster is summarizing a weather-predicting equation that considers many possibilities, including prevailing winds, weather in nearby geographical areas, humidity, pressure, and other variables. What the weather person is actually reviewing is a distribution of possible outcomes. By applying a statistical inference to this range of possible outcomes, the weather forecaster is able to determine the percentage of likelihood that rain will occur.

The man-on-the-street may be irritated at such a forecast, wishing instead that the weather forecaster would say definitely that an umbrella is necessary. This same individual probably does not realize that a medical doctor is making the same kind of decision during a medical diagnosis. The physician is not always certain what is causing the problem and selects the most likely possibility from a range of probable causes.

Risk and Reward in Lending

The underlying concept to lending is aversion to the risk of a wide range of outcomes; lenders prefer predictable outcomes. The presence of risk means that the outcome can be accurately forecast only as a range of possibilities. Accommodating a wide range of possible outcomes requires that the average return or yield on that investment be greater than the return on an investment in which the range of possibilities is much narrower. In other words, risky loans require a higher interest rate.

Consider an everyday example, deciding whether it is safe to jaywalk across a busy highway. At 2 in the afternoon on a bright, clear day, most people probably would consider it safe to ignore the traffic signal and jaywalk to save a few minutes of time. But at 7:30 on a rainy, winter-dark night, most people probably would decide that the risk is not worth the saving in time. The additional risk factors that most people are likely to have considered in the second situation include the possibility of

- slipping on the road,
- not seeing an oncoming vehicle,
- not being seen by an oncoming vehicle,

- being struck by an oncoming vehicle driven by an intoxicated driver, and
- being struck by an oncoming vehicle that is unable to stop on the slick road.

These factors would cause an individual to reconsider the value of the one or two minutes gained by running against the red signal. In this case, the advantage gained by getting across the street is insufficient to warrant the downside potential of being struck or of falling down. Other factors, however, such as not having an umbrella and wishing to keep dry a brand-new "dry-clean only" suit, might increase the payoff sufficiently to make the risk worthwhile.

This comparison of rewards for undertaking specific risks is frequently described as the *risk-reward calculation* and implies that there are methodologies to quantify uncertainty: if greater risk should produce greater rewards, then there must be a system for comparing various risks.

Risk Related Definitions

A *probability distribution* is a statement of the different potential outcomes and the probability percentage of each one happening. It can be expressed graphically as a probability distribution curve. Additionally, the *expected return* from an investment is the weighted average return; it is calculated as the sum of all of these potential returns weighted by their percentage probability of happening. Essentially, this is the equivalent of the simple mean when all outcomes are equally likely. Thus, the *expected return*, the *average*, and the *mean* are all interchangeable terms. Unfortunately, these terms do not fully describe the probability distribution. This is true, surprisingly enough, even though the mean of the different sets of observations relating the two variables may be identical.

Upon reflection, this should not come as a complete surprise. For example, a college classroom could have the same average age as the audience at a rock concert, although it is more likely that the age range actually observed at the rock concert would be much wider than the age range in the college classroom. There ought to be some method to assess the degree of risk (or range of variation) within any distribution of outcomes, and there is. Statisticians measure this degree of variability by calculating how much an individual observation differs from the mean, which is called *standard deviation*. The standard deviation is the square root of the variance, which is the sum of the squared deviations from the mean.

Empirical analysis has demonstrated that investors require that stocks exhibiting variability in yields (yields include dividends and changes in stock prices) must produce higher returns on average. For instance, in the long run, higher returns can be earned on computer stocks than on public utility stocks, which are regulated monopolies. Also, while the standard deviation of a series of observations (for example, the various prices and returns of a group of stocks over time) may be measured, an additional calculation is required to be able to compare the information between groups of variables or groups of firms. The calculation of the *coefficient of variation* assists in this project. The coefficient of variation is the ratio of the standard deviation of returns to the expected value. In other words, it gives the percentage from the mean of the standard deviation rather than just the raw numbers. It is similar to getting a common-size analysis on a balance sheet.

Exhibit 9.2 shows the relationship between average returns on a long-term basis and the standard deviation of those returns on a long-term basis. The Financial Analysts Research Foundation showed the interrelationship between the extremely high expectations for high returns on small stocks and the very wide standard deviation. This contrasts with the low mean rate of returns of U.S. Treasury bills and a standard deviation that is also very narrow and tight. A calculation of the coefficient of variation in these cases shows that the coefficient of variation for the small stocks would be 37.3 ÷ 12.1, or approximately 300 percent. The same calculation for U.S. Treasury bills would produce a coefficient of variation of approximately 100 percent.

Exhibit 9.2

Historical Relationship Between Risk and Return

Statistical distribution parameters of investment total annual returns, 1926-1981

Series	*Mean Returns*	*Standard Deviation (%)*	*Distribution*
Common Stocks	9.1	21.9	
Small Stocks	12.1	37.3	
Long-term Corporate Bonds	3.6	5.6	
Long-term Government Bonds	3.0	5.7	
U.S. Treasury Bills	3.0	3.1	
Inflation	3.0	5.1	
			− 0 +

Source: R. Ibbotson and R.A. Sinquefield, *Stocks, Bonds, Bills and Inflation:* "The Past and the Future" (Charlottesville, Va.: Financial Analysts Research Foundation, 1982).

This information exemplifies why banks are willing to finance the purchase of U.S. Treasury bills at a relatively high percentage of the bills' current market value. It also shows why financing small stocks would be viewed as an extremely risky proposition. The distributions for small stocks are flat in comparison to the peaked curve demonstrated by U.S. Treasury bills. The observed returns of the latter are all close to the mean, showing little variation and, thus, little risk. Graphically, the standard deviation is an extremely interesting and good measure of the extent of variability of returns.

The second principle demonstrated in these drawings is that a considerable amount of time must be taken into account to achieve the various mean returns. Diversification of investment is an alternative way to maintain equilibrium in any specific portfolio. While the statistical patterns may indicate long-term outcomes, they do not necessarily give a clear indication of what will be happening on any specific day. This is especially true with regard to small stock investments.

The difference in risk between the mean yield required in the market for common stocks and that required in the market for U.S. Treasury bills is the market premium. Sometimes called systematic risk, this risk cannot be diversified against (by buying lots of different stocks) because it is inherent in all market portfolios. In contrast, the remaining risk—unsystematic, or individual-firm risk—is the risk induced by individual management strategies.

The study of debt-repayment capacity indicates the typical desire of analysts for a simple *go* or *no go* quantification method in decision making. Naturally, this is similar to the conflict between

- ❒ going to the effort of projecting funds flows and then considering how they might evolve into best and worst cases, an exercise often requested by senior credit officers, and
- ❒ just calculating simple current and debt-to-worth ratios and matching them to a predetermined guideline considered to be foolproof, such as two-to-one and one-to-one, respectively.

While the latter alternative appears much safer and is actually similar to investing only in U.S. Treasury bonds, investors with more sophisticated analyses will be able to achieve higher returns by devising means of dealing with variability in these returns. Reviewing probability distributions by examining not only the mean outcome but also the standard deviation allows profound understanding of risk and leads to better decisions about that risk. Those investors who prefer the former approach may be trying to hold to unrealistically high standards while losing reasonable types of business.

Probability Distribution Curves

The above conclusion forces credit analysts to examine additional statistical concepts. Most executives pale at the thought of looking at probability distribution curves, but it is imperative to address two important issues:

1. The extremely high likelihood that any distribution that occurs in human affairs is likely to be shaped as a normal distribution.
2. Decision makers can develop confidence limits that allow them to make *yes* or *no* decisions and obtain greater insight by matching
   - ❐ risk-taking inclinations with
   - ❐ risks of any particular investment, as well as
   - ❐ suitable returns to the risks that are undertaken.

An example of the absence of suitable returns given the risks that are undertaken in current practice is the extremely close ranges of lending rates used by most lending institutions over the range of customer quality, from risky to stable. Rates offered most customers fluctuate within a percentage point of prime, whereas the difference in yields between common stocks and small stocks is 3 percent (see Exhibit 9.2). If credit analysts can accustom themselves to this broader understanding of risk and returns, they may be able to make wiser choices for the individual financial institutions and the individual firms.

There appears to be a strong steeple or stepped-tower pattern evident in the discrete observations of long-term corporate bonds, long-term government bonds, and U.S. Treasury bills. The distributions of outcomes and their related number of occurrences with regard to common stocks and small stocks are less easily characterized. The graphic interpretation relates more variability to the wider and lower curves. The higher variability exhibited by the stocks also means that the standard deviation will be larger.

In an attempt to more closely identify the ranges of various types of distributions, Karl Gauss (1777 to 1855), thc most important of statistically oriented mathematicians, discovered the formula that describes the so-called *normal distribution*. This formula defines the range of outcomes most frequently produced by biologically based activities. It is typically shown in the shape of a bell, where most of the measured activities are close to the mean or average. In a few cases they deviate more, and in some rare cases the measured values will be very different from the mean. In fact, in the mathematical description, the tails of the curve never actually touch the horizontal plane.

Relating to the application of this concept are the empirical studies showing that humans appear to be good at estimating a single standard deviation from the mean of a normal distribution. Human beings describe it as a range beyond which they would be mildly surprised if it occurred. The normal distribution produces the following sets of probabilities:

Standard Deviation	*Confidence Limits*
1	68.26%
2	95.46%
3	99.74%

These distributions hold no matter how squat the bell-shaped curve appears. Consider extremely wide distributions, for example those in small stocks. When the 37.3 percent is multiplied by 3 to include 3 standard deviations, the result includes the farthest observation to the right of the mean because the total would be approximately 124 to the right of the 0 point. (This is 111.9 plus the 12.1 mean.) In comparison, for the common stock alternative, 3 times 22 plus the mean of 9.1 equals 75.1 to the right of the 0 point. The vast majority of observations are included within three standard deviations of the mean. Thus, while the observations may not conclusively indicate a precise normal curve shape, its rules with regard to the standard deviations and the percentages of occurrences they embrace may be extremely valuable for many distributions.

Combining Probabilities with Useful Risk Judgments

Credit analysts frequently are interested in only one of the tails of the probability distribution curve: *the likelihood of failure*. Naturally, this increases the degree of confidence that may be obtained, given a certain number of standard deviations from the mean.

For example, managers might be interested in determining within certain confidence limits the chance that the funds flow will fall below a certain level. (The term *confidence limits* is interchangeable with the percentages encompassed by the various standard deviations.) Perhaps the need to comply with the repayment commitments of a new loan requires the firm to have this minimum funds flow from operations. Assuming that the lender is concerned only with answers in one tail (the down side), and because the entire upper side distribution above the mean (where the firm far exceeds the minimum) is of no worry, each standard deviation level provides greater confidence than indicated above.

Exhibit 9.3 shows the percentages remaining in a single tail, given various numbers of standard deviations from the mean. For a single standard deviation, all of the possible events have been incorporated, shy of only 15.77 percent of the total possibilities. Thus, after determining the value of a standard deviation of a series of observations as well as the average of those observations, an analyst could conclude that with confidence limits of 84.23 percent (1-15.77 percent), any new observation will be above an amount equal to the mean less the value of that single standard deviation. For those who are extremely risk averse (or stuck with low loan pricing), two standard deviations would include 97.72 percent (1-2.28 percent) of all the possibilities, and so on.

Single Tail Probabilities

Exhibit 9.3

NORMAL PROBABILITY DISTRIBUTION TABLE

Number of Standard Deviations from the Mean	Chance of a result less than those included (One Tail)	Number of Standard Deviations from the Mean	Chance of a result less than those included (One Tail)	Number of Standard Deviations from the Mean	Chance of a result less than those included (One Tail)
0.10	46.02%	1.10	13.57%	2.10	1.79%
0.20	42.07%	1.20	11.51%	2.20	1.39%
0.30	38.21%	1.30	9.68%	2.30	1.07%
0.40	34.46%	1.40	8.08%	2.40	0.82%
0.50	30.85%	1.50	6.68%	2.50	0.62%
0.60	27.43%	1.60	5.48%	2.60	0.47%
0.70	24.21%	1.70	4.46%	2.70	0.35%
0.80	21.19%	1.80	3.59%	2.80	0.26%
0.90	18.41%	1.90	2.87%	2.90	0.19%
1.00	15.77%	2.00	2.28%	3.00	0.13%

To apply this conclusion to the above example, assume that the analyst possesses a series of observations (at least as long as a business cycle) of the industry's cash flows and has determined their standard deviation. The analyst can express within specific confidence limits (probability) that future various funds flow outcomes will exceed a hypothetical danger point when funds flow is inadequate for repaying debt or for paying fixed charges.

With the danger point known, its relationship to the value of a single standard deviation can be used to calculate the number of standard deviations below the mean. Then the confidence interval can be determined. Conversely, if a certain confidence interval is desired, based upon the lender's aversion to risk, the calculation can be reversed. For example, an 84.23 percent confidence limit would include all flows above the mean less one standard deviation.

Recalling Exhibit 9.2 and the many hundreds of observations that were available to the researchers preparing those calculations, the analyst may be concerned about applying the observations to a specific series of data for which there may be very few discrete observations. This can be a serious problem, and in sets containing fewer than 20 observations, the so-called *population* standard deviation calculation should not be used. Instead, use the *sample* standard deviation, which corrects for there being so few observations that they might not be sufficiently descriptive of the overall normal curve and of the standard deviations.

To calculate the sample standard deviation, take the standard deviation and multiply it times the square root of the quotient of the total number of entries divided by the sum of the total number of entries minus one. This enlarges the standard deviation to account for smaller samples.

Another tool, sometimes called the *student's "T" distribution* after William S. Gosset, another mathematician, is available for calculating the sample standard deviation. Exhibit 9.4 is a table somewhat comparable to Exhibit 9.3, except that it contains the additional variable of the number of observations. To learn how to use this table, assume that the lender wishes to achieve 90 percent assurance that cash flow will cover fixed charges, but there are only 10 previous observations. Now, move down the "10 observations" column to the row where 9.75 percent appears (row 14). Compare this to the "No. of Standard..." column where 1.4 standard deviations is indicated. The answer is that the funds flow would remain above 1.4 standard deviations below the mean 90 percent of the time. Thus, if the example had a mean cash flow of $20,000 and a standard deviation of $5,000, 90 percent of the time cash flow will remain above $20,000 - 1.4 x $5,000 = $13,000. If this is sufficient, there is a 90 percent assurance of repayment.

Alternatively, if the analyst divides the fixed charges ($9,000) by the standard deviation ($5,000) and derives a multiple of 1.8 times, then it is apparent that the fixed charges will be met 95 percent of the time. (Go down the "No. of Standard . . . " column to the row with 1.8, then over to the "10 observations" column to find 5.14 percent, the chance of failure; confidence of success is therefore 94.86 percent.)

Iota Coefficient

This section develops the *Iota coefficient* as a methodology for increasing the analyst's understanding of the reliability of any firm's forecast of funds flow from operations. It discusses the concept of identifying the variability of funds flow from operations from year to year for specific industries. By evaluating these variations, an analyst may apply the various industry risks identified in the first section of this chapter in a quantitative way to any given firm's forecast of funds flow.

Need for Historical Data

Statistical data that may be serviceable as industry data over time have already been identified in this book. Chapter 6 discussed comparing intercompany firms with the Robert Morris Associate's statistics. Taking the variations of funds flow items over a period long enough to include a full business cycle within that industry, it is possible to derive the standard deviation of these funds flow variables. Further, it is a simple matter to generate for each industry a coefficient of variation that, given a specified confidence interval, would make it possible to calculate the probability of a shortfall from the funds flow forecast produced by the analyst using the forecasting techniques in chapters 7 and 8.

Student's "T" Distribution

Exhibit 9.4

Given a small sample, the following table predicts the chance that a result less than those included may occur. (One Tail).

No. of Standard Deviations from the Mean	*The number of observations*					
	2	*3*	*4*	*5*	*6*	*7*
	Probability of an outcome less than those identified (One Tail)					
0.1		46.43%	46.00%	45.97%	45.94%	45.93%
0.2	43.74%	43.03%	43.30%	43.13%	43.01%	42.94%
0.3	40.75%	39.63%	40.61%	40.28%	40.08%	39.95%
0.4	37.97%	36.62%	37.91%	37.44%	37.15%	36.95%
0.5	35.00%	33.57%	35.22%	34.60%	34.22%	33.96%
0.6	32.93%	30.52%	32.52%	31.76%	31.29%	30.97%
0.7	30.62%	28.13%	29.82%	28.92%	28.36%	27.98%
0.8	28.66%	25.88%	27.13%	26.08%	25.43%	24.99%
0.9	26.83%	23.63%	24.43%	23.24%	22.50%	22.00%
1.0	25.00%	21.37%	20.89%	20.40%	19.57%	19.01%
1.1	23.67%	19.53%	18.86%	18.20%	17.53%	17.06%
1.2	22.34%	18.32%	17.31%	16.31%	15.53%	14.99%
1.3	21.01%	17.10%	15.76%	14.41%	13.52%	12.91%
1.4	19.80%	15.89%	14.20%	12.52%	11.52%	10.83%
1.5	18.94%	14.68%	12.65%	10.63%	9.52%	8.75%
1.6	18.09%	13.47%	11.48%	9.50%	8.85%	8.41%
1.7	17.24%	12.25%	10.50%	8.75%	7.92%	7.42%
1.8	16.39%	11.04%	8.77%	6.50%	5.64%	5.48%
1.9	15.54%	9.83%	7.70%	5.57%	5.34%	5.14%
2.0	14.83%	9.44%	7.39%	5.33%	5.04%	4.81%
2.1	14.39%	8.96%	7.02%	5.08%	4.75%	4.48%
2.2	13.94%	8.47%	6.65%	4.83%	4.45%	4.14%
2.3	13.49%	7.98%	6.78%	4.58%	4.16%	3.81%
2.4	13.04%	7.49%	6.30%	4.34%	3.86%	3.48%
2.5	12.59%	7.00%	5.81%	4.09%	3.56%	3.14%
2.6	12.14%	6.51%	5.33%	3.84%	3.27%	2.81%
2.7	11.70%	6.03%	4.84%	3.59%	2.97%	2.48%
2.8	11.25%	5.54%	4.36%	3.35%	2.67%	2.14%
2.9	10.80%	5.05%	3.87%	3.10%	2.38%	1.81%
3.0	10.35%	4.56%	3.38%	2.85%	2.08%	1.58%

This coefficeint of variation could reasonably describe the possible outcomes of a subject firm's funds flow, anticipating that industries having a reputation for being relatively risky would, indeed, have a relatively higher coefficient of variation than industries that have a reputation for being stable. As you examine the industries discussed in this section, recognize that further research clearly needs to be undertaken to assess whether calculations made using older historical data are indeed capable of being verified using current outcomes.

Determining the Iota Coefficient

This section uses Robert Morris data as industry input to determine the Iota coefficient for two industries. There is a problem identifying the funds-flow numbers within the data sheet and finding a comparable alternative in the firm under study. For example, with the individual firm, the taxes paid by a firm are an expense that is deducted before the gross cash flow is calculated. Of course the change in the deferred tax account is added back into the generation of the gross cash flow, so that only the actual taxes paid are taken

The number of observations					
8	9	10	11	12	13
Probability of an outcome less than those identified (One Tail)					
45.91%	45.92%	45.90%	45.90%	45.90%	45.90%
42.88%	42.85%	42.81%	42.79%	42.78%	42.78%
39.84%	39.79%	39.72%	39.68%	39.65%	39.63%
36.81%	36.72%	36.63%	36.57%	36.52%	36.47%
33.78%	33.65%	33.54%	33.45%	33.39%	33.29%
30.74%	30.58%	30.45%	30.34%	30.27%	30.21%
27.71%	27.52%	27.36%	27.23%	27.14%	27.05%
24.68%	24.45%	24.27%	24.12%	24.01%	23.91%
21.64%	21.38%	21.18%	21.01%	20.88%	19.72%
18.61%	18.31%	18.09%	17.89%	17.75%	17.14%
16.71%	16.45%	15.69%	14.92%	14.62%	14.56%
14.58%	14.28%	14.05%	13.82%	13.74%	13.33%
12.45%	12.11%	11.81%	11.48%	11.15%	10.66%
10.32%	9.93%	9.75%	9.68%	9.58%	9.48%
8.19%	7.76%	7.46%	7.26%	2.58%	8.31%
8.07%	7.81%	7.59%	7.41%	7.26%	7.14%
7.03%	6.73%	6.48%	6.27%	6.11%	5.96%
5.34%	5.23%	5.14%	5.05%	4.95%	4.79%
4.98%	4.85%	4.74%	4.50%	4.35%	4.26%
4.62%	4.46%	4.03%	3.88%	3.74%	3.63%
4.26%	4.07%	3.88%	3.50%	3.12%	3.00%
3.89%	3.69%	2.86%	2.68%	2.51%	2.37%
3.53%	2.98%	2.28%	2.25%	2.21%	2.14%
3.17%	2.69%	2.22%	2.07%	1.92%	1.84%
2.81%	2.41%	2.02%	1.83%	1.63%	1.54%
2.44%	2.13%	1.82%	1.58%	1.34%	1.24%
2.08%	1.85%	1.61%	1.33%	1.05%	0.97%
1.72%	1.56%	1.36%	1.15%	0.89%	0.84%
1.55%	1.28%	1.13%	0.99%	0.77%	0.71%
1.39%	1.20%	1.01%	0.82%	0.64%	0.57%

into account. This level of detail is unfortunately unavailable in the Robert Morris statistics since the income statistics end before taxes are considered. Consequently, to generate the funds-flow calculations, the only option is to ignore taxes. This largely resolves the problem of the provision-for-taxes numbers on the income statement being unrelated to the actual taxes paid.

Thus, follow these steps to begin a compilation that is as close as possible to the funds flow concept:

1. Choose the percentage of sales value next to the "Operating Profits" caption on the Robert Morris sheet. This gives the first major component, free from nonrecurring items and the tax problems just mentioned.

2. Now, add to that the percentage of sales value for depreciation, depletion, and amortization to achieve a relatively close approximation to the funds flow concept keynoted above as the principal identifier of debt-repayment capacity.

3. Complete the other columns and formula calculations in Exhibit 9.5. A bottom section has been added to simplify another step of calculating the funds flow given different confidence intervals.

Industry Risk Analysis and Funds Flow Forecasting

Exhibit 9.5

INDUSTRY RISK ANALYSIS AND FUNDS FLOW FORECASTING

INDUSTRY: SIC #:

SUBJECT FIRM:

STEP ONE: DETERMINE THE SAMPLE COEFFICIENT OF VARIATION OF THE INDUSTRY

COLUMN:

1	2	3	4	5	6
				Calculation of Standard Deviation	
Year	Operating Profit as a % of Sales	Depreciation & Other as a % of Sales	Funds Flow as % of Sales (1+2)	Average of Column 4	Deviation (Column 4 - Column 5)
19					
19					
19					
19					
19					
19					
19					
19					
19					
19					
		TOTAL			VARIANCE

FORMULAS:
(1) Expected Value (Ave): Total Col 4 / # Entries In Col 4
(2) Standard Deviation: Square Root Of Weighted Ave Variance
(3) Sample Standard Deviation (Corrects For Small Samples)
Multiply the standard deviation times the square root of the quotient of the total # of entries divided by the sum of the total entries - 1.
(4) Coefficient of Variation: Sample Standard Deviation / Ave
(This is the percentage variability for each standard deviation from the mean, THE IOTA FACTOR)
NOTE: You may wish to weight some of the cash flows more heavily than others.

STEP TWO: CALCULATE THE FIRM'S ESTIMATED FUNDS FLOW AND REEVALUATE BASED ON INDUSTRY COEFFICIENT OF VARIATION

Column:

1	2	3	4	5
			Subject Firm's Probable Funds Flow Range	
Subject Firm's Estimated Funds Flow	Coefficient of Variation Multiplier	Confidence Interval (Approx.)	High Column 1 + Column 2*1	Low Column 1 - Column 2*1
	0.67	75.0%		
	0.84	80.0%		
	1.04	85.0%		
	1.14	87.5%		
	1.28	90.0%		
	1.44	92.5%		
	1.64	95.0%		
	1.92	97.5%		

An example of the above is shown in Exhibit 9.6, in which the funds-flow variations in the women's dress industry (Standard Industrial Code No. 2335) over a full business cycle, 1978 to 1987, are presented as enumerated above. This particular industry is well known to be relatively high in risk. Therefore, a relatively high coefficient of variation is expected.

Exhibit 9.6

Analysis of Funds Flow Variations in the Women's Dress Manufacturing Industry

COLUMN: 1	2	3	4	5	6	7
				Calculation of Standard Deviation		
Year	Operating Profit as a % of Sales	Depreciation & Other as a % of Sales	Funds Flow as % of Sales (1 + 2)	Average of Column 4 - Column 5)	Deviation (Column 4 Squared)	Variance (Column 6
1978	3.6	0.6	4.2	5.18	-0.98	0.9604
1979	3.7	0.5	4.2	5.18	-0.98	0.9604
1980	4.8	0.8	5.6	5.18	0.42	0.1764
1981	3.9	0.6	4.5	5.18	-0.68	0.4624
1982	5.9	0.6	6.5	5.18	1.32	1.7424
1983	5.3	0.8	6.1	5.18	0.92	0.8464
1984	7.2	0.7	7.9	5.18	2.72	7.3984
1985	3.5	0.8	4.3	5.18	-0.88	0.7744
1986	3	0.6	3.6	5.18	-1.58	2.4964
1987	4.2	0.7	4.9	5.18	-0.28	0.0784
		TOTAL	51.8		Variance	1.5896

FORMULAS:
(1) Expected Value (Average): Total Col. 4 / Number Entries In Col. 45.1800
(2) Standard Deviation: Square Root Of Weighted Ave. Variance (Col. 7) 1.2608
(3) Sample Standard Deviation (Corrects For Small Samples)
Multiply the standard deviation times the square root of the quotient of the total number of entries divided by the sum of the total entries minus one. 1.3290
(4) Coefficient of Variation: IOTA factor 0.2566
Sample Standard Deviation / Expected Value

Funds Flow to Current Portion Long-term Debt	**3.6**
Debt to Worth	**1.3**

Continue to calculate as follows:

1. Calculate the expected value or average of all of the funds-flow yearly observations. This equals 5.18 percent, shown in column 5.
2. Next, subtract this expected value from each funds-flow observation to find the individual differences. To do this, subtract column 5 from column 4 and place the results in column 6.
3. Determine the variance, first, by squaring the differences found in column 6, and, second, by weighting them according to their likelihood of occurrence. In this case, each variance is assumed to be equally likely, so all the variances are merely averaged to equal the variance of 1.59 at the bottom of column 7.
4. Next, calculate the standard deviation by taking the square root of the variance to equal 1.26.
5. Now calculate the sample standard deviation, correcting for small samples by multiplying the standard deviation times the square root of the total number of entries divided by the sum of the total entries minus one, which results in 1.329.

6. Finally, calculate the coefficient of variation of the sample standard deviation by dividing the sample standard deviation by the mean, which results in 25.66 percent. Now, considering that only the lower tail is a problem, divide the result by 2, which results in 10.45 percent.
7. As an aside, if there have been unusual years, unrelated to the business cycle, it might be advisable to give some of the funds flows more weight than others.

Applying the women's dress manufacturing industry's very high Iota coefficient of 25.66 percent will sharply reduce the high confidence interval of the availability of funds flow. Assume that the analyst is reviewing the funds flow forecast of a particular women's dress manufacturer and that the manufacturer's forecast had already been evaluated from the point of view of the reliability of its own data. Now there needs to be agreement on a confidence interval that takes into account the various aspects of the riskiness of the industry and their possible impact on the forecast funds flows, especially on the downside.

Consider, for the sake of the example, that, in view of the firm's depth of management and position in the market, only one standard deviation would be necessary in validating the funds flow forecast. This means that the analyst could be approximately 81.91 percent sure of incorporating the possible variations of one tail with a sample of 10 observations. (See Exhibit 9.4 and the intersection of the "1.0" row in the "No. of Standard Deviations . . . " column with the "10 observations" column.) Thus, only 87.17 percent of the forecast funds flow might be present in any one year for debt repayment. (This figure is 100 percent less one-half the 25.66 percent found above.) The next step is for the analyst to test this result against the firm's fixed charges at the present time. If the forecast funds flow reduced by 12.83 percent is still sufficient to cover the fixed charges, then the dress manufacturer is capable of handling more debt.

Assuming that the lender wishes to be more confident of having anticipated all the possible events, then a higher confidence limit must be chosen. By picking three standard deviations (refer to Exhibit 9.4), the analyst could be 99 percent certain (with 10 observations) that all possibilities have been met. By multiplying 3 times 12.83 percent, the analyst finds that the dress manufacturer's debt-repayment requirement must be held to less than 61.51 percent of the analyst's forecast of funds flow (100 percent less 38.49 percent) if the lender wishes to be 99 percent sure of repayment.

Another element to be remembered here is that the type of financing naturally will affect the debt-repayment requirements. For example, a firm that is arranging a 30-year mortgage will be able to satisfy the fixed-charge coverage ratio with much less funds flow. Contrast this with a firm agreeing to repay all its term debt on a 2-year basis.

Exhibit 9.7

Analysis of Funds Flow Variations in the Long-distance Trucking Industry

COLUMN: 1	2	3	4	5	6	7
				Calculation of Standard Deviation		
Year	Operating Profit as a % of Sales	Depreciation & Other as a % of Sales	Funds Flow as % of Sales (1 + 2)	Average of Column 4	Deviation (Column 4 - Column 5)	Variance (Column 6 Squared)
1978	5.5	4	9.5	9.65	-0.15	0.0225
1979	5.9	4.5	10.4	9.65	0.75	0.5625
1980	5.3	4.7	10	9.65	0.35	0.1225
1981	4.8	4.8	9.6	9.65	-0.05	0.0025
1982	5.6	4.6	10.2	9.65	0.55	0.3025
1983	3.5	4.6	8.1	9.65	-1.55	2.4025
1984	4.2	4.8	9	9.65	-0.65	0.4225
1985	5.2	4.7	9.9	9.65	0.25	0.0625
1986	4.7	5	9.7	9.65	0.05	0.0025
1987	4.9	5.2	10.1	9.65	0.45	0.2025
		TOTAL	96.5		Variance	4.105

FORMULAS:

(1) Expected Value (Average): Total Col. 4 / Number Entries In Col. 4	9.6500
(2) Standard Deviation: Square Root Of Weighted Ave. Variance (Col. 7)	0.6407
(3) Sample Standard Deviation (Corrects For Small Samples) Multiply the standard deviation times the square root of the quotient of the total number of entries divided by the sum of the total entries minus one.	0.6754
(4) Coefficient of Variation: IOTA factor Sample Standard Deviation / Expected Value	**0.0700**
Funds Flow to Current Portion Long-term Debt	**1.6**
Debt to Worth	**2.2**

Contrast the analysis of the dress manufacturers with the analysis of the funds flow variations in the long-distance trucking industry, as shown in Exhibit 9.7. Here, the result of the coefficient of variation is only 7 percent. (Recall that this time period even includes the deregulation of the long-distance trucking industry.) Here, being 99 percent sure would eliminate only 10.5 percent of the firm's own previously estimated funds flow from availability for debt repayment.

Preliminary Validation of the Iota Coefficient

A possible area of research is to compare the Iota coefficient with existing popular ratios. In such a comparison, the underlying assumption is the efficient-market hypothesis. That is, if the industry has been supplied with the correct amount of credit, given its level of risk, it should be possible to find that the debt-to-worth ratio is lower in the women's dress manufacturing industry than it is in the long-distance trucking industry, where the variability is less. Exhibit 9.8 shows that this hypothesis is true. The average of 1981 through 1987 ratios of earnings coverage of interest expense and funds flow to current portion of long-term debt are both significantly higher in the dress manufacturing business than in the long-distance trucking industry. Obviously, the debt-to-worth ratio is much lower in the women's dress manufacturing industry.

Exhibit 9.8

Comparison of Iota Coefficient with Popular Ratios

SIC No.	Coefficient of Variance	EBIT* to Interest	Funds Flow to CPLTD*	Debt to Worth
2335	25.66%	3.52	3.6	1.3
4213	7.00%	2.24	0.6	2.2

* EBIT = Earnings before interest and taxes

* CPLTD = Current portion of long-term debt

Clearly, lenders have identified the risk inherent in the two different industries. It is relatively easy to see that the funds flow provided principally by depreciation not only builds the total funds flow of the trucking industry, but also helps maintain its even values so that the variability of funds flow is significantly less than that of operating profit by itself.

Conclusion

Whether the Iota coefficient will be countenanced by additional research is still an issue. Nevertheless, it has become increasingly important that analysts be able to quantify their risks, and there are few alternatives to the Iota coefficient available at this time. Even if it achieves a prominent place in analytical guides of the future, the Iota coefficient should be only the first in many statistical applications to assist the financial analyst. It may stimulate others to attempt to quantify risks and show that industry statistical information can satisfy this need.

SUMMARY OF IMPORTANT CONCEPTS

Determine which of the advanced analytical techniques presented in this chapter—working investment analysis, sensitivity analysis, sustainable growth, probability analysis—are appropriate in a given situation. These techniques are usually applied along with the basic techniques presented in the previous chapters—income statement analysis, balance sheet examination, cash flow analysis, use of ratios, long-term forecasting, and cash budgets—to form a complete analytical picture.

Working investment analysis provides the credit analyst with a quick way of roughly calculating the financial consequences of growth in a company's working assets (accounts receivable and inventory). This enables the lender to easily assess the level of financing required based on various sales projections.

Sustainable growth measures a company's ability to grow within the constraints of given debt-to-worth and other relationships. It assumes that increased sales require increased fixed assets, which is not true for all companies. However, it does show the effect of growth on a company's financial leverage—which is usually a primary constraint on growth.

Sensitivity analysis allows the lender to test the validity of projections, such as those used in creating pro forma financial statements, by analyzing a range of scenarios. It allows the lender to focus on a company's primary areas of vulnerability to see how changed assumptions would affect the company's financial performance.

Probability analysis applied to forecasting can enable simple optimistic-pessimistic scenario analysis to actually specify a range of likely cash flows given a degree of confidence. Applied on an industry basis, it can replace simple industry benchmarks with analysis covering business cycles and their consequences on various industries.

The credit analyst's proficiency in using these more-advanced techniques will increase only with experience. The various formulas and calculations presented in this chapter should not be regarded as useful only in unusual circumstances. Rather, they should be used routinely to further the scope of financial statement analysis.

This text provides a solid foundation in the various steps of financial statement analysis that must underlie any lending decision. The credit analyst should not, however, expect to become proficient in financial statement analysis on the basis of the materials presented in this text alone. Rather, the basic skills learned here must be honed through diligent application, further study, and practical experience. In addition, many other skills that are crucial in commercial lending, such as structuring and negotiating loans, must also be acquired. Only with this breadth of knowledge and experience can the credit analyst expect to make sound lending decisions that will benefit both the bank and those companies seeking financing.

EXERCISES

Important Terms to Define

working investment analysis
sensitivity analysis
standard deviation
normal distribution
risk-reward calculation
sustainable growth analysis
probability distribution
coefficient of variation
Iota coefficient
expected return

Dependable Doors Case Study

1. Calculate working investment for 1991 and for 1992 (projected).
2. Calculate Dependable Doors' working investment need based upon 1991's figures and comment upon any differences in management's 1992 projected need.
3. Do a most-likely and a pessimistic case sensitivity analysis on Dependable Doors to determine how much financing will be required and compare your conclusion to management's projected financing need. Use the following variables to do your analysis:

Item	Management's projection		Most Likely	Pessimistic
Sales	50% =	30,000	25%	5%
COGS	73% =	21,900	76%	78%
Acct. Rec.	51 DOH* =	4,200	60 DOH	75 DOH
Inventory	81 DOH =	5,639	85 DOH	95 DOH
Acct. Pay	28 DOH =	1,958	25 DOH	20 DOH
Accruals		782	700	500
Working Inv.		7,099		
Net Profit Margin	3% =	1,080	2.5%	2.0%
Financing Required		6,019		

*Days on Hand

The answers to these Dependable Doors questions appear in the appendix.

Engraph Case Study

1. Calculate working investment at Engraph in 1990 and 1991.
2. Why do you think working investment declined from 1990 to 1991?

ANSWERS TO QUESTIONS ABOUT THE DEPENDABLE DOORS CASE STUDY

Chapter 2 The Industry Environment

1. What type of operating cycle does Dependable Doors have?

Dependable Doors starts with cash, trade credit, or bank financing to purchase raw materials. The raw materials probably would be aluminum, wood, cements, plastics, glues, paints, and so on. In the manufacturing cycle, these raw materials are converted into finished goods inventory (doors), which are then sold on account to building suppliers and commercial contractors. The company collects these accounts receivable and pays off any outstanding debt. The cycle then begins anew.

2. Do you think Dependable Doors has a typical distribution of assets and liabilities? Please explain.

Yes. In 1991 the company had the following distribution: 47 percent fixed assets and 23 percent inventory. That distribution is fairly typical of a manufacturer. Dependable Doors is also fairly highly leveraged (1.97 percent), which is also typical of a manufacturer. The fixed asset and leverage position of the company has changed over the last few years due to the acquisition of the new St. Louis plant.

3. What type of financing needs might you expect with a company like Dependable Doors?

Because Dependable Doors is a manufacturer, the company would probably need short-term borrowing to finance inventory and receivables during the operating cycle. This would probably be financed with a line of credit. In addition, a company like Dependable Doors can have long-term financing needs for equipment purchases or for plant improvements.

4. As a lender, what other types of industry risks might concern you?

Manufacturers of doors are very dependent on housing starts. It is most likely a very cyclical industry, doing well during economic upturns and the reverse during recessions. It also seems to be a competitive industry: over 250 companies manufacture patio doors. However, Dependable Doors' size should help offset some of this risk.

5. What kind of operating cash flow cycle might you expect to see with Dependable Doors and how might this differ from its accounting for income?

Given that the company is a manufacturer, a typical cycle would be for it to start with cash, trade credit, or bank financing to buy raw materials. With Dependable Doors these raw materials might be various metals, wood, cements, glues, plastics and paints. By means of the manufacturing process, these raw materials would be converted into inventory, which would be sold to customers to create accounts receivable. When these accounts receivable are collected, cash is generated and loan or trade creditors are paid off. Therefore, at various points during its operating cash flow cycle, Dependable Doors could be inventory or accounts receivable rich and have a cash shortage.

Under the accrual method of accounting for income, this cash shortage would not be reflected. In fact, the company could be showing a net accrual profit and be short of cash.

Chapter 3 The Balance Sheet

1. Looking at the balance sheet, evaluate the management philosophy of Dependable Doors (hint—make sure you consider working investment).

Working Investment has increased from 1990 to 1991. It is calculated as follows:

Step 1 - Calculate Trading Assets.

Trading Assets	*1991*	*1990*	*1989*
Accounts Receivable	4,161	3,662	3,422
Inventory	4,118	4,095	2,661
Trading Assets	8,279	7,757	6,083

Step 2 - Calculate Spontaneous Finance.

Spontaneous Finance	*1991*	*1990*	*1989*
Accounts Payable	1,434	1,530	558
Accruals	589	519	558
Spontaneous Finance	2,023	2,049	1,116

Step 3 - Calculate Working Investment.

Working Investment	*1991*	*1990*	*1989*
Trading Asset	8,279	7,757	6,103
Spontaneous Finance	2,023	2,049	1,116
Working Investment	6,256	5,708	4,978

Working investment has been increasing from 1989 to 1991, which means that management used more long-term debt or equity to fund the current assets in the trading cycle and relied less on spontaneous finance. It also means that the company is becoming less liquid.

A review of the equity section shows that in 1991, as both common stock and paid-in-surplus increased, management issued more common stock. The decline in retained earnings was due to a loss in 1990 and a prior-period adjustment, probably due to the stock issuance.

Leverage has increased from 0.78 in 1989 to 1.97 in 1991. The company is relying more on debt and less on internally generated funds.

2. From a collateral point of view, how marketable are the assets of Dependable Doors?

Cash is probably very marketable. However, an analyst should check to see if any of it is pledged in the form of compensating balances. In addition, Dependable Doors has a large Canadian customer. If Dependable Doors is paid in Canadian dollars, some of the payment could be subject to devaluation. An analyst would have to ask management for details of the company's terms with the Canadian customer.

An analyst would really need to get an aging of accounts receivable to determine how comfortable to feel about the current receivables. In addition, a lot of Dependable Doors' receivables are to contractor's, which would probably cause most banker's some concern.

3. Spread and common-size the balance sheet.

Dependable Doors Balance Sheet

Company Name: Dependable Doors
Balance Sheet Date:
Rounded to: millions (000,000's)

	31-Dec-89		31-Dec-90		31-Dec-91	
ASSETS	**$**	**%**	**$**	**%**	**$**	**%**
1 Cash	109.0	1.1%	409.0	2.3%	548.0	3.0%
2 Marketable Securities		0.0%		0.0%		0.0%
3 Accounts Receivable—Trade	3,422.0	34.0%	3,662.0	21.0%	4,161.0	23.1%
4 Inventories: Raw Materials		0.0%		0.0%		0.0%
5 Inventories: Work in Process		0.0%		0.0%		0.0%
6 Inventories: Finished Goods	2,661.0	26.4%	4,095.0	23.4%	4,118.0	22.9%
7 Subtotal Inventories	2,661.0	26.4%	4,095.0	23.4%	4,118.0	22.9%
8 Prepaid Expenses		0.0%		0.0%		0.0%
9 Other Current		0.0%	297.0	1.7%	426.0	2.4%
10 Total Current Assets	6,192.0	61.5%	8,463.0	48.4%	9,253.0	51.4%
11 Property, Plant & Equipment	3,503.0	34.8%	8,285.0	47.4%	8,294.0	46.1%
12 "Capital" Leased Equipment		0.0%		0.0%		0.0%
13 "Operating" Leased Equipment		0.0%		0.0%		0.0%
14 (Less Depreciation)		0.0%		0.0%		0.0%
15 Subtotal Net Prop, Plant & Equip.	3,503.0	34.8%	8,285.0	47.4%	8,294.0	46.1%
16 Investments and Advances		0.0%		0.0%		0.0%
17 Long Term Marketable Securities		0.0%		0.0%		0.0%
18 Affiliate & Sundry Receivables		0.0%		0.0%		0.0%
19 Net Assets/Discontinued Operations		0.0%		0.0%		0.0%
20 Other Noncurrent Assets	378.0	3.8%	725.0	4.1%	442.0	2.5%
21 Intangibles (Patents & Rights)		0.0%		0.0%		0.0%
22 Goodwill (Resulting from Mergers)		0.0%		0.0%		0.0%
23 Total Fixed Assets	3,881.0	38.5%	9,010.0	51.6%	8,736.0	48.6%
24 TOTAL ASSETS	10,073.0	100.0%	17,473.0	100.0%	17,989.0	100.0%
LIABILITIES						
25 Notes Payable	400.0	4.0%	1,800.0	10.2%	2,500.0	13.9%
26 Accounts Payable —Trade	558.0	5.5%	1,530.0	8.8%	1,434.0	8.0%
27 Taxes and Accrued Expenses	847.0	8.4%	519.0	3.0%	589.0	3.3%
28 Other Current		0.0%		0.0%		0.0%
29 Current Portion L-T Debt (Operating)	86.0	0.9%	134.0	0.8%	147.0	0.8%
30 Total Current Operating Liabs.	1,891.0	18.8%	3,983.0	22.8%	4,670.0	26.0%
31 Current Portion L-T Debt (Remaining)		0.0%		0.0%		0.0%
32 Deferred or Unearned Income		0.0%		0.0%		0.0%
33 Long Term Debt— Unsecured		0.0%		0.0%		0.0%
34 Long Term Debt—Secured	2,355.0	23.4%	6,762.0	38.7%	6,615.0	36.8%
35 Capital Lease Obligations		0.0%		0.0%		0.0%
36 Present Value of Operating Leases		0.0%		0.0%		0.0%
37 Other Noncurrent Liabilities		0.0%		0.0%		0.0%
38 Total Senior Term Debt	2,355.0	23.4%	6,762.0	38.7%	6,615.0	36.8%
39 Subordinated Debt		0.0%		0.0%		0.0%
40 Unfunded Pension Obligations		0.0%		0.0%		0.0%
41 Deferred Taxes (Debt Portion)	364.0	3.6%	740.0	4.2%	963.0	5.4%
42 TOTAL LIABILITIES	4,610.0	45.8%	11,485.0	65.7%	12,248.0	68.1%
EQUITY						
43 Deferred Taxes (Equity Part)		0.0%		0.0%		0.0%
44 Minority Interest		0.0%		0.0%		0.0%
45 Preferred Stock		0.0%		0.0%		0.0%
46 Common Stock	2,724.0	27.0%	2,724.0	15.6%	3,369.0	18.7%
47 Retained Earnings	2,739.0	27.2%	3,264.0	18.7%	2,372.0	13.2%
48 (Treasure Stock & Other Reductions)		0.0%		0.0%		0.0%
49 Net Worth	5,463.0	54.2%	5,988.0	34.3%	5,741.0	31.9%
50 TOTAL FOOTINGS	10,073.0		17,473.0		17,989.0	

Accruals and current-year income taxes have been added together because current-year income taxes should also be considered an accrual.

Reserve-deferred income taxes have been spread on the debt portion of the balance sheet because depreciation exceeds capital expenditures, which is one sign that growth in the firm is slowing and the deferred taxes might actually start coming due.

Common stock and paid in surplus have been added together for easier analysis.

4. How does the balance sheet of Dependable Doors compare with RMA industry statistics?

Look at the 1990 statement studies under the 10M to 25M sales category to compare Dependable Doors and other companies for that year. It is immediately obvious how different Dependable Doors is in 1990 compared with the industry. Just look at Dependable Doors' total current assets of 48 percent compared to the industry average of 73.1 percent. This variance from the industry average was caused by the purchase of the St. Louis plant, which caused a large increase in the company's fixed assets (47 percent) compared with the industry average (18 percent).

However, looking at Dependable Doors prior to the purchase of the St. Louis plant shows that the company tracks much closer to the industry average, with the exception of its investment in fixed assets, which is still somewhat higher than the industry.

5. As a lender, how do you feel about the trends in Dependable Doors' balance sheet?

The fixed asset increase in 1990 caused by the purchase of the St. Louis plant shifted the balance sheet dramatically. Long-term debt increased to fund this expansion. Trading assets in the form of receivables and, particularly, inventory also increased in this year. The increase in inventory was due to the additional capacity at the St. Louis plant and the fact that the projected sales increase never materialized in 1991. In addition, what frequently happens after an acquisition is that a company is initially saddled with excess inventory that takes some time to work down. These increases in inventory were funded by the increases in notes payable and accounts payable. From a lender's perspective, the decline in the company's equity accounts would be of concern.

6. Do the notes to the financial statement provide any information that can be of assistance in an examination of the balance sheet?

Note 3 reveals that the changes due next year in the deferred tax account will not have a significant affect on the company.

Note 4 reveals that the inventory is valued at first in, first out. This means that the inventory figure on the balance sheet is probably close to current replacement cost.

Note 7 explains why the company had a tax refund in 1990. The company does not explain the tax refund in 1991. However, the income statement shows that the company had a loss in 1991.

Chapter 4 The Income Statement

1. Spread and common-size the income statement numbers.

Company Name: Dependable Doors Rounded to: (000's)				
	Year Ending 31-Dec-90		Year Ending 31-Dec-91	
INCOME STATEMENT	$	%	$	%
1 Net Sales (Revenues)	$20,540.0	100%	$20,055.0	100%
2 Cost of Goods Sold (Less Dep)	$15,194.0	74.0%	$15,703.0	78.3%
3 Depreciation Expense		0.0%		0.0%
4 Gross Profit	$5,346.0	26.0%	$4,352.0	21.7%
5 Selling Expense	$1,529.0	7.4%	$1,443.0	7.2%
6 General & Admin. Expense	$2,410.0	11.7%	$2,485.0	12.4%
7 Officers' Compensation		0.0%		0.0%
8 Other Operating Expenses		0.0%		0.0%
9 Operating Income	$1,407.0	6.9%	$424.0	2.1%
10 Other Non-Operating Income		0.0%		0.0%
11 (Interest Expense)	($635.0)	-3.1%	($833.0)	-4.2%
12 Interest Income		0.0%		0.0%
13 (Other Non-Operating Expense)		0.0%		0.0%
14 (Plant Closings & Writedowns)		0.0%		0.0%
15 Earnings on Equity Investments		0.0%		0.0%
16 Profit Before Tax	$772.0	3.8%	($409.0)	-2.0%
17 Income Tax	$103.0	0.5%	($234.0)	-1.2%
18 Income Fr Continuing Operations	$669.0	3.3%	($175.0)	-0.9%
19 Net Profit fr Discont Operations		0.0%		0.0%
20 Gain (Loss) on Sale of Operations		0.0%		0.0%
21 Income (Loss) Before Extraordin.	$669.0	3.3%	($175.0)	-0.9%
22 Extraordinary Income (Loss)		0.0%		0.0%
23 Net Profit	$669.0	3.3%	($175.0)	-0.9%

2. Do a three-year trend analysis on the income statement.

Sales growth from 1989 to 1990 increased about 5 percent, but from 1990 to 1991 it decreased about 2.3 percent. The reason for this drop was an overall sluggish economy. The gross margin has decreased almost 5 percent over the last three years. This decline was caused by the company's inability to pass on skyrocketing costs, its need to hold down prices in order to maintain its market share, and increased overhead costs associated with its increased capacity.

In 1990 this decrease in the gross margin, combined with increases in both selling and general and administrative expenses, caused the operating profit to decline 31 percent. The purchase of the new St. Louis facility and the resulting increases in inventory and receivables caused increased borrowing and, consequently, increased interest expense. This translated directly to the bottom line, and net profit dropped 34 percent.

Selling expenses declined in 1991 as the company attempted to get a better handle on its costs. Despite this slight drop, the operating profit (also known as the cushion) was only 2 percent of sales. Remember that out of this cushion the company has to pay taxes and interest and, it is hoped, have enough left over to finance capital expenditures and pay dividends. The $1,000,000 decline in gross profit, combined with a $200,000 increase in interest expenses, resulted in a pretax loss of $409,000 in the fiscal year 1991. The impact of the loss was softened by tax benefits that resulted in a $175,000 after-tax loss.

3. Does the company have sufficient profitability to service its debt?

Remember that the interest expense has already been taken out of the net profit figure. Because of this, the company was able to service interest in both years. In 1991 the company had a loss and was unable to service the current portion of long-term debt (CPLTD) of $134,000 (remember 1990 CPLTD is as of 31 December 1990 and will actually be paid in 1991). Net profit in 1990 of $669,000 was sufficient to service the principal of $86,000 (1989 CPLTD).

Profitability is important because it is through long-term profits (evidenced in cash) that companies are able to service term debt.

The traditional method of determining whether there is enough coverage of debt is to add net income to depreciation. To determine the depreciation figure, look at the statement of cash flows.

It is important to note at this point that net profit does not repay loans; cash repays loans. This point was examined in the chapter on cash flow analysis.

4. How does Dependable Doors compare to the industry with respect to its income statement?

Looking at RMA statistics in the 10M to 25M sales range shows that in 1990 Dependable Doors had a 4 percent profit before tax figure that was right on the industry average of 4 percent. Dependable Doors' total operating expenses of 19 percent were less than the industry average of 22.3 percent. However, its interest expense of 3 percent was significantly higher than the industry average of 0.3 percent. (All other expenses on the RMA form include interest expense.) Looking back to the balance sheet shows that the higher levels of inventory in 1990 were the primary reasons for the additional borrowing and, consequently, the higher interest expense.

5. **Do the notes to the financial statement provide any information that can be useful in an examination of the income statement?**

Note 3 explains the revenue recognition policy of the company.

Note 4 explains that the company uses FIFO to value inventory, which means that the company uses the oldest costs to determine cost of goods sold. This will cause the net profit figure to be higher than under LIFO. It will also result in the company's paying higher taxes.

Chapter 5 The Cash Flow Statement

1. **Using Dependable Doors' statement of cash flows, analyze the company's cash flows from operating activities for 1990 and 1991.**

In 1990 Dependable Doors' biggest source of cash was spontaneous financing in the form of accounts payable. The company was able to finance a lot of its inventory increase in this manner because the increase in inventory used the largest amount of cash. This inventory buildup was caused by the purchase of the new facility in St. Louis, which had excess inventory, and by the company's decision to build up inventory in anticipation of a sales turnaround. Net income was also a big source of cash. However, depreciation and the change in deferred taxes also provided the company with additional sources of cash. Both of these sources resulted from the purchase of fixed assets related to the new St. Louis facility.

In 1991, all of the accounts related to the trading cycle (receivables, inventory, and payables) were drains on cash, as was the net loss. These cash outflows were offset by cash inflows in the form of increases in depreciation and deferred taxes. This is a worrying trend because depreciation and deferred taxes will not continue to grow at this rate without additional expansion of fixed assets. The buildup in receivables was caused by the company's giving more favorable terms to buyers in order to maintain market share. The company cannot continue to sustain losses and remain viable as long-term debt is amortized by profits evidenced in cash.

2. **Does Dependable Doors have sufficient cash from operations in 1990 and 1991 to service its debt?**

In 1990 the company generated $468,000 in cash from operations, and the current portion of long-term debt (CPLTD) was $86,000 (remember that 1990's CPLTD repayment will be year-end 1989's CPLTD figure). In 1991 the company generated $230,000 in cash from operations, and the CPLTD was $134,000. Therefore, in both years the company was able to pay off its debt amortization with cash from operations. Payment of interest was already factored when net income was calculated.

3. Compare the traditional method of calculating cash flow with the statement of cash flows for both 1990 and 1991.

The traditional method of calculating cash flow is as follows:

	Traditional Method		Using Statement of Cash Flows
		1990	
Net Income	$669,000		
Depreciation	$750,000		
Total	$1,419,000		$468,000
		1991	
Net Income	($175,000)		
Depreciation	$859,000		
Total	$684,000		$230,000

It is quickly apparent that the traditional method of calculating cash flows can give a skewed picture of the actual amount of cash available to service debt. In fact, the difference for 1990 was almost $1,000,000. The reason for the difference is that the traditional method does not consider key balance sheet changes.

4. Analyze Dependable Doors' cash flow from investing activities.

In 1990, the biggest use of cash on the entire statement was in fixed-asset expansion caused by the purchase of the plant in St. Louis. There was also a cash drain caused by a change in noncurrent assets (frequently, these are sundry receivables).

In 1991, fixed assets continued to drain cash, in the amount of $868,000. A cash inflow was caused by the change in noncurrent assets.

5. Analyze Dependable Doors' cash flow from financing activities in 1990 and 1991.

In 1990, Dependable Doors used long-term debt to partially fund the increase in fixed assets. The balance of the increase in fixed assets was funded by an increase in notes payable.

In 1991, the increase in the capital accounts was used to finance the fixed asset increase, and the increase in notes payable was used to finance the payment of dividends.

There seems to be a financing mismatch in both years. It is also important to note that, despite a loss, the company increased dividend payments (to $717,000) in 1991.

6. **Analyze the dividends payments on the statement of cash flows in light of changes in the equity accounts on the balance sheet. What do you think happened between 1990 and 1991?**

The balance sheet shows that retained earnings declined from 1990 to 1991. Adding back the loss for the year and the payment of dividends shows how the decline occurred. The company offset this decline in retained earnings by issuing more common stock.

Chapter 6 Ratios

1. **Calculate the liquidity and activity ratios for Dependable Doors over the last three years. Calculate the activity ratios in terms of days on hand.**

Days on Hand	*1989*	*1990*	*1991*
Current Ratio	3.27	2.12	1.98
Quick Ratio	1.87	1.10	1.10
Accounts Receivable DOH	63.	64.	75.
Inventory DOH	67.	97.	94.
Accounts Payable DOH	13.	36.	32.

2. **Discuss the trends in the liquidity and activity ratios in light of what has been happening with Dependable Doors over the last three years.**

Both the current and quick ratios have been declining over the last three years in spite of increases in both receivables and inventory. This is because current liabilities in the form of accounts payable and notes payable have risen even higher as a percentage of total assets. The company has been using short-term debt to finance some of its fixed-asset expansion.

The accounts receivable days on hand (ARDOH) has been increasing over the last years as a result of Dependable Doors' having loosened its terms of sales in order to retain its existing market share. Inventory days on hand (INVDOH) has also increased, the result of Dependable Doors' purchase of the St. Louis facility and retaining higher inventory levels in anticipation of sales increases that never materialized. Accounts payable days on hand (APDOH) also increased as the company sought to get the trade to pay for some of the increases in inventory.

An examination of the timing differences over the last three years reveals that the company definitely required some additional financing because of these overall changes.

	1989	1990	1991
Accounts Receivable DOH	63	64	75
Inventory DOH	67	97	94
– Accounts Payable DOH	–13	–36	–32
Timing Difference	117	125	137

3. Calculate appropriate leverage ratios for Dependable Doors over the last three years and discuss their significance.

	1989	1990	1991
Debt to Worth	.84	1.91	2.13
Debt to Capitalization	.33	.56	.57

The company's total debt to net worth has increased over the last three years as the company has had to take on additional debt to pay for its acquisition of the St. Louis facility and for increased receivables and inventory.

The debt-to-capitalization ratio has also increased as more of the company's permanent capital is financed with debt as opposed to shareholder's investment. This is also because of the reasons stated above.

4. Calculate the coverage ratios for Dependable Doors over the last three years and comment on their significance.

The ratio is calculated as follows:

$$\frac{\text{Net income} + \text{Depreciation} + \text{Other noncash charges}}{\text{Current maturities of long-term debt}}$$

1989 $\quad \frac{1014 + 760 + 170}{86} = 22.6$

1990 $\quad \frac{669 + 750 + 376}{134} = 13.4$

1991 $\quad \frac{(175) + 859 + 223}{147} = 6.2$

Even though the ratio has been declining in the last two years, it is more than sufficient to service debt.

The times-earned-interest ratio is calculated as follows:

$$\frac{\text{Profit before tax + Interest expense}}{\text{Interest expense}}$$

The ratios for the three years were: 1989, 8.6; 1990, 2.2; 1991, .5

The ratio shows that Dependable Doors did not earn enough to cover its interest expense in 1991. However, this ratio can be misleading. If the income tax refund it received because of the loss in 1991 is considered, the company had more than enough cash to cover interest expense.

5. Calculate the profitability ratios of Dependable Doors and explain the trends over the last three years.

The return on sales from 1989 to 1991 was 5 percent, 3 percent, and (1) percent, respectively. This return was fairly good for 1989, but it was not very good for subsequent years.

The return on assets ratio is calculated as follows:

$$\frac{\text{Net profit + Interest expense - Tax benefits of interest expense}}{\text{Average total assets}}$$

1989 $\frac{1014 + 241 - .44 \times 241}{10073} = .114$

1990 $\frac{669 + 635 - .13 \times 635}{17473 + 10073/2} = .054$

1991 = Net loss

These returns are not very good if alternative investments are considered.

The return on equity is calculated as follows:

$$\frac{\text{Net profit}}{\text{Average net worth}}$$

The ratios for 1989 and 1990 were .19 and, .12, respectively. There was a loss in 1991.

The return in 1989 was good, but in subsequent years it was terrible.

6. How does Dependable Doors compare to industry averages? Explain any divergences from the norm.

Looking at the liquidity and activity turnover ratios shows that Dependable Doors tracks fairly closely to the industry norm with respect to liquidity.

However, the activity ratios, especially receivables days on hand and inventory days on hand, begin to show serious divergences from the norm after the acquisition. Accounts payable days on hand approximates the industry norm.

The debt-to-worth leverage ratio is slightly above the industry norm. This is due to recent borrowing to fund the fixed-asset expansion and timing differences in the company's working capital accounts.

The coverage ratios, all above the industry norm, indicate that Dependable Doors has enough cash to service its debt and interest payments. The company has been generating a lot of excess cash through depreciation caused by fixed-asset purchases.

Chapter 7 Cash Budgets

Review the cash budget supplied by the management of Dependable Doors.

1. Do you detect any seasonality in the sales pattern of Dependable Doors?

Yes, Dependable Doors' peak cash receipts are from March through June. However, its sales peak is probably in either January or February through May or June because there is a lag between when a sale is made and when cash is collected.

2. What ramifications do Dependable Doors' annual projections have on the company's projected monthly cash needs?

Dependable Doors has projected annual levels of growth in all key variables, such as gross margin, accounts receivable days on hand, inventory days on hand, and so on. If the company is incorrect in its assumptions, there will be ramifications for its cash budgeting needs throughout the year.

In the February cash budget, for example, the cumulative funding requirement is $5,136,000. This requirement is based upon a production policy that creates a seasonal inventory buildup before the peak selling season. Thus, inaccurate sales forecasts could lead to overproduction of inventory.

3. After examining the monthly cash budget submitted by Dependable Doors, do you think the company's debt is structured correctly?

Probably not. Seasonal financing loans should be able to pay out at least one month out of the year. An examination of the cumulative funding requirement on the cash budget shows that Dependable Doors is never able to fully pay off its short-term debt requirements. Therefore, assuming that this budget is correct (in actuality, an analyst probably would rework these numbers based upon his or her own scenario), Dependable Doors' debt should be restructured so that a portion of line is structured as long-term debt. In addition, two of the principal payments of its long-term debt are now scheduled for months in which its cash position is low. It probably makes sense to reset the timing of principal repayment to months when the cash position is stronger.

4. Prepare your own cash budget for Dependable Doors.

Chapter 8 Pro Forma Forecasting Analysis

Management provides you with the following information about its expectations for the company in 1992:

1. Sales are expected to increase 50 percent due to the expected recovery in the housing market, the company's geographic expansion into Texas and Canada, its sales of steel products to new markets, its full use of production facilities, and its introduction of new products.
2. The gross profit margin is going to increase to 27 percent of sales due to increasing economies of scale in the new production facility and to the company's ability to raise prices in the upcoming boom market.
3. Selling expenses will decline to 5 percent of sales because of increasing sales volume per salesperson.
4. General and administrative expenses will decline slightly to 12 percent of sales due to increasing efficiency in the St. Louis plant.
5. Interest expense is expected to increase to $1,116,000 because of anticipated higher inventory levels, which will be funded with short-term debt.
6. Income taxes are expected to be 3 percent of sales.
7. Cash at year end 1992 is projected to be $300,000.
8. Accounts receivable days on hand are projected to be 51 days as the company improves the collection of receivables and institutes a new policy that salespeople do not get commissions on accounts that are over 60 days overdue.
9. Inventory days on hand are projected to be 81 days as the company eliminates some of the obsolete inventory at the St. Louis plant and gets its new inventory control system up and running.
10. Accounts payable days on hand are projected to be 28 days.

11. Fixed assets are not expected to grow next year, and depreciation expense is projected to be $660,000.
12. Other fixed assets are projected to remain the same as the prior year.
13. Accruals are expected to increase 33 percent over the prior year.
14. No new long-term debt is anticipated next year because the company plans to focus its attention on absorbing the St. Louis facility, increasing sales, and reducing expenses.
15. Deferred income taxes are expected to be 6 percent of total assets.
16. The capital accounts are not expected to grow next year.

Questions

1. On the basis of the financial statements and the forecasts provided by management, prepare a pro forma income statement and balance sheet for 31 October 1992.

Dependable Doors
Pro Forma Balance Sheet
(in thousands of dollars)

	1992	*Percent*
Cash	300	2
Accounts Receivable	4,200	23
Inventory	5,639	31
Current Assets	10,139	56
Fixed Assets—Net	7,634	42
Other Assets	442	2
Noncurrent Assets	8,076	44
Total Assets	18,215	100
Notes Payable to Banks	1,117	6
Accounts Payable	1,958	11
Accruals	782	4
CMLTD	147	1
Current Debt	4,004	22
Long Term Debt Secured	6,468	36
Total Debt	10,472	58
Reserve—Deferred Income Taxes	1,066	6
Capital Stock—Common	1,320	7
Paid-in-Surplus	2,049	11
Retained Earnings	3,308	18
Net Worth	6,677	36
Total Liabilities and Net Worth	18,215	100

Dependable Doors
Pro Forma Income Statement
(in thousands of dollars)

	1992	*Percent*
Net Sales	30,000	100
Cost of Goods Sold	21,900	73
Gross Profit	8,100	27
Selling Expenses	1,600	5
General and Administrative Expenses	3,440	12
Total Operating Expenses	5,040	17
Operating Profit	3,060	10
Interest Expense	1,116	4
Profit before Tax	1,944	6
Income Taxes	864	3
Net Profit after Tax	1,080	3

The calculations to arrive at the pro forma statements are as follows (your numbers may differ slightly due to rounding):

1. Using management's assumptions, calculate the sales increase.
2. Using management's assumptions, calculate cost of goods sold by subtracting the projected gross profit from sales.
3. Using management's assumptions, calculate projected selling expense.
4. Using management's assumptions, calculate general and administrative expense. Subtract both selling expense and general and administrative expense from gross profit to arrive at operating income.
5. Using management's assumptions, list projected interest expense.
6. Calculate profit before tax by subtracting interest expense from the operating income figure.
7. Using management's assumptions, calculate income taxes.
8. Subtract income tax from profit before tax to arrive at net profit.
9. Using management's assumptions, list the projected cash figure.
10. Using management's assumptions, calculate the projected accounts receivable figure.
11. Using management's assumptions, list the projected inventory figure.
12. Using management's assumptions, list the projected accounts payable figure.
13. Using management's assumptions, calculate projected capital expenditures.
14. Using management's assumptions, calculate other assets.
15. Add up total noncurrent assets.

16. Add up total assets.
17. Using management's figures, calculate accruals.
18. Using management's assumptions, calculate current portion of long-term debt (CPLTD) and long-term debt.
19. Add up total current liabilities.
20. Using management's assumptions, calculate deferred income taxes.
21. Using management's assumptions, list common-stock accounts.
22. Calculate the change in retained earnings by adding net income to retained earnings of the prior year and subtracting any declared dividends.
23. If total assets are less than total liabilities, plug the balancing figure into marketable securities. If total liabilities are less than total **assets**, plug the balancing figure into notes payable.
24. Common-size the figures on the balance sheet and income statement.

Remember that, if assets exceed liabilities, the balancing figure is notes payable. If liabilities exceed assets, the balancing figure is marketable securities. This is the way most major software programs work (TurboFast, MAPS, FAMUS, and others). In reality, an analyst probably would discuss the situation with the customer in advance and structure the debt either short term or long term, as needed.

On the job, when doing a pro forma balance sheet and income statement, a credit analyst would carefully examine each of the assumptions made by management. Then, interpreting the information provided by management, the analyst would create his or her own assessment of what was going to happen over the course of the next year. This analysis would be based upon management's past success in projecting future events as well as the analyst's assessment of the marketplace and external environment.

2. How much additional borrowing requirement will Dependable Doors have if the gross margin is 25 percent?

Projected Sales	$30,000,000
Gross margin	x .25
Projected margin	$ 7,500,000

Company's original projected margin at 27%	$ 8,100,000
New projected margin	−7,500,000
Additional borrowing requirement	$ 600,000

3. **Prepare another pro forma balance sheet and income statement using your own assumptions about the future for Dependable Doors.**

Chapter 9 Other Analytical Techniques

1. **Calculate working investment for 1991 and for 1992 (projected).**

Working Investment (Projected)	*1991*	*1992*
Accounts Receivable	4,161	4,200
Inventory	4,118	5,639
Trading Assets	8,279	9,839
Accounts Payable	1,434	1,958
Accruals	589	782
Spontaneous Finance	2,023	2,740
Trading Assets	8,279	9,839
Spontaneous Finance	2,023	2,740
Working Investment	6,256	7,099

2. **Calculate Dependable Doors' working-investment need based upon 1991's figures and comment upon any differences in management's 1992 projected need.**

$$\text{Working investment percentage} = \frac{\text{Working investment}}{\text{Sales}} \times 100$$

$$\frac{6{,}256}{20{,}055} \times 100 = 31\%$$

$$\text{Management's projected percentage} = \frac{7{,}099}{30{,}000} \times 100 = 24\%$$

The company obviously thinks it can cut down on its working investment need through more efficient management of the timing differences in Accounts receivable days on hand (DOH), inventory DOH, and accounts payable DOH.

3. **Do a most-likely and pessimistic-case sensitivity analysis on Dependable Doors to determine how much financing will be required and compare your conclusion to management's projected financing need. Use the following variables to do your analysis:**

Item	Management's projection	Most Likely	Pessimistic
Sales	50% = 30,000	25%	5%
COGS	73% = 21,900	76%	78%
Acct. Rec.	51 DOH* = 4,200	60 DOH	75 DOH
Inventory	81 DOH = 5,639	85 DOH	95 DOH
Acct. Pay	28 DOH = 1,958	25 DOH	20 DOH
Accruals	782	700	500
Working Inv.	7,099		
Net Profit Margin	3% = 1,080	2.5%	2.0%
Financing Required	6,019		

*Days on Hand

Item	Management's projection	Most Likely	Pessimistic
Sales	50% = 30,000	25% = 25,069	5% = 21,058
COGS	73% = 21,900	76% = 19,052	78% = 16,425
Acct. Rec.	51 DOH = 4,200	60 DOH = 4,121	75 DOH = 4,327
Inventory	81 DOH = 5,639	85 DOH = 4,437	95 DOH = 4,275
Acct. Pay	28 DOH = 1,958	25 DOH = 1,304	20 DOH = 900
Accruals	782	700	500
Working Inv.	7,099	6,554	7,202
Net Profit Margin	3% = 1,080	2.5% = 627	2.0% = 421
Financing Required	6,019	5,927	6,781